M000076925

What's in the Bible for . . . ™

Couples

Larry & Kathy Miller

CARTOONS BY
Reverend Fun
(Dennis "Max" Hengeveld)
Dennis is a graphic designer
for Gospel Films and the
author of *Has Anybody Seen
My Locust?* His cartoons can
be seen worldwide at
www.reverendfun.com

STARBURST PUBLISHERS®

P. O. Box 4123, Lancaster, Pennsylvania 17604

To schedule author appearances, write:

Author Appearances
Starburst Publishers
P.O. Box 4123
Lancaster, Pennsylvania 17604
(717) 293-0939

www.starburstpublishers.com

CREDITS:
Cover design by David Marty Design
Text design and composition by John Reinhardt Book Design
Illustrations by Bruce Burkhart and Melissa A. Burkhart
Cartoons by Dennis "Max" Hengeveld

Unless otherwise noted, or paraphrased by the author, all Scripture quotations are from the New International Version of The Holy Bible.

Scripture taken from the HOLY BIBLE: NEW INTERNATIONAL VERSION®, NIV®. Copyright © 1973, 1978, 1984 by International Bible Society.

Reverend Fun cartoons ©Copyright Gospel Films Incorporated.

To the best of its ability, Starburst Publishers® has strived to find the source of all material. If there has been an oversight, please contact us, and we will make any correction deemed necessary in future printings. We also declare that to the best of our knowledge all material (quoted or not) contained herein is accurate, and we shall not be held liable for the same.

First Printing, February 2001

ISBN: 1-892016-02-8
Library of Congress Number 00-108569
Printed in the United States of America

READ THESE PAGES BEFORE YOU READ THIS BOOK . . .

Welcome to the *What's in the Bible for . . .*™ series. This series is the result of a belief that no matter who you are—teenager or senior, pastor or plumber—the Bible is the most important book for you to read and understand.

You could open up to the first page of the Bible and start plowing through, but let's be honest. Doing so can be a little overwhelming. Don't worry. This book combines bullet points, expert quotes, sidebar help, and cartoon humor so your time in the Bible will be enjoyable and meaningful. Have fun as you learn the Word!

On this page and the next you'll find information about the *What's in the Bible for . . .*™ and *God's Word for the Biblically-Inept*™ series. Please note the "Title Code" of each book. This code along with page numbers is used throughout each series, allowing easy reference from one book to another.

What's in the Bible for . . .™ Couples   WBFC
Larry and Kathy Miller
(trade paper) ISBN 1892016028 $16.95

What's in the Bible for . . .™ Women   WBFW
Georgia Curtis Ling
(trade paper) ISBN 1892016109 $16.95

What's in the Bible for . . .™ Mothers   WBFM
Judy Bodmer
(trade paper) ISBN 1892016265 $16.95

What's in the Bible for . . .™ Teens   WBFT
Mark Littleton and Jeanette Gardner Littleton
(trade paper) ISBN 1892016052 $16.95

• **Learn more at www.biblicallyinept.com** •

See page 351 for Purchasing Information.

IT'S THE BIBLE MADE EASY!

The *God's Word for the Biblically-Inept*™ series is already a best-seller with over 100,000 books sold! Designed to make reading the Bible easy, educational, and fun, this series of verse-by-verse Bible studies, topical studies, and overviews mixes scholarly information from experts with helpful icons, illustrations, sidebars, and time lines. It's the Bible made easy!

God's Word for the Biblically-Inept™ Series

The Bible by Larry Richards	IBSN 0914984551	**GWBI**	**$16.95**
Daniel by Daymond R. Duck	ISBN 0914984489	**GWDN**	**$16.95**
Genesis by Joyce Gibson	ISBN 1892016125	**GWGN**	**$16.95**
Health & Nutrition by Kathleen O'Bannon Baldinger	ISBN 0914984055	**GWHN**	**$16.95**
John by Lin Johnson (Available Spring 2001)	ISBN 1892016435	**GWJN**	**$16.95**
Life of Christ, Volume 1, by Robert C. Girard	ISBN 1892016230	**GWLC**	**$16.95**
Life of Christ, Volume 2, by Robert C. Girard	ISBN 1892016397	**GWLC2**	**$16.95**
Men of the Bible by D. Larry Miller	ISBN 1892016079	**GWMB**	**$16.95**
Prophecies of the Bible by Daymond R. Duck	ISBN 1892016222	**GWPB**	**$16.95**
Revelation by Daymond R. Duck	ISBN 0914984985	**GWRV**	**$16.95**
Romans by Gib Martin	ISBN 1892016273	**GWRM**	**$16.95**
Women of the Bible by Kathy Collard Miller	ISBN 0914984063	**GWWB**	**$16.95**

New Titles Are Coming!

Starburst Publishers will continue expanding the *What's in the Bible for . . .*™ and *God's Word for the Biblically-Inept*™ series. Look for these future titles:

- **What's in the Bible for . . . Families**
- **Mark—God's Word for the Biblically-Inept**
- **Acts—God's Word for the Biblically-Inept**

For Purchasing Information, see page 351 • Learn more at **www.biblicallyinept.com**

CHAPTERS AT A GLANCE

PART TWO: **FAMILY TIES**

PART THREE: "DOIN' WHAT COMES NATURALLY"

PART FOUR: HURDLES OF HONEYHOOD

ILLUSTRATIONS

For a preview of the icons in this book, check out the sidebar in this Introduction!

INTRODUCTION

WHAT'S IN THIS CHAPTER

Here We Go

Welcome to *What's in the Bible for . . .™ Couples*. If you are part of a couple, then this book is for you! We are excited that you picked up this book because it means you are interested in strengthening your relationship.

Relationships with members of the opposite sex are not always blissful, but we can still choose to bless our boyfriend or girlfriend, fiancé or fiancée, husband or wife. In this unique book you'll find insights, encouragement, and instruction for doing exactly that. You've just discovered a REVOLUTIONARY COMMENTARY™ that will enhance your understanding of the Bible and improve your relationship!

1 Samuel 25:2–4 A certain man in Maon, who had property there at

Why Look to the Bible?

The Bible is the number one best-selling book of all time. No matter how often it has been renounced, no matter how many people have conspired to destroy Christianity, God has made sure his Word has not only survived, but thrived. Once someone reads the Bible, they see its <u>truth</u>, and it is particularly applicable to those looking for help for their marriage. God wants to offer practical ideas for every couple, and the Bible offers <u>wisdom</u> and insights for all of life.

There are a lot of books on the market about marriage, but God's perspective as revealed in the Bible is right from the creator of marriage himself. He knows exactly what couples need! And it's never too late for any marriage—no matter how hopeless it seems. With God there is always <u>hope</u>.

self-concept: our view of ourselves

☞ **GO TO:**

Psalm 119:159–168 (truth)

Proverbs 1:2 (wisdom)

Jeremiah 29:11 (hope)

Henry Cloud and John Townsend: As the Bible teaches, make the most of today, for the days are evil (Ephesians 5:16). What you take initiative to deal with today will affect the rest of

What Others are Saying:

Couples in the Bible

☞ **Check It Out:**

1 Samuel 25:2–44

Marriage God's Way—

She Says . . .

He Says . . .

your married life. And what you ignore or are afraid to address will do the same.[1]

The Bible is about people and their relationships with God and each other. From couples like Abraham and Sarah, David and Abigail, and Priscilla and Aquila, we learn how to deal with conflict, restore love, make loving choices, and enjoy sex. Other issues like finances, spiritual intimacy, and friendships are also covered in the Bible, and you'll find them included here also.

Don't be hesitant. God's medicine contained in this inspirational and encouraging guidebook will give you the courage to make positive changes in your life. It's all here—wrapped in fascinating stories of biblical couples. They may have lived long ago, but what they faced is as fresh as today's newspaper. You'll find laughter, love, and life-giving support on every page. Dig in!

How to Use
What's in the Bible for . . .™ Couples

To make the most of the wonderful possibilities herein, we suggest the following:

- Sit down with this book and your Bible.
- Start the book at chapter 1.
- As you read through each chapter, read the "Check It Out" passages in conjunction with the Couples of the Bible feature.
- Use the sidebar loaded with icons and helpful information to gain a knowledge boost.
- If you want to do further research, look up the "GO TO" verses.
- Answer the Study Questions and review with the Chapter Wrap-Up.
- Then go on to the next chapter.

It really is simple! If you prefer, you can go immediately to a subject that is of interest to you. Then, by all means, go to the chapter that will best meet your needs. If you want to deepen your sexual relationship, go to that section. If you need help with the in-laws—so they don't become outlaws—go to that chapter. Let God guide you, but be sure to read everything eventually. Even if you're already married, don't ignore the chapters on engagement. We've included information throughout this book that will strengthen any couple, no matter where they are in their relationship. Don't miss any of it!

Why Use the New International Version (NIV)?

We want this book to be easy to read and understand; that's why we chose to use the New International Version (NIV) of the Bible. It is a scholarly translation that accurately expresses the original Bible in clear and contemporary English.

TAKE IT FROM THEM

The Features

This book contains a variety of special features that can help you learn. They're illustrated in the outside column of this introduction and in the following sample page. Here they are again, with a brief explanation of each.

Sections and Icons	*What's It For?*
What's in This Chapter	the most prominent points of the chapter
Here We Go	a chapter warm-up
Bible Quote	what you came for—the Bible
Commentary	our thoughts on what the verse means
What Others Are Saying	if you don't believe us, listen to the experts
Go To	other Bible verses to help you better understand (underlined in text)
What?	the meaning of the word (bold in text)
Check It Out	related Bible passages you should look up
Couples in the Bible	focuses on special couples from the Bible
Marriage God's Way	specific application of Scripture to marriage
He Says . . . She Says	personal stories from our marriage
Think about It	some interesting points to mull over
Take It from Them	other couples' ideas for living out God's principles
Key Point	a major point in the chapter
Remember This	take special note
Warning	something to beware of
Study Questions	questions for discussion, study, and digging deeper
Chapter Wrap-Up	the most prominent points revisited
Kathy and Larry's Bookshelf	favorite books we recommend

KEY POINT

Seek to grow up emotionally and spiritually as much as possible before getting married.

REMEMBER THIS

STUDY QUESTIONS

CHAPTER WRAP-UP

KATHY & LARRY'S

BOOKSHELF

A Special Word about "Take It from Them"

We are very grateful to the husbands and wives who were willing to submit stories about their marriages. They have vulnerably shared from their own struggles and victories. You'll find their stories throughout our book, and you will be amazed at how much you relate to them and are energized by their ideas for practicing God's love in marriage.

A Word about Words

As you read *What's in the Bible for . . . Couples*, you'll notice some interchangeable words: Scripture, Scriptures, Word, Word of God, God's Word, etc. All of these terms mean the same thing and come under the broad heading of "the Bible."

In most cases, the New Testament phrase "*the Scriptures*" refers to the Old Testament. Peter indicated that the writings of the apostle Paul were quickly accepted in the early church as equal to "*the other scriptures*" (2 Peter 3:16). Both Testaments consistently demonstrate the belief that is expressed in 2 Timothy 3:16, "*all Scripture is God-breathed.*"

One Final Tip

There's a wonderful promise given when we turn to the Bible to answer life's questions. As we read the inspired Word of God, God promises that his Word will make a distinct difference in our lives, and he is present whenever we read it.

As you read, pray, and open your heart to God, ask him to speak to you. You will find your life enriched and changed forever as you find out what's in the Bible for couples!

Here's a Sample Page!

Bible Quote: This is where you'll read a quote from the Bible.

> **James 1:5** If any of you lacks wisdom, he should ask God, who gives generously to all without finding fault, and it will be given to him.

Decisions, Decisions: In or Out?

James, the brother of Jesus, is writing to the new believers who were scattered about the Roman world (see GWBI, pages 213–214) when they fled from persecution. James knows that godly wisdom is a great gift. He gives a simple plan to get it: need wisdom, ask for it. God will give it to us.

Up 'til now we've concentrated on finding the wind sails of your drifting marriage and overcoming marita lems. But you may be the reader who is shaking her head, thinking that I just don't understand what you're going through. Yo can't take the abuse any longer; you've forgiven the **infidelity** time after time; and in order for you and your children to survive, you see no alternative but divorce.

So let me make this clear: in no way am I saying to allow your husband to abuse you or your children. If the abuse continues, get out and seek profess keep the only dam physical a

When you feel you've depleted all of your options, continue to ask God for wisdom in order to have the knowledge to make the right decisions. Wise women seek God. God is the <u>source</u> of wisdom and wisdom is found in Christ and the Word.

Gary Chapman, Ph.D.: Is there hope for women who suffer physical abuse from their husbands? Does reality living offer any genuine hope? I believe the answer to those questions is yes.[6]

Give It Away

You don't have to be a farmer to understand what the Apostle Paul wrote to the Corinthian church (see illustration, page 143). A picture is worth a thousand words, and Paul is painting masterpiece. He reminds us of what any smart farmer knows in order to produce a bountiful harvest, he has to plan for it

Commentary: This is where you'll read commentary about the biblical quote.

"What?": When you see a word in bold, go to the sidebar for a definition.

infidelity: sexual unfaithfulness of a spouse

"Go To": When you see a word or phrase that's underlined, go to the sidebar for a biblical cross-reference.

☞ **GO TO:**

Psalm 111:10 (source)

REMEMBER THIS

What Others are Saying:

What Others Are Saying: This is where you'll read what an expert has to say about the subject at hand.

MONEY, MONEY, MONEY • 5

127

Feature with icon in the sidebar: Throughout the book you will see sections of text with corresponding icons in the sidebar. See the chart on page xiii for a description of all the features in this book.

Part One

HOME BEGINNINGS AND HOME IMPROVEMENTS

REVEREND FUN

After the wedding at Cana, Jesus was flooded with wedding invitations . . . but they always included a special request that he bring his own water.

1 PREPARING FOR MARRIAGE

Here We Go

It's happened in many different ways over the years. A boy and girl see each other in the fields, knowing their parents have chosen them for each other. A man spots a beautiful woman across the dance floor. A high schooler tells her girlfriend, "There's this new guy in my chemistry class. I've just got to introduce you to him." Lifelong friends suddenly see each other with new eyes. A blind date sends a man to a woman's front porch and there are instant fireworks.

Falling in love is always fresh and new to those who encounter it, yet the experience goes all the way back to the very beginning of creation. The Bible has a lot to say about love, from courting to marriage. In this chapter, we will explore God's invention of marriage and what the Bible says about preparing for marriage.

Neil Clark Warren: Every person I know yearns for love! And the most obvious place to search for it is in marriage. In fact, more than 90 percent of all the people in the United States will marry at least once during their lifetime.[1]

What Others are Saying:

MARRIAGE: GOD'S INVENTION

> **Genesis 2:18** The Lord God said, "It is not good for the man to be alone. I will make a helper suitable for him."

Single Adult Male Seeks Member of the Same Species

☞ **GO TO:**

Genesis 1:22
(populating)

God knew Adam would never be happy alone. Not only that, <u>populating</u> the earth would be a little awkward too! Adam wasn't meant to be the only person on earth. All along God had a plan to match Adam with someone spectacular, but he didn't create Adam's companion right away. First, he wanted to make Adam aware of his need.

REMEMBER THIS

Adam and Eve were God's unique design for populating the earth. He wanted them to experience the joy of emotional and sexual **intimacy**.

Think about It

intimacy: *closeness*

progeny: *descendants*

If God had somehow made it possible for Adam to have **progeny** without a counterpart, Adam might never have experienced the joys and challenges of having an intimate companion. God instilled in Adam a desire to share his life with another person. Although there are some Christians who feel called to <u>remain single</u> and serve him without distractions, more often than not people want to get married.

☞ **GO TO:**

1 Corinthians 7:32
(remain single)

> **Genesis 2:19–20** Now the Lord God had formed out of the ground all the beasts of the field and all the birds of the air. He brought them to the man to see what he would name them; and whatever the man called each living creature, that was its name. So the man gave names to all the livestock, the birds of the air and all the beasts of the field. But for Adam no suitable helper was found.

Adam Fills Out the Name Tags

Adam had the incredible responsibility of naming all the animals. He must have felt affirmed because not once did God interrupt him and say, "Are you sure you want to call that a . . . hippopotamus?" Adam's God-given creativity—just like his heavenly Father's creativity—was being used to the max.

Think about It

Even though this must have been a rewarding task for Adam, when all the animals had finished parading in front of him, the biblical text suggests Adam felt lonely. He'd never noticed that feeling before. What was that pain in his chest? He would have to think of a new word to describe it. "Aloneness? Yes, that's it," we can imagine him thinking. "Lonely? That's it, too. Solitary. . . Forlorn . . . Whatever it is, I don't like it."

What Others are Saying:

Michelle McKinney Hammond: When God brought the animals to Adam for a closer look before the great naming ceremony began, I think Adam finally noticed that there were male and female of everything—made for one another! It must have been a startling revelation.[2]

Marriage God's Way—To capture what the Bible means when it refers to a "suitable helper," think of a tailor specifically designing and sewing a suit to fit a man's build. Where the man is thinner, the tailor takes in more fabric. Where the man has worked on building his muscles, the tailor allows for more space. In marriage, God wants each of us to be "fitted" with a spouse who will be strong where we are weak and who will let our strengths offset their weaknesses. When we seek a person who "**complements**" our strengths and weaknesses, we are seeking a "suitable helper."

complements: provides balance

> **Genesis 2:21–25** So the Lord God caused the man to fall into a deep sleep; and while he was sleeping, he took one of the man's ribs and closed up the place with flesh. Then the Lord God made a woman from the rib he had taken out of the man, and he brought her to the man. The man said, "This is now bone of my bones and flesh of my flesh; she shall be called 'woman,' for she was taken out of man." For this reason a man will leave his father and mother and be united to his wife, and they will become one flesh. The man and his wife were both naked, and they felt no shame.

An Operation with a Welcome "Side Effect"

That must have been quite some operation—with only God's natural **anesthesia**. But Adam was thrilled when he woke up and saw what was standing before him. She wasn't like any of the animals

anesthesia: numbing effect

☞ **GO TO:**

Genesis 1:31 (good)

at all! She could talk. She could smile. She could wrap her arms around him. Suddenly, that new feeling he'd been trying to get rid of—loneliness—was gone! For the first time, he felt fulfilled and complete. God had indeed made something "good."

What Others are Saying:

Liz Curtis Higgs: Why the man's rib? Perhaps because when it comes to the human skeleton structure, one rib isn't exactly a load-bearing wall. Plus, from an emotional standpoint, God wisely chose the bone nearest the man's heart as a gentle reminder to keep his helpmate close by his side—physically, emotionally, spiritually.[3]

Larry Crabb: Our personal needs for security and significance can be genuinely and fully met only in relationship with the Lord Jesus Christ. To put it another way, all that we need to function effectively as persons (not necessarily to feel happy or fulfilled) is at any given moment fully supplied in relationship with Christ and in whatever he chooses to provide.[4]

Even though God put a desire in Adam and in many others to have a lifelong companion, ultimately only God can fulfill us. God wants us to enjoy our spouse, but our husband or wife can never <u>fill</u> the unique "God-shaped vacuum" that is within each of us.

It's hard for us to comprehend how Adam and Eve could be naked without **shame**. Because of the hurtful things that happen to each of us, we bring into marriage a sense of shame and distrust. Adam and Eve had not experienced such pain. They had not been hurt by people's uncaring remarks or endured physical or sexual abuse of any kind.

God's original plan was that each person would offer **untainted** personhood to his or her spouse, but because of the choices Adam and Eve made later, and because of the choices each of us makes, we can't bring that kind of innocence to our spouses. Yet, God knew sin would happen and in his mercy uses our struggles to draw us closer to him and to our spouses.

REMEMBER THIS

☞ **GO TO:**

Psalm 46:10 (fill)

Think about It

shame: *humiliation*

untainted: *pure*

How It Began for Us

She Says . . .

KATHY: My friend Margie and I had never been to a water polo game, but it seemed like a good idea for a Friday evening. Once we arrived at the indoor pool, I lost track of Margie in the crowd, but saw Frank, a friend of mine from church. As we talked, I quickly noticed the handsome guy standing next to him. Frank introduced his friend, Larry, and explained that they played water polo for their high school. I liked Larry immediately and when the game started, I made sure I followed him and Frank up into the stands to watch the game. I wanted to keep Larry's attention, hoping he would ask me out on a date, so I asked him questions about water polo. Larry was pleased to answer my questions and we got along well. I just knew he'd ask me out.

When the game ended, we climbed down the stands and instead of asking for my phone number, all I heard was, "Bye! Nice talking to you!"

I was devastated. "That's the story of my life," I thought. "I get a nibble and the hunk jumps off my line!"

He Says . . .

LARRY: When I first saw Kathy I was impressed! She was attractive, articulate, and attentive. During the evening she asked a lot of questions, and it was clear she was interested in me. We hit it off. As we warmed up to each other, I wanted to ask her out, but fear grabbed my heart. What would I do if she rejected me in front of Frank? I couldn't take the risk so we parted after the game. Later I asked Frank for Kathy's number, but he didn't know it. I called every "Collard" in the phone book and finally found her.

PREPPING FOR MARRIAGE

> **Esther 2:12** Before a girl's turn came to go in to **King Xerxes**, she had to complete twelve months of beauty treatments prescribed for the women, six months with oil of <u>myrrh</u> and six with perfumes and cosmetics.

King Xerxes: king of Persia

☞ **GO TO:**

Matthew 2:11 (myrrh)

Primping Esther-Style

The Book of Esther tells the story of how a young woman named Esther was chosen by God to save his people—the Jews—from **extinction**. As **Haman**, an enemy of the Jews, was plotting to influence King Xerxes to have all Jews murdered, God was preparing Esther, a Jewish woman, for her role in the failure of Haman's plan. After King Xerxes' wife, Vashti, was dethroned as queen, a new queen was to be chosen.

The Jewish historian Josephus believes there were as many as four hundred women, including Esther, called to the palace to be "queen for a day" in the king's chambers. Each candidate was given beauty treatments with spices and oils, like myrrh (see illustration below).

The king immediately fell in love with Esther and declared her the new queen. Esther had been prepared both physically and emotionally—even spiritually—to be the best she could be as she met the king. Just like Esther prepared herself for twelve months before her special day, each of us must prepare ourselves to be the best potential mate we can be.

extinction: being brought to an end

Haman: an official in King Xerxes' court

☞ **GO TO:**

Esther 1:9 (Vashti)

What Others are Saying:

Wayne Barber, Eddie Rasnake, and Richard Shepherd: It was one thing to be one of the prettiest girls in the city. It was yet another to stand out when placed beside all the prettiest girls of the known world. Initially she was selected for her external beauty, but ultimately it was the internal beauty of her character that set her apart from the rest of the beautiful women.[5]

Myrrh

Myrrh is a well-known gum resin from an Arabian plant that is used as a perfume.

The Tease Disease

KATHY: We had been dating steadily for a long time and had talked at length about getting married. One day at church Larry joked to our friend in front of me that he didn't think he'd ever get married. I was furious! I had to leave immediately for work, but as soon as I got there, I called him at church and yelled, "So you don't think you'll ever get married, huh?" and slammed down the phone.

LARRY: Dan, Kathy, and I stood there talking, and the topic of discussion turned to marriage. As often happens when young men talk about marriage, the negative aspects came up. Even though Kathy and I had spent hours discussing the topic, my teasing comment was directed right at her.

I was looking for a similar response from Kathy. When she did not react with another tease but a frown instead, I knew I was in trouble. When she called me, just to hang up, my suspicions were confirmed! Later, after my apology, we patched up the rift.

I have learned teasing usually works between male friends. Teasing sometimes works well with a mix of men and women friends. However, take it from me, teasing rarely works with your spouse or fiancée. Too often I've seen what I intended as lighthearted comments inflict pain on the one I love. While I have dramatically reduced these comments, I still find myself slipping into a teasing mode on occasion.

I'm still trying to make my home a tease-free environment.

It must have seemed like an incredibly long time for Esther to prepare to meet the king. Would her skin really be that much softer with twelve months of treatment as opposed to six? But Esther wasn't just being prepared physically through the wait, she was being prepared emotionally, too. Maybe she originally thought, "Well, let's just get this over with!" But through waiting and preparing, she could learn to trust God even more—and that prepared her for the difficulties she would face later.

An engaged couple can patiently use the preparation time before marriage. In waiting, they aren't just preparing for the wedding, they are preparing themselves for marriage as they learn to interact with each other and better handle difficult situations.

She Says . . .

He Says . . .

Couples in the Bible

☞ **Check It Out:**

Esther 1–2

Focus on being a perfect spouse. We don't mean "perfect" in the sense of having no faults or difficulties. Since no one is perfect, we see "perfect" as being willing to grow and change within marriage. Marriage is a process, and as long as we see the need to respond to our mate with love and understanding, we're being perfect—or as perfect as we can get on this earth!

LOOKING INWARD

Galatians 5:22 But the fruit of the Spirit is love, joy, peace, patience, kindness, goodness, faithfulness, gentleness and self-control. Against such things there is no law.

Full of Fruit

characteristics:
distinguishing traits or qualities

An emotionally healthy person exhibits **characteristics** that provide the background for a healthy, successful marriage. Strive to have the following traits:

- Loving, even when our intended isn't lovable
- Joyful with gratitude for however our future mate can meet our needs
- Peaceful, even when stress is overwhelming
- Patient, even when disappointment strikes
- Kind, even when kindness is not returned
- Generous by desiring the best for our future spouse
- Faithful by keeping our promises, even when those promises suddenly seem insignificant
- Gentle in responding to the cares and concerns of our beloved
- Self-controlled in our reaction to opposing viewpoints

REMEMBER THIS

Will we have these wonderful responses all the time? No. That would require perfection and none of us is perfect. But to the degree that we can respond with God's power, we can identify how ready we are to enter the stressful world of marriage.

Marriage Is Not a Pain Reliever

Those who are single sometimes think that marriage is the only state of being that will bring true happiness. Although marriage is a wonderful gift from God for many, he is the best gift and he offers himself to everyone. If you think, "I can't be happy or content until I get married," then you are setting yourself up for unrealistic expectations that marriage may not be able to meet.

Mary Whelchel: When we think of marriage as an essential, we start to make an idol out of it. It becomes more important to us than anything else. That's idolatry, and God simply does not tolerate idolatry in our lives. He is a jealous God, and he demands first place in our thoughts, our ambitions, our desires, our devotion.[6]

What Others are Saying:

Iron the Wrinkles before Wearing the Shirt

It's easy to think you and your fiancé aren't getting along because you can't yet live in the same house, or you don't have enough time together. You may even be separated by distance because of your job and think, "When we can enjoy each other unhindered, we'll get along better."

Having disagreements is natural in any relationship, but the time to work on them is before you say "I do," not after the honeymoon. Don't sweep issues under the rug thinking you can work on them more when you're husband and wife.

If you disagree on how many children to have, find out how important it is now—not after you're committed in marriage. If you don't know how your conflicting job schedules are going to work out, sort it through before life gets so busy you can't find the time to talk about it. If you see areas of misunderstanding occurring over and over again—like one of you frequently saying, "You never care about my feelings"—then seek some counseling to work through it.

Neil Clark Warren: But inevitably, marriage only intensifies problems. The stress of marriage, the **vulnerability** of living with someone day in and day out, the weight of responsibility, the fear of failure, the realization that marriage isn't a cure-all—all these combine to thrust existing problems to the forefront.[7]

What Others are Saying:

vulnerability: *being honest and open*

When Sally and Bobby were engaged, they discussed having children. Sally had grown up in a family that highly valued children and came away thinking she would be fulfilled when she got married and had children. Sally couldn't imagine not having children.

Bobby grew up as an only child and had no desire to have children. When he expressed this, Sally couldn't comprehend his viewpoint. She rationalized, "He's got to be kidding. Oh, he'll change his mind later. He doesn't understand. He just doesn't know what he wants." Instead of taking his comments at face value, she disrespectfully discarded the importance of his opinion.

After Sally and Bobby had been married for two years, Bobby reluctantly agreed to have children. Sally was glad when he was willing to be flexible on this issue. And when their first child, a daughter, was born, Bobby fell in love with her.

Sally and Bobby were fortunate this issue didn't become a wedge between them. Sometimes people don't want to change their opinion and these issues become sources of discord. That's why it's so important to explore any areas of disagreement before marriage.

Do You Like Yourself?

Many people get married hoping the love of their spouse will boost their own sagging self-image. But it takes two healthy people to face and conquer the challenges that marriage brings.

**What Others
are Saying:**

self-concept: our view of
ourselves

Neil Clark Warren: The **self-concept** is at the very center of every person's emotional and mental functioning. It is so central that any relationship between two people can be no healthier than the two "selves" involved.[8]

> **1 Samuel 25:2–4** A certain man in Maon, who had property there at Carmel, was very wealthy. He had a thousand goats and three thousand sheep, which he was shearing in Carmel. His name was Nabal and his wife's name was Abigail. She was an intelligent and beautiful woman, but her husband, a Calebite, was surly and mean in his dealings. While David was in the desert, he heard that Nabal was shearing sheep.

Different Kinds of Baggage

Nabal brought anger and tension into his marriage with Abigail. Abigail contributed intelligence and beauty. Everything that we are is brought into a marriage. In order to prepare for marriage, we must be the best we can be before taking our vows.

The Bible talks about a couple who met under some very tense circumstances, yet because of the healthiness of the woman's character, her "enemy" became her second husband.

In the time when David was traveling throughout the land, trying to avoid being killed by King Saul, he sent some of his followers to Nabal, a man of Maon, who was shearing his sheep in Carmel. David asked for help to feed his traveling band of supporters—a common courtesy that was granted almost without exception. But Nabal responded sharply, saying, "Who is this David? Who is this son of Jesse? Many servants are breaking away from their masters these days. Why should I take my bread and water, and the meat I have slaughtered for my shearers, and give it to men coming from who knows where?" (1 Samuel 25:10b–11).

When David's men returned to their master with Nabal's message, David was furious and swore that he would kill Nabal and all his family. But Nabal had one asset that he wasn't even aware of—his wife, Abigail. When Abigail learned of how Nabal had treated David's servants, she quickly went into action. She took bread, wine, sheep, grain, raisins, and pressed figs, and following the servants—without telling Nabal—she approached David.

What a woman of wisdom, humility, and tact! As an emotionally healthy woman, she

- took quick <u>action</u>,
- was willing to humble herself,
- was truthful about her husband,
- communicated her inability to **intercede** previously,
- gave a compliment to David about his future **dynasty** and purpose in life, and
- acknowledged God's work in David's life.

David was so impressed with her that later, as soon as he heard of Nabal's death, he <u>proposed</u> and she accepted his offer of marriage.

Couples in the Bible

☞ **Check It Out:**

1 Samuel 25:2–44

intercede: intervene

dynasty: kingdom

☞ **GO TO:**

Daniel 11:32 (action)

1 Samuel 25:39 (proposed)

> **2 Peter 1:3** His divine power has given us everything we need for life and godliness through our knowledge of him who called us by his own glory and goodness.

Our Provider

God created us perfectly, but our original parents made wrong choices that caused imperfection in his creation. God knows that we are needy people. He wants us to learn to depend only on him to fill that neediness. He is more than powerful enough to provide.

Think about It

Since each of us marries a person who is imperfect, it's unrealistic to assume marriage will bring us a solution to our own low self-esteem. If our spouses can't even meet all of their own needs, how can we expect them to meet all of ours? We must enter marriage with a healthy self-concept obtained through some combination of self-examination, repentance, counseling, and support from friends. The greatest gift we can give to our future spouse is knowing who we are "in Christ." The first chapter of Ephesians lists some wonderful ways God views us:

- Verse 4: chosen before foundation of the world
- Verse 5: **predestined** to be adopted as God's children
- Verse 6: **recipients** of God's grace
- Verse 7: forgiven and redeemed
- Verse 9: knowing God's will
- Verse 11: recipients of God's spiritual and eternal inheritance
- Verse 13: secure and sealed in our eternal destiny through the Holy Spirit

predestined: chosen formerly

recipients: receivers

If we can allow these truths to sink deeply into our spirit, we will feel loved, cherished, and important. As a result, we won't need to get our emotional needs met by our spouse—we'll already be filled with God's unconditional love.

Does this mean we can't get married until we become perfectly secure in God's love? No, otherwise no one would ever get married. But we should grow toward that security as much as possible before marrying another imperfect person.

KEY POINT

Seek to grow up emotionally and spiritually as much as possible before getting married.

There is a kind of inner security in healthy people. They are not always thinking that their worth as a person is on the line, that they have to be "right" in order to be acceptable and valuable.[9]

Marriage God's Way—What you are and what you lack, you bring to the marriage. The more you lack in spiritual and emotional healthiness, the more you'll struggle in marriage. Look for patterns of anger, insecurity, dishonesty, fear of vulnerability, or pride that could make your marriage more difficult. If you recognize these things in yourself, find out why and work at changing.

STUDY QUESTIONS

1. When God talks about a "helper suitable" for Adam, what does he mean?
2. Why did God give Adam the experience of naming the animals before he created Eve?
3. What does the word "woman" mean?
4. How long did Esther prepare before meeting the king, and what were her beauty treatments?
5. How did Abigail reveal her quality personality?

CHAPTER WRAP-UP

- God knew Adam would never be satisfied living by himself, or find fulfillment in the animals, so God showed Adam he needed a woman as he named the animals. God created the woman to be a complement for the man.

- Just as Esther took a long time in preparing to meet with the king, an engaged couple should take the time to become the best they can be before marriage.

- An engaged couple should evaluate their relationship to discover whether they are spiritually and emotionally prepared for the challenge of marriage. They should work on reducing destructive patterns within themselves.

KATHY & LARRY'S  BOOKSHELF

Here are some of our favorite books on preparing for marrying:

- *Common Mistakes Singles Make*, Mary Whelchel, Fleming H. Revell Company. Shows you how to recognize and prevent problems that Christian singles encounter.
- *Finding the Love of Your Life*, Neil Clark Warren, Ph.D., Focus on the Family Publishing. Ten principles for choosing the right marriage partner.
- *Finding Love (Again!)*, Connie Merritt, BookPartners. The dating survival manual for women over thirty.
- *What to Do until Love Finds You*, Michelle McKinney Hammond, Harvest House. Getting ready for Mr. Right.

2 EENEY, MEENEY, MINEY, MO: CHOOSING A SPOUSE

Here We Go

While you're working on being the best person you can be, it's important that you evaluate the kind of person you want to marry. God has made each person different. We tend to be attracted to the person who offers a "complement" to our personality, temperament, and needs. Being aware of the true person inside your potential spouse will give you the insight you need to choose wisely.

Yet, no one is perfect. No one will be able to meet all your needs. Therefore, the "perfect" spouse is the one God has chosen for you. God wants to be involved in every aspect of your relationship as it heads toward the wedding altar. This is for keeps! So choose wisely.

GOD KNOWS BEST!

> **Psalm 73:23–24** Yet I am always with you; you hold me by my right hand. You guide me with your counsel, and afterward you will take me into glory.

A Wonderful (Premarital) Counselor

Every area of our lives is important to God. Example after example of how God leads and directs people is detailed in the Bible. In Bible times, parents arranged marriages for their children many

☞ **GO TO:**

Genesis 12:1;
Exodus 3:17 (example)

This illustration portrays a
typical wedding procession
where the bridegroom
accompanied his bride to his
home. Everyone in the town
took the time to celebrate
and escort the new couple.

years before the wedding (see illustration above). People didn't
have much choice back then, but today we must seek God's help
to find the right person for us.

Some Christian teachers believe God ordains one person meant
for each of us. Other Christian leaders believe many different
people could well fit God's purpose. The Bible doesn't clearly state
God's method, but regardless, it's an important choice.

**What Others
are Saying:**

Talmud: Jewish Scriptures

M. Blaine Smith: Here it is striking that Scripture never specifically states that God predestines a man and woman for each other
in marriage. Even though this belief was deeply embedded in Jewish tradition and reflected in a number of sayings and anecdotes
in the **Talmud**, the Holy Spirit did not choose to state matters so
specifically in the inspired Scripture.[1]

Many a Christian marries an unbeliever intending to help **convert** that person. It's easy to assume our great love will cause unbelievers to see their need of __salvation__, but if anything, unbelievers who marry Christians have one less reason to convert—they no longer need to convert for the purpose of winning a Christian spouse.

A believer's commitment to God can **wane** as an unbelieving spouse's viewpoint wars against a Christian one. Tension may arise after the wedding when the Christian wonders why his or her spouse isn't keeping a promise to depend upon God. In either case, the outcome is a weakened relationship with one's spouse or with God.

> **2 Corinthians 6:14–15** Do not be **yoked** together with unbelievers. For what do righteousness and wickedness have in common? Or what fellowship can light have with darkness? What harmony is there between Christ and __Belial__? What does a believer have in common with an unbeliever?

Oil and Water Don't Mix

God's primary instruction for a person seeking a spouse is this: Don't marry an unbeliever. No matter how perfect the other person seems, if s/he doesn't share your faith in Christ, that person is off limits. A Christian marrying someone who doesn't know God is like trying to mix oil and water. It makes for an incompatible union (see illustration, page 20). The apostle Paul wrote that such relationships can draw a person away from their devotion to God. *"But I am afraid that just as Eve was deceived by the serpent's cunning, your minds may somehow be led astray from your sincere and pure devotion to Christ"* (2 Corinthians 11:3).

M. Blaine Smith: While scholars argue over whether Paul had marriage in mind in this statement, it is unimaginable that a relationship as binding as marriage wouldn't fall within his boundaries of concern here. The imagery in being unequally yoked is profound and helpful to keep in mind—a horse and ox attached to the same cart and attempting to pull it at different paces is simply not effective.[2]

REMEMBER THIS

☞ **GO TO:**

John 3:3 (salvation)

convert: change their perspective

salvation: depending upon Jesus to get to heaven

wane: weaken

yoked: bound together

Belial: pagan god

☞ **GO TO:**

Deuteronomy 13:13 (Belial)

☞ **GO TO:**

Genesis 3:20 (Eve)

serpent: Satan disguised as a snake

What Others are Saying:

Couples in the Bible

☞ **Check It Out:**

1 Kings 16:29–33

Baal: *foreign god*

Asherah: *a Canaanite goddess*

☞ **GO TO:**

Leviticus 25:23;
  Numbers 36:7 (sell)

1 Kings 21:13 (stoned)

1 Kings 21:19 (lick)

Ahab, king of Israel, was raised in the ways of Jehovah, yet he turned away from worshiping his God after marrying Jezebel, a foreign princess from Sidon. Jezebel worshiped idols in honor of her country's god, Baal (see illustration, page 21). She influenced Ahab to worship her gods, and as a result Ahab "*set up an altar for **Baal** in the temple of Baal that he built in Samaria. Ahab also made an **Asherah** pole and did more to provoke the Lord, the God of Israel, to anger than did all the kings of Israel before him*" (1 Kings 16:32–33).

After Jezebel influenced Ahab to worship her gods, Ahab ruled his country with lies and deceit. One time, Ahab was unhappy because Naboth, an Israelite, wouldn't sell him a piece of land. Even though God had determined in the law that a man couldn't <u>sell</u> his family's land, Ahab still wanted it. When Jezebel heard about it, she took matters into her own hands. She created lies about Naboth and as a result, he was <u>stoned</u> to death. Upon hearing the news, Ahab confiscated the land.

After that, Elijah predicted Ahab would die in such a way that dogs would <u>lick</u> up his blood. He also said God would cut off Ahab's descendants from Israel. This was so sobering to Ahab that he repented of his evil, and God honored his repentance.

Ahab's repentant heart indicates he might have been a godly king without Jezebel's evil influence. Each of us is responsible for our own actions, but we are still influenced by the wickedness of others. Jezebel influenced Ahab for evil; Ahab was not successful in influencing Jezebel for good.

Baal

This drawing shows the god Baal, thought to influence weather, seasons, and fertility. Worship of Baal involved ritual prostitution meant to encourage Baal to mate with his "spouse" Asherah, bringing rain and fertility.

Sidon was an ancient Phoenician city built on a promontory and small island. It was twenty miles north of Tyre and today is called Saida, part of the Republic of Lebanon. Genesis 10:15 identifies Canaan as the father of Sidon, who established the city. Sidonians worshiped Baal and Ashtoreth, two gods whom worshipers believed required animal sacrifice and sensual interactions, including prostitution, in their temples. Earlier in Israel's history, <u>Solomon</u> had been influenced by Sidonian cults.

Jesus called the wicked, hypocritical teaching of the Pharisees "<u>**leaven**</u>," which, without careful attention, could permeate the disciples' thinking. Likewise, the ungodly perspective of an unbelieving spouse can cause a Christian spouse to accept ideas that are dishonoring to God.

> **Genesis 24:4** "But will go to my country and my own relatives and get a wife for my son Isaac."

Think about It

☞ **GO TO:**

1 Kings 11:5–7 (Solomon)

Luke 12:1 (leaven)

REMEMBER THIS

leaven: *yeast*

☞ **Check It Out:**

Genesis 24:1–67

Here Comes the Bride

This story of Abraham, his servant, Rebekah, and Isaac is a beautiful account of a father who wanted the best for his son, a servant who honored his master and prayed for direction, a woman who was willing to go on an adventure, and a son who received the gift of a wife that his father provided. Each person trusted God, facing the challenges that came their way.

In his old age, Abraham sent his servant to find a bride for Isaac from among his relatives in the city of Nahor in the land of Mesopotamia. When the servant arrived there, pausing at a well, he prayed for God's guidance and immediately met a very helpful woman named Rebekah, who offered to water his camels from the well (see illustration below). To his delight he discovered that she was Abraham's great-niece—the granddaughter of Abraham's brother, Nahor. The servant proposed marriage to Rebekah and her family on Isaac's behalf, and she left her family and country to become Isaac's wife. When they were united, Isaac quickly fell in love with Rebekah.

What Others
are Saying:

William L. Coleman: There are too many couples heading for the altar who do not really love each other. The pressures of life have pushed them together, and their lack of commitment may eventually catch up with them and completely gut their relationship.[3]

David and Heather Kopp: Genesis reveals that Isaac and Rebekah went on to have struggles in their marriage, mostly over their children. This doesn't mean they were wrong for each other. It simply reminds us that even a marriage "made in heaven" must be lived out day-by-day on earth—with and in spite of our human shortcomings.[4]

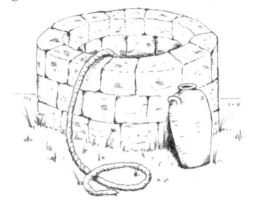

Well

Rebekah probably drew water from a well similar to this one.

The story of finding a wife for Isaac can also be viewed as an analogy for how God makes his children a <u>bride</u> for Christ. God the heavenly Father sent his Holy Spirit to the church so that it would become the bride of Christ. In like manner, God wants to guide each of his children to the spouse of his choosing.

Think about It

☞ **GO TO:**

Revelation 21:9 (bride)

LOVE BAROMETER: HOW DOES YOUR BELOVED MEASURE UP?

> **1 Corinthians 13:4–8a** Love is patient, love is kind. It does not envy, it does not boast, it is not proud. It is not rude, it is not self-seeking, it is not easily angered, it keeps no record of wrongs. Love does not delight in evil but rejoices with the truth. It always protects, always trusts, always hopes, always perseveres. Love never fails.

Perfect Love, the Reader's Digest™ Version

If you're wondering what kind of spouse you'll make or whether the fiancé or fiancée you love will be a good spouse, check out the wisdom of God's basic description of love. He characterizes love in such a way that you can evaluate whether you're giving and receiving true love.

William L. Coleman: Sometime when you are asking yourself what kind of a partner you will make, read 1 Corinthians 13:4–8. It is the world's greatest description of love. Take a brief survey of what love does and apply it to your coming marriage.[5]

What Others are Saying:

Mary Whelchel: Remember that when our emotions are involved in a situation, it's very easy to lose perspective. Someone once told me, "Emotions and feelings have zero IQ," and I think that's a good thing to remember. You cannot trust your emotions. They're dumb sometimes! Those juices get flowing, those romantic notions start whirling around in your head, and you can lose perspective in an instant.[6]

"Love is blind," someone once said, and actually, it's true. When we're dating and falling in love, we tend to overlook the characteristics of our loved one that could potentially create difficulty in our future marriage. We might think:

- "Oh, they'll change and become more patient."
- "It can't really be bad to be jealous, can it?"
- "He seems so insecure at times, but my love for him will overcome that."
- "She sometimes overreacts to my suggestions, but she means well."

If negative characteristics are deeply seated in your spouse to be, you may be in for very difficult times.

Marriage God's Way—If we're wise, we will diminish the "love is blind" syndrome by comparing our potential spouse's behavior to the characteristics of 1 Corinthians 13:4–8. Take each characteristic of love named in that passage and rate your future spouse on a scale of 1 to 10, with 1 being negative and 10 being positive. Be aware: Assessments like these are difficult when struck with the love bug. You will need to think clearly, so pray beforehand, asking God to help you to be honest and fair.

Love Characteristic	Rating
Love is patient	1 2 3 4 5 6 7 8 9 10
Love is kind	1 2 3 4 5 6 7 8 9 10
Love does not envy	1 2 3 4 5 6 7 8 9 10
Love does not boast	1 2 3 4 5 6 7 8 9 10
Love is not proud	1 2 3 4 5 6 7 8 9 10
Love is not rude	1 2 3 4 5 6 7 8 9 10
Love is not self-seeking	1 2 3 4 5 6 7 8 9 10
Love is not easily angered	1 2 3 4 5 6 7 8 9 10
Love keeps no record of wrongs	1 2 3 4 5 6 7 8 9 10
Love does not delight in evil but rejoices with the truth	1 2 3 4 5 6 7 8 9 10
Love always protects, always trusts, always hopes, always perseveres	1 2 3 4 5 6 7 8 9 10
Love never fails	1 2 3 4 5 6 7 8 9 10

If the results tip toward the negative end of the scale, *stop* and consider whom you are planning to marry. It may be that your insecurities or needs are causing your blindness to potential problems. God desires the very best for you. Consider getting wise counsel in order to discuss these issues before you marry. (For another checklist of questions to help you decide the wisdom of marrying a certain person, see WBFT, page 202.) The heartache of a broken engagement will pale in comparison to the agony of an unhappy or failed marriage. God will strengthen you to do the right thing as you seek him.

> **Ruth 3:7–13** When Boaz had finished eating and drinking and was in good spirits, he went over to lie down at the far end of the grain pile. Ruth approached quietly, uncovered his feet and lay down. In the middle of the night something startled the man, and he turned and discovered a woman lying at his feet. "Who are you?" he asked. "I am your servant Ruth," she said. "Spread the corner of your garment over me, since you are a **kinsman-redeemer**." "The Lord bless you, my daughter," he replied. "This kindness is greater than that which you showed earlier: You have not run after the younger men, whether rich or poor. And now, my daughter, don't be afraid. I will do for you all you ask. All my fellow townsmen know that you are a woman of noble character. Although it is true that I am near of kin, there is a kinsman-redeemer nearer than I. Stay here for the night, and in the morning if he wants to redeem, good; let him redeem. But if he is not willing, as surely as the Lord lives, I will do it. Lie here until morning."

Love Is Not Self-Seeking

In Ruth's day, if a man died, one of his relatives had to marry his wife and buy his property to keep it in the family. This relative was known as the kinsman-redeemer.

Boaz wanted to be Ruth's kinsman-redeemer, but there was another man who by law was supposed to have the opportunity

KEY POINT

Engaged people should be honest about the weaknesses they see in their potential spouses.

WARNING

☞ **GO TO:**

Leviticus 25:25 (kinsman-redeemer)

kinsman-redeemer: *relative who delivered a person from poverty by paying debts or buying land*

☞ **GO TO:**

Leviticus 20:10 (law)

Think about It

What Others
are Saying:

☞ **GO TO:**

Matthew 1:18 (Joseph)

compassionate: *wanting the best*

Couples in the Bible

☞ **Check It Out:**

Ruth 1–4

destitute: *desperately poor*

glean: *harvest the grain left over by the reapers*

☞ **GO TO:**

Job 24:6 (glean)

Ruth 2:20 (praised)

Ruth 4:17 (Obed)

first. Boaz trusted God enough to release control and to see what God had in mind for them.

Many years later in biblical history, Mary, the mother of Jesus, told her fiancé, Joseph, that she was pregnant. Joseph was required by <u>law</u> to expose her as a sinful woman so that she would be stoned to death. His love for her caused him to ignore the law, for he had another plan. Matthew 1:19 tells us, *"Because Joseph her husband was a righteous man and did not want to expose her to public disgrace, he had in mind to divorce her quietly."*

M. Blaine Smith: It is of considerable interest to me that both <u>Joseph</u> and Boaz were willing to accept even the ending of the relationship, as painful as the option might be. This is always the response of **compassionate** persons, when they know it's in the best interest of the other. It's in the unhealthy, addictive relationship that one feels that he or she must hold on (no matter what the cost) to the other.[8]

Ruth and Boaz met under unusual circumstances. Ruth was a foreigner who arrived in Israel with her mother-in-law, Naomi, after the deaths of Naomi's and Ruth's husbands. Ruth and Naomi were **destitute**. Ruth willingly went to the fields to **glean** grain for them to eat (see illustration, page 27). She unknowingly sought food in the fields owned by Boaz, a "kinsman-redeemer" of Naomi. When Naomi found out where Ruth gleaned, she <u>praised</u> God for guiding Ruth to that particular field. Naomi then instructed Ruth to gain Boaz's attention and indicate her desire to marry. Naomi told her to lay down beside Boaz on the threshing floor and cover herself with his garment. This was not intended to be a sexual advance. It was a custom of the time, which would have been intrepreted as a marriage proposal as well as a request for protection.

Since Boaz was older than Ruth, he was impressed that she chose him instead of a younger man. He acknowledged her wonderful qualities and told her he wanted to marry her, but he knew another, closer relative should have the opportunity first. Later, he made the closer relative aware of his opportunity to redeem Naomi and marry Ruth, but the man declined. That freed Boaz to marry Ruth. In time, Ruth gave birth to <u>Obed</u>, who was the grandfather of King David and in the lineage of Jesus Christ (see Matthew 1:5).

Reaper

After the reapers finished harvesting the fields as shown in this illustration, the poor could walk through the fields, gathering any grain left behind. This was called "gleaning."

True love wants only the best for the object of its affection, even if it means releasing the loved one. If your future mate will do anything to hold on to you, even at your expense, that's not healthy love.

REMEMBER  THIS

LOVE'S FOUNDATION: CRUMBLING OR LOTS IN COMMON?

> **Judges 16:4–6** Some time later, he fell in love with a woman in the Valley of Sorek whose name was Delilah. The rulers of the Philistines went to her and said, "See if you can lure him into showing you the secret of his great strength and how we can overpower him so we may tie him up and subdue him. Each one of us will give you eleven hundred shekels of silver." So Delilah said to Samson, "Tell me the secret of your great strength and how you can be tied up and subdued."

Delilah's Deception

The story of Samson's love for Delilah is a powerful lesson in the importance of **compatibility**. Samson was a Jew who was raised in a devout family. At birth, his parents dedicated him to serve God.

compatibility: ability to get along in harmony

Honestly evaluate the quality of your future mate's love.

shackles: chains used to confine arms or legs

What Others are Saying:

Think about It

inerrancy: no mistakes or errors

Delilah, on the other hand, was from another country where Jehovah was not worshiped. She had completely different values, and they had little in common. Samson was raised to be honest, and Delilah was deceitful. She didn't want the best for Samson and "loved" him only for her own gain. She charmed him into telling her the secret to his strength. What did Samson get from his lack of wisdom? One shaved head, two blind eyes, and **shackles**.

M. Blaine Smith: Maturity and lifestyle factors make an enormous difference in the ability of two people to live effectively together in marriage. In considering your compatibility with someone, it's as important to look carefully at how ready both of you are for marriage.[9]

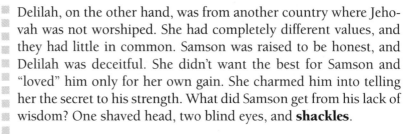

Marriage God's Way—God not only wants men and women to join themselves in marriage to other Christians, he wants them to marry those with compatible similarities.

Consider these areas to determine your compatibility:

- *Physical:* Whether you have a strong physical attraction to your future mate or not, the important thing is your willingness to make a commitment of physical intimacy solely with that person for the rest of your life.

- *Intellectual:* It's not so important that you and your beloved have the same level of education, but that you find conversation stimulating and that your growth— emotional, intellectual, and spiritual—is encouraged. If he or she is threatened by your desire to expand your interests and knowledge, it may be that he or she will stifle you in marriage.

- *Emotional:* An emotionally mature person knows himself or herself. He or she understands personal weaknesses and is working toward becoming a better person rather than blaming others, seeking to escape, or denying the existence of a problem.

- *Spiritual:* Even if you're both Christians, there are essential issues to consider: viewpoint on the **inerrancy** of Scripture, gender roles and expectations, commitment to spiritual growth, and agreement about ethics and values.

Don't let the love for your loved one blind you to potential difficulties. Often new love emphasizes the commonalities and ignores the differences. Consider putting yourselves into unusual circumstances so that you can see how each of you respond. By honestly evaluating how you relate to each other, you'll be prepared for future difficulties.

WARNING

Barbara and Orris had not formed a spiritual oneness with their former spouses, so that was high on their list of priorities when they began dating. Orris set the pace early in their relationship by suggesting that they pray together. To actually pray out loud together was a delightful first for Barbara. At her suggestion, they began reading the same sections of Scripture on their own, using *The One Year Bible*. Then they talked about what they had read when they were together.

*TAKE IT
FROM THEM*

In preparation for marriage, they read Christian books on marriage, discussing what they learned and applying it to their particular situation. Having experienced divorce, they both knew a successful, enduring marriage must include God. As they read, talked, and prayed, Barbara and Orris realized that with their strong-willed natures, God's standards and God himself needed to be central in their marriage.

It took time for Barbara to accept the fact that she wouldn't be #1 in Orris's life, because that position belonged exclusively to God. But they discovered that the closer they got to God, the closer they became to each other. They visualized that concept through the image of a triangle with God at the top and the couple at opposite ends of the base. As the two individuals move up the sides of the triangle getting closer to God, they are also growing closer together.

Because Barbara and Orris desired to follow God's direction in their marriage, they included Proverbs 3:5–6 in their wedding ceremony: *"Trust in the Lord with all your heart and lean not on your own understanding; in all your ways acknowledge him, and he will make your paths straight."* Putting God at the top of their relationship gave them a strong base for what has become an enduring, happy marriage.

NOT TEMPERAMENTAL, JUST A TEMPERAMENT

stature: height

> **Luke 2:52** And Jesus grew in wisdom and **stature**, and in favor with God and men.

The Perfect Model

As Jesus grew up, he was a model of wisdom, physical bearing, and love—both with God and his fellow man. Even as a young person, Jesus exhibited physical, emotional, and spiritual healthiness. We can assume he took good care of his body, respecting it as the **temple** of the Holy Spirit. He exhibited wisdom by making good choices. He was aware of his special relationship with God, his heavenly Father, and he knew how to respond to people in a way that showed them God's love. As a result, he pleased God and was respected by others as someone with integrity.

☞ GO TO:

1 Corinthians 3:16 (temple)

temple: dwelling place

If Jesus had married, he would have been the perfect husband. Although none of us will be perfect here on earth, we can grow in wisdom and in favor with God and men. As we do we will please our spouse or make the perfect "catch" for a future spouse.

What Others are Saying:

M. Blaine Smith: There is considerable benefit to understanding each other's personalities, to be sure. But the value comes in helping you understand where your potential for conflict will lie rather than in giving you a magical answer about whether or not to marry.[10]

Marriage God's Way—Jesus would be the perfect spouse if he could have married. Yet, an expressed opinion is that most likely any woman who married him still wouldn't have been satisfied. That's just like relationships, isn't it? We're never satisfied with what we have—even if it's perfect. Yet, Jesus' personality can be an important measure for an engaged couple. They can evaluate how closely their potential mate resembles Jesus in action and attitude and also assess their beloved's strengths and weaknesses.

Jesus was the perfect human being—yet fully God. We cannot expect our future mate to be perfect like him, but we can evaluate Jesus' strengths to gain an understanding of the four basic **temperaments**, which some call **personality styles** (see WBFW, pages 106–107). They are the viewpoints about life that motivate how we respond to circumstances and people. Each personality or temperament has both strengths and weaknesses.

Here is a summary of the four basic temperaments:

- *Sanguine:* outgoing, desires fun, is emotional, outspoken, and relationship-oriented
- *Melancholy:* introverted, desires perfection, is organized, **pessimistic**, and task-oriented
- *Phlegmatic:* introverted, desires peace, is unemotional, pessimistic, and relationship-oriented
- *Choleric:* outgoing, desires power or control, is outspoken, strong-willed, and **optimistic**

Instead of displaying the attitude, "Now that you know why I act that way, you'll just have to accept me the way I am," we can choose to think of others. We can respond through the power of the Holy Spirit in a way that would help meet their needs and overcome the weaknesses of our temperament. That's called "**versatility**."

The Perfect Personality

Jesus didn't exhibit weaknesses of any of the temperaments, but he demonstrated all the strengths of all four temperaments. He truly was the perfect person.

With <u>children</u>, he was the sanguine: lively and fun. His ability to teach effectively, especially with <u>parables</u>, shows his strength in organization and attention to detail—like the melancholy temperament. Jesus was most like a phlegmatic when he was able to <u>sleep</u> in a boat when the disciples thought the boat would be tossed over in a storm. And finally, he operated as a choleric when he confidently and forcefully threw the <u>money-changers</u> out of the Temple. He took quick action and wasn't afraid of anyone.

REMEMBER THIS

temperaments: one's customary frame of mind or natural disposition

personality styles: individual temperaments and behavior

pessimistic: focuses primarily on the gloomy or bad

optimistic: focuses primarily on the cheerful or good

versatility: capability of change

☞ **GO TO:**

Matthew 18:2 (children)

Matthew 13:18 (parables)

Matthew 8:24 (sleep)

Matthew 21:12 (money-changers)

Think about It

Knowing your future spouse's temperament will help you understand them. Many people believe that the person they love looks at life the same way they do, but that's usually not the case. Not understanding their way of thinking will lead to assumptions and misunderstandings when they react out of *their* perspective of life, not *your* perspective.

What's Temperament Got to Do with Anything?

He Says . . .

LARRY: When I first dated Kathy, I was impressed with the energy and flexibility she demonstrated. If there were some minor conflict between us, she readily faced the problem and even offered compromises that suited both our interests.

But after we were married a while, things began to change . . . things like when Kathy consistently squeezed the toothpaste tube in the middle, in obvious rebellion to my careful instruction. Imagine my surprise when I found my compromising and flexible bride was no longer interested in making any changes. **Status quo** was now her goal in life.

status quo: *keep the same*

I'd never heard of the different temperaments when we were dating. Although Kathy demonstrated versatility during that time, there were plenty of warning signs that popped up to reveal her desire to be perfect, but my love-blinded eyes just didn't see them. Years later when we learned about the temperaments, I was identified as a choleric, whereas Kathy tested as a melancholy. We began to understand the different perspective we each had.

Women normally see a man's potential and hope he will change after marriage. Men, on the other hand, fall in love with a woman just as she is and expect her to stay the same throughout marriage.

She Says . . .

KATHY: When Larry and I were engaged, I thought my eyes were open to any weaknesses Larry might have. I even considered writing down the imperfections in him so that later, if those things upset me, I would remember that I went into marriage with my eyes open.

The real surprise came when the things I loved about Larry before we married became sources of irritation. As a result, I went into marriage with two strikes already against me: the weaknesses I was aware of and the lack of knowledge about how strengths might be taken to extremes.

I loved Larry's take-charge personality when we were dating. He organized our dates and I felt secure, knowing I wouldn't have to make decisions. I didn't know, though, that he would take that temperament characteristic and tell me how to stack the glasses in the kitchen cupboard. Nor did I expect him to comment on how much toilet paper or tissues I used in the bathroom. Yet, Larry had an opinion about that and . . . everything else.

Had I known about the temperaments before we got married, I could have gone into marriage more knowledgeable and less defensive over Larry's self-assuredness. Instead of accepting his confidence as the way God had made him, I took it personally, got angry, and believed he loved me less.

TAKE IT FROM THEM

After Charles and Karen studied the personalities/temperaments, their marriage radically changed for the better. They understood how they could complement each other instead of looking at their differences as annoyances. However, they still have moments when they forget what they learned! When they notice one of them trying to take control, usually in a negative way, they stop right away and remind themselves that they're having a "pantry moment."

That phrase developed because Charles, the melancholy perfectionist, likes compartments in the pantry, dishwasher, and refrigerator to be maintained in a categorical and orderly fashion (small items on top, canned goods in a row, cups and saucers in their proper slots in the dishwasher, etc.). Karen, the fun-loving sanguine, is more interested in getting things put away—but not necessarily in a perfect way—so that she can get on to what is "fun."

When Karen is out of town, Charles straightens up everything in the pantry, fridge, and dishwasher. When Karen is home, she tends to forget the "rules" and just puts things behind the closed doors. This bugs Charles! Yet, his precision bugs Karen! However, they have learned that this can work in their favor.

When they start to argue, they stop and remind themselves that they're having a "pantry moment." That's a signal to get to the bottom of the communication difference rather than trying to control each other. Karen and Charles's marriage is now more calm, warm, caring, and intimate. They rarely fight because they understand each other's personality in a deeper way, and they see it as a blessing instead of a source of competition. Charles brings the order, Karen supplies the fun.

STUDY QUESTIONS

1. How do we know God is interested in whom we marry according to Psalm 73:23–24?
2. According to 2 Corinthians 6:14–15, God does not want Christians to marry whom and why?
3. How was Jezebel a destructive influence on Ahab and why?
4. In what way does the story of how Rebekah came to be Isaac's wife relate to a Christian's quest for a spouse?
5. What are the characteristics of true love as defined in 1 Corinthians 13:4–8?
6. How do we know Delilah did not really love Samson?
7. How was Jesus the perfect man?

CHAPTER WRAP-UP

- God knows the best person for you to marry. He promises to guide you to that person just as Abraham's servant was led to the wife that Isaac could love. Although in Bible times a spouse was chosen by the parents, today we can look to God our heavenly Father to choose the best person for us. His choice will always be another Christian because believers are incompatible with unbelievers.

- God gives us the characteristics of true love in 1 Corinthians 13:4–8, and those qualities are the ones we should seek in a potential spouse. No one will be able to love us perfectly, but we can open our love-blinded eyes by asking ourselves how close that person's love comes to God's definition of love.

- It's important to evaluate how compatible you are with the person you're thinking about marrying. If a couple has too many differences and not enough in common, they may find it difficult to make marriage work. Pleasant emotion is not always enough to overcome differences.

- We certainly won't find a "perfect" spouse, but by understanding temperaments, we can prepare ourselves to understand the differences of our fiancé or fiancée. We will then be less likely to become angry or defensive when they do something we don't understand or that contradicts our viewpoint.

KATHY & LARRY'S BOOKSHELF

Some of Kathy and Larry's favorite books about engagement:

- *Should I Get Married?*, M. Blaine Smith, InterVarsity Press. Wisdom for making choices about marriage.
- *The Engagement Book*, William L. Coleman, Tyndale House Publishers. Preparing for the love of a lifetime.
- *Playing the Tuba at Midnight*, Roberta Rand, InterVarsity Press. The joys and challenges of singleness.
- *Single Adult Passages*, Carolyn A. Koons and Michael J. Anthony, Baker Book House. Uncharted territories for singles.

3 IN HOT PURSUIT OF PURITY

WHAT'S IN THIS CHAPTER

- The Purpose of Purity
- Temptation 101
- Passionate Patience

Here We Go

You have found the love of your life. He or she is everything you want or could have hoped for. God has answered your prayer for a worthy husband or wife and you are thrilled. You love each other so much that there's an electricity and passion between you. You can't wait for your wedding night! But at times, it seems so far off and there's so much passion between you that it's hard to resist touching and getting physically intimate. You don't want to go too far, but it's just so hard to combat those intense desires.

What can you do?

Such passion *is* hard to resist, yet God wants to help you do exactly that. He created your body to desire physical intimacy as a commitment of your love, but he wants you to save that fabulous experience for marriage. Let's see how God wants to help you keep yourself and your beloved pure.

THE PURPOSE OF PURITY

> **1 Thessalonians 4:3–5** It is God's will that you should be **sanctified**: that you should avoid sexual **immorality**; that each of you should learn to control his own body in a way that is holy and honorable, not in passionate lust like the **heathen**, who do not know God.

sanctified: free from sin

immorality: sex outside of marriage

heathen: unbelievers

Satan Is in the Premarital Counseling Business

premarital sex: sex before marriage

It may be hard to comprehend or even accept, but God does want you to avoid **premarital sex**. Regardless of how much you love your fiancé or fiancée, God knows what's best, and he wants you to remain pure until the night of your wedding. Having control over your body and its passions takes a lot of trust and dependence on the Lord, but when you have this self-control, it is a demonstration to others of God within you.

The world says sex before marriage is alright. Some people go so far as to say it's a good idea to have sex before marriage, and here are some reasons they typically give:

- You'll find out whether you and your potential spouse are sexually compatible.
- You're going to have sex eventually, so why wait?
- You should practice so that being married for the first time is great.
- It's not healthy to deny your normal sexual urges.
- You're just satisfying a biological urge, so commitment isn't necessary.

Yet, these are all lies created by Satan to steal the joy of purity. Satan is the "father of lies." There is nothing more joyful or satisfying than offering your purity to your new husband or wife on your wedding night. That doesn't mean everything will be perfect on your wedding night, but it does mean you won't carry into your honeymoon any baggage of guilt or shame.

☞ **GO TO:**

John 8:44
(father of lies)

What Others are Saying:

repress: reject

Josh McDowell and Paul Lewis: The Playboy philosophy, among many other voices, has led millions to believe that God is anti-sex, and that the Bible is negative on sexual enjoyment and fulfillment. They've asserted that to be a Christian believer, one would have to deny and **repress** his sexual urges. Nothing could be further from the truth.[1]

Carolyn A. Koons and Michael J. Anthony: We Christians are called to be stewards of all our gifts—including our sexuality. This involves acknowledging that we have been entrusted with a gift of great value: our sexual nature. We can choose to allow our sexuality to control us or, instead, we can consider it as one more resource available for investment in God's kingdom.[2]

Marriage God's Way—God created sex for our pleasure and enjoyment. Scripture tells us, *"For this reason a man will leave his father and mother and be united to his wife, and they will become one flesh. The man and his wife were both naked, and they felt no shame"* (Genesis 2:24–25). As sexual beings, Adam and Eve, who are referred to in this verse, were not afraid or ashamed of their bodies and their sexuality. God wanted them to enjoy each other and their bodies.

God delights in giving good gifts to his children, and one of them is sex—within the context of marriage. Outside marriage, sex is destructive and will not accomplish God's purposes. He designed sex as a means of uniting our souls together. When sex takes place outside of marriage, there is fear involved. The woman, for example, might be afraid of having sex without the assurance that the man will stay with her. Within marriage, sex can be a deeply spiritual experience.

KEY POINT

God created sex as a great gift for his creation.

REMEMBER THIS

☞ **GO TO:**

James 1:17 (good gifts)

TEMPTATION 101

> **Genesis 3:1–5** Now the serpent was more crafty than any of the wild animals the Lord God had made. He said to the woman, "Did God really say, 'You must not eat from any tree in the garden'?" The woman said to the serpent, "We may eat fruit from the trees in the garden, but God did say, 'You must not eat fruit from the tree that is in the middle of the garden, and you must not touch it, or you will die.'" "You will not surely die," the serpent said to the woman. "For God knows that when you eat of it your eyes will be opened, and you will be like God, knowing good and evil."

☞ **GO TO:**

Genesis 2:17 (die)

Lies-s-s-s-s-s

Satan, in the form of a snake, tempted Eve in the Garden. He made her doubt God's goodness by questioning what God had said. That's why Satan asked Eve, "Did God really say?" Satan has continued to tempt people throughout the ages by the same method. He wants to destroy an unmarried person's purity by making them

☞ **GO TO:**

Job 1:6–12; Matthew 4:1; 1 Corinthians 7:5 (tempt)

think that God is withholding something good from them—sex. Satan is the great <u>deceiver</u> who delights in questioning God's motives and his love.

What Others are Saying:

☞ **GO TO:**

Revelation 12:9 (deceiver)

Josh McDowell and Paul Lewis: God isn't *against* sex. He's so *for* it that he wants every man and woman to understand how to get the most out of it. He wants them to realize it's not a casual toy; it's a fundamental pleasure to be carefully cherished, no matter how gratifying a "quick fix" might seem.[3]

Liz Curtis Higgs: By twisting the Lord's decrees, Satan also tossed out one of the big stumbling blocks he still uses with great success today—making God look less than fair, kind, or loving.[4]

> **Genesis 3:6** When the woman saw that the fruit of the tree was good for food and pleasing to the eye, and also desirable for gaining wisdom, she took some and ate it. She also gave some to her husband, who was with her, and he ate it.

KEY POINT

Temptation focuses on what we don't have and ignores what God has already given us.

Sugar-Laced Poison

When Satan tempts, he offers something that seems "pleasing" and "desirable." When Satan tempts a couple with sex, he makes it seem like they can't live without it and that it's the ultimate pleasure—which they are missing. Yes, sex *is* pleasurable, but the pleasure is not worth disobeying God.

What Others are Saying:

Liz Curtis Higgs: The tree that had been in the middle of everything, yet obediently avoided—for how long we don't know— suddenly, that tree was *it*. The all-consuming, gotta-have-it thing. The problem here involved taking her eyes off what was good and acceptable, and putting them on what she *knew*, absolutely, to be forbidden.[5]

Albert Y. Hsu: The first step to a healthy approach toward sexuality is to recognize that sexual expression is not essential for life. Jesus himself is our example for living the single life without sexual activity.[6]

Society and the media, especially movies, portray sex as if no one can possibly live without it, and that with it, life will be abundant with joy. Yet, only a relationship with God can meet such a claim. Sex is a **temporal** pleasure that is wonderful, but spiritual oneness with God is more important and more valuable.

temporal: short-lived

Marriage God's Way—The word for "wisdom" in this passage refers to the idea of being "in the know." Another one of Satan's whispered lies about sex outside of marriage is that we can't be "in the know" about whether or not this person is the one to marry unless we experience sexual intimacy with him or her. This isn't true because good sex doesn't have as much to do with compatibility as it does with serving the other person.

God wants married couples to grow and develop their sexual artistry within the safe atmosphere of marriage. Outside that boundary, members of a couple who have sex do not feel free to be who they really are because they are worried about whether their performance is acceptable.

> **Genesis 3:7–13** Then the eyes of both of them were opened, and they realized they were naked; so they sewed fig leaves together and made coverings for themselves. Then the man and his wife heard the sound of the Lord God as he was walking in the garden in the cool of the day, and they hid from the Lord God among the trees of the garden. But the Lord God called to the man, "Where are you?" He answered, "I heard you in the garden, and I was afraid because I was naked; so I hid." And he said, "Who told you that you were naked? Have you eaten from the tree that I commanded you not to eat from?" The man said, "The woman you put here with me—she gave me some fruit from the tree, and I ate it." Then the Lord God said to the woman, "What is this you have done?" The woman said, "The serpent deceived me, and I ate."

The Birth of Shame

After Adam and Eve sinned by eating the forbidden fruit, Satan's promise came true: their eyes were opened. But it wasn't what they expected (see GWWB, pages 10–16). Instead of true wisdom, they lost their innocence about life and their trust of each other. Now they were uncomfortable with each other's bodies, and they tried to hide from each other. Then they tried to hide from God.

What Others are Saying:

Liz Curtis Higgs: Now fallen, Adam, who had named every animal in the garden, had to find a name for what they did: *sin*. A name for what they felt: *shame*. A name for the consequences: *separation*.[7]

Joseph M. Stowell: Realizing their shame and loss, Adam and Eve tried to cover their sin by sewing fig leaves together. Our world still specializes in fig leaves, because there is no hope of significance apart from God. When sin is present, as it is in all of us, there is also no hope of restoration to him in and of ourselves and therefore no hope of true, shameless significance. That is why redemption is such a pivotal and wonderful reality. The marvel of it all is that God has taken the initiative.[8]

WARNING

☞ **GO TO:**

Genesis 3:14–24
(consequences)

God does want us to desire wisdom, but true wisdom comes from knowing God—not from having sex with somebody. Proverbs 1:7 says, *"The fear of the Lord is the beginning of knowledge, but fools despise wisdom and discipline."* Disobeying God's commands will never give us true wisdom or joy, but seeking and obeying God will.

Disobedience brought <u>consequences</u> that Adam and Eve never anticipated. They were banished from the Garden of Eden. Adam had to work hard to bring food from the ground. Eve became submissive to her husband, and was fated to have pain during childbirth.

Disobeying God's laws always brings consequences. Couples who have sex before marriage may carry guilt into the wedding day. A man and woman who have premarital sex may become distrustful of each other. Their "knowledge" of each other is no longer innocent and could influence their ability to enjoy sex when married.

A Consequence We Never Anticipated

LARRY: After dating and falling in love with Kathy, I found myself overwhelmed by the desire for sex. As we continued to struggle I wanted to move up the wedding date. The cycle was vicious, and I judged myself a weak leader. It never occurred to me that making myself accountable to a small group of men could have made a difference.

Since 1994 I have been a part of a small group of men. We are wholly committed to our mutual spiritual growth. Before this group, I faced life alone. I shared with no one. Now, years later, I find the daily struggle to walk with Christ less harsh and victories more frequent. Truly, a small group of committed men makes each man stand a little taller and walk a little straighter. I wish that I'd had that support and accountability when Kathy and I were dating.

KATHY: Larry and I struggled with our sexual desires while we were dating, wondering if we would be able to stay pure until our wedding day. When we experienced the failure of going beyond the boundaries we had set for ourselves, we would both become upset. I had a hard time believing God could forgive us since it seemed like we fell too often. It was so hard to resist, yet I knew God wanted us to stay pure.

When we finally married, I didn't realize our sexual wanderings before marriage would influence our relationship. I had developed a great bitterness toward Larry, without realizing how deep it was, because he didn't have more self-control. I blamed myself tremendously, also, but I thought he was primarily responsible.

My resentment and guilt about our failings influenced me so that I couldn't enjoy sex as much after we were married. It just didn't seem right to enjoy something we had previously struggled against. I also found that my body wasn't as responsive as before marriage. It wasn't until doing research for our book, *When the Honeymoon's Over,* that I learned that the **illicitness** of our touching before marriage had become a stimulus in itself. It also became a trigger for responding. After Larry and I got married the illicit trigger was no longer there to cause a strong reaction.

It took several years for me to work through my guilt and anger towards Larry. I finally put it behind me when I truly accepted God's forgiveness. Then I was free to forgive Larry and myself. My sexual response improved over the years, but I missed out on greater enjoyment in the beginning because of our history while dating.

He Says . . .

She Says . . .

KEY POINT

Satan's promises never come true in the way he suggests.

illicitness: *unlawful*

PASSIONATE PATIENCE

> **Genesis 29:16–20** Now Laban had two daughters; the name of the older was Leah, and the name of the younger was Rachel. Leah had weak eyes, but Rachel was lovely in form, and beautiful. Jacob was in love with Rachel and said, "I'll work for you seven years in return for your younger daughter Rachel." Laban said, "It's better that I give her to you than to some other man. Stay here with me." So Jacob served seven years to get Rachel, but they seemed like only a few days to him because of his love for her.

And You Thought Sitting at Stoplights Was Bad

The Bible is honest in sharing the sexual immorality of many people in the history of God's people, but there was one person who waited seven years to sexually enjoy the woman he was madly in love with: Jacob! Jacob agreed to work for seven years in order to earn his marriage to his beloved Rachel, and he kept both of them pure during that time. He loved her so much that the long seven-year wait was worth it to him.

What Others are Saying:

sanctity: value and purity

KEY POINT

The first step to purity is to believe it's possible.

Joy Jacobs and Deborah Strubel: We must see ourselves as God sees us: as unique, created, loved beings. We are not animals. We are capable of reasoning and weighing the possible consequences of our actions before we perform them. When we start with correct beliefs about the **sanctity** of human life, we can translate those beliefs into correct attitudes and proper actions. Only when we accept responsibility for our actions and their consequences will we be empowered to change.[9]

Mary Whelchel: That's because we have been infiltrated with the world's view, to the point that purity of thought and life is considered a joke, something possible only for weird people who don't live in the real world. That's a satanic lie, and our enemy has sure done a good job of putting that one over on us![10]

One of Satan's lies regarding sexual purity is, "No one else has enough self-control to resist, why do you think you can?" Yet many people do resist every day—our society just doesn't celebrate their dependence upon God. From the movies, other media, books, and pornography, you'd think that "everyone's doing it," but there are many who are not. Thankfully, there are also those who are vocal in encouraging people to "just say no!"

REMEMBER THIS

> **Genesis 34:1–2** Now <u>Dinah</u>, the daughter Leah had borne to Jacob, went out to visit the women of the land. When Shechem son of <u>Hamor</u> the **Hivite**, the ruler of that area, saw her, he took her and **violated** her.

☞ **GO TO:**

Genesis 30:21 (Dinah)

Genesis 33:19 (Hamor)

Genesis 36:2 (Hivite)

Dinah Was in Danger

Although Dinah didn't choose to be raped, she placed herself in a dangerous place: among the neighboring women whose customs were immoral. As a result, she was powerless to resist the advances of a man who was stronger than she.

Hivite: *a nation in Canaan*

violated: *raped*

Mary Whelchel: When you think you "can handle it," when you assume that you know how far to go, when you believe that it would never happen to you, you're in trouble. The only cure here is prevention, and the only way you can prevent sexual involvement with someone to whom you are attracted is to eliminate the opportunity.[11]

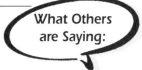

What Others are Saying:

Keith Miller and Andrea Wells Miller: But whatever decision you make, I'd suggest you make it before the evening begins, since the sex drive is so strong that it may be impossible to make a decision to set limits after you begin touching in a potentially loaded sexual situation.[12]

KEY POINT

The second step to purity is to avoid dangerous situations.

Marriage God's Way—One of the best ways to keep your commitment to sexual purity is to set **parameters** for the activities you will engage in and the places you will go. If you have your own apartment, don't have that special person over and fill the house with lighted candles. Don't just let your dates happen, where inactivity may cause temptation to increase. Instead,

parameters: boundaries

plan your dates and keep busy with activities. Even doing useful things like helping at a shelter for the homeless or sorting clothes at a thrift store can be fun. Don't go to places like the local mountain lookout or a dark corner of a house where temptation lurks. And if temptation is really starting to overwhelm you, consider not being alone together.

TAKE IT FROM THEM

Sam and Gail dated for four years before they decided to get married. From the beginning, they struggled with sexual temptation. They were so much in love that they wanted to experience everything that could draw them closer. As Christians, they kept trying to resist their sexual urges, but they often went farther in their necking and touching than they desired. Although they didn't have intercourse, they felt guilty about their lack of self-control. They wondered if they could resist "going all the way" the next time.

Gail found herself feeling suspicious of Sam's intentions. She thought, "Maybe he just loves me for the physical contact he gets. Or maybe he doesn't really love me at all and is just using me. If he can't resist me now, maybe he won't be able to resist the advances of another woman after we're married."

Sam felt guilty also. He knew he loved Gail and found it almost impossible to resist touching her when they were together. He prayed again and again for strength but felt powerless at times.

Sam and Gail almost had intercourse one time and realized they had to take drastic steps to prevent that situation again. From that point on, they set up guidelines for their dates together. They would only double date, not be alone, and plan activities for their times together. They also involved their church's youth pastor in holding them accountable by checking in with him weekly. He and his wife were always available if they needed prayer support or to talk about their struggle.

Sam and Gail were successful in resisting the temptation that almost overwhelmed them, and on their wedding night they prayed together, thanking God for the closeness they could enjoy without guilt.

> **2 Peter 1:5–8** For this very reason, make every effort to add to your faith goodness; and to goodness, knowledge; and to knowledge, self-control; and to self-control, perseverance; and to perseverance, godliness; and to godliness, brotherly kindness; and to brotherly kindness, love. For if you possess these qualities in increasing measure, they will keep you from being ineffective and unproductive in your knowledge of our Lord Jesus Christ.

With Self-Control You're on a Roll

Scripture stresses self-control for the sake of representing Christ. Those engaged in sexual activity outside of marriage prevent the Holy Spirit from using them. They can't grow in their ability to receive the <u>fruit of the Spirit</u> because God is not in charge of their lives. It's not a happy place to be because guilt and condemnation replace God's joy.

Josh McDowell and Paul Lewis: But why wait? I think one reason is to build self-control; something all of us need a little more of. There are many times after you're married when you cannot have sex due to illness, separation, or some stages of pregnancy. When you learn to control your sex life before marriage, you can control it afterwards. And this self-control adds the factor of trust to a relationship.[13]

Jim Talley and Bobbie Reed: Learning to live out our commitment to obedience is a major step in our spiritual growth. When we learn how to exercise self-control in sexual matters, we can use the same techniques to master anger, language, and other tendencies to excess.[14]

Purity has many advantages:

- With purity, it is easier to determine whether your beloved is the right person for you to marry. Sexual contact creates a <u>bond</u> that is painful to break. Moreover, after premarital sex a feeling of obligation makes it difficult for the couple to discern whether they are truly right for one another.
- With purity, you avoid the consequences of disease and pregnancy. You also avoid having to make a decision about aborting a child. Purity is easier! Sexual immoral-

☞ **GO TO:**

Galatians 5:22–23 (fruit of the Spirit)

What Others are Saying:

KEY POINT

The third step to purity is to focus on the advantages of purity.

Think about It

☞ **GO TO:**

Genesis 2:24 (bond)

ity complicates life, creating decisions that God never intended for an unmarried couple to make.

☞ **GO TO:**

Galatians 5:23
(self-control)

- Purity cultivates the spiritual fruit of <u>self-control</u>. Self-control is useful in other areas of life as well, like finances and physical health.
- Purity enables the bride and groom to offer themselves to each other with no strings attached. No other lover has invaded their memories. No one else can be held up for comparison.

> **Ephesians 5:1–4** Be imitators of God, therefore, as dearly loved children and live a life of love, just as Christ loved us and gave himself up for us as a fragrant offering and sacrifice to God. But among you there must not be even a hint of sexual immorality, or of any kind of impurity, or of greed, because these are improper for God's holy people. Nor should there be obscenity, foolish talk or coarse joking, which are out of place, but rather thanksgiving.

A Single Spark Can Destroy a Forest

☞ **GO TO:**

2 Corinthians 10:5
(captivate)

God says we shouldn't speak of that which is immoral. That seems a little drastic, but if we completely ignore immorality, it can't <u>captivate</u> our minds. If we envision kissing or touching our beloved in his or her absence, we'll have a hard time resisting in his or her presence.

Couples in the Bible

☞ **Check It Out:**

2 Samuel 13:1–22

King David had many children with several different wives. Amnon and Tamar were two of those children. Tamar was the beautiful sister of Absalom, another of David's sons. Amnon fell in love with Tamar but couldn't figure out a way to make Tamar return his love. He was so frustrated he became physically ill.

Amnon's friend Jonadab came up with a plan to help Amnon. He advised Amnon to pretend he was sick and to ask Tamar to prepare some food for him. When Tamar came to help him, he grabbed her. Tamar pleaded with him to let her go, telling him she would even be willing to request that he ask for her hand in marriage, but he refused to listen. He forced himself upon her and raped her.

Instead of continuing to love her, he suddenly hated her and threw her out of his room. She never married, living the rest of her life in her brother Absalom's house. Absalom knew what had happened, and years later, murdered Amnon in revenge.

What started out as simple thoughts, escalated into lust, and ended in <u>destruction</u>. Proverbs 23:7 tells us, *"For as he thinks within himself, so he is"* (NASB). What we think about, we will act upon. That is certainly true with our sexuality.

☞ **GO TO:**

James 1:15
(destruction)

Michelle McKinney Hammond: That rape started in Amnon's thought life. The Bible states that he fantasized about her to the point of illness! By the time he got near her, he was beyond rational thinking. And you know the rest of the story: Death, sponsored by runaway imaginations.[15]

What Others are Saying:

Elisabeth Elliot: A touch that might become exciting is the beginning of sexual foreplay. This is the way God arranged things. Any such encounter may start the fire running in one's veins. Divine Wisdom purposed that one thing should lead to another. The act begins in thought. When the first touch occurs, momentum gathers.[16]

KEY POINT

The fourth step to purity is to control your thoughts.

Exposing ourselves to sexual ideas through movies, the Internet, magazines, or pornography creates a stronghold in our minds that will encourage sexual behavior with our future husband or wife. Second Corinthians 10:5 admonishes us: *"We demolish arguments and every **pretension** that sets itself up against the knowledge of God, and we take captive every thought to make it obedient to Christ."* We do that by making a moment-by-moment choice to focus on that which is honoring to God.

WARNING

pretension: wrong motive

STUDY QUESTIONS

1. Based on 1 Thessalonians 4:3–5, what are two reasons God wants us to avoid sexual immorality?
2. How did Satan first tempt Eve?
3. How does everything forbidden look when temptation strikes?
4. Why was Jacob willing to work for Rachel's hand in marriage and how long did he wait?
5. How did Dinah put herself in a dangerous position to be sexually violated?
6. What advice does Scripture give about sexual immorality?

- God created sex for the pleasure of people who are married. He wants us to abstain from sexual intimacy when we're not married because he knows doing so is what's best for us. With abstinence, we honor him in the eyes of others, we grow closer to him in obedience, and we develop self-control, the fruit of the Holy Spirit.

- Satan is an expert at temptation. He tells us that God doesn't want the best for his people. He tempted Eve to eat the forbidden fruit, and he tempts singles to have sex by telling them God is withholding something good from them.

- It is possible to resist sexual temptation by first understanding that many people practice abstinence, even though society gives the impression that it's impossible. It's also necessary to avoid situations or places that make sexual temptation more compelling. Understanding the advantages of purity also helps. Finally, refraining from thinking about sex when it's not appropriate diminishes temptation.

KATHY & LARRY'S  BOOKSHELF

Kathy and Larry's favorite books about staying pure:

- *Givers, Takers and Other Kinds of Lovers*, Josh McDowell and Paul Lewis, Tyndale House Publishers. Answers basic questions about love and sex.

- *Quest for Love*, Elisabeth Elliot, Fleming H. Revell Company. True stories of passion and purity.

- *The Single Experience*, Keith Miller and Andrea Wells Miller, Word Books. Feelings as a single in a doubles world.

- *Single, Whole & Holy*, Joy Jacobs and Deborah Strubel, Horizon Books. Christian women and sexuality.

- *Singles at the Crossroads*, Albert Y. Hsu, InterVarsity Press. A fresh perspective on Christian singleness.

4 MAXIMIZING MARRIAGE

Here We Go

If you want a successful and happy marriage, you and your spouse must work hard at making your marriage a priority. When you were first married, it may have been difficult to believe your marriage would ever fade into the background, but life has a way of demanding time and attention that distracts us from marriage, causing it to sink lower and lower on the ladder of importance.

You will need to discover your mission as a married couple and share your values and goals with each other. Only through mutual sharing will you and your mate keep going in the right direction, as you seek God's will and plan for you.

SETTING YOUR PRIORITIES

> **John 8:14** Jesus answered, "Even if I testify on my own behalf, my testimony is valid, for I know where I came from and where I am going. But you have no idea where I come from or where I am going."

Jesus Had a Plan

Jesus was a person with a mission in life. His mission was to <u>please</u> his heavenly Father. He knew he would accomplish that mission with a plan <u>directed</u> specifically by his Father.

Marriage needs the same thing. Without a plan, we'll never know whether our marriage is traveling in the direction we de-

☞ **GO TO:**

John 5:30 (please)

John 4:34 (directed)

☞ **GO TO:**

Colossians 1:10
(pleasing, bearing,
growing)

sire. God's plans for your life and marriage include these things: <u>pleasing</u> God, <u>bearing</u> fruit, and <u>growing</u> in the knowledge of God; <u>serving</u> others in love; <u>sharing</u> God's love with others; and <u>selfless</u> giving of yourself.

What Others
are Saying:

Colossians 5:13
(serving)

Matthew 28:19–20
(sharing)

Philippians 2:4 (selfless)

Roger and Donna Vann: Jesus had a very clear sense of his life purpose. When he reached the end of his life, he told his Father that he had completed his assigned tasks (John 17:4). How did the Lord know he'd finished his life work? He had a sharp picture of what it was. And he fulfilled his purpose by living according to his priorities, according to the values he knew were important.[1]

Priorities are those things that should take **preference** over everything else. Something of highest priority is not that which takes up the most time, but that which cannot be sacrificed for less important things.

Reflect on what is important for you in each of these categories. We've put in some ideas that you can reflect on or add to:

- *God:* My desire is to walk in <u>fellowship</u> with him by immediately <u>confessing</u> any sin and <u>seeking</u> his will for my life.
- *Spouse:* I do my best to make my husband or wife feel like he or she is the most important human in my life.
- *Children:* I want to respond to my children in such a way that they know they are important, second only to my spouse.
- <u>Work</u>: I want to see work as an opportunity to represent God through wise planning and loving responses.
- *Church:* I will serve the Lord in positions and activities as God directs.
- *Unbelievers:* I am prepared to foster relationships with the goal of representing Christ and looking for opportunities to share Christ with them.

Think about It

preference: *one's first choice*

☞ **GO TO:**

1 John 1:3 (fellowship)

1 John 1:9 (confessing)

Matthew 6:33 (seeking)

Colossians 3:23 (work)

TAKE IT
FROM THEM

In raising their children, Ted and Patty have tried to instill the priority of reaching out to others. One way they have done this is to host an annual neighborhood drop-in at Christmas. The week after Thanksgiving the family personally delivers invitations throughout the neighborhood. This annual event is a highlight for their family and for those in their neighborhood as well. Further, Ted and Patty stress an attitude of generosity by making their yard available to neighborhood children; often coordinating games or activities all can do together! Not only is it fun to share their resources in this way, it has strengthened their children's ability to reach out to others.

Priscilla and Aquila (see WBFW, pages 33, 169–170, 203), of **Asia Minor** and formerly of Pontus, were a Jewish couple in the early church whose priority was to serve Christ. Around 50 A.D., the Roman emperor <u>Claudius</u> called for all Jews to leave Rome because of their constant rioting against his rule at the instigation of Chrestus—possibly another name for Christ. Priscilla and Aquila were forced to travel to **Corinth** to live where they ministered for Christ. <u>Tentmakers</u> by profession, they may have come to know Christ through fellow tentmaker, the apostle Paul (see illustration, page 54).

After they came to know Jesus as their Savior, they traveled, sometimes with Paul, to many places sharing Christ. Priscilla and Aquila truly had a common goal: to serve God. At one time they <u>risked</u> their lives to save Paul, and they encouraged a spiritually immature missionary/evangelist, <u>Apollos</u>, to know Christ in a more personal way. Tradition indicates that they were both **martyred** for their faith in Christ.

ACHIEVING YOUR GOALS

> **Proverbs 28:19** He who works his land will have abundant food, but the one who chases fantasies will have his fill of poverty.

Be a Fan of the Plan

<u>Solomon</u>, who wrote the wise sayings in the Book of Proverbs, knew that work is what puts food on the table. Get-rich-quick schemes never have done a very good job at getting people rich. This verse points not only to the importance of working, but also to the importance of wise work. To work wisely, one needs a plan, and this is as true for marriage as it is for plowing a field.

KEY POINT

God has a purpose for each marriage.

☞ **Check It Out:**

Acts 18:2; Romans 16:3–5

Couples in the Bible

Asia Minor: the peninsula between the Black Sea and the Mediterranean Sea that includes most of Turkey

Corinth: a prominent Greek city located south of the narrow isthmus connecting central Greece with the Peloponnesus

martyred: killed

☞ **GO TO:**

Acts 16:2 (Claudius)

Acts 18:1 (Corinth)

Acts 18:3 (tentmakers)

Romans 16:4 (risked)

Acts 18:24 (Apollos)

2 Samuel 5:14 (Solomon)

Solomon: king of Israel

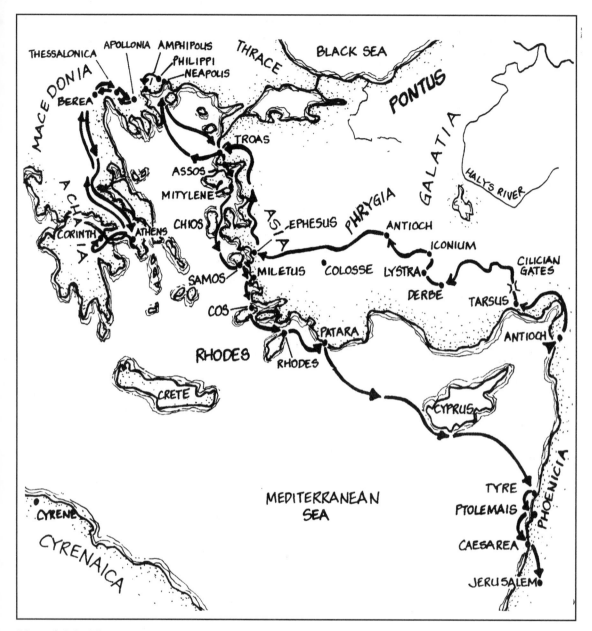

Map of Asia Minor

This map shows Pontus and Corinth, where Aquila and Priscilla served Christ. It also shows Paul's third missionary journey when Paul met Aquila and Priscilla.

Bill and Pam Farrel: To get on the same page of life, you'll need to find out what is really important to each of you. Often arguments and misunderstandings develop because we assume we know what is important to one another. But priorities are deceptive. They shift around like the pea in the shell game. You don't want to be guessing when you dovetail your life together; you want to know what is important.[2]

Harville Hendrix: My second order of business with couples is to help them define their relationship vision. Before I hear all the things they don't like about their marriage, I want to hear how they would like it to be. Defining the vision turns their energy away from past and present disappointments toward a more hopeful future. Achieving their vision is the goal of therapy.[3]

Think about It

One of the best ways a husband and wife can focus on their goals is through a "Family Mission Statement." Businesses have them to give direction and security. A couple can take advantage of one also.

How to develop a Family Mission Statement:

1. Each person writes several sentences beginning with "We . . . ," such as "We pray together three times a week," "We enjoy camping together," "We go to church together," "We have a date night once a week," or "We eat dinner with the kids five times a week."

2. Compare your sentences for matches.

3. Develop additional statements on which you both agree.

KEY POINT

Make a reasonable plan and do it!

4. Reform the statements into a Mission Statement of one paragraph. Example: "We are committed to representing God in our relationship and in the choices we make. We enjoy spending time together and will have a date night every other week. Our desire is to work through our disagreements while holding hands and reminding each other that we want the best for each other. We love each other and nothing will drive us apart."

When creating such statements and working toward your Mission Statement, it's a good idea to be reasonable in your expectations. Instead of thinking unrealistically ("We will pray together every day for an hour"), start with a small goal like praying together for five minutes twice a week and build

REMEMBER THIS

your way up. You'll find that your goals and the fulfillment of your Mission Statement will be more easily attainable.

TAKE IT FROM THEM

Sharon and Gary have learned to make a plan and work with it by watching their two cats. Cleopatra and Nefertiti are inseparable and, for the most part, extremely compatible. Sharon and Gary love watching them interact. Cleo and Neffie have taught Gary and Sharon:

- To be kind.
- To share the blanket on cold nights.
- To refrain from biting or scratching when spats arise.
- To cooperate: two cats accomplish more than one.
- Never to disturb another's nap.
- To play together.
- To cuddle close on tough days.
- To approach the other with purrs, not complaints, to obtain the best reaction.
- To explore the world together. It's more fun.
- To share your tuna.

commit: entrust

incorporate: include

sovereign: in charge

> **Proverbs 16:3 <u>Commit</u>** to the Lord whatever you do, and your plans will succeed.

God: The Master Planner

As Christians, we must surrender our will and entrust all our plans to God, especially regarding marriage. That means we must seek his plans for us and then **incorporate** them. Those plans will surely succeed because God is **<u>sovereign</u>** over everything that happens in our lives. He has the <u>power</u> and <u>wisdom</u> to fulfill every need. We just need to cooperate by asking his guidance.

☞ **GO TO:**

Psalm 37:5 (commit)

Daniel 5:21 (sovereign)

Job 36:22 (power)

Job 9:4 (wisdom)

The word "commit" means literally "to roll." Visualize pushing a boulder onto new ground and then removing your hands. As we "roll" our burdens and plans to God for safekeeping, we remove our hands, and trust he will do what only he knows is best.

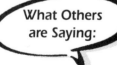

What Others are Saying:

Roger and Donna Vann: The solution isn't to throw out planning, but to be sure to commit our plans to the Lord. It's a mistake to assume that the Holy Spirit's leading is always "spontaneous," unless we revise our understanding of "spontaneity." Instead of avoiding the whole process of prioritizing, goal setting and planning, we simply need to remember that the Holy Spirit is our "management consultant." We must be sure to listen to his directions at the beginning, middle, and end of the planning process. That's the balance.[4]

David and Claudia Arp: Write down both short- and long-term goals. Maybe you want to work on your communication skills, or maybe you want to start the habit of dating. Presently, we are working on establishing boundary lines between our work in marriage education and our own marriage, so one of our goals is to plan a getaway with one rule—we won't talk about our work, only about us![5]

What Others
are Saying:

Some people are short-range planners; others are long-range planners. As a result, some think it's "not in their genes" to discern the direction of their marriage. Although it takes time and effort to establish goals and priorities, it's possible and essential for everyone to do so. Consider setting goals in the areas of finances, spiritual life, family, and your future.

Think about It

Marriage God's Way—Some people think that if you're serious about letting the Lord lead, you shouldn't plan ahead. That's like saying God didn't have a plan for Jesus' trip to earth. Did God just say, "Well, Son, do the best you can and we'll see how it goes." No! The Father knew everything he wanted the Son to accomplish and that's how Jesus <u>knew</u> he'd accomplished the plan.

Yes, we need to let the Holy Spirit lead—but he can lead through planning, not just spontaneous living.

☞ **GO TO:**

John 17:4 (knew)

When Richard and Kathryn were engaged, she resented his pastor's requirement that they take his counseling course. For four months they met, talked, and were given homework. Before each meeting, Richard and Kathryn went over their homework together. It became a special time, different from their courting. They truly got to know one another. Before they were married, they had already discussed their personalities, their goals, ways to resolve conflicts, sex, children, in-laws, and finances.

After their marriage, it seemed natural to continue. Now, twice a year, they have a planning session. They take time

**TAKE IT
FROM THEM**

away and discuss their goals, their accomplishments, and areas they'd like to work on together and individually. When time allows, they complete their planning session with a play session—dinner, antiquing, or picnicing . . . something fun to seal their intimate time together.

Richard and Kathryn recently celebrated their twentieth anniversary with no serious marriage problems, so it seems their pastor knew best—even if Kathryn didn't believe it in the beginning.

Date Your Mate

He Says . . .

LARRY: After seven hard years of marriage, I finally saw the light. I needed to put as much planning and energy into our marriage as I did into dating. Now we make it a priority to get away several times each year . . . always alone and away from home! Whether attending a marriage conference, taking a mini-vacation, or just getting a weekend away, we are committed to focused time alone. Sometimes we go to a hotel in the area and work on one of our book topics or re-work our marriage talks. Sometimes we go away only to play. Regardless, we always make lots of time for us.

She Says . . .

KATHY: I look back over our thirty years of marriage and have many wonderful memories of those times away. Some of my favorites are the week-long vacations we took when our children went to church youth camp. After dropping them off at camp, we drove away with a sigh of relief and in anticipation of our private time together. Quite often, Larry would golf and I would lie by the pool, anticipating our afternoon and evening of play and lovemaking.

Other times in the year we attended conferences or hung out for a weekend at a distant hotel. I always came away from our times together loving Larry even more than before.

☞ **GO TO:**

Genesis 17:11
(circumcision)

worship: revere

HOLDING ON TO YOUR VALUES

Philippians 3:3–11 For it is we who are the <u>circumcision</u>, we who **worship** by the Spirit of God, who glory in Christ Jesus, and who put no confidence in the flesh—though I myself have reasons for such confidence. If anyone else thinks he has reasons to put confidence in the flesh, I have more: circumcised on the eighth day, of the people of Israel, of the tribe of Benjamin, a Hebrew of Hebrews; in regard to the law, a **Pharisee**; as for **zeal**, <u>persecuting</u> the church; as for legalistic **righteousness**, faultless. But whatever was to my profit I now consider loss for the sake of Christ. What is more, I consider everything a loss compared to the **surpassing** greatness of knowing Christ Jesus my Lord, for whose sake I have lost all things. I consider them rubbish, that I may gain Christ and be found in him, not having a righteousness of my own that comes from the **law**, but that which is through faith in Christ— the righteousness that comes from God and is by faith. I want to know Christ and the power of his resurrection and the fellowship of sharing in his sufferings, becoming like him in his death, and so, somehow, to attain to the resurrection from the dead.

Pharisee: *Jewish religious leaders/teachers*

zeal: *passion*

righteousness: *doing the correct thing*

surpassing: *above and beyond*

law: *Jewish rules*

☞ **GO TO:**

Acts 9:5 (persecuting)

Flushing Bad Values

When Paul was a Pharisee, he enjoyed the best of life: wealth, position, ambition, and heritage. He was even an "**evangelist**" for the Jewish way of life calling for and <u>participating</u> in the killing of Christians. Yet, once he came to know Christ personally in a dramatic <u>encounter</u> with the risen Jesus, his value system changed. What was important to him before became not just insignificant but meaningless—rubbish! The word "rubbish" was originally translated in the King James Version as "dung" or "manure."

Now that's a change in values!

evangelist: *person who tries to influence the attitudes of others*

☞ **GO TO:**

Acts 7:58; 8:3 (participating)

Acts 9:3–8 (encounter)

Gary Smalley: What a man values, he takes good care of. Or as Christ said, "Where your treasure is, there will your heart be also" (Matthew 6:21). If your hobby is fishing, you probably hesitate to loan out your rod and reel. If you enjoy hunting, you probably know how to carefully oil and polish guns. Based on the amount of time you spend on each activity, your wife can sense which is most important to you. If she doesn't feel that you are as careful with her as you are with other interests, she will know she is not as important.[6]

What Others are Saying:

What you really value
is where you'll put the
greatest interest.

Marriage God's Way—Just as Paul made a change in his values, marriage requires husbands and wives to put aside what was previously important and put greater value on their spouses. As singles, they could do what they wanted without consideration of others, but once married, they must consider the opinions and feelings of their mates. That can be a difficult choice, but the rewards are well worth it.

Sincerely evaluating where your marriage is on your list of priorities can be difficult, but by asking for God's enlightenment, it can be done. Ask yourself questions like:

- Am I easily irritated when my plans must be changed for the good of our marriage?

- Do I invest time and energy into the growth of our relationship?

- Am I willing to change my mind about something regarding my marriage if the Lord reveals it, or do I remain selfish or stubborn?

- Am I willing to be accountable to a mentor or counselor if difficulties arise that we can't solve ourselves?

If your answers reveal that your own priorities are taking precedence over those of your marriage, make some changes. What one thing could you do this week to begin that process?

STUDY QUESTIONS

1. Why is it important to make plans for the success of your marriage?
2. Why is a Family Mission Statement important for a couple to develop?
3. What does the word "commit" mean when used in Proverbs 16:3, and how can a couple apply it to their plans?
4. How can a couple apply Paul's comments in Philippians 3:3–11 about priorities in their former life be compared to their priorities after knowing Christ?

- Priorities are those things that take preference over other things. Each couple needs to decide what is important to them.

- Solomon encouraged people to work their land in order to achieve success, and the same principle applies to marriage. The way to "work the land" in marriage is to have a Family Mission Statement that will bring focus to the relationship and offer an opportunity for dialogue about priorities.

- The way we keep priorities in order is to commit our plans to the Lord. Committing means to "roll" those plans over to God, entrusting that he can direct and be in sovereign control of everything that happens.

- The apostle Paul provides an example of how knowing Christ can change our value system. Couples can set aside attitudes that prevent them from making their marriage a priority.

KATHY & LARRY'S  BOOKSHELF

Some of Larry and Kathy's favorite books about making marriage a priority:

- *Secrets of a Growing Marriage*, Roger and Donna Vann, Here's Life Publishers. Building our commitment to love.

- *Marriage Moments*, David and Claudia Arp, Servant Publications. Heart-to-heart times to deepen your love.

- *The Joy of Committed Love*, Gary Smalley, Zondervan Publishing House. A valuable guide to knowing, understanding, and loving each other.

5 WORDS! WORDS! WORDS!

WHAT'S IN THIS CHAPTER

- Say What You Mean and Mean What You Say
- Stop Finding Fault
- Good Words Make Good Relationships
- Put a Knife to Strife

Here We Go

Words are some of the most powerful things on earth. With them we can hurt or heal, encourage or correct, and express ourselves with effectiveness or futility. They are especially powerful in the marriage relationship because we know our spouses so well. A few words from us can hurt deeply or help greatly.

There is enormous power in words! Proverbs 18:21 warns us, *"The tongue has the power of life and death, and those who love it will eat its fruit."* The Bible often illustrates how words are instruments of good or evil for couples. Let's dig into the treasure chest of God's Word to see what we find about the power of words.

SAY WHAT YOU MEAN AND MEAN WHAT YOU SAY

> **Proverbs 10:20** The tongue of the **righteous** is **choice** silver, but the heart of the wicked is of little value.

righteous: *those who seek God*

choice: *pure*

☞ **GO TO:**

1 Corinthians 3:12 (silver)

aptly: *appropriately*

Are Your Words Silver or Tin?

At the core of a successful marriage is a couple who understands the value and power of words. Words can hurt or heal, they can encourage or discourage, and they can express love or hate. A wise husband or wife uses words that are valuable—like pure silver as Solomon says. In another proverb, he says, *"A word **aptly** *spoken is like apples of gold in settings of silver"* (Proverbs 25:11). But if a mate uses words to hurt or control, those words are not only worthless but also can damage the relationship.

What Others
are Saying:

quells: diminishes

Dan B. Allender and Tremper Longman III: Marriages are challenged in many ways. How we talk to each other reflects the quality of our relationship as well as the depth of our character. Good speech **quells** chaos and promotes joy and life; bad speech produces chaos and leads to despair and death. The book of Proverbs teaches this well. *"The tongue has the power of life and death, and those who love it will eat its fruit"* (Proverbs 18:21).[1]

☞ GO TO:

Proverbs 31:26
  (opens her mouth)

Wayne Barber, Eddie Rasnake, and Richard Shepherd: "She opens her mouth in wisdom." Don't you wish that came out every time you opened your mouth? Remember that wisdom is not simply knowledge, but is knowledge made practical—it is application-focused truth. Not only that, but her teaching is flavored with kindness. What a beautiful balance is seen here! Wisdom given without kindness can hurt more than help. But this woman's wisdom is shared with a kind heart, making it much easier to swallow.[2]

Couples in the Bible

☞ **Check It Out:**

Proverbs 31:10–31

*compiled: put together
from several sources*

The unnamed woman in Proverbs 31 is a model for all women. Commentators believe that she wasn't actually *one* person, but a vision **compiled** by Solomon's mother for the kind of woman Solomon should seek. In Proverbs 31:10–31, Solomon describes his mother's idea of a perfect woman, an intimidating comparison for most women. But God intended her as an example, rather than a source for comparison.

The Proverbs 31 woman is described as noble, hardworking, industrious, and energetic. She is a wife, mother, businesswoman, and community worker. She confidently goes about her tasks, yet doesn't neglect reaching out to the poor with help and encouragement. She sews fine linens and even sells them at a profit. Her own clothing identifies her as someone who is self-assured and powerful in the community.

In biblical times, all fabrics had to be made from natural materials. Linen was woven from thread spun from the flax plant (see illustration, page 65); wool, from sheep; silk, from worms; sackcloth, from goat hair; and cotton, from plants. The well-to-do wore clothing made from "fine" linens, whereas the poor wore fabric of a coarser quality.

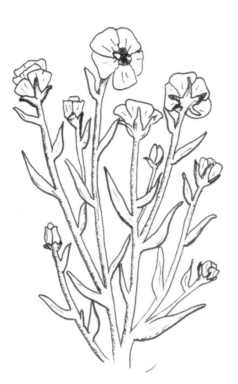

Flax Plant

Flax was separated from its seeds, laid in the sun to dry, and immersed in water to soften for crushing. Then the flax fibers were beaten out of the woody stems and woven into thread.

In the description of this godly woman, her husband is a leader of the city. Solomon writes, *"Her husband is respected at the city gate, where he takes his seat among the elders of the land"* (Proverbs 31:23). Taking his place at the city gate indicates he had power and authority, for that is where governmental decisions were made (see illustration, page 66). Because of his position she is also influential, and because she is highly respected in the community her husband in turn receives respect from others. Both husband and wife bring benefits to each other.

The Proverbs 31 woman also possesses great emotional strength, which reflects her faith in God. Her husband praises her because *"she brings him good, not harm, all the days of her life"* (Proverbs 31:12). Solomon writes of her, *"She speaks with wisdom, and faithful instruction is on her tongue"* (Proverbs 31:26).

Marriage God's Way—Solomon described good communication at great length. He suggests the following ways to say what we mean and mean what we say:

Those in authority made
governmental decisions as
they gathered at the city
gate, as depicted in this
illustration.

Proverbs	Effective Communication
10:19	Don't talk too much
10:32	Seek to understand rather than to be heard
12:17	Speak the truth
12:18	Guard what you say, being sensitive to others
12:25	Give encouragement through your words
13:3	Avoid saying the wrong thing
13:14	Encourage others to make wise choices
14:23	Don't talk just for the sake of talking
15:23	Speak that which is correct for the circumstances
15:28	Think before you speak
16:24	Encourage and affirm to promote well-being
16:28	Refrain from gossip
18:13	Listen before speaking
26:4–5	Don't reply in kind to unkindly remarks
28:9	Pray first in order to listen for God's input

discerning: wise

When the guidelines in Proverbs are followed, **discerning** husbands and wives will be aware of the power of their words and be sensitive to how their words are being received.

Joan and Emmitt had a disagreement and went to bed upset. Joan prayed that the Lord would reveal to each of them who was correct. In the middle of the night, Emmitt awakened Joan telling her he'd had a dream that he was wrong. He asked for her forgiveness. Since then, they are committed to praying—sometimes individually and sometimes together—before talking things over. God has helped them to be open to hearing the other's opinion. Sometimes an impression, a dream, a revelation, a small voice, or an inner conviction persuades one of them that they have been wrong. This has really made God the third partner in their marriage.

TAKE IT FROM THEM

STOP FINDING FAULT

2 Samuel 6:16–23 As the **ark** of the Lord was entering the **City of David**, <u>Michal</u> daughter of Saul watched from a window. And when she saw King David leaping and dancing before the Lord, she despised him in her heart. They brought the ark of the Lord and set it in its place inside the tent that David had pitched for it, and David sacrificed **burnt offerings** and **fellowship offerings** before the Lord. After he had finished sacrificing the burnt offerings and fellowship offerings, he blessed the people in the name of the Lord Almighty. Then he gave a loaf of bread, a cake of dates and a cake of raisins to each person in the whole crowd of Israelites, both men and women. And all the people went to their homes. When David returned home to bless his household, Michal daughter of Saul came out to meet him and said, "How the king of Israel has distinguished himself today, disrobing in the sight of the slave girls of his servants as any **vulgar** fellow would!" David said to Michal, "It was before the Lord, who chose me rather than your father or anyone from his house when he appointed me ruler over the Lord's people Israel—I will celebrate before the Lord. I will become even more undignified than this, and I will be humiliated in my own eyes. But by these slave girls you spoke of, I will be held in honor." And Michal daughter of Saul had no children to the day of her death.

☞ **GO TO:**

Exodus 25:1–40 (ark)

1 Samuel 14:49 (Michal)

Genesis 8:20 (burnt offerings)

Exodus 20:24 (fellowship offerings)

ark: portable chest holding the Ten Commandments and other items

City of David: *Jerusalem*

burnt offerings: *sacrificed animals burned on altar*

fellowship offerings: *bread or animals dedicated to God*

vulgar: *tasteless*

Love Turns Cold

☞ **GO TO:**

1 Samuel 17:4 (Goliath)

1 Samuel 25:44 (Phalti)

reverberated: sounded

Michal fell in love with David even before he was king. She most likely heard the story of his victory over <u>Goliath</u>, which **reverberated** throughout Israel. When Michal's father, King Saul, heard of their love for each other, he tried to have David killed. When that didn't work, Saul was forced to keep his promise and give Michal to David as his first wife. In time, Michal was given to another man, <u>Phalti</u>, as a wife but David eventually succeeded in getting her back.

Why did Michal react so strongly to David's dancing and rejoicing as he accompanied the Ark of God? Did she consider his behavior unseemly for a king? Was she jealous of the attention other girls were giving David? Was she embarrassed because of David's undignified actions? We know that she didn't share David's close relationship with the Lord. She might have been envious of his faith and the openness with which he could worship God.

What Others are Saying:

Gary Smalley: One husband won his wife back partly through creative praise. He bought 365 pieces of wrapped candy, wrote a special message on every wrapper, and then sealed them again. She opened one piece every day and read what he appreciated about her for a full year.[3]

☞ **GO TO:**

Philippians 4:4
    (rejoice always)

Florence Littauer and Marita Littauer: For those who wish to communicate on a positive level, we need to "<u>rejoice always</u>, again I say rejoice." We need to repay bad with good and not fall into the negative traps gaping before us. The world desperately needs cheerful people who will smile and spread joy wherever they go. Are you that kind of person? Do you get up each day and look forward to blessing others?[4]

Marriage God's Way—Michal found fault with David for his joyous dance. Chances are that wasn't the first, or only, time she had criticized him. Criticism can be defined as "finding fault." Instead of focusing on the positive, criticism focuses on the negative—and expresses it in a tone of voice lathered with anger and resentment. The Bible mentions many different causes of a critical spirit.

Cause	Reference	Verse
Envy	Proverbs 14:30	*A heart at peace gives life to the body, but envy rots the bones.*
Discontentment	Proverbs 17:1	*Better a dry crust with peace and quiet than a house full of feasting, with strife.*
Quarrelsome spirit	Proverbs 17:19	*He who loves a quarrel loves sin; he who builds a high gate invites destruction.*
Control	Proverbs 19:19	*A hot-tempered man must pay the penalty; if you rescue him, you will have to do it again.*
Pride	Proverbs 30:11–13	*There are those who curse their fathers and do not bless their mothers; those who are pure in their own eyes and yet are not cleansed of their filth; those whose eyes are ever so **haughty**, whose glances are so **disdainful**.*

If husbands or wives have perfectionistic expectations, they may become critical. They may believe that by pointing out wrongs their spouse can "become perfect, " or they may criticize their mate in an attempt to increase their own self-esteem.

Some people really believe criticism is effective. When initial criticism doesn't work, a husband or wife may think that more criticism will help, and nagging is born. The Bible calls nagging "quarreling." *"A quarrelsome wife is like a constant dripping on a rainy day; restraining her is like restraining the wind or grasping oil with the hand"* (Proverbs 27:15–16). No one likes a dripping faucet, and no one likes to hear repeated criticisms—especially from the person who is supposed to be most loving.

To avoid being critical, a spouse needs to, most of all, <u>trust God</u>. When we feel responsible for changing a person, we can easily nag and become demanding. Trusting that God knows best how to influence and change a person can help us release control and develop a positive attitude.

Encouragement is the key to avoiding criticism, as we'll see in the next section.

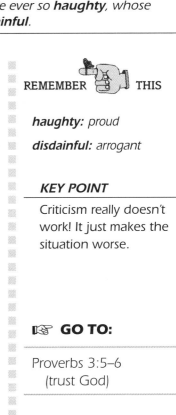

REMEMBER THIS

haughty: proud

disdainful: arrogant

KEY POINT

Criticism really doesn't work! It just makes the situation worse.

☞ **GO TO:**

Proverbs 3:5–6 (trust God)

But It's Never Good Enough!

LARRY: Early in our marriage, Kathy's critical tongue would strike at any time. It seemed there was little I did that pleased her. If I took some time for myself, it would only give her more ammunition to attack my motives. One of her favorite sayings was, "If you really loved me you would. . . ." She seemed to think I could read her mind. Of course, when I couldn't, she was unhappy. This criticism eroded my self-esteem and angered me. I found myself spending more time away from home, just to find peace and pleasure. The more Kathy nagged me, the further I went from her.

When Kathy started controlling her critical tongue, I found myself drawn back toward a loving relationship with her. The qualities that first attracted me toward her resurfaced. I was again interested in spending time with her.

KATHY: From the beginning, I thought it was my job to offer "constructive criticism" to Larry so that he could become the best person he could be. My perfectionistic expectations didn't allow me to appreciate what he did or who he was. After all, something could always be done just a little bit better, why not strive for that? I couldn't understand why Larry was not grateful for my wisdom. When he seemed to pull away from me, I just figured he couldn't handle my great ideas. In time I learned that words of encouragement, not criticism, drew him closer to me. I learned to diminish my perfectionistic expectations so that I could give praise, even when something wasn't done "perfectly."

Recently, I asked Larry to clear the bathroom sink drain. He took out the sink stopper and put it aside after cleaning out the sink. I thought, "Well, he hasn't finished the job yet so I better not thank him. He might think he's done." But I knew that was a form of criticism. I wouldn't be appreciating what he had already done for me. So I gave him a big kiss and thanked him for a clean drain. He put the stopper back several days later, but my covenant not to criticize eliminated any irritation. Of course, that doesn't mean I won't ask again, but I'll do it with patience.

Early in their marriage Ellis would listen to Donna's list of chores and become frustrated. He finally told her to make a written list for him. She has discovered three ways she can communicate about the chores:

1. Put a "honey do" list on the refrigerator.
2. Place a job request by his breakfast plate.
3. Ask the Lord to remind him.

TAKE IT FROM THEM

She has also learned to give him time to relax after work and not to make more than one request at a time. Donna can sort through several projects at once, but Ellis prefers to concentrate on only one task at a time and asks Donna to remind him about a second project after the first one is done.

Another couple, Virginia and David, who have been married forty-six years, find that reiterating the message they hear helps to clear up potential misunderstandings. Asking questions such as, "Is this what you meant?" or "Do I hear you saying thus and so?" helps to clarify meanings. For instance, if one of them comes in from the garage and says, "Boy, this garage is sure dirty!" The other one can clarify the information by querying, "Are you saying I should have cleaned the garage?" Then the other one can respond, "No, I was just thinking out loud and meant I really needed to get busy myself!" For Virginia and David, doing this eliminates lots of hard feelings.

They also keep communication lines open by using word pictures. Sometimes a logical person, like David, does not understand a feeling person, like Virginia. But when Virginia says, "I feel like a basketball," David, a sports enthusiast, understands that Virginia is feeling bounced around.

GOOD WORDS MAKE GOOD RELATIONSHIPS

> **Hosea 2:14–16** Therefore I am now going to **allure** her; I will lead her into the desert and speak tenderly to her. There I will give her back her vineyards, and will make the Valley of <u>Achor</u> a door of hope. There she will sing as in the days of her youth, as in the day she came up out of Egypt. "In that day," declares the Lord, "you will call me 'my husband'; you will no longer call me 'my master.'"

☞ **GO TO:**

Exodus 22:16; Judges 14:15; 16:5 (allure)

Joshua 7:24 (Achor)

allure: charm

Give a Vision with Your Words

In the Book of Hosea, God wants to express his love for his spiritual "wife," the people of Israel. Yet they are separated from him because of their lustful worship of false gods. He wants to declare his love for them and offer them hope, so he tries to attract them with tender words. By alluring them into the desert—an emotional desert in this case—there would be no distractions of "city life." He wanted his people to leave their busyness behind and to focus completely on him.

John Trent: One communication tool in relationships is so powerful that it can move right past a person's defenses and boost his sense of worth and value. The tool is so easy to use that it's already an everyday part of your conversations, yet so potentially life-changing that the greatest communicators of all time have used it to rally masses and direct entire movements. The tool is the practice of praise, and this time-tested and God-honored way of talking has a marvelous effect on those who are insecure.[5]

Charlie Shedd: Varnish always melts under heat. You can only tell him he isn't wonderful where he isn't if you have told him he is wonderful where he is. Most husbands now and then overpraise themselves. When yours does this too much, it may mean that he needs more of your praise.[6]

God's example of using tender words to "allure" his beloved creation to return his love helps us see the benefit of encouraging words, rather than criticism. By focusing on the positive and giving appreciation even for the imperfect things our spouse does, we strengthen our marriage.

Think about It

Couples in the Bible

☞ **Check It Out:**

Job 1:1–2:10

Sometimes it's hard to give encouragement. In the midst of great misery, Job's wife lost her ability to trust God and to remain positive. God had given Satan permission to test Job and as a result, Satan killed Job's ten children and destroyed his flocks. Then, since Job didn't sin in reaction to all this tragedy, Satan asked for and received permission from God to physically assault Job's body with illness. He was stricken with painful sores from the soles of his feet to the top of his head.

As Job's wife saw all that was happening, she could no longer contain her grief. She blamed God in her heart and cried out to Job, *"Are you still holding on to your integrity? Curse God and die!"* (Job 2:9). Job replied, *"You are talking like a foolish woman. Shall we accept good from God, and not trouble?"* (Job 2:10a). Scripture then says, *"In all this, Job did not sin in what he said"* (Job 2:10b).

It would be hard to blame Job's wife for her outburst. Her grief over the loss of her children must have broken her heart. Both she and Job needed reassurance, not discouragement at this time. Proverbs 10:21 says, *"The lips of the righteous nourish many, but fools die for lack of judgment."*

Eventually, God restores Job's wealth and gives him ten more children with, it is believed, the same wife. Although she hadn't been able to give Job perfect support, she stayed by his side, and they weathered the storm together. Encouraging words can make the storm less threatening as a couple encourages each other with the truth: God is <u>in charge</u>—even when it seems he is not.

☞ **GO TO:**

1 Chronicles 29:11–12 (in charge)

PUT A KNIFE TO STRIFE

> **Proverbs 20:3** It is to a man's honor to avoid strife, but every fool is quick to quarrel.

Avoid Strife? Is It Possible?

If you're married, you're going to have conflict. It's impossible for two individuals to live together and make decisions that affect both of them without having disagreements. So how can the Bible help us to avoid strife?

The word *strife* refers to an expression of **enmity**. Yes, we will have disagreements with our spouse, but we are to work through the conflict and not let issues divide us. We are supposed to remain friends. That *can* be done!

enmity: animosity

David Augsburger: Conflict, resolved creatively, results in greater intimacy, understanding, and acceptance. Is that not sufficient reason for welcoming it, if not eagerly, at least without fear?[7]

What Others are Saying:

antidote: *remedy*

elixir: *cure-all*

predisposes: *prepares, inclines*

Bill and Lynne Hybels: We have observed that in addition to knowing practical tools for conflict resolution, nearly all couples who survive the minor and major conflicts of married life have discovered a key **antidote** for marital demise. It is called *the spirit of reconciliation.* This **elixir** produces a heart condition that **predisposes** people toward reconciliation and revolutionizes the way they approach conflict.[8]

Duos Display Do's and Don'ts

Conflict fills the pages of the Bible. We can learn ways to avoid and resolve conflicts from the following biblical couples.

• *Abraham and Sarah:* Sarah finally gave birth to their son, Isaac, but Abraham's son Ishmael, by the substitute wife Hagar, made fun of Isaac. Sarah was so angry about Isaac's mistreatment that she told Abraham that Hagar and Ishmael should be thrown out of their household. Although Abraham was distressed because he loved Ishmael, he listened to God's directions and sent Hagar and Ishmael away according to Sarah's plan.

We can learn from them that seeking God during disagreements will strengthen us to do the right thing—even if it's against our will (Genesis 21:1–14).

• *Jacob, Rachel, and Leah:* Jacob had two wives, Rachel, whom he loved, and Leah, who could give him children. The two wives fought constantly, as Leah tried to gain Jacob's love through bearing him a lot of children and Rachel felt threatened. Eventually, Rachel did have two children, Joseph and later Benjamin. Rachel died while giving birth to Benjamin. In great sorrow Jacob buried Rachel. The Bible doesn't record a single instance where Jacob addressed the conflict within his family. He was not much of a leader.

We can see from Jacob that we should avoid being passive when there are conflicts in our home. We must be active in finding solutions to our disagreements, not in trying to avoid them (Genesis 29:31–30:24). (To discover more lessons from this family, see GWWB, pages 75–81.)

• *Moses and Zipporah:* Moses and his wife, Zipporah, disagreed when God directed Moses to perform <u>circumcision</u> on his sons. The Lord was insistent, and he threatened Moses' life. Zipporah was so angry that she cut off their sons' foreskins and threw them at Moses' feet.

Zipporah is an example to us that anger is not the best way to deal with conflict (Exodus 20:24–26).

☞ **GO TO:**

Genesis 17:11
(circumcision)

- *Xerxes and Esther*: A valuable example of creativity in conflict resolution was exhibited when Queen Esther risked her life to present a problem to King Xerxes. Esther attained the king's attention when she **piqued** his curiosity with a dinner invitation rather than immediately presenting her problem. At the dinner, he offered Esther half of his kingdom to find out what was so important. She again stalled him with another dinner invitation, which again he accepted. In the meantime, God was preparing Xerxes' heart to accept a solution.

piqued: stimulated

Esther is an example of how God may suggest unique and creative ways to resolve a conflict (Esther 5–7).

TAKE IT FROM THEM

Sue and Gil designed a unique way to deal with fixing blame. Since neither wanted to take blame and often it wasn't clear who was to blame, they now take turns. Sue will say, "OK, I'll take the blame this time because you took it last time." Gil will do the same when it's his turn. As a result, they are less opposed to taking blame.

Gary and Sharon have another way to deal with blame. When they have a disagreement, one of them pretends that the argument is their fault. Once they stop placing blame, the issues become clearer. Anger and blame only deepen a dilemma, but not fixing blame helps bring focus back to resolving the issue.

Satan wants to destroy happy marriages. Blame and fault-finding are one of his many weapons. If he can cause couples to focus on pointing fingers at each other, he will diminish the glory that God receives from a good marriage.

REMEMBER THIS

> **Ephesians 4:26–27** "In your anger do not sin": Do not let the sun go down while you are still angry, and do not give the devil a foothold.

Turn Fighting to Fun

The key to conflict resolution is to negotiate a solution as quickly as possible. Otherwise, Satan has an opportunity to bring resentment, discouragement, and hopelessness into our marriage. Getting angry with our spouse over an issue is not sinful, but if we don't deal with our feelings quickly, they can turn into sins like bitterness and selfishness. By working through our differences as soon as possible, we gain greater strength and intimacy in our marriage.

David Augsburger: Life without confrontation is directionless, aimless, and passive. When unchallenged, human beings tend to drift, to wander, or to stagnate. Confrontation is a gift. Confrontation is a necessary stimulation to jog one out of mediocrity or to prod one back from extremes. Confrontation is an art to be learned.[9]

Bill and Lynne Hybels: When the spirit of rebellion reigns in a marriage, every little conflict escalates into a war of harsh accusations. But when the spirit of reconciliation prevails even major conflicts can be discussed constructively and worked through.[10]

Think about It

In order to evaluate whether you operate out of a spirit of rebellion or a spirit of reconciliation, consider these two perspectives.

Spirit of Rebellion	Spirit of Reconciliation
Wants his or her own way no matter what	Wants the best for both self and spouse
Always thinks he or she is right	Sees the value of spouse's perspective
Refuses to confront or work together	Is willing to listen and negotiate
Focuses only on the inadequacies of the spouse	Understands that both partners are a part of the problem—and the solution

KEY POINT

Seek a compromise by praying, listening, reflecting, forgiving, talking calmly, and negotiating.

Marriage God's Way—Couples can overcome conflict by applying these biblical principles:

- *Begin with prayer.* Ask for God to direct your thinking. Surrender to God your own hardened desires and requirements. Trust that God wants the best for both of you (Psalm 37:5).

- *Reaffirm your love for each other.* Never mention divorce as an option. Even if you can't say, "I love you" out loud, think it as a choice of your will. You don't have to feel it, just decide to love (1 John 3:10).

- *Listen—really, really listen.* No matter how much you want

WHAT'S IN THE BIBLE FOR . . . COUPLES

to defend yourself, listen to what your spouse has to say (Proverbs 18:13).

- *Repeat what your partner said in your own words.* Instead of expressing your opposing opinion, share what you heard your partner say (Proverbs 18:2).

- *Avoid extremist words like never, always, all the time, constantly, etc.* Even if you think your spouse "never" or "always" does a certain thing, being reasonable will facilitate discussion (Philippians 4:8).

- *Use "I messages" instead of "you messages."* Say, "I feel angry when my opinions aren't considered important" instead of, "You make me angry when you ignore me." Focusing on your own feelings and desires rather than blaming the other person will diminish defensiveness (Proverbs 16:21).

- *Express forgiveness.* Most of the time, a hurt or misunderstanding was unintentional. Even if it was intentional, forgiving that person is required because God has forgiven you for so much (Ephesians 4:32).

- *Talk calmly.* No matter how hard it seems, make a commitment to talk at a calm level. Remind yourself that anger doesn't get you the results you need or desire (Proverbs 15:1).

- *Negotiate.* Both husband and wife should make a separate list of acceptable solutions, then compare the lists and find some common ground. Both need to be willing to give up some of their desires or needs to find greater common ground. Then find a solution you both can accept (Philippians 2:3–4).

- *Seek help if necessary.* Professional Christian counseling can be useful and needed. Ask your pastor for a recommendation (Proverbs 11:14).

Most of the conflicts a couple have will be forgotten a year later. Although issues seem important at the time, in the light of eternity—or even in five years—their importance will diminish. We will feel foolish if we are reminded about how upset we were over something small. In light of eternity, it's worth it to settle our differences.

WARNING

Patty and Ted have sought to develop listening skills by utilizing a simple technique they call a "2 x 2." When used in conflict resolution, a 2 x 2 works like this: for two minutes one of them shares the issue that is on his or her mind, and the listening spouse cannot interrupt. After the two minutes are up, the listening spouse repeats back what he or she heard. Once that person has finished repeating, the one who first shared can clarify if needed. If not, the dialogue moves to the other spouse and the process is repeated.

Another couple, Brenda and Paul, often begin a discussion on a potentially difficult issue by saying, "I want to share with you how I feel, not for your approval, criticism, or opinion, but just to let you in on how I feel." They've found that defusing a situation at the beginning prevents it from escalating to misunderstanding and hurtful words.

STUDY QUESTIONS

1. According to Proverbs 10:20 and Proverbs 25:11, how important are words?
2. Who criticized David as he danced joyfully unto the Lord, and why do you think she did that?
3. How does God woo his children to love him, and how is that an example for a married couple?
4. How can a couple work and talk through their conflicts?
5. What does the Bible say about anger, and what does Ephesians 4:26–27 say we should do about it?

CHAPTER WRAP-UP

- Words are an important aspect of a marriage. They can heal or injure, support or destroy, and express love or hate. There are many examples in the Bible of people who used their words to bring good, but one of the finest is the woman in Proverbs 31 who always spoke with wisdom and kindness. The more husbands and wives resemble that example, the more they will bless and strengthen their marriages.

- Criticism is usually not constructive and actually harms a marriage relationship. We may think we're encouraging someone to do better or improve, but actually it discourages him or her instead. A wise mate will focus on the positive while gracefully making suggestions for improvement.

- Husbands and wives may be hesitant to give compliments, thinking their mate will give up trying to be better. But if God woos his children to him with kind words then so should we. By expressing appreciation for what our spouse does, even if it's not perfect, we will encourage him or her to do more.

- It will take hard work and selflessness, but a couple can work through their differences and conflicts. They should practice the biblical principles of beginning with prayer, reaffirming their love for each other, and really, *really* listening to their spouse. After listening, they can repeat in their own words what they heard, and then communicate their needs without extremist words and with "I messages." Ultimately, they must forgive their spouse for whatever inadequacies their mate has and choose to focus on the positives in their relationship.

KATHY & LARRY'S  BOOKSHELF

Some of Kathy and Larry's favorite books about communication:

- *Talking So People Will Listen*, Florence Littauer and Marita Littauer, Vine (Servant). You can communicate with confidence.

- *Love for All Seasons*, John Trent, Moody Press. Eight ways to nurture intimacy.

- *Fit to Be Tied*, Bill and Lynne Hybels, Zondervan Publishing House. Making marriage last a lifetime.

- *Caring Enough to Confront*, David Augsburger, Gospel Light. How to understand and express your deepest feelings toward others.

6 THE CIRCLE OF LOVE

Here We Go

There's a saying, "Love makes the world go 'round." And of course, we know it makes marriage a whole lot better! Most marriages start with each person being desperately in love. We believe with all our hearts that our great love for each other will solve every problem and overcome any disagreement. But one day after the honeymoon . . . something happens. Talk about disillusionment! We suddenly see our spouse through different eyes, and we wonder how we could have been so blind.

Thus begins a cycle that will reoccur throughout our marriage. Our challenge is to learn how to keep committed and stay focused on love—and it isn't easy. Let's see what God's Word has to say about making the decision to love and seeing our spouse through God's eyes.

CHOOSING TO LOVE

> **Romans 5:8** But God demonstrates his own love for us in this: While we were still sinners, Christ died for us.

Love Doesn't Always Feel Good

God most likely didn't feel "good" that every single person on earth was a sinner, yet he made a choice to demonstrate his **unconditional** love by sending Jesus to die on the cross so that each person could be <u>set free</u> from the **bondage** of sin. That's the same <u>kind of love</u> that God wants each of us to have for our spouse. That's the most difficult kind of love! Yet, it's the true kind of love.

unconditional: without conditions or expectations

bondage: held captive

☞ **GO TO:**

Romans 6:18 (set free)

Romans 8:21 (bondage)

1 John 3:10 (kind of love)

What Others are Saying:

stabilize: secure

H. Norman Wright: The love which is needed to **stabilize** a marriage is the type of love God displays to each of us—unconditional commitment to an imperfect person. Unconditional love takes energy and effort. It means caring about the other person as much as you care about yourself.[1]

Willard F. Harley Jr.: Romantic love is what we experience when someone meets our needs. But that isn't enough. We also need caring love, which is a decision to try to contribute to someone's happiness or help someone avoid unhappiness.[2]

Think about It

catapults: throws

disillusionment: unhappiness

Every marriage cycles through different stages of love. It all starts with romance—that fabulous feeling when we figure our future mate is fantastic. We can't imagine ever being unhappy with him or her. After marriage, we begin to see faults and weaknesses we never noticed before. We are amazed that our spouse has changed! But the fact is, they haven't changed. We're just being "real" for the first time with each other. This **catapults** us into some degree of **disillusionment**. We may feel slight disillusionment, a little irritated, or aggravated at some of the actions or reactions of our spouse. But deep disillusionment may make us seriously wonder if we married the "right" person or if our marriage can survive.

The way to move out of disillusionment into true love is to consciously decide to love our spouse, even when we don't feel like they deserve it. Making a decision to love doesn't depend upon feelings. Instead, it's a choice made with our mind.

Making Love a Choice

She Says . . .

KATHY: When Larry and I had been married seven years, we were in deep disillusionment. I had expected Larry to be my Prince Charming by meeting all my needs, but instead, he seemed to focus on everything else while working at two jobs and pursuing his hobby of flying. He was never home. But I was stuck at home with a two-year-old daughter and an infant son, and I wasn't happy about it. In fact, I was so angry that I prayed that the plane in which Larry was flying would crash.

One day God whispered to my heart, "Kathy, I want you to tell

Larry that you love him!" I was shocked because it wasn't true. Would God want me to be a hypocrite and say something untrue? I replied, "No, God, I won't." When he whispered the same message again, I refused again, telling myself that Larry might misinterpret my comment and think I approved of everything he was doing wrong in our marriage. God persisted, "Then think it the next time you see Larry." I was surprised that thinking "I love you" could be worthwhile, but then I realized Larry wouldn't hear me and therefore wouldn't be able to use it against me. So I agreed.

When Larry returned home from a flying trip that evening, I looked him straight in the eye, gulped, and thought, *I love you.* I paused and then added, *but I don't really.* In that moment God was asking me to make a decision to love. For the first time, I chose to love Larry even when I didn't think he was lovable. And as I continued to do that, I felt my love for him return. I was amazed! It made a difference in my heart and in my mind.

LARRY: Deep disillusionment? You bet! It seemed nothing I did pleased Kathy. Criticism, sarcasm, and nagging seemed to be Kathy's most mature assets. The more she tried to pull me closer, the further I drifted away. When we married I made a promise that I would never divorce Kathy, so I finally came to the conclusion, "This is the best it's going to be." I put more energy and effort into pleasing myself through my career and recreational activities.

At the time Kathy made the choice to love me I noticed a change. I wasn't aware of her decision; however, I was a recipient of its consequences. Kathy became less demanding. The nagging stopped, and within a short time, I began remembering the reasons I fell in love with her. When she stopped being negative, I found myself more interested in strengthening our marriage. I remembered something Josh McDowell said in a speech during my college days: "Love causes creative changes in the one who is loved." Kathy's behavior actually influenced how I approached our marriage. I began listening to her and enjoyed spending more time with her. I wanted to get closer to the wife of my youth.

During that time of deep disillusionment, Kathy and I were totally consumed with our own needs to the exclusion of the other. Our self-centeredness blinded us to our responsibility to serve the other. Kathy took the first step, and I found it irresistible not to respond in a positive manner. It was a slow, steady process that developed into the vibrant and robust marriage we experience today.

He Says . . .

**TAKE IT
FROM THEM**

Joan and Emmitt have been married fifty-one years, and they make a daily decision to sacrifice and be patient and forgiving. Emmitt often whispers in Joan's ear in the middle of the night, telling her that when he is away from her, she is all he can think about. Joan gets goose bumps when she's with Emmitt and tells him so. They try to make a phone call during the day to their beloved, tape a card to the mirror, or plan a surprise candlelight dinner. At times, Joan has received a surprise rose on her pillow. They know it takes effort to stay in love, but they report it's well worth it.

> **1 Corinthians 13:4–8** Love is patient, love is kind. It does not envy, it does not boast, it is not proud. It is not rude, it is not self-seeking, it is not easily angered, it keeps no record of wrongs. Love does not delight in evil but rejoices with the truth. It always protects, always trusts, always hopes, always perseveres. Love never fails.

Just Do It!

When the apostle Paul wrote that description of love, he didn't include, "love is a feeling." Yet many people think of it that way. But that isn't God's way of describing love. Instead, he characterizes it in the choices that love makes: responses like being patient and kind—just like God himself, who always does the <u>right thing</u> regardless of the way he's treated by others.

☞ **GO TO:**

Romans 3:21
(right thing)

What Others
are Saying:

James Dobson: There are times in every good marriage when partners feel as though they will never love the other again. Emotions are like that. They flatten out occasionally like an automobile tire with a nail in the tread. Riding on the rim is a pretty bumpy experience for everyone on board. Set your jaw and clench your fists. Nothing short of death must ever be permitted to come between the two of you. *Nothing!*[3]

REMEMBER  THIS

God wants us to love the same way he does. Unconditional love says, "You don't have to perform to my needs in order for me to love you." It has no conditions or expectations that our mate will act a certain way before we will love them. Unfortunately, because we are needy people, we tend to require our spouse to return our love in a certain way, but that's dangerous. Everyone will disappoint us at times because they are just as needy as we are. We can recognize their inability, knowing God will <u>meet</u> our true needs.

Only God is capable of meeting our needs completely. Although he often provides love and joy through another person, no one except God is selfless enough to want the <u>very best</u> for us all the time. When we take our eyes off our spouse as the one responsible for our happiness and look to God instead, we will experience the best kind of satisfaction.

Marita and Chuck have learned to make love a choice. When Marita was forming her personal mission statement, she read a portion of Ephesians 5:1–2 in *The Message*. It said: *"Observe how Christ loved us. His love is not cautious but extravagant. He didn't love in order to get something from us but to give everything of himself to us. Love like that."* She knew she wanted her personal mission to be to love her husband with extravagance—whether she was doing the dishes, washing laundry, or cooking breakfast!

But her extravagant love was challenged when Chuck hung his large, bright-red, radio controlled model airplane in the family room from the peak of the cathedral ceiling. To protect it, he covered it with large dry-cleaning bags with lettering on them. She felt that she had loved enough in agreeing to have it hang there; it seemed too much to have unsightly plastic bags hanging from the ceiling. But she had decided to love extravagantly and was ready to accept the dry cleaning bags.

Meanwhile, God had begun working in Chuck's heart. He decided to replace the bags with clear plastic wrap that molded to every curve. Marita rejoiced that God had met her needs even as she chose to love fully.

Loving fully doesn't mean we never express our desires, opinions, or needs. But it does mean expressing them without anger, and then allowing God to bring the results he wants. That's very difficult and will stretch our trust in God to the max, but it can be done <u>in God's power</u>.

☞ GO TO:

Philippians 4:19 (meet)

Think about It

☞ GO TO:

John 10:10 (very best)

TAKE IT FROM THEM

REMEMBER THIS

☞ GO TO:

Philippians 4:13 (in God's power)

Couples in the Bible

☞ **Check It Out:**

Hosea 1:1–11

What Others
are Saying:

Hosea was a prophet of God who ministered to the northern kingdom of Israel during the reign of Jeroboam II (782–753 B.C.). During that time, God was disgusted with Israel's moral corruption and spiritual adultery in the midst of a financially prosperous time. God asked Hosea to marry Gomer, a prostitute whom God knew would not give up her sinful ways. God intended for Hosea's marriage to an unfaithful wife to be an object lesson for Israel of their disloyalty to him. Even though Gomer was unfaithful time and time again, God gave Hosea the ability to unconditionally love her and to receive her back when she temporarily repented. Hosea's example represents God's ability to love his people even when we are disobedient and disloyal. That's the kind of love that God wants each of us to have for our spouse.

David and Heather Kopp: Hosea's forgiveness of Gomer illustrates God's heart toward Israel—and toward us. He doesn't stop loving us and pursuing us while he waits for us to come to our senses. Like Gomer, we're capable of terrible sins against our marriage. But by God's grace, we are also like Hosea, candidates for a love that reaches further.[4]

LOVE LINGO

John 3:16 For God so loved the world that he gave his one and only Son, that whoever believes in him shall not perish but have eternal life.

Love at Its Best

☞ **GO TO:**

John 10:14 (lay down)

When God wanted to show us his great love, he knew that we would recognize it through sacrifice: the life and death of his Son, Jesus Christ. When someone is willing to <u>lay down</u> his or her life for another, that is the ultimate in love. Anyone would value love like that!

When it comes to one person's love for another, it becomes more complicated because we each have our own definition or expression of love. We each have a unique way that we want to be loved. Most of the time, we go into marriage thinking that everyone's "love expression" is the same as ours. Therefore, we can easily misinterpret our spouse's actions. Because we don't express our love the way our spouse does, we often don't recognize when he or she is showing love. We may wonder why our spouse doesn't love us, when actually they do love us—we just don't recognize it. We need to communicate our own "love needs" and then identify the ways our spouse loves us—in their own manner. We also need to love them the way they want to be loved.

What Others are Saying:

Chuck and Barb Snyder: Take a moment right now and try to determine what your mate's love language is. Usually a person will have one special way—one "language"—in which they best understand love.[5]

Rich Buhler: Unfortunately, few of us realize this language barrier. Since we've spent a lifetime developing a language of love, we tend to think that everyone in the world speaks the same language—ours. Everyone, that is, except the person we married![6]

Think about It

Because we think everyone has the same definition of love or "love language," we don't think it's necessary to ask our mate about theirs. We just assume we already know. But most of the time when we think we're making our spouse feel loved through what we're doing, they don't have a clue—and are not giving us credit!

A husband working at two jobs may think he's showing his wife love because he's working so hard to provide for her, but that wife may prefer that he work at only one job and help her around the house. Another wife may think that baking a pie is communicating her love, but her husband may be starving sexually and wishing she save more energy for the bedroom.

Women tend to see love in romantic things, such as flowers, dinner out, time away from the children, unexpected gifts and cards, and lots of conversation! Men tend to view love in a wife's interest in sex, in togetherness at sporting events or watching sports on TV, and in a husband's hobbies.

KEY POINT

Ask, don't assume, about your spouse's definition of love.

ATTITUDES THAT DIMINISH LOVE

Many attitudes diminish our ability to make that crucial decision to love. Throughout years of marriage, we must make a choice to love. If we harbor negative attitudes, it will be hard to choose to love our spouse. We begin to see through eyes that have only one perspective: ours! Let's examine some attitudes that deplete our gracious love toward our spouse.

> **1 Corinthians 12:4–6** There are different kinds of gifts, but the same Spirit. There are different kinds of service, but the same Lord. There are different kinds of working, but the same God works all of them in all men.

Different Isn't Wrong

God made each of us different, and he equipped us with different talents and gifts. When we're first attracted to our future mate, we focus primarily on the things we have in common. We disregard our differences as unimportant or we think those irritations won't bother us. We show our future spouse our best side by graciously accepting them as they are.

Soon after the wedding and honeymoon, we begin to see those small differences as big deals! If our husband was always a few minutes late when we were dating, it was no big deal. After we're married, if he's always making us late for church, we can't stand it. If our wife talked a lot to her friends when we were dating, we called it "friendliness" and loved it. But within the context of marriage, we can't understand why she talks so many hours on the phone—and doesn't give us the attention we deserve. Some people get upset when the toilet tissue roll is put on "incorrectly;" other people are upset that the toothpaste tube gets squeezed in the middle. Everything becomes a big deal.

Yet so much of life is insignificant, and creating tension about it within marriage isn't worth it! Doing things differently—as long as Scripture doesn't call it sinful—is just different, but not wrong!

What Others are Saying:

☞ **GO TO:**

Genesis 2:18 (help-meet)

homogenate: *make the same*

James Dobson: It is important to understand some of the ways men and women are unique if we hope to live together in harmony. Genesis tells us that the Creator made two sexes, not one, and that he designed each gender for a specific purpose. Take a good look at male and female anatomy and it becomes obvious that we were crafted to "fit" together. This is not only true in a sexual context but psychologically as well. Eve, being suited to Adam's particular needs, was given to him as a "<u>help-meet</u>." How unfortunate has been the recent effort to deny this uniqueness and **homogenate** the human family! It simply won't square with the facts.[7]

Donald R. Harvey: Within marriage, we need to accept the fact that there are going to be differences between our mates and us. Recognizing these differences, and then trying to adjust to them in a cooperative fashion, is our goal. By so doing we demonstrate respect for one another and behave in love.[8]

Marriage God's Way—Many Scriptures tell us to <u>accept</u> one another—faults and all. We can do that by seeing the advantages of the very things we dislike about our spouse. If she talks too much, you don't have to talk so much at parties—and you probably like that. If he's constantly out in his workshop, appreciate the results of his handiwork for your home. Remember to appreciate and praise those activities and characteristics your spouse values. If those activities become excessive, use the confronting techniques we recommended in the previous chapter.

> Each of us married our spouse with the unconscious desire to have them "<u>complement</u>" our weaknesses. If we begin to **disparage** the strengths that we need, we won't be as open to having God use those characteristics to develop our own character. Over time, we should become more like the good qualities in our spouse that magnify our weaknesses. If we don't, we won't become well-rounded, well-balanced people.

It took several years for Paul and Brenda to appreciate each other's style. For example, Paul quietly mulls a matter over before packaging his feelings into words. On the other hand, Brenda liberally vents her thoughts as they come to mind and then eventually arrives at solid opinions. Paul has learned to tolerate Brenda's outpouring of disconnected words, knowing she is processing toward a conclusion. He doesn't take her headstrong comments personally. Brenda has learned to respect Paul's temporary silence, not interpreting it as sulking, but as his way of getting in tune with his feelings. She then listens closely when he shares. Because neither style is wrong nor right, it is this mutual understanding that has contributed to their twenty-two years of marital friendship.

What Others are Saying:

☞ **GO TO:**

Romans 14:1; 15:7 (accept)

WARNING

☞ **GO TO:**

1 Corinthians 12:22–23 (complement)

disparage: belittle

TAKE IT FROM THEM

KEY POINT

Appreciate your differences—they are God's tools for change.

> **1 Samuel 1:4–8** Whenever the day came for Elkanah to sacrifice, he would give portions of the meat to his wife Peninnah and to all her sons and daughters. But to Hannah he gave a double portion because he loved her, and the Lord had closed her womb. And because the Lord had closed her womb, her rival kept provoking her in order to irritate her. This went on year after year. Whenever Hannah went up to the house of the Lord, her rival provoked her till she wept and would not eat. Elkanah her husband would say to her, "Hannah, why are you weeping? Why don't you eat? Why are you downhearted? Don't I mean more to you than ten sons?"

Are Feelings Really That Important?

In Israel, a barren woman was considered deprived of children by God because she was sinful. The women who had a lot of children were considered more blessed and favored by God. Hannah deeply grieved over her barrenness. She felt worthless and unloved, even though Elkanah obviously did many loving things for her.

What Others are Saying:

David and Heather Kopp: He could have shamed her for her "inadequacy" or even divorced her. Instead he loved Hannah for *who* she was far more than for *what* she could or could not give him. And so Elkanah tried to fill her emptiness with gifts of comfort, affirmation, and honor. The extra portion he gave her "because he loved her," sounds trivial. But it was a tender act, worthy to be recorded in the Bible for all time.[9]

Think about It

Elkanah performed many loving acts but could have really shined by reflecting back Hannah's feelings. What he said made her feel as if she were wrong for feeling the way she did. Instead of invalidating her feelings, he could have said something like, "Hannah, I can certainly understand how distraught this makes you feel. I really want you to have a child too. You are valuable to me regardless, but I see how important it is to you."

Marriage God's Way—Reflecting the feelings of our spouse back to them fulfills Romans 12:15, *"Rejoice with those who rejoice; mourn with those who mourn."* When we discount our mate's feelings by trying to fix their problem without listening to their heart, or by telling them they shouldn't feel a certain way, we belittle an important aspect of that person. But when we identify and welcome their feelings, we actually help them work through difficult feelings faster.

What Others are Saying:

Bill and Pam Farrel: After a significant amount of sharing, when you think you have a good idea of what is motivating your spouse, describe a time in your life when you think you have felt the same way. When you are done describing this event, ask your spouse, "Is that what it is like for you?"[10]

> **Ephesians 5:28–30** In this same way, husbands ought to love their wives as their own bodies. He who loves his wife loves himself. After all, no one ever hated his own body, but he feeds and cares for it, just as Christ does the church—for we are members of his body.

Stop Being So Selfish!

This Scripture refers to married men, but of course, it's a message for everyone—especially those who are married. We each go into marriage thinking our mate will meet all of our needs. Do we think, "I'm going to be selfless and always meet my spouse's needs"? Not too often! Yet, that is God's call for us. We won't do it completely or perfectly, but that should be our goal: to become more and more unselfish.

KEY POINT

Our selflessness creates greater godly character.

Marriage God's Way—We are to love our spouse even as we love <u>ourselves</u>. We usually take *very* good care of ourselves! That's the same care God wants us to give our spouse. Even though that's a tall order, in God's power we can do it. We may be afraid that our needs will be ignored, but God tells us that he'll provide all of our true needs. *"And my God will meet all your needs according to his glorious riches in Christ Jesus"* (Philippians 4:19). If we trust God enough to believe that, we will be able to give abundantly to our spouse.

☞ **GO TO:**

Leviticus 19:18; Matthew 19:19 (ourselves)

What Others are Saying:

Think about It

☞ **GO TO:**

Philippians 2:3 (selfless)

He Says . . .

She Says . . .

Bill and Lynne Hybels: But six months after the wedding, they [husband and wife] retire their servant's uniforms. Suddenly it's every man for himself; every woman for herself. They hide the uniforms in the back of the hallway closet, and with them the warm feelings that service engenders. If a husband and wife want to heat up those feelings again, they need to squeeze themselves back into those uniforms, blow the dust off the shoulders, and get back to serving.[11]

Often, we justify our selfishness, blaming our spouse for not meeting our needs. Yet, God wants us to grow in our dependence upon him. What better way to do that than to be challenged to act in an unnatural way—unselfishly. If the challenge to be <u>selfless</u> is looked upon as surrendering to God, we will see the benefit and maybe be more willing to do it.

I'm Going to Outserve You!

LARRY: Like a knife, the words of Wellington Boone cut at my heart: "Guys, if you want to be a godly man, you must outserve your wife!"

I was sitting in the Los Angeles Coliseum with 70,000 other Promise Keepers. The stadium was very quiet. I wasn't the only man struck by the power and simplicity of the statement. After twenty-five years of marriage, there was no doubt that year after year Kathy had outserved me. I committed right then to outserve Kathy.

When I got home that evening, I walked up to Kathy and said, "Honey, for over twenty-five years you have outserved me in our marriage. It was you who gave and I who benefited. I am sorry because I took your loving choices for granted. I am putting you on notice, I'm going to outserve you for the next year." I knew I couldn't make up for twenty-five years of sacrifice with just one year of service, but that was how I expressed my commitment. Maybe I subconsciously was hedging my decision with the time limit, but I was serious. Things were going to change in my home.

KATHY: And they did! I was amazed when Larry expressed his new commitment with such fervor and passion. I wondered if he would actually be able to keep his promise, but he did. He began doing things for me that relieved many of my stresses. For instance, he began doing the weekly food shopping—something I dislike doing—so that I could spend more time writing. He was more caring and considerate. He looked for little opportunities to please me. He actually *was* outserving me, and I was so grateful! At the end of the year, I said to him, "Larry, you said you would outserve me and you have. Thank you!" In the years since then, we tease each other about trying to outserve each other.

> **Matthew 5:5** Blessed are the meek, for they will inherit the earth.

Who's Responsible for My Happiness?

Our happiness, which in Jesus' Sermon on the Mount is called "blessedness," is not dependent on someone or something else; it's dependent on our attitude. When we are "meek," we are surrendered to God's plan for providing for our needs and happiness. That doesn't mean that he will provide all of our wants or desires, but it does mean God will provide for our true needs.

Tim Woodroof: Primarily, meekness is a posture we adopt in the presence of God. The humility and submissiveness implied by meekness is evidenced first and foremost in our demeanor before the Father. Meekness is surrender, **abdication**, and yielded obedience—but not the kind given by the weak to people who are stronger and more powerful. Meekness is bowing the knee to God. It's the surrender of self-will to God's will.[12]

What Others are Saying:

abdication: abandonment

Michelle McKinney Hammond: Whatever you do, don't imagine you can change a man or that all of a sudden the light will go on and he will immediately become a new person. Forget it! People generally are who they are. Any changes made will only be by the hand of God, and even those will take time. God is extremely patient; how patient are you?[13]

Believing that my spouse is responsible for my happiness feeds the lie that I must change my spouse so that I can be happy. If our husband or wife is not living up to our expectations, we can begin to think that's the reason we're not happy. But the truth is, we can be happy, joyful, and content regardless of how we are treated. Our attitude is a choice—not an automatic response to another person's behavior.

Think about It

Couples in the Bible

☞ **Check It Out:**

1 Samuel 25:3–39

There is a difference between happiness and joy. Happiness is an emotion, and joy is a choice of meekness: believing that God knows best in allowing the circumstances of my life. If we believe happiness and joy are the same, we'll be constantly disappointed because events in life don't always lead to good feelings.

Abigail was married to Nabal, a mean and angry man. Yet, Abigail was described as intelligent and beautiful. She was humble and wise when dealing with Nabal's uncouth response to David, as David fled King Saul. Abigail had a cheerful countenance in the midst of dealing with her hard-hearted husband. Her happiness was not dependent upon her husband. After Nabal died, David saw her worth—both inside and out—and offered to marry her.

STUDY QUESTIONS

1. In what way did God make a choice to love us, and how is that an example for husbands and wives?
2. How does the Bible characterize love based on 1 Corinthians 13:4–8?
3. What did God use to express his love for us, and how does that apply to marriage?
4. How can couples appreciate their spouse's differences?
5. How can a couple incorporate Romans 12:15 into their relationship?
6. How can a husband or wife judge whether they are loving their mate according to God's way described in Ephesians 5:28–30?

CHAPTER WRAP-UP

- Husbands and wives need to make a choice to love their mates because they won't always have good feelings. God is the example for making that loving choice because he chose to love us by sending Jesus to die on the cross. God wants us to love with a godly love.

- Every person has his or her own opinion about how he or she wants to be loved. What speaks love to one person might not be meaningful to another. Husbands and wives need to learn their spouse's love language and then fulfill it—even if it's not their own personal definition of love.

- Couples can easily get frustrated with each other if they don't understand that different isn't necessarily wrong. There are many ways to accomplish something or to look at something—as long as it isn't against Scripture. Couples can learn to appreciate the different perspective their mate brings to their relationship. Husbands and wives—especially wives—feel loved when their spouse acknowledges their feelings and lets them know it's OK to feel that way. Being selfless is one of the greatest challenges in marriage, yet when we make the choice to be selfless, we bless our spouse, draw closer to God, and develop spiritual character.

KATHY & LARRY'S  BOOKSHELF

Some of Kathy and Larry's favorite books about responding with love:

- *Love for a Lifetime*, James Dobson, Multnomah. Building a marriage that will go the distance.
- *Romancing Your Marriage*, H. Norman Wright, Regal Books. How to better understand and respect your marriage partner.
- *Love Life for Every Married Couple*, Ed Wheat and Gloria Okes Perkins, HarperCollins. How to fall in love and stay in love.
- *Incompatibility: Grounds for a Great Marriage!*, Chuck and Barb Snyder, Questar. Personality differences can enhance marriage intimacy.

7 CRAVING SPIRITUAL INTIMACY

Here We Go

When we marry, we may not know exactly what we're craving, but it's actually spiritual intimacy: to be one in spirit with our spouse. We long to be understood and loved, to be able to share our innermost being with our beloved and to receive his or her acceptance. And we want our spouse to share with us in the same way. Many times, though, we don't know how to achieve such intimacy, and we are easily hurt by the unintentional things our spouse does. Our spirit, so willing to openly share, now shrinks back, uncertain of the reception we'll receive.

Yet, God desires for us to experience a oneness with our spouse—because he wants us to represent the oneness between him and his <u>bride</u>, the church. With his help, we can open our spirits again to be intimate with our thoughts and feelings, and also be able to receive our mate's tentative sharing. There is hope! Let's find out God's recipe for intimate married spirits.

☞ **GO TO:**

Revelation 19:7 (bride)

SHARING MY SOUL

> **Genesis 2:22–25** Then the Lord God made a woman from the rib he had taken out of the man, and he brought her to the man. The man said, "This is now bone of my bones and flesh of my flesh; she shall be called 'woman,' for she was taken out of man." For this reason a man will leave his father and mother and be united to his wife, and they will become one flesh. The man and his wife were both naked, and they felt no shame.

Wow! No Shame!

God intended from the beginning for husband and wife to experience a spiritual and physical oneness. More than the sexual oneness we usually think of, God desired for his beloved human creation to experience oneness with each other on a spiritual level. A couple is to relate to each other without fear or embarrassment. We are not to be self-conscious but spouse-conscious, focusing on the best for our mate. In spiritual oneness we are to expose our innermost being freely with each other, experiencing no hesitation or embarrassment.

Adam and Eve, as described in this passage, were completely **vulnerable** with each other—both physically and spiritually. They didn't think about themselves, only the other.

vulnerable: exposed

What Others are Saying:

Linda Dillow: The first husband and wife experienced nakedness in all areas: a physical, emotional, intellectual, and spiritual transparency between husband and wife: no masks, no barriers, only communion and companionship. They were unashamed. They enjoyed an intimacy where there was no fear to reveal, a transparency that led the other into the deep crevices of life. Neither partner feared to let the other see the good, the bad, the indifferent.[1]

David and Claudia Arp: In the first book of the Bible we are given the secret for making marriages last. Genesis 2:24 challenges us to leave our homes and families of origin, cleave to each other, and become one. Cleaving gives the picture of sticking together, both in easy times and hard times. It's joining wings and permanently flying together![2]

Think about It

A slippery toddler, who runs around the house after his bath, has no sense of his nakedness. He never wonders what people will think of him. He doesn't cover parts of his body in embarrassment. He feels free to run from his mother's efforts to put on his clothes. It feels good to be **unfettered** by the restrictions of clothes. That's how Adam and Eve felt. That is how God desires a married couple to be: open and honest with each other without worrying what the other person thinks. Unfortunately, careless words, unkind remarks, insensitive reactions, and selfishness often crush that freedom. The spirit of the wounded mate closes up like a flower sens-

unfettered: free

ing darkness. Forgiveness and understanding are the keys to protecting spiritual oneness.

Marriage God's Way—Spiritual oneness can come from having a biblical view of God's purpose for marriage. The Bible sheds light on God's intentions:

- *Genesis 1:28:* Marriage serves the purpose of creating children.
- *Genesis 2:18–24:* God designed the idea of marriage because he knew a man and woman would need each other.
- *Genesis 24:58–60:* God intended marriage to require a commitment of one man to one woman for all their lives.
- *Song of Songs 1:15–16:* God desires a man and woman to experience the feelings of love and affection.
- *Jeremiah 33:10–11:* God conceived marriage to be a source of joy and celebration.
- *Malachi 2:14–15:* A godly marriage is God's ideal atmosphere for raising godly children.
- *Matthew 5:32:* Infidelity and divorce have far-reaching negative implications from which God wanted to protect his created beings.
- *Matthew 19:6:* Marriage is a lifetime responsibility.
- *Romans 7:2–3:* Only death should end a marriage.
- *Ephesians 5:21–33:* Within marriage, there should be love to the point of sacrifice.
- *Hebrews 13:4:* Marriage should be regarded as beneficial and valuable.

Dave and Jan Stoop, in their book, *The Intimacy Factor,* identify nine myths about intimacy that should be avoided:

1. If the other person really loves me, he or she will always know what I want or need to be happy.
2. The best indicator of a good marriage is a good sex life.
3. The level of satisfaction and intimacy automatically increases over the years of the relationship.

KEY POINT

Forgiveness and understanding are the keys to protecting spiritual oneness.

4. It doesn't matter how I behave, the other person should show love for me simply because we are married to each other.

5. If we are really close, we should be able to point out each other's errors and shortcomings without feeling threatened.

6. My spouse either loves me or doesn't; whichever, there is nothing I can do to make it any different.

7. The more we can disclose—both good and bad information—to each other, the closer we become.

8. Keeping the feelings of romantic love alive is necessary to fuel an intimate relationship.

9. I have to feel love toward the other person before I can help the relationship become closer.

> **Ephesians 5:31–32** "For this reason a man will leave his father and mother and be united to his wife, and the two will become one flesh." This is a profound mystery—but I am talking about Christ and the church.

One Plus One Equals Three

When a couple becomes one flesh and experiences physical and spiritual unity, what happens to one of them affects the other. If the husband experiences a bad time at work, his wife feels his pain. If the wife hurts from a disappointing relationship with a friend, the husband sympathizes with her when she talks about it. When this kind of unity develops between two people, they express and share each other's experiences.

That is the same oneness that God wants modeled for Christ and his bride, the church. They become so close and connected that they each are affected by what the other does. Jesus loves the people comprising his bride, the church, so much that he sacrificially gave his life for her. Likewise, the people of God should be willing to sacrifice their own lives in order to show the union they have with Jesus. When unbelievers see this kind of unity, they are amazed and, hopefully, drawn to that kind of loving communion.

☞ **GO TO:**

John 3:16 (gave his life)

John 17:23 (unity)

validate: prove

What Others are Saying:

Larry Crabb: He also wants our relationship to **validate** the claims of Christianity to a watching world as an example of the power of Christ's redeeming love to overcome the divisive effects of sin. In

John 17:21, Jesus poured out his heart to the Father: "I pray . . . that all of them may be one, Father, just as you are in me and I am in you. May they also be in us so that the world may believe that you have sent me." Christ's prayer for oneness refers first of all to our relationships to other believers; but marriage, with its unique opportunity for intimacy, also offers a convincing demonstration of the power of Christ's love to enable people to experience true relationship.[3]

What Others are Saying:

Wayne Barber, Eddie Rasnake, and Richard Shepherd: God designed the husband and wife relationship to be a bond of oneness, and through that a deepening and growing relationship. He uses this relationship as a picture of the oneness with him for which mankind was created.[4]

Unity between a husband and wife is also supposed to reflect the unity between the members of the **Trinity**. God the Father, God the Son, and God the Holy Spirit are all in perfect union in their purposes, desires, and actions. If a husband and wife are able to accomplish such a challenge in a world of marital dissension, then they can give credit to God for their ability to work together. Will their marriage be perfect? Of course not. They will disagree and even argue. But if they can <u>work things out</u> and have a common purpose, they are far ahead of many married couples—and their example can represent God to a hurting world.

REMEMBER THIS

Trinity: the three persons or roles of God: Father, Son, and Holy Spirit

☞ **GO TO:**

Proverbs 17:1 (work things out)

INSTRUCTIONS FOR INTIMACY

If our desire is for marital intimacy, then we need to know how to develop tools for reaching that goal. It won't be easy and it requires hard work, but it is possible. By following God's principles, we will achieve his goal of achieving intimacy of the soul.

> **1 Corinthians 7:3–5** The husband should fulfill his marital duty to his wife, and likewise the wife to her husband. The wife's body does not belong to her alone but also to her husband. In the same way, the husband's body does not belong to him alone but also to his wife. Do not deprive each other except by mutual consent and for a time, so that you may devote yourselves to prayer.

Make Prayer a Priority

abstaining: *going without*

The apostle Paul didn't mean that a couple should pray together only when **abstaining** from sexual union. He was saying that at times "fasting" from sex would make their prayers more powerful through their sacrifice and through the added time to spend in prayer.

Prayer between a husband and wife is one of the most powerful disciplines of intimacy. To be able to appear in God's presence together and seek him for their needs is a bonding experience. Plus, we tend to be more honest when we come before our Father. Praying together can even tenderize our hearts so that any anger or irritation will diminish.

What Others are Saying:

David and Claudia Arp: We are convinced that having a spiritual dimension in marriage actually increases marital satisfaction. Research says we are right! Did you realize that couples who frequently pray together are twice as likely to describe their marriages as highly romantic?[5]

H. Norman Wright: As the level of communication deepens between you and God, you will begin to experience a greater strength and courage to deepen the levels between you and your partner. God's plans for your marriage are best fulfilled when each of you are opened to his presence and guidance. Prayer, then, is the first step toward marital intimacy.[6]

Think about It

For many couples, the idea of praying together sends shivers throughout their bodies—and we're not talking fun shivers! For some people there is a discomfort connected with praying in a group and outright fear of opening up to pray with their spouse. How can we begin learning to pray together? Consider these ideas:

- Pray silently and separately and then give a brief summary of what you prayed.

- In each other's presence, pray a verse or two of Scripture out loud or silently about the situation you want to bring before the Lord.

- Find a book that contains prayers and read them out loud. We suggest the series of books by Lee Roberts such as *Praying God's Will for My Husband* or *Praying God's Will for My Wife* (Thomas Nelson Publishers).

- Each pray only one sentence out loud to begin getting used to praying together.
- Find the time that works best for both of you.
- Read a book about prayer together and discuss it.
- To avoid one person "outpraying" the other, make a list of concerns to be prayed about, then each pray about half the concerns.
- Don't use prayer as a way to change or attack your mate.

If a husband or wife is more talkative or **vivacious** than the spouse, they may **inadvertently** belittle the quiet mate by praying too long or too expressively. As a result, the less-verbal person may feel like he or she isn't praying as "correctly" or as beautifully. The quiet person is less motivated to try this precious discipline of intimacy because he or she doesn't want to appear silly, unspiritual, or stupid. The more talkative mate must be sensitive to the insecurities of the quiet one. Rather than "modeling" a beautiful or powerful prayer through **verbosity**, the talkative spouse is actually discouraging the mate. By restraining the length of the prayer or by making it simpler, the person praying will encourage the spouse to communicate in prayer more often.

It is important to give up our perfectionistic expectations that prayer must be a certain length or said in a certain way in order to be the "right" kind of prayer. By releasing our unrealistic expectations, we'll be willing to accept however our spouse can participate. God is pleased with any efforts we give him. We don't need to "perform" in a certain way. All that is required is a <u>clean</u> heart.

Praying together is a great tool for conflict resolution. It is a powerful means of releasing our own agenda, hearing our spouse, and then listening to God's direction. When we're so determined to believe that our opinion is right and good, surrendering our own opinions before God in prayer enables us to hear and receive our mate's ideas.

WARNING

vivacious: outgoing

inadvertently: without meaning to

verbosity: many words

 GO TO:

Psalm 51:2 (clean)

REMEMBER THIS

Marriage God's Way—Another method to deepen the spiritual relationship between a husband and wife is to enjoy devotions together. Reading God's Word draws couples together as they find nuggets of wisdom they can apply to themselves and their lives. Just like prayer, this may take some cooperative effort in finding the devotional activity that is best for you. You might try a Bible study you do individually and later share your answers. Read a daily devotional book together, or attend a couples' Bible study group.

After Thirty Years, We Learned to Pray Together

He Says . . .

LARRY: Most of my career as a policeman has been spent working nights. When I would get home around 3:00 A.M., Kathy was asleep. When I awoke mid morning, Kathy was busy with the kids or her writing. Making consistent shared prayer a priority was merely a goal for many years. We would often pray before bed on my days off, but often I would stay up late and Kathy would go to sleep, exhausted from the day. It wasn't until I started working days that a breakthrough occurred. We now set our alarm twenty minutes early and use that time to pray and share before the day starts.

She Says . . .

KATHY: Over the years, we tried to find a method and time that would enable us to spend quality devotional time together. We knew how important it was, but when things didn't work smoothly, my perfectionism made me want to give up, and if I judged that quality was lacking, I felt frustrated. I tried to be satisfied with small steps, but it was hard, and unfortunately, I communicated my dissatisfaction—which discouraged Larry from continuing. But over the last few years, we've found great spiritual oneness in waking up early to spend time in prayer. It starts our day with a positive perspective and increases our security in God's control over the day. It gives us the opportunity to know the other's concerns and feel unified in bringing them to God. Morning devotions have become a new dimension that we both always wanted and have finally found.

TAKE IT FROM THEM

Donna and Ellis made prayer a greater priority after their son was born with special needs. Every evening, they prayed together for wisdom and God's help in dealing with his special gift. They sensed a oneness of purpose as they sought God's guidance, especially since they disagreed on the proper approach to their son's problems. Donna thought they should be more strict, but Ellis thought they should be lenient. The contrast in their perspective forced them to pray for strength and wisdom from God and actually drew them closer than if they hadn't had that challenge.

Another couple, Ted and Patty, have solidified a prayer-based intimacy in their relationship over their twelve-year marriage. Early on, they began a nightly habit of reflecting over their day together. As they did, they would sit on the sofa, pull out their prayer journal (which was simply a colorful notebook), and take turns sharing from their day, jotting down both the thanksgivings and the prayer requests. When finished, they take a few moments to pray for the things shared, thanking the Lord for the blessings and lifting before him the concerns of their hearts. This time together enables them to see blessings as well as needs and concerns they might otherwise have missed, and has empowered them to know more deeply how to pray for one another throughout the day. They are amazed as they look back over their prayer journal, because it chronicles how God has been faithful in helping and protecting them over the years.

> **Proverbs 18:13** He who answers before listening—that is his folly and his shame.

Listen! Don't Fix!

Solomon wrote about the importance of listening, and that is especially important for developing spiritual intimacy. When our beloved spouse listens to us while we are talking, we experience closeness because they are showing they love and care about us. When we know our mate is really, *really* listening to us, we feel valued. But if our mate tries to tell us what to do to solve the problem (before we're ready for a solution), or they cut off communication in some other way, we feel trivialized and confused.

Bill and Pam Farrel: A key principle in promoting intimacy is permission. If your spouse senses permission to share more without being judged or prematurely "fixed," new information will be shared. This new information will lead you to a better understanding of what your spouse is all about at the emotional level of his or her life that motivates actions and decisions.[7]

What Others are Saying:

James Dobson: What is the solution to such communicative problems at home? As always, it involves compromise. A man has a clear responsibility to "cheer up his wife which he hath taken" (Deuteronomy 24:5). He must not claim himself "a rock" who will never allow himself to be vulnerable again. He must press himself to open his heart and share his deeper feelings with his wife. Time must be reserved for meaningful conversations.[8]

REMEMBER   THIS

Most of the time, the temptation to solve a spouse's problem is a man's need to be the hero in his wife's life. Usually, a man doesn't operate out of emotion, but out of logic. "She has a problem. I know how she can fix it. I don't need to hear anything else. I will be her hero with my ideas to make her feel better." He doesn't understand that she'll feel "better" after sharing her heart and feelings. When she has talked through her feelings, she will be able to listen to a solution or suggested insights. A husband can show his love and interest by leaning toward his wife and having eye contact as she shares with him. That will make her feel loved and important.

Marriage God's Way—Prayer is so important to God that he stores his children's prayers in heaven right before his throne. Revelation 5:8 tells us, *"And when he had taken it, the four living creatures and the twenty-four elders fell down before the Lamb. Each one had a harp and they were holding golden bowls full of incense, which are the prayers of the saints."* When the Israelites were traveling in the wilderness, God gave them the dimensions and directions for <u>building</u> an altar of incense (see illustration, page 107). Maybe that description is similar to the bowls holding our prayers in heaven.

☞ **GO TO:**

Exodus 30:1–6
(building)

WARNING

The apostle Peter wrote, *"Husbands, in the same way be considerate as you live with your wives, and treat them with respect as the weaker partner and as heirs with you of the gracious gift of life, so that nothing will hinder your prayers"* (1 Peter 3:7). It's not a surprise that Peter focused on men, warning them about the importance of treating their wives with respect. For if a wife isn't treated well, she likely won't cheerfully or enthusiastically affirm her husband's prayers—and those prayers will be hindered. First Peter 3:7 seems to indicate that God might

Golden Altar of Incense

The Israelites made the altar of incense of acacia wood, two cubits high, one cubit wide, and one cubit broad, with a top and horns. It was covered with gold and only incense was allowed to burn on it both morning and night. The Bible refers to prayers of Christians as incense.

not be as willing to answer prayers of a husband who doesn't treat his wife kindly.

Here are some things *not* to say when your spouse shares intimately with you:

REMEMBER THIS

- I wouldn't worry about that.
- You shouldn't feel that way.
- If you'll only do what I say, you won't feel that way anymore.
- I know what you're feeling.
- There's really no reason for you to feel that way, look at the facts.

Instead say this:

- Repeat key words or phrases your spouse has said and then say, "Tell me more."
- Summarize what you think they've said, and ask, "Is that what you are saying?"
- Give constant eye contact while your spouse talks and don't interrupt, but do nod and smile or frown according to their sharing. Proverbs 25:20 says, *"Like one who takes away a garment on a cold day, or like vinegar poured on soda, is one who sings songs to a heavy heart."*

H. Norman Wright in his book, *Romancing Your Marriage*, suggests that couples spend an entire day together in order to develop intimacy! They must stay in the same room together for twelve hours with no other people, books, television, radio or stereo, or telephone calls. It's all right for the couple to be silent at times, and in the beginning, they will most likely feel awkward and self-conscious. Communication must be about something personal pertaining to themselves, not to the children, the house, or work. Wright says, "Most couples experience a deepening of feelings as the hours pass and they begin to share in a way they have not experienced before. Some couples pray together, sing together, make love, or enjoy any combination of many intimate expressions. Many have made the twelve-hour retreat a biannual or annual event in order to continue developing intimacy in their relationship."

TAKE IT FROM THEM

Anita and Dave had parents who modeled good communication, so after several years of marital problems, they sought counseling. Their therapist taught them basic listening and reflecting skills. Initially, they felt awkward discussing vulnerable and unfamiliar concepts like feelings and needs, but they became more proficient by practicing. Their nightly "check-in" is their main source of emotional intimacy. In the evening, either Anita or Dave goes first, stating their current feelings, while the other listens closely or asks questions for clarification. The roles are then reversed. Next, they list their needs and the things they are thankful for, ranging from the philosophical (God's love) to the practical (having enough Kleenex in the flu season). This end-of-the-day exchange helps them to reconnect. They end the exchange with prayer together, giving each other a compliment and a goodnight kiss. Ten or fifteen minutes is all it takes, depending on how often they go on tangents! Here's the order of their "check-in":

1. feelings
2. needs
3. gratitude list
4. marital goals
5. prayer
6. compliment
7. kiss

BE BEST BUDDIES

> **Song of Songs 5:16** His mouth is sweetness itself; he is altogether lovely. This is my lover, this my friend, O daughters of Jerusalem.

You Mean *Like* My Mate Too?

Couples who enjoy a spiritual oneness are those who don't just love each other, they like each other too. They are best friends. That can be a tall order. If we often have to make a choice to *love* our mate, how can we also *like* them? There are keys for making our mate our best friend—just like Solomon wrote in his romantic song above.

KEY POINT

Make your mate your best friend.

Bill Hybels: We have friends who always discuss their Friday night date during dinner on the previous Monday. They look through the entertainment section of the Sunday newspaper, consider various options, decide together what they want to do, and then have all week to anticipate their plans.[9]

Chuck and Barb Snyder: You need to verbally say to each other—actually repeating your marriage vows—that no matter what happens you will not leave the other person or seek a divorce. You WILL work things out even though there may be times when you feel like walking away.[10]

 **Marriage God's Way**—Couples that are best friends share:

- *Companionship:* have common activities they enjoy together.
- *Communion:* encourage their spouse's spiritual walk (Hebrews 10:24).
- *Communication:* share who they are and what they need (Proverbs 16:21).
- *Commitment:* express their desire to keep their spouse as their highest priority (Hebrews 13:4).
- *Candor:* speak the truth in love (Ephesians 4:15).
- *Comfort:* bear one another's burdens (Galatians 6:2).

Couples in the Bible

☞ **Check It Out:**

Acts 18:2, 18, 26;
Romans 16:3;
1 Corinthians 16:19;
2 Timothy 4:19

**TAKE IT
FROM THEM**

• *Championship:* they are on each other's "emotional team" and they may even play sports together.

Priscilla and Aquila became Christians during the time of the apostle Paul, several years after Jesus' resurrection. From the biblical account of their activities, they seemed to be best friends. They were in business together as tentmakers and evidently became Christians at about the same time. After becoming Christians, they were involved side by side in ministering to different groups of Christians, even sponsoring a church in their home. They went on missionary trips with Paul and endangered their own lives for his sake. In every account of them in the Bible, they are mentioned together. They truly shared a common goal and purpose: their love of Christ and their passion to share him with others. That's a firm friendship.

Ken and Suzy retain their friendship through spontaneous prayer, especially when a seed of bitterness springs up within one of them. Suzy remembers a day when she had thorns of anger ready to rip Ken's flesh because of resentment. Feeling more like an enemy of Ken than a friend, she sensed God's nudge in her heart prompting her to say, "Ken, let's pray." They both knelt, and Suzy poured her heart out to God, sharing her anguish with Ken through God's filter of prayer. That snipped off the rough edges of her bitterness and allowed Ken to respond kindly to her frustration. When they rose from their knees, Suzy felt like a new woman. She smiled and hugged her husband, silently thanking God, and knowing they would have continued responding as adversaries instead of friends if they hadn't prayed.

> **Genesis 26:8–9** When Isaac had been there a long time, Abimelech king of the Philistines looked down from a window and saw Isaac caressing his wife Rebekah. So Abimelech summoned Isaac and said, "She is really your wife! Why did you say, 'She is my sister'?" Isaac answered him, "Because I thought I might lose my life on account of her."

Keep the Pizzazz in Marriage

Isaac and Rebekah were such lovers that, even in a public place, it was apparent. What Abimelech observed isn't clear, but it was obvious to him that they were married rather than being brother and sister as Isaac had said. Isaac had called Rebekah his sister so that Abimelech wouldn't kill him trying to get his beautiful wife to join his harem.

Bill Hybels: Too many spouses do little more than give each other an obligatory kiss when they part ways in the morning and then repeat the routine when they greet one another at night. Their lips touch, but they barely even know it. It has become an involuntary response. Adding a little variety to touching can take it out of the autopilot realm and put the feeling back in it.[11]

Ed Young: There is not a woman alive who does not know the difference between affection, period, and affection, comma. The affection that satisfies your wife's desire has no strings attached. A hug is a hug, not a prelude to sex or the announcement that you have just bought a boat. The husband who seldom touches his wife except as an entrée to lovemaking needs to understand that he is depriving her of something as important to her as sex is to him: the knowledge that she is loved and appreciated, period.[12]

Think about It

If Isaac and Rebekah kept the pizzazz in their marriage through "caressing," then so should we! Although affection is most often the primary desire of the wife, many men favor it also. Let's face it, most men prefer sex to affection (That's why we've included a whole section on it!), but women love affection. It prepares them for a sexual encounter. When a husband puts his arm around his wife, or takes her hand in public, he is saying—as far as she is concerned:

- You are important to me.
- I will take care of you.
- I want the best for you.
- You can be secure in my love.

She feels important and valued as he makes that effort to caress her.

KEY POINT

Giving affection develops spiritual oneness.

Because women often think of affection, wives conclude that it's also on the minds of their husbands. A wife walking down the street beside her husband may have a desire for him to put his arm around her or take her hand. Because she is thinking about it, she assumes he is thinking about it also! When she doesn't receive the affection she craves, she believes he is deliberately withholding something through a conscious choice!

But he isn't thinking the same thing at all! That's like saying, "I was just thinking of a blue elephant, weren't you?" Men don't think of giving affection readily, but they can be coached. As a wife takes his hand or slips her arm under his with a smile, she will remind him graciously and gently that she has that need. Over time, he might actually think about it, maybe as often as he thinks of a blue elephant!

LEADERSHIP, HEADSHIP, OR SINKING SHIP

> **Ephesians 5:25–33** Husbands, love your wives, just as Christ loved the church and gave himself up for her to make her holy, cleansing her by the washing with water through the word, and to present her to himself as a radiant church, without stain or wrinkle or any other blemish, but holy and blameless. In this same way, husbands ought to love their wives as their own bodies. He who loves his wife loves himself. After all, no one ever hated his own body, but he feeds and cares for it, just as Christ does the church—for we are members of his body. "For this reason a man will leave his father and mother and be united to his wife, and the two will become one flesh." This is a profound mystery—but I am talking about Christ and the church. However, each one of you also must love his wife as he loves himself, and the wife must respect her husband.

Taking the Lead

God takes marriage seriously. Throughout Scripture the husband's role is specific and purposeful: take leadership. When this is done biblically, a couple will experience greater spiritual oneness. Yet, throughout history husbands have struggled with how to lead. Here, Paul lays an important foundation for leadership in the home. Husbands must love their wives like Jesus Christ did the church. Wow, what a tall order! There are three things to remember from this passage:

1. A godly leader is willing to make sacrifices. Jesus was willing to sacrifice everything for the church. This required intimate knowledge of those needing his intervention and contradicts the modern notion that the man's home is his castle and those living there serve his needs. We must see our responsibility to sacrifice.

2. A godly leader is willing to outserve his wife. Self-centeredness sabotages the ability to meet our wife's needs. Other-centeredness energizes the leader and is demonstrated when the well-being of the wife is the primary importance.

3. A godly leader cares for his wife as he cares for his own body. A wife needs not fear submitting to such a man.

James Dobson: If his family has purchased too many items on credit, then the financial crunch is ultimately his fault. If the family never reads the Bible, or seldom goes to church on Sunday, God holds the man to blame. If the children are disrespectful and disobedient, the primary responsibility lies with the father . . . not his wife. In my view, America's greatest need is for husbands to begin guiding their families, rather than pouring every physical and emotional resource into mere acquisition of money.[13]

What Others are Saying:

God calls all husbands, with the cooperation of wives, to exert leadership to ensure that their partnership serves the purposes of God and not the whims of either partner. Male domination is sin. Leadership has nothing to do with superiority. Submission has nothing to do with inferiority. Male leadership treats the wife as an equal partner and affirms her value and contribution to the marriage.

REMEMBER THIS

Legitimate criticism erupts across our society today because husbands are either (1) preoccupied with success; (2) passive and uninvolved in the family; or (3)

WARNING

too authoritative and overbearing. Make no mistake; all three struggles involve moral failure, not biblical principles. The Bible clearly tells men first to love their wives with a sacrificial love. In chapter 6, we defined love as a choice for the highest good of another. In marriage, such a love leaves little room for passivity or preoccupation. Such a love rejects the notion that self-interest and domination are biblically supported. Such a love demands a servant's heart. When a wife sees her husband outserving her, she becomes more willing to submit to his leadership.

What Is Leadership Anyway?

He Says . . .

LARRY: I remember struggling with the concept of leadership in my home. Many men face the same uncertainty. I once asked a group of men to define what it means to provide leadership in the home. We all sat around for a few minutes forming weak, general answers such as "setting the tone" or "being the leader." Duh! It became clear they were comfortable with the big picture but weren't clear on the specifics. I later asked the same question to a group of women. I received quick responses: does what is asked, takes initiative in family prayer, fixes things around the house. The women knew exactly what leadership looked like in the home.

Facing the responsibility of leading Kathy like Christ leads the church, I find myself stepping carefully when there is disagreement. I have learned that Kathy and I make excellent decisions together. I trust her insight and depend upon her sharing. Rarely do we disagree, and when we do I move slowly and prayerfully.

She Says . . .

KATHY: In excited anticipation of eventual retirement, Larry and I began looking at, dreaming about, and planning the possibilities. Soon, we were seriously considering buying property. As we discussed different possibilities, I really thought buying property would be the best option. Yet, Larry began backing away. I was disappointed. Although it would involve taking a risk, I—the cautious one—was willing to do it. I shared my readiness, but Larry continued to hesitate. Although buying the property was important to me, I realized the Lord was acting through Larry to slow us down. I knew from past experience that God could change Larry's mind if he desired, so I was able to relax and trust that God was leading through Larry. We still don't know what we'll do in the future, but we're confident that God will guide us.

SUBMISSION IS NOT AN IMPOSSIBLE MISSION

> **Ephesians 5:22–24** <u>Wives, submit</u> to your husbands as to the Lord. For the husband is the head of the wife as Christ is the head of the church, his body, of which he is the Savior. Now as the church submits to Christ, so also wives should submit to their husbands in everything.

☞ **GO TO:**

Colossians 3:18;
1 Peter 3:1
(wives, submit)

Submitting Is Not Being a Doormat

No issue in the church today is challenged by our culture more than the issue of submission. The Bible consistently proclaims that the wife should submit to her husband. However, by God's decree, the wife is told to possess an <u>inner quality</u> that gently affirms his leadership. Submission is, first of all, an attitude of the heart that desires cooperation out of <u>love</u> and respect for God's plan for the family, and second, out of love and respect for the husband. This will give him the freedom to grow personally and then to lead the family maturely.

☞ **GO TO:**

1 Peter 3:1–4
(inner quality)

Titus 2:4 (love)

What Others are Saying:

Wayne Grudem: What submission does not mean:

1. Submission does not mean putting a husband in the place of Christ.
2. Submission does not mean giving up independent thought.
3. Submission does not mean a wife should give up efforts to influence and guide her husband.
4. Submission does not mean a wife should give in to every demand of her husband.
5. Submission is not based on a lesser intelligence or competence.
6. Submission does not mean being fearful or timid.
7. Submission is not inconsistent with equality in Christ.[14]

KEY POINT

To the degree that a wife trusts God is the degree she'll be able to submit to her husband.

Life Application Bible:
Submission
Functional—a distinguishing of our roles and the work we are called to do

Relational—a loving acknowledgment of another's value as a person

Reciprocal—a mutual, humble cooperation with one another

Universal—an acknowledgment by the church of the all-encompassing lordship of Jesus Christ[15]

Submission can be thought of as a protection for women, especially if they are being ruled by their emotions. Eve neglected to ask Adam's opinion about Satan's offer, and her emotional reaction of wanting the forbidden fruit created havoc. The concept of the Eastern sheepfold (see illustration below) can help us see submission in a positive light. A sheepfold is a place of shelter for the sheep safe from the attacks of wild beasts. Such sheepfolds were usually low, flat buildings surrounded by a stone wall. The wall had a layer of thorns on top to discourage wild beasts from jumping over.

Submission looks as painful and unattractive as that layer of thorns, but it protects wives from the "wild beasts" of wrong choices. Considering a husband's perspective protects from Satan's attacks.

Think about It

☞ **GO TO:**

Genesis 3:1–6 (Eve)

KEY POINT

Two heads making a decision really are better than one.

Eastern Sheepfold

Illustration shows the low wall that protects the sheep from wild beasts.

Donna and Ellis believe communication is vital to marriage. They discuss their plans openly without either one feeling threatened. They believe that God made the husband as head of the family for a purpose, but that a wise husband will listen to his wife's input. If they can't agree on a decision that needs to be made, Ellis will make the final choice. Yet, Donna promises not to say, "I told you so" or "I knew that wouldn't work," if the plan turns sour. Donna realizes that *"Wives, submit to your husbands as to the Lord,"* (Ephesians 5:22 and Colossians 3:18) means she is to submit to the Lord by submitting to her husband. What a wonderful revelation! She recognizes that when she fits properly into Ellis's decisions, God, to whom he is accountable, can work with him.

TAKE IT FROM THEM

STUDY QUESTIONS

1. How can spiritual oneness be described?
2. Why is it important for Christian couples to have a "one flesh" kind of experience?
3. What is the only act that Scripture encourages married couples refrain from in order to spend more time in prayer and to become in more spiritual tune with each other?
4. Husbands frequently want to just "fix" their wives' problems instead of doing what important thing?
5. Who in the Bible called her spouse her "best friend"?
6. How did Abimelech know that Isaac and Rebekah were actually married and not brother and sister as Isaac had claimed?
7. What does God want husbands to do that Christ modeled for them?
8. If a husband is the head, what is the role of the wife?

CHAPTER WRAP-UP

- God wants husbands and wives to feel safe with each other and to be able to share themselves intimately—everything that they are. One of God's purposes for the spiritual and emotional oneness between a husband and wife is that it represents the kind of unity that Christ has with believers, who make up his church. God wants others, especially unbelievers, to see that and desire to come to know Christ as their Lord and Savior.

- Prayer should be such a priority for couples that at times they will even abstain from sexual encounter in order to spend more time in prayer. Prayer helps a couple to feel closer to each other by bringing their concerns together before God. It also helps to diminish conflict because when in prayer with someone, it's hard to stay angry. Reflecting your mate's feelings back to them after listening closely to what they are saying can help develop spiritual intimacy. Sometimes that can be difficult, especially for a husband who wants to fix his wife's problems with logical answers. A wife really needs to be listened to first before solutions are offered.

- God desires a husband and a wife not just to love each other, but to like each other and be best friends. That takes hard work by learning to communicate, encourage, speak truth in love, and bear one another's burdens. Affection and touch are essential for making a woman feel loved and valued, thus developing and deepening her desire for spiritual oneness with her husband. Without it, she will feel hurt and be tempted to emotionally withdraw from him.

- A husband's leadership is not achieved through superiority, but rather a choice of loving his wife sacrificially through service and sensitive attention to her ideas in order to lead her into greater spirituality and closeness with the Lord.

- A wife's desire to submit will be strongest when she realizes that through it she is submitting to God. A wife will be able to submit to her husband to the degree that she trusts God. And, although involved in the decision process, if a decision needs to be made and there is not agreement between a husband and wife, the wife should allow the husband to make the final decision.

KATHY & LARRY'S  BOOKSHELF

Kathy and Larry's favorite books about spiritual intimacy:

- *The Intimacy Factor*, David Stoop and Jan Stoop, Thomas Nelson Publishers. Becoming one in spirit and soul.

- *Marriage in the Whirlwind*, Bill and Pam Farrel, InterVarsity Press. Seven skills for couples who can't slow down.

- *Intimate Allies*, Dan B. Allender and Tremper Longman III, Tyndale House Publishers. Rediscovering God's design for marriage and becoming soul mates for life.

- *Getting the Love You Want*, Harville Hendrix, Ph.D., Harper-Collins. A guide for couples.

- *Recovering Biblical Manhood & Womanhood*, John Piper and Wayne Grudem, eds., Crossway Books. Interesting discussions about headship and submission.

Part Two

FAMILY TIES

REVEREND FUN

"I just don't think it's right that our young little Junior is learning about the birds and the begats in the fourth grade."

8 IN-LAWS, NOT OUTLAWS

Here We Go

Being married can seem like such a simple concept: "I'll get married and live happily ever after with the man (or woman) of my dreams." We quickly learn that we are not only marrying our spouse but a family with a history and an influence over our spouse that we will never fully understand. We don't just marry one person; we marry a complex host of people who have both direct and indirect influence upon them. And they marry us with our whole set of family dynamics, too. Moreover, each of us thinks our family looks at life correctly! Do we smell a scent of possible difficulty here—or is it an odor?

The Bible addresses even these complications. Scripture has practical help for dealing with in-laws without treating them as outlaws.

CUT THE APRON STRINGS

> **Genesis 2:22–24** Then the Lord God made a woman from the rib he had taken out of the man, and he brought her to the man. The man said, "This is now bone of my bones and flesh of my flesh; she shall be called 'woman,' for she was taken out of man." For this reason a man will leave his father and mother and be united to his wife, and they will become one flesh.

Get Outta There!

Even before there were parents, in-laws, or the proverbial bad mother-in-law, God said that when a man and woman marry, they are to leave their parents. How interesting that God was subtly pointing out a solution to a yet unknown potential problem: dependency upon parents after marriage. Such a relationship with parents can be unhealthy and detrimental to the new family unit.

Interestingly, in the Near Eastern homes of Jews, a son didn't physically leave his house after marriage. During the engagement period, he built a house adjacent to his parents' home and separated it by a courtyard. Then when his house was ready, he went to get his bride and brought her to that house—just yards from his parents. Only the bride physically left her parents. The new bride became her mother-in-law's helper around the home of her husband's parents. We don't know whether that cultural tradition was really the way God intended things to be, but we do know from Genesis 2:22–24 that God wanted a new bride and bridegroom to emotionally separate from their parents.

<table>
<tr><td>

What Others are Saying:

</td><td>

Robert Hemfelt, Frank Minirth, and Paul Meier: When you say the appropriate and deliberate good-bye to your parents (and stepparents and foster parents and surrogate parents, if such exist), you must fill the blank parent-space somehow. The correct filler is God, the ultimate parent.

You see, saying good-bye to parents is more than just saying good-bye to parents, for parents are a shadow of God. When you were very small, you viewed them as if they *were* God. Now you are saying that no human being is adequate to kiss the hurt and make it better. You are saying good-bye to the myth that human resources are adequate. That is painful and wrenching. You have arrived at the place where no other human being can be God in your life.[1]

Max Lucado: God has proven himself as a faithful father. Now it falls to us to be trusting children. Let God give you what your family doesn't. Let him fill the void others have left. Rely upon him for your affirmation and encouragement."[2]

</td></tr>
</table>

emancipated: set free

autonomy: self-rule

proximity: nearness

James Dobson: If either the husband or wife has not been fully **emancipated** from their parents, it is best not to live near them. **Autonomy** is difficult for some mothers (and fathers) to grant, and close **proximity** is built for trouble.[3]

A couple may not have "left" one or more of their parents if they are still financially dependent or if they are living in their old family home with their parents. Dependency could also be indicated by a grown child's inordinate need to check in with their parents for their approval. What an adult child does isn't as important as the attitude with which they do it.

- Does a wife call her mother daily because she enjoys talking with her mom or because she's afraid her mother will be angry if she doesn't?
- Does a son call his parents frequently because they are ill or because he is made to feel guilty if he doesn't?

It's possible for the adult child never to have "left" emotionally, even if his or her parents are dead. Maybe that adult child is still confined emotionally to them by feelings of inadequacy or the need to obtain their love. If they are deceased, their loving approval never comes. As a result, the adult child may not be able to accept his or her mate's love and God's unconditional love.

Think about It

KEY POINT

God's best plan is for newlyweds to both physically and emotionally leave their parents.

Marriage God's Way—If one or both sets of parents have real needs, husbands and wives can find it difficult to balance their need to "leave and cleave" with the needs of the parents. Focusing **inordinately** on a parent's need rather than the needs of the spouse will create friction and prevent a couple from bonding as necessary in God's original plan. Couples must learn to put their spouse ahead of the needs of their parents, and although difficult, decline a parent's request when necessary.

inordinately:
unnecessarily

Of Course, I Am My Own Man

LARRY: When Kathy and I got married, I went directly from living with my parents to living with Kathy, and I became a police officer. I was ready to spread my wings and focus on my new bride. I gave little thought to pleasing my parents. They went out of their way to make sure the "break" was complete and final.

On the other hand, I remember feeling surprised by the frequent calls from Kathy's mother. I knew Kathy felt obligated to keep the conversation open, and I was a little troubled by the

He Says . . .

intrusion. As I look back I see there could have been a middle ground: more contact with my parents and less with Kathy's.

KATHY: Early in our marriage, I would have said that I had emotionally left my parents, but I would have been denying the truth. In reality, I often chose my mother's preferences over Larry's. I felt obligated to please my parents even if it meant disregarding Larry's ideas. Larry was raised as an only child in a family that didn't often get together with extended family. But my family loved getting together with grandparents, aunts, uncles, and cousins for barbecues or outings. I loved family gatherings because we had so much fun, but Larry didn't feel that way in the beginning. If my family was having a gathering and Larry didn't want to attend, I would needle him until he gave in. I loved my family, but also I wanted to avoid admitting that we couldn't attend. It just didn't sound loving to me. I was still seeking my family's approval.

In time, as I matured, I realized that Larry must come first. I remember the first time I told my mother that we wouldn't be in attendance. I felt tense, but my mother handled it just fine. "No problem," she replied. I was surprised and relieved that it hadn't become a big deal. I began to see that I was putting this pressure on myself—my family wasn't putting it on me. I finally felt like I'd cut the apron strings.

TAKE IT FROM THEM

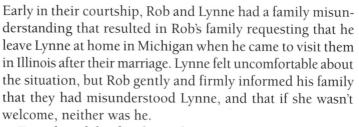

Early in their courtship, Rob and Lynne had a family misunderstanding that resulted in Rob's family requesting that he leave Lynne at home in Michigan when he came to visit them in Illinois after their marriage. Lynne felt uncomfortable about the situation, but Rob gently and firmly informed his family that they had misunderstood Lynne, and that if she wasn't welcome, neither was he.

Even though his family tried many times to convince him to come without Lynne, it was a full year before Rob went to Illinois. When he went, he took Lynne with him. Rob's decision to stand by Lynne helped to soften his family's stubborn opinion that no one was good enough for "our Rob." His family came to see that "Lynne must be good enough; he's holding out for her." Lynne, Rob, and his family have enjoyed thirty-two years together. Had Rob not held out, the misunderstandings might have stretched over years!

BECOME FRIENDS—NOT JUST FAMILY

> **Deuteronomy 5:16** Honor your father and your mother, as the Lord your God has commanded you, so that you may live long and that it may go well with you in the land the Lord your God is giving you.

Honor Doesn't Mean Dependency

God thought that this statement was so important that he included it in a very select number of rules for living: the Ten Commandments. If someone hasn't left their parents physically or emotionally, they could easily misunderstand God's intention. Honoring one's parents does not mean doing everything they say or letting them run one's life. That wasn't God's aim.

Robert Hemfelt, Frank Minirth, and Paul Meier: The greatest honor you can give your parents is to become all the person God intended you to be. If unfinished business, emotional baggage, hinders your growth as a Christian, it is important that you shed that baggage. That means you must lovingly but firmly deal with that business. We can't think of a better way to honor parents than to develop your natural gifts.[4]

Kathy Collard Miller: The Hebrew word for *honor*, *kavod*, has a two-sided meaning. It means to "reverence" and "to be heavy." Together these meanings indicate that honoring means we "give weight" to someone as being valuable and important. It can also indicate that honoring can be a heavy responsibility—something not easily done. We all can relate to that since none of us have perfect parents. There is always going to be something that we feel disappointed or upset about with our parents.[5]

We become friends with our parents and parents-in-law when we have a proper relationship with them: by honoring them for their important contribution in our lives but not allowing them to control us. A healthy relationship provides us the power to honor them because we aren't filled with anger, resentment, bitterness, or fear. Forgiving them for the ways they have hurt us in the past or the ways they have been imperfect will free us from bitterness.

> **What Others are Saying:**

REMEMBER THIS

KEY POINT

You can't force your parents to have a healthy relationship with you, but you can respond to them in a healthy way—regardless of their reaction.

Penny was very close to her father-in-law but unfortunately, that was not the case with her mother-in-law. Penny endeavored to develop a relationship with her, but living hundreds of miles from her didn't make the feat easy. When Penny and her husband visited them, she tried to spend time alone with her mother-in-law, hoping they could talk and develop some type of relationship. It just didn't happen.

Her mother-in-law always ended up with an excuse to be alone, or she disappeared someplace by herself. The relationship wasn't bad—just nonexistent. Since her mother-in-law wouldn't participate in any conversations with her, even when they were alone, Penny concluded that her mother-in-law didn't like her. Their last conversation before her mother-in-law died was on the telephone. Penny's last words to her were "I love you."

After her mother-in-law died, Penny discovered that her mother-in-law had indeed liked her. In fact, several people remarked about how much her mother-in-law had liked and admired Penny. She showed that love by bequeathing a precious Shirley Temple doll to Penny for her doll collection.

Penny found out too late that her mother-in-law was painfully shy. Had she known that, Penny would have done more to start a relationship with her. Now she doesn't have that opportunity.

Honor Has Healthy Highlights

When we value our parents without allowing them to control us, we are able to be emotionally healthy, possibly resulting in a longer life. No longer emotionally tied to our parents through an unhealthy dependence upon their approval or control, we rid ourselves of negative emotions like anger, resentment, and bitterness that bring illness and stress. Although Deuteronomy 5:16 is not a promise of long life, it is God's assurance that our life will have the qualities of joy and peace.

**What Others
are Saying:**

Robert Hemfelt, Frank Minirth, and Paul Meier: The notion of emotionally leaving home is nothing new. The "leave your parents and cleave to your wife" principle goes clear back to Genesis 2:24. As you say that fond farewell to Mom and Dad, you enjoy better intimate relationships with other persons in your life—spouse, kids, co-workers—in addition to that deeper relationship with God.[6]

Stuart Briscoe: Deuteronomy 5:16 further expands this commandment to say, "Honor your father and your mother, as the Lord your God has commanded you, so that you may live long and that it may go well with you." In other words, honor *them* so that *you* may have emotional stability.[7]

> **1 Timothy 5:8** If anyone does not provide for his relatives, and especially for his immediate family, he has denied the faith and is worse than an unbeliever.

Honor Means Care

God wants us to provide for the care of our parents when they need us; however, that shouldn't be done to the detriment of the care of our own families. Our own spouse and children must come first, but there are times when the care of elderly or ill parents will require more time than usual. In the midst of that, we should not be taking care of them out of an unhealthy guilt over the past or out of fear. It should be done out of love, as a way to represent God's love.

Jill Briscoe: I began to ask God to radically change my attitude toward my mother-in-law. Is it realistic to expect to love other people's relatives as much as your own, I worried? But this was Stuart's mom, not just anybody's relative. That was a starting place. I could love and care for her because I loved and cared for him. I could start by doing it for Stuart, and hopefully I would end up doing it for her![8]

Marriage God's Way—Even as we seek to forgive and then care for our parents, we'll also use some of these other ways to honor them:

- listen
- share their life and activities
- don't argue
- phone "home"
- visit in person
- send cards
- overlook annoyances like repeating something to a deaf father or wiping up milk spilled by trembling hands

Couples in the Bible

☞ **Check It Out:**

Ruth 1:1–19

Although Ruth and Naomi were not a married couple, they have much to model for us about a caring relationship with parents, especially in-laws. Naomi and her husband were Jews living in Moab, because of a famine in Judah. While there, their two sons, Mahlon and Kilion married Moabite women, Ruth and Orpah. After living there for ten years, Naomi's husband and both sons died. Destitute and hearing that Judah was no longer experiencing a famine, she prepared to return to her homeland, encouraging Ruth and Orpah to return to their parents, which Orpah did.

But Ruth refused to go even when Naomi told her she could offer her no future. In reply, Ruth uttered the words to her mother-in-law that have often been used to represent the commitment of a wife to her husband: *"Don't urge me to leave you or to turn back from you. Where you go I will go, and where you stay I will stay. Your people will be my people and your God my God. Where you die I will die, and there I will be buried. May the Lord deal with me, be it ever so severely, if anything but death separates you and me"* (Ruth 1:16–17). Her devotion was rewarded. After returning to Judah with Naomi, Ruth married a relative of Naomi's and became the mother of Obed, who was in the line of David and the lineage of Jesus.

Ruth could give that kind of devoted attention to her mother-in-law because she wasn't married. That kind of devotion would not be appropriate between a married daughter and mother because it would prevent her from "leaving and being one" with her husband. The loving, caring attitude of Ruth for her mother-in-law represents the kind of love and attention that God wants children to give their parents and parents-in-law.

What Others are Saying:

Jill Briscoe: I reflected how like Naomi and Orpah's relationship Mother's [mother-in-law] and mine had been. Naomi and Orpah had a "nothing much" sort of relationship. Nothing like the one that existed between Ruth and her mother-in-law. Coming to a crossroads, Orpah kissed Naomi and went her own way. Ruth, on the other hand, clung to Naomi and committed herself unreservedly to her for the rest of her life.[9]

TAKE IT FROM THEM

Patti and Randy lived with his mother in the same house for years and since have bought two condos side by side. Randy's mother is eighty-four years old, and the three of them could write the book on living and loving together! Their best advice is "release anger and resentment because love covers a multitude of sins." That love philosophy saw them through ten years of living with Randy's father who had Alzheimer's. They also discovered the importance of laughter and humor. Patti has learned to chuckle and remind herself how imperfect she is! She's found out that even an aging parent doesn't want her advice unless he or she asks.

A WONDERFUL WAY FOR WISDOM

> **Proverbs 15:22** Plans fail for lack of counsel, but with many advisers they succeed.

Take Advantage of Their Advice

The wisdom of our elders, including our parents and in-laws, is invaluable. Unfortunately in our society, those who have gained the most wisdom are respected the least. The young, though inexperienced and idealistic, are considered knowledgeable, while those who have experienced life and gained so much insight are thought of as "out of step."

Stuart Briscoe: I have a theory that many people need counseling today because they have gotten away from their extended families. It used to be that the "young-timers" could get an awful lot of common-sense teaching from the old-timers. Without those extended families, today's young people have lost that depth of experience.[10]

Moses shows us how he avoided stress because he honored his father-in-law, Jethro, by listening to Jethro's advice. Moses served the Lord from morning until evening as a judge for the people. It was a never-ending task. When Jethro saw what was happening, he inquired why Moses was doing this.

Moses replied, *"Because the people come to me to seek God's will. Whenever they have a dispute, it is brought to me, and I decide between the parties and inform them of God's decrees and laws"* (Exodus 18:15–16).

Jethro replied: *"What you are doing is not good. You and these people who come to you will only wear yourselves out.*

What Others are Saying:

Couples in the Bible

☞ **Check It Out:**

Exodus 18:13–27

The work is too heavy for you; you cannot handle it alone. Listen now to me and I will give you some advice, and may God be with you. You must be the people's representative before God and bring their disputes to him. Teach them the decrees and laws, and show them the way to live and the duties they are to perform. But select capable men from all the people—men who fear God, trustworthy men who hate dishonest gain—and appoint them as officials over thousands, hundreds, fifties and tens. Have them serve as judges for the people at all times, but have them bring every difficult case to you; the simple cases they can decide themselves. That will make your load lighter, because they will share it with you. If you do this and God so commands, you will be able to stand the strain, and all these people will go home satisfied" (Exodus 18:17–23).

Moses wisely saw Jethro's wisdom and honored him by following his advice. As a result, Moses was alleviated of the stress of too much work.

In contrast, in Genesis 13:1–18, Lot has an opportunity to ask his wise Uncle Abram for advice in choosing the best place to live. Instead he chooses that which was appealing to the <u>lust of his eyes</u> and settled in Sodom. In time, his family was destroyed because of his unwise choice. Lot neglected to take advantage of Abram's knowledge. We need to consider the value of wisdom and knowledge that our parents and in-laws have gained over the years. We'll also be training our children to listen to us in our old age!

HELPFUL HINTS FOR HONORING

Not everyone enjoys a wonderful relationship with their parents and in-laws; therefore, we can look to the Bible in dealing with problems that surface. Several people in the Bible had difficult situations also, so we can learn how to respond from them.

> **Matthew 10:37** Anyone who loves his father or mother more than me is not worthy of me; anyone who loves his son or daughter more than me is not worthy of me.

REMEMBER   THIS

☞ **GO TO:**

1 John 2:16
(lust of his eyes)

KEY POINT

Our elders have much to offer us. We should listen to them!

Put Jesus First

Those who feel obligated to please the unreasonable demands of their parents or in-laws can take Jesus' command to heart. No one, not even a parent or a spouse, should be more important than obeying Jesus and having a relationship with him. Jesus <u>said</u> to separate from our parents!

Stuart Briscoe: In other words, Jesus said, "Don't **deify** the family. Don't make the family the number-one consideration. I am the number-one consideration; I am the Lord, not your kids. I am the Lord, not your family. I am the Lord, not your marriage. I will be the Lord of your children, your household, your marriage. But I will never surrender my Lordship to any or all of these things."[11]

If you are following your parents' demands at the cost of loving Jesus, your husband, or your children, then you are not following God's command to put him first and to put your immediate family second. You are actually sinning. You must trust God enough to risk your parents' wrath and seek God's approval rather than your parents' approval. It's hard, but it can be done.

> **Ruth 1:19–21** So the two women went on until they came to Bethlehem. When they arrived in Bethlehem, the whole town was stirred because of them, and the women exclaimed, "Can this be Naomi?" "Don't call me Naomi," she told them. "Call me Mara, because the Almighty has made my life very bitter. I went away full, but the Lord has brought me back empty. Why call me Naomi? The Lord has afflicted me; the Almighty has brought misfortune upon me."

Choose to Love

Ruth and Naomi's story is a good one for those who struggle with parents or in-laws because Ruth models a loving example of dealing with an angry and bitter woman. In spite of how "unlovable" Naomi was, Ruth chose to stay with her. Ruth further honored Naomi by following her advice and being patient with her. Ruth could focus on Naomi with a whole heart because she wasn't married.

☞ **GO TO:**

Mark 10:7–8 (said)

What Others are Saying:

deify: set something up as a god

Think about It

connotations: meanings

REMEMBER THIS

Ruth Stafford Peale: Stop thinking of your marriage partner's relatives as a special breed known as in-laws (a term with faintly unpleasant **connotations**) and think of them simply as human beings with flaws and imperfections but also lovable qualities.[12]

Observe the positive and negative qualities of your in-laws as a means of getting to know your spouse better. By understanding their perspective, you will better relate to the viewpoint of your spouse. Look into their history for spiritual, emotional, and physical patterns that will give you insights into your mate's way of thinking. As you come to understand the differences in thinking between you and your mate, you will realize that your mate responds from the influence of his family's thinking rather than in purposeful opposition to yours.

> **Ephesians 4:15** Instead, speaking the truth in love, we will in all things grow up into him who is the Head, that is, Christ.

Speak the Truth in Love

foibles: mistakes

Talk with your mate about both of your parents but do it in love. Talk openly about family **foibles** without name calling, yelling, or becoming defensive. Avoiding defensiveness may be difficult because we tend to take whatever is said about our families personally—even if we don't like them ourselves!

What Others
are Saying:

Ruth Stafford Peale: We agreed not to get angry or defensive when the subject of in-laws came up, but to treat it as a kind of good-humored verbal pillow-fight in which either of us could say anything within reason and not do any damage to the fabric of our own marriage.[13]

WARNING

idiosyncrasies: unusual ways of viewing life

Realize that every family has its strengths and weaknesses. Your spouse's observations may shed light on some unhealthy family attitudes that you've never realized. Be gentle as you point out observations about your spouse's family. They will be more receptive if you speak without condemning their family's **idiosyncrasies**.

Marriage God's Way—After David was <u>chosen</u> to be king of Israel, he <u>killed</u> Goliath and was given King Saul's daughter Michal for his <u>wife</u> as a reward. As David became more victorious in battle, Saul was <u>jealous</u> of his son-in-law and not only threatened to <u>kill</u> him, but actually tried to do so many times. As a result, David was constantly on the run, always trying to avoid Saul's malicious efforts. Talk about in-law problems!

Only David's trust in God enabled him to resist taking drastic action against Saul in anger. Even David's friend Abishai urged him to kill Saul. But David responded, *"Don't destroy him! Who can lay a hand on the Lord's anointed and be guiltless? As surely as the Lord lives, . . . the Lord himself will strike him; either his time will come and he will die, or he will go into battle and perish. But the Lord forbid that I should lay a hand on the Lord's anointed. Now get the spear and water jug that are near his head, and let's go"* (1 Samuel 26:9–11). David recognized that God had placed Saul in a position of power over him for a purpose.

We can apply the same kind of trust in dealing with our parents and in-laws. God chose those particular people to be a part of our lives. So when we are tempted to speak with **rancor** or hold resentment toward them, we can do as David did and entrust our parents and in-laws to God's hands. We should ask, "Lord, what qualities do you want to develop in me because of the people you have placed in my life?" God is always interested in strengthening our character and drawing us closer to him. Having parents and in-laws who are less than perfect will help to fulfill that purpose in our lives.

STUDY QUESTIONS

1. God wanted to avoid parental and in-law problems, so he commanded newly married couples to do what?
2. Even though a married couple will "leave" their parents, what does God always want them to do?
3. How does God want us to respond to our relatives, and if we don't, what action, in effect, have we taken?
4. How can couples honor their parents?
5. If we are concerned that we are dishonoring God by not conforming to our parents' demands, what command of Jesus should we take comfort in?
6. When a parent is depressed or unhappy, how should we respond? Who gives us a good example of how to do that?

☞ **GO TO:**

1 Samuel 16:13 (chosen)

1 Samuel 17:49 (killed)

1 Samuel 18:27 (wife)

1 Samuel 18:8–9 (jealous)

1 Samuel 19:1–24 (kill)

rancor: hostility

7. In order to work through potential conflicts with parents, a couple can discuss their family backgrounds, but how should they do this?

CHAPTER WRAP-UP

- God wants a newly married couple to start their married life in a healthy way by recognizing that their new husband or wife is their first priority, rather than their parents.

- Even though parents should not be a first priority to a married couple, God still wants them to respond to their parents with honor by providing for the needs of parents in a way not detrimental to the needs of their own family. By doing so, healthy relationships will be formed.

- Those who seek the counsel of their parents and in-laws show their own wisdom by taking advantage of those who have gained knowledge and insights in their long lives.

- No one is supposed to be more important in our lives than Jesus. If we are feeling obligated to meet the demands of a parent, then we are, in effect, making them a god in our lives. We can free ourselves from feeling obligated or seeking their approval by obeying and seeking the approval only of Jesus. A couple can gain insight into unhealthy viewpoints within their families if they consider the objective perspective of their mate. Such sharing should be done in a loving and gentle method to avoid defensiveness.

KATHY & LARRY'S  BOOKSHELF

Kathy and Larry's favorite books about family relationships:

- *Since Life Isn't a Game, These Are God's Rules*, Kathy Collard Miller, Starburst. Finding joy and fulfillment in God's Ten Commandments.

- *Smoke on the Mountain*, Joy Davidman, Westminster Press. An interpretation of the Ten Commandments.

- *The Ten Commandments*, Stuart Briscoe, Harold Shaw Publishers. Playing by God's rules.

- *Pulling Together When You're Pulled Apart*, Stuart and Jill Briscoe, Victor Books. The Briscoes' personal story of strengthening their marriage.

9 IT'S ALL IN THE CHURCH FAMILY

Here We Go

We need each other, and couples especially need godly friends who will challenge them to live for God and work hard at their marriage. Friends serve as wonderful sources of objectivity and new perspective, providing the encouragement we each need. Marriage is hard. It's encouraging to know we're not alone as we navigate through the **shoals** of marital challenges.

We, too, impact others through our own example and encouragement of others. We can mentor others and share ideas as we all work toward marital fulfillment. Let's see how we can take full advantage of friendships.

shoals: *shallow waters*

CHOOSING WISE FRIENDS

> **Proverbs 22:17–19** Pay attention and listen to the sayings of the wise; apply your heart to what I teach, for it is pleasing when you keep them in your heart and have all of them ready on your lips. So that your trust may be in the Lord, I teach you today, even you.

Prove Yourself Wise

God says <u>repeatedly</u> in the Bible that there is value in the advice of counselors, and without it, it's almost impossible to be successful—and that certainly applies to marriage. The wise couple will recognize their need of godly friends who can encourage them to grow in their relationship.

☞ **GO TO:**

Proverbs 15:22; 22:17 (repeatedly)

Kay Arthur: First Corinthians 15:33 gives this clear word: "Do not be deceived: 'Bad company corrupts good morals.'" Righteousness is living morally according to God's standard. What friends do you have who distract you or pull you away from your pursuit of holiness? Are you in a yoke with someone who is drawing you away from the Lord—keeping you away from his yoke?[1]

Think about It

Scripture speaks strongly of the wisdom of seeking the help and advice of others. Consider these verses from the book of Proverbs.

Proverbs	Wise Words
11:14	*For lack of guidance a nation falls, but many advisers make victory sure.*
12:5	*The plans of the righteous are just, but the advice of the wicked is deceitful.*
12:15	*The way of a fool seems right to him, but a wise man listens to advice.*
13:10	*Pride only breeds quarrels, but wisdom is found in those who take advice.*
13:14	*The teaching of the wise is a fountain of life, turning a man from the snares of death.*
15:12	*A mocker resents correction; he will not consult the wise.*
15:22	*Plans fail for lack of counsel, but with many advisers they succeed.*
18:15	*The heart of the discerning acquires knowledge; the ears of the wise seek it out.*
21:2	*All a man's ways seem right to him, but the Lord weighs the heart.*

REMEMBER THIS

KEY POINT

Every couple needs the advice and counsel of others.

TAKE IT
FROM THEM

Each one of us has a stake in other couples' marriages. Especially for couples who are believers, we are all a part of the Body of Christ. If one member suffers, so do the rest. If one couple is struggling, then it affects us all. We need to keep accountable to others and seek their strength and help, but the most important reason to seek those friendships is so that our strong marriage will be a witness of the strength of the Body of Christ to unbelievers. First Corinthians 12:26–27 tells us, *"If one part suffers, every part suffers with it; if one part is honored, every part rejoices with it. Now you are the body of Christ, and each one of you is a part of it."*

Eva Marie enjoyed having lots and lots of friends, while Dennis only wanted one: Eva Marie. After many years of misunderstandings they finally came to a compromise. Dennis learned to allow other friends into his life, and Eva Marie learned that (other than Jesus) she would never have a better friend than Dennis. Eva Marie realized that all too often women are more open and honest with their friends than with their husbands. This is not God's plan. Eva Marie still has friends, of course, but she makes Dennis her primary friend.

> **2 Corinthians 6:14–18** Do not be yoked together with unbelievers. For what do righteousness and wickedness have in common? Or what fellowship can light have with darkness? What harmony is there between Christ and **Belial**? What does a believer have in common with an unbeliever? What agreement is there between the temple of God and idols? For we are the <u>temple</u> of the living God. As God has said: "I will live with them and walk among them, and I will be their God, and they will be my people. Therefore come out from them and be separate, says the Lord. Touch no **unclean** thing, and I will receive you. I will be a Father to you, and you will be my sons and daughters, says the Lord Almighty."

Belial: a worthless person; also used to refer to Satan

unclean: forbidden by God to be eaten or touched

☞ **GO TO:**

1 Corinthians 3:16 (temple)

Be Finicky about Finding Friends

Scripture tells us not to seek strength from those who don't know Christ. Being yoked with unbelievers doesn't refer just to marriage but to friendships and business alliances as well. The apostle Paul wrote a general guideline that applies in all aspects of life, and it certainly applies to a couple seeking friends in order to strengthen their marriage. Does that mean we shouldn't associate with unbelievers at all? No, it doesn't. As <u>lights</u> in the world to represent Christ, we want to seek friendships with unbelievers, but they should not be our primary source of friendship or advice. They view life from an earthly perspective, and God wants us to look at life with a heavenly one. Only Christians can truly give us that eternal perspective.

☞ **GO TO:**

Matthew 5:14 (lights)

Marriage God's Way—There will be some unbelievers who have successful marriages. They may even follow godly principles without giving credit to God. Certainly, they can be helpful. Their experience of overcoming difficulties will be helpful, but God's wisdom resides in those who know him.

Couples in the Bible

☞ **Check It Out:**

Esther 5:1–14

diabolical: evil

Couples should be careful whom they pick as friends. Even a Christian couple may not always give wise advice. Current conflicts or human flaws may warp their view of what is right. We should remember to examine all advice in the light of God's Word. The best mentors are those couples who have been successful in facing temptation and who point us to the source of the best marital wisdom: God.

In the Book of Esther, Haman sought to destroy all the Jews living in Persia. Haman hated them, primarily because a Jew named Mordecai would not bow down to pay him homage as one of King Xerxes' high officials.

God protected his people, the Jews, from Haman's **diabolical** plan by placing Esther, a Jewish girl, in King Xerxes' court as his queen. When Esther learned of Haman's plan, to which the king had agreed, she invited Haman and the king to a banquet. Haman was thrilled. He boasted to his family and friends about his wealth and the honor the king and queen had given him. But Mordecai still refused to bow before him. Whenever he thought about that, Haman was disgusted. Haman's friends and wife said, "Have a gallows built, seventy-five feet high, and ask the king in the morning to have Mordecai hanged on it. Then go with the king to the dinner and be happy." The biblical text says, "This suggestion delighted Haman, and he had the gallows built."

Through God's sovereign plan, Haman's murderous plot against the queen and her people was revealed. The king sided with Esther and Mordecai and used the gallows to take Haman's own life. The evil suggestion of his wife and friends resulted in Haman's own destruction.

None of us need friends like that. If Haman's friends had been good, they would have pointed out the destructive nature of hatred. We each need to have friends who will tell us the truth so that we can make godly, rather than evil, choices.

The friends we choose could indeed bring good or destruction into our lives and marriages.

FINDING A CHURCH THAT FITS

> **Hebrews 10:25** Let us not give up meeting together, as some are in the habit of doing, but let us encourage one another—and all the more as you see the Day approaching.

We need each other. Christians need other Christians. If a piece of wood stays in the fireplace, it will continue to burn alongside other burning wood, but if it is removed, it won't burn as brightly. It may even lose its flame. Likewise, a Christian glows brightest with God's love when it is stoked with the example and support of other Christians. That's encouragement—when the good model of others fuels us.

What Others are Saying:

Paul Tournier: A bringing together of faith and marital life is needed, so that faith may bring its incomparable transforming power and its understanding, and so that marital life may attain its fullness.[2]

Think about It

Finding a church home where you "fit" and can grow can be a daunting experience at times. Depending on how many churches are available in your area, you may have few or many choices. These guidelines may help you find the right church:

- *Does this church teach from the Bible?* Some churches just give practical principles without actually referring to the Bible. Make sure they refer to the Bible and believe that a person must be **born again** in order to be a Christian.

☞ GO TO:

John 3:3 (born again)

born again: receiving Christ as Savior

- *Does this church offer the kind of programs that will strengthen your marriage and family?* Of course, God could want you to go to a church that is just starting which doesn't have many programs in place, but as a rule, you'll want to find a church which corresponds to the needs of your family. If you have children in school, a church of only elderly believers may not give you the support you need.

KEY POINT

It's essential that each couple be involved in a local church.

- *Don't wait to find the "perfect" church—otherwise you may never join a church!* Understand that each church has its strengths and weaknesses. Find the one that will help you grow in your faith and love for God.

- *Look for a church that desires to spread the Gospel to those who don't know God.* You may find your spiritual growth, and that of your marriage, diminished if there are not opportunities to share your faith with others in the community or the world.

Deb and Ken both grew up in the same area where they were married. They chose to be married at Ken's church because he had a close relationship with his pastor. During their engagement when they attended Ken's church, Deb felt like an outsider. When they attended Deb's church, Ken felt like an outcast. So they compromised by visiting several neutral churches. They chose a Bible teaching church in a denomination that was new to both of them, and they have been active members there for twenty years.

Being involved in a church is a wonderful experience, but it can also become a distraction from the very thing it should be encouraging: couple togetherness. When couples begin to spend more time at church than they do with each other, God's original plan isn't being followed. God intends for church activities to encourage couples love not to detract from it. Make wise choices about how involved to become in your church body. Only take on what God wants you to do. Anything else won't honor him and can actually be detrimental to your family. That's never God's intention.

Church Friends for One or Two?

LARRY: Shift work at the police department always presented challenges for church attendance because I was either working or sleeping during that time. Kathy would go alone and complain at times. I wasn't too sympathetic to her concerns because she knew being a police officer involved weekend and night shifts. However, one result of my absences became apparent. I found myself judging others, and my willingness to mix with Christian friends diminished. Critical thoughts seemed to push loving thoughts away. I knew I was becoming self-absorbed. By the time my schedule changed and I got weekends off, I had learned a valuable lesson. Attending church with Kathy gave me more than a chance to worship and receive instruction. My judgmental spirit melted away as I was surrounded by those loving friends at church.

KATHY: For so many years I attended church alone and hated it. How I wanted Larry beside me! I longed for us to develop more Christian friends—and reach out to unbelievers as a couple. Yet, Larry couldn't see the need and was content to just work and sleep. I tried to invite friends over, but with Larry's changing hours it was hard to maintain a consistent social life.

When God answered my prayer for Larry to have more stable hours, we began attending church services together and meeting in an adult Sunday School class. We developed friendships with some wonderful couples. Now Larry is just as enthusiastic as I am about building those relationships and reaching out to others.

EXALTING GOD TOGETHER

> **Psalm 34:3 Glorify** the Lord with me; let us **exalt** his name together.

Reach Out Together

The Psalmist saw the value of two people lifting up God's glory together. He wanted someone else to join him because there is power in praising God together—and in having a ministry together. If God calls a husband and wife to minister together, their oneness will testify to God's ability to create a successful marriage.

David Augsburger: In the New Testament, husband-wife relationships first are elevated to partnership. Men/women functioned in co-ministries as did Aquila and Priscilla. The apostles traveled with their wives in mission journeys, a strangely revolutionary action for those times.[3]

Jerry and Mary White: The word ministry scares many people, but to minister is simply to serve. That is the root meaning of the word. A ministry is a service to others—in this case, a spiritual service. It has nothing to do with being a full-time pastor, missionary, or Christian worker. Ministry is the task of every believer.[4]

☞ **GO TO:**

1 Peter 2:12 (glorify)

Psalm 30:1 (exalt)

glorify: *make God's goodness noticeable*

exalt: *make the truth apparent*

What Others are Saying:

☞ **GO TO:**

1 Corinthians 9:5 (apostles)

When we think of ministering together, we most often think of formal, full-time ministry, but "ministry" can happen in large and small ways. It's just a matter of being available to do whatever God wants you to do. It could be asking a couple who are struggling in their marriage to dinner. Just listening to them, even if you don't have formal counseling training, will be valuable. Couples can visit the aged or serve in the nursery together. A couple could lead a Bible study together in their home. A married team has great power in serving together.

TAKE IT FROM THEM

In the early days of their thirty-year marriage, any discussion of ministry together caused conflict between Andi and Lee. Their gifts were so different that they didn't know how to combine them. Andi led worship, prayer groups, and Bible studies. Lee served people in practical ways. He pulled cars out of ditches, fixed broken pipes, and didn't mind washing dirty dishes. But those things didn't fulfill Andi's definition of "ministry," and she didn't think they were ministering together. Andi also believed that what they did do together— invite people into their home—didn't qualify as ministry. But eventually, Andi and Lee realized they were indeed in a "ministry" of hospitality.

KEY POINT

Ministry is doing anything that helps other people.

Now, they team up, first praying about to whom God wants them to extend an invitation, then whoever has time does the grocery shopping. If Andi is cooking, Lee mops the floor and vacuums. If he wants to cook then she does other things. After the guests leave, Lee often does the dishes while Andi straightens the house. They are now able to appreciate their differences and see how they complement each other in this unique ministry together.

Think about It

David and Claudia Arp suggest a marriage ministry called "Couples' Nights Out." That is an opportunity for couples to build their marriages and enrich their relationship. The program is launched with a short video, where the Arps introduce a dating theme based on a skill from their Marriage Alive Seminars. Each couple then spends time alone, while their children are cared for. David and Claudia recommend one and one-half hours for the date. Because couples also meet other couples who are working on their marriages, there is accountability and encouragement. If you feel the Lord is calling you to organize such an opportunity for couples, contact the Arps at www.marriagealive.com.

David and Claudia Arp: As we have worked with couples in the church over the past twenty-five years, we have observed over and over that doing what we know—not knowing what to do—is the fundamental dating problem. Couples' Nights Out gives husbands and wives the opportunity to immediately apply what they are learning.[5]

> **Amos 3:3** Do two walk together unless they have agreed to do so?

Make Sure You Agree

Walking together as a couple in ministry is something that requires agreement. Both the husband and wife have to agree that God is calling them to participate. Often, one spouse feels led to reach out and if the other spouse doesn't sense the same calling, it can bring conflict. It may be that God is calling both partners but one may be hesitant. He or she may feel inadequate and unqualified. She may think she will be required to "perform" in ways that are uncomfortable, like speaking in front of a group. Or he may sense an inappropriate motive in his spouse's desire to minister. Many things can be going on, but God doesn't want one partner to force the other to agree. The eager spouse can be confident that if God is truly calling them, God will influence the reluctant spouse to recognize the vision. In the meantime, the other spouse should wait.

Roger and Donna Vann: Reaching out to others essentially involves giving of yourselves; it's bringing the little that you have and holding it out in open hands before God and asking him to take it and multiply it. Perhaps you shouldn't attempt to reach out if your marriage is presently on shaky ground, yet you can't wait until your home situation is "perfect" before you plunge in. Nothing is quite as refreshing to a stagnant marriage as two partners united in stretching out their hands to others, in Christ's name![6]

Couples in the Bible

☞ **Check It Out:**

Acts 18:24–26

What Others
are Saying:

☞ **GO TO:**

Romans 16:4 (sacrifice)

Couples in the Bible

☞ **Check It Out:**

Judges 4

emulate: imitate

What Others
are Saying:

☞ **GO TO:**

Judges 4:9 (lead)

Ministry Done Right

Priscilla and Aquila ministered together. They opened their home for a church group meeting, they traveled with the apostle Paul to preach, and they gently directed the ministry of a young evangelist named Apollos. Some commentators also believe they carried one of Paul's letters to foreign countries. They seemed to be in perfect unity in their ministry and were so united that they were willing to <u>sacrifice</u> their lives for Paul's.

Bob and Cinny Hicks: Everywhere Priscilla and Aquila went, a ministry happened. When we meet them in Corinth they are inviting Paul into their home. Paul then takes them with him to Ephesus and leaves them there to initiate the ministry (Acts 18:19). Later they have a church in their home (1 Corinthians 16:19). In fact, wherever we find them they are ministering through their home. They obviously viewed their marriage as their ministry; though their profession was tentmaking, their vocation (calling) was church-making.[7]

Deborah and her husband, Lappidoth, didn't necessarily minister together, but they had ministries that most likely overlapped. Deborah was called a prophetess and her husband was a city official. Both gave advice as they sat at the city gate. They are an example of two secure and strong individuals who supported each other in their individual ministries, as evidenced in Deborah's military activity. She prophesied that the Israelites should fight against the Canaanites. When her country's leader, Barak, asked her to travel to the battle with the army, she did so (see illustration, page 145).

Deborah and Lappidoth are an example of a couple who served together independently. They encouraged each other in their individual ministries and are an example of strength that others can **emulate**.

Georgia Curtis Ling: Deborah was a homemaker who counseled those who sought her advice. This led her to a position as one of the Judges of Israel. Her wisdom was needed in time of war and Deborah learned to <u>lead</u> an army to victory.[8]

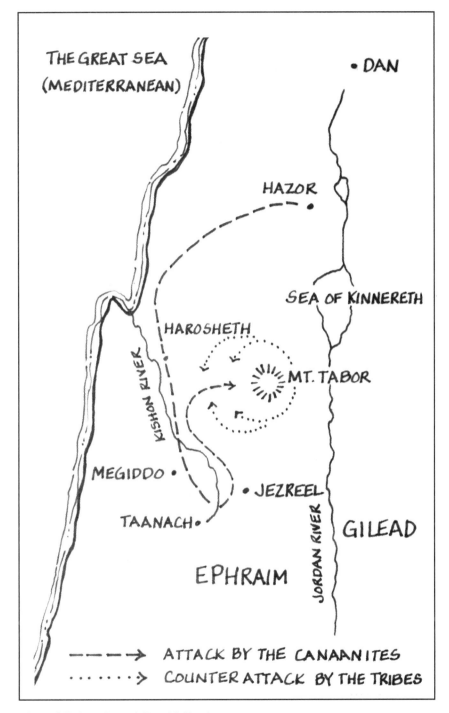

THE GREAT SEA (MEDITERRANEAN)

• DAN

HAZOR

SEA OF KINNERETH

HAROSHETH

MT. TABOR

KISHON RIVER

MEGIDDO •

• JEZREEL

TAANACH •

JORDAN RIVER

GILEAD

EPHRAIM

– – – –→ ATTACK BY THE CANAANITES

· · · · · ·> COUNTER ATTACK BY THE TRIBES

Map of Deborah and Barak's Battle

This map shows the route where Deborah and Barak led the Israelites in battle against the Canaanites.

Years ago when Paul accepted a pastorate in the mountains of southern Idaho, Brenda eagerly supported him. She went on hospital visits and calls with him and preached in his place when he was sick. Years later when Brenda felt God calling her into the ministry of public speaking, Paul heartily supported her. Today, he accompanies her on speaking engagements and prays for and encourages her. Together, they have been each other's biggest cheerleaders in answering God's unique call to them as individuals.

Ministry Done Wrong

Couples in the Bible

☞ **Check It Out:**

Acts 5:1–11

Ananias and Sapphira conspired to lie about selling a parcel of their land, saying they were giving the proceeds to the church. Although they weren't obligated to make the gift, they lied and that became the problem. Peter, possibly through the inspiration of the Holy Spirit, knew they had lied about their "investment" in the ministry. When they were confronted— even after several opportunities to declare the truth—they again lied and both were struck dead by God. They are a bad example of a couple in ministry, and their poor choice forever holds them up to ridicule.

ROBUST REASONS FOR REACHING OUT

breaking of bread:
communion with or
without a common meal

> **Acts 2:42–47** They devoted themselves to the apostles' teaching and to the fellowship, to the **breaking of bread** and to prayer. Everyone was filled with awe, and many wonders and miraculous signs were done by the apostles. All the believers were together and had everything in common. Selling their possessions and goods, they gave to anyone as he had need. Every day they continued to meet together in the temple courts. They broke bread in their homes and ate together with glad and sincere hearts, praising God and enjoying the favor of all the people. And the Lord added to their number daily those who were being saved.

Talk about Powerful Ministry!

The early believers in the church knew how to minister to each other. Without any seminars on "How to Start the Early Church" or books on "God and the Early Church," these first believers in Jesus, out of the love and gratitude they had for God, met together and gave of themselves not just generously, but sacrificially. . . to the point of *everything*! They bonded because of a common belief in Jesus' sacrificial death and resurrection, their joint prayer, and their experience of seeing God's miraculous works. They reached out to one another in a healthy, unselfish manner.

What Others are Saying:

Liz Curtis Higgs: God delights in seeing us share our time, money, and resources for no reason other than the joy of giving. When our motives are pure, then giving is not only easy, it's downright fun. When we give with an expectation of receiving **accolades** or seeing our names carved in stone, though, the joy is gone, chased away by fear and a hunger for approval that can never be satisfied.[9]

accolades: *praise*

James, the brother of Jesus and an early church father, warned of selfish motives. In his letter to the various churches, he wrote, *"What causes fights and quarrels among you? Don't they come from your desires that battle within you? You want something but don't get it. You kill and covet, but you cannot have what you want. You quarrel and fight. You do not have, because you do not ask God. When you ask, you do not receive, because you ask with wrong motives, that you may spend what you get on your pleasures"* (James 4:1–3). We need to heed his warning and have selfless motives when we seek to minister as a couple. Otherwise, the only fruit we'll reap will be contention and strife.

REMEMBER THIS

KEY POINT

There are many good reasons and benefits for reaching out to others as a couple, but we should make sure we have pure motives.

Here are other good reasons to minister:

- Christ's love **compels** us (2 Corinthians 5:14). We've experienced so much of God's love and grace in our marriages that we can't help but share it with others—especially those who are struggling in their marriages.
- We've experienced the blessings of being ministered to (2 Corinthians 1:3–5). When we see the wonderful benefits in our own relationship because of the time and effort another couple gave to us, we are motivated to help others.

Think about It

compels: *forces*

- We learn how to distinguish between burdens and loads (Galatians 6:2–5). Burdens are those struggles that God wants us to help carry for others. Loads are those things God wants people to depend totally upon him for—without our assistance. God doesn't want us to minister in every situation, and it can take practice to learn when and how much to help. If we try to <u>rescue</u> hurting people at every opportunity, they will look to us rather than to God. If we try to help when God wants the person to look only to him, we become worn out and that person doesn't grow in a healthy manner.

☞ **GO TO:**

Proverbs 19:19 (rescue)

TAKE IT FROM THEM

Rob and Lynne have been in ministry for twenty-three years. Rob has learned to value Lynne's viewpoint as a woman—as a complement to his viewpoint as a man. When counseling a couple, Rob has often requested Lynne's presence so that she might discern and interpret the wife's feelings and thinking. It also prevents the wife from feeling that she is being "ganged up on." Rob and Lynne's partnership has been appreciated and respected by others.

> **Job 16:2** I have heard many things like these; miserable comforters are you all!

Don't Be Miserable Comforters

Job and his wife were in the darkest time of their lives, and friends showed up to help them. At first those friends did the right thing—they kept quiet! They commiserated with their friend. But then they began to blame Job for his tragedies. Even though Job expressed his conviction that there was no unconfessed sin in his life, his friends thought that he wouldn't be experiencing the loss of family, possessions, and health if he hadn't sinned. They believed that trouble meant a person was sinful. Their comments inspired Job's remark in the verse above. When we minister as a couple, we want to avoid being that kind of "comforter."

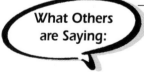

What Others are Saying:

Bob and Cinny Hicks: When a husband and wife open their hearts to God, the doors of their home usually follow. As a team they open themselves to people, allowing who they are and what they have in their marriage to minister to others.[10]

From the responses of Job's friends, we can learn that the wrong attitudes prevent us from being the helpful mentors that God wants us to be. Here is a list of bad concepts that Job's friends exhibited:

Think about It

Reference	How to Be a Miserable Comforter
Job 4	Believe the innocent do not suffer, therefore the one suffering must be guilty.
	Give pat answers without compassion.
	Tell, don't ask.
	Assume the one suffering hasn't already tried to seek God.
Job 8	Misunderstand and twist words to suit one's own opinions.
	Predetermine guilt rather than keeping an open mind.
	Don't want to hear the sufferer's feelings or doubts.
Job 11	Say God isn't reachable or knowable.
	Say, "If only you would. . . ."
Job 18	Accuse without really listening.
Job 22	Say the same thing over and over again.
Job 25	Make broad statements without taking the situation into consideration.
Job 32	Talk excessively.

Instead, couples who are mentoring others can be great listeners, empathize with the feelings the couple expresses, expect and think the best of the other people, and ask lots of questions.

The hardest thing to do as we counsel others, even as friends, is to resist telling them what they should do or how they should act. We may think we know what's best, but they must seek God and depend upon his power to make changes.

We may even feel compelled to rescue them, but the consequences of a bad choice may be what God is using to create change in their lives. Proverbs 19:19 warns us, *"A hot-tempered man must pay the penalty; if you rescue him, you will have to do it again."* We must allow God to work instead, even as we offer support and unconditional love.

REMEMBER THIS

1. What does wisdom come from according to Proverbs 22:17–19?
2. When seeking friends, especially as a source for wisdom about marriage, what principle should a couple follow?
3. Why does God want couples to become involved in a church?
4. What is one purpose for couples in sharing their life with others?
5. How did the early church minister to each other?
6. How were Job's friends "miserable comforters"?

CHAPTER WRAP-UP

- Couples need each other. Without the help and support of others, we may not be as happy or successful in marriage. The Bible repeatedly says that wisdom comes from seeking the advice and counsel of those who are wise.

- Wise couples know that it's essential that they become involved in a local church. Such involvement is a source of encouragement for their marriage and an opportunity to share their own wisdom with other couples.

- As a couple shares with others, they will credit God for the work that he has done in their lives. That will bring glory to the Lord and cause others to think highly of God's mighty power and love. When a couple wants to glorify God, they can be assured that there are many ways of ministering. Even inviting another couple over for dinner can be a ministry.

- There are many reasons for reaching out to other couples. There is great joy in seeing the changed lives of others, yet we must have pure motives and not look to our own gain. Passing along the wisdom that we've received from others gives a sense of satisfaction, knowing God has used us in other people's lives.

KATHY & LARRY'S  BOOKSHELF

Kathy and Larry's favorite books about friendship and ministry as a couple:

- *The Encyclopedia of Christian Marriage*, compiled by Cecil Murphey, Fleming H. Revell. Advice from experts on marriage and family.

- *The Marriage Builder*, Larry Crabb, Zondervan Publishing House. A blueprint for couples and counselors.
- *Love Is a Choice*, Robert Hemfelt, Frank Minirth, and Paul Meier, Thomas Nelson Publishers. Recovery for codependent relationships.
- *Rise Above*, Gwen Shamblin, Thomas Nelson Publishers. God can set you free from your addictions and compulsions forever.

10 LOVE THAT CHILD

Here We Go

Children are a blessing and a challenge. They can be a source of great joy and delight within a marriage, and can be used by God to develop character and bring needed changes within us. What parent hasn't squealed with delight at their child's first step and swelled with pride when his child hits a home run. Our lives are intricately tied to our children's, for they are a part of us. They can strengthen a marriage or divide it.

Since we want our children to strengthen, not divide, our relationship, we can seek God's wisdom in raising our children and in loving them the way they deserve. They are gifts from God. Psalm 127:3 says, *"Sons are a heritage from the Lord, children a reward from him."*

LOVE NO MATTER WHAT

> **Psalm 89:30–34** If his sons forsake my law and do not follow my **statutes**, if they violate My decrees and fail to keep my commands, I will punish their sin with the rod, their iniquity with flogging; but I will not take my love from him, nor will I ever betray my faithfulness. I will not violate my covenant or alter what my lips have uttered.

statutes: rules

Withdrawing Love Isn't Very Loving

God offers each of us an unconditional kind of love. It is not based on our performance—whether good or bad—but upon God's own character. God never stops loving his children or expressing that love—even when we are disobedient. He will give consequences for that disobedience, but he will not stop loving us.

Ross Campbell: Unconditional love means loving a teenager, no matter what he looks like, no matter what his assets and liabilities are, no matter how he acts. This does not mean you always like his behavior. Unconditional love means you love him even when you detest his behavior.[1]

 **Marriage God's Way**—Some parents try to control their children's behavior by withdrawing the love their children need. If their child is good, the parent treats them well, but if the child disobeys, the parent withdraws by acting cold or not talking to the child. Trying to make them regret their disobedience through withdrawing love opposes God's loving example. A parent should give consequences for a child's disobedience, but should still give affection and consistent love. That should never change—regardless of the child's performance.

TAKE IT FROM THEM

Like most families, Ted and Patty have a full schedule of activities: homework, church activities, athletic events, get-togethers. They have found that it is easy to "manage" their children through the events of life yet fail to "relate" with their children in the midst of life. In order to carve out quality time with their kids, they routinely set Friday evenings aside as "movie night." After dinner they bathe the children, pop popcorn, turn off all the lights, settle onto the family room carpet, and watch a family flick together. That is a highlight for all of them! They often use Sunday evenings as game night, taking time to enjoy one another through playing a game in which every family member can participate. In the midst of busy weeks, they look forward to evenings they can spend together!

KIDS WILL BE KIDS

1 Corinthians 13:11 When I was a child, I talked like a child, I thought like a child, I reasoned like a child. When I became a man, I put childish ways behind me.

A Child Is a Child

The apostle Paul gave the characteristics of a child: a child talks, thinks, reasons, and acts like a child. Parents have trouble remembering that at times. It's easy to think that a child should act and think like an adult—but a child can't! A child only has the maturity level to see things through a childlike frame of reference. Parents set themselves up for frustration when they expect their child to act more mature than is reasonable.

Children differ in their developmental growth, and it is destructive to compare one child with another—whether within the same family or with other children. Child-development books are a helpful resource for judging age-appropriate behavior; however, caution must be exercised when comparing children's behavior and standards. A child may progress faster or slower than the book indicates and still be within the normal range.

James Dobson: I must make it clear that the compliant child is not necessarily wimpy or spineless. That fact is very important to our understanding of his nature and how he differs from his strong-willed sibling. The issue under consideration is focused on the strength of the will—the inclination of some children to resist authority and determine their own course, as compared with those who are willing to be led. It is my supposition that these temperaments are prepackaged before birth and do not have to be cultivated or encouraged. They will make themselves known soon enough.[2]

Jesus' treatment of the disciples as they develop slowly in their spiritual growth is a good model for <u>parents</u> who want to be patient. He isn't frustrated with the disciples nor does he give up on them. He continues to encourage them toward greater faith and dependence on God, even when he <u>knows</u> they are going to fail him. In his power he sees their potential. Parents can take clues from Jesus and be enabled to really love their children when they too focus on their child's potential.

KEY POINT

Parents should be patient and understanding by allowing their children to act like children.

REMEMBER THIS

What Others are Saying:

Think about It

☞ **GO TO:**

Luke 9:12–14 (parents)

Matthew 26:30–35 (knows)

ANGER DANGER

exasperate: *frustrate, discourage, make resentful*

> **Ephesians 6:4** Fathers, do not **exasperate** your children; instead, bring them up in the training and instruction of the Lord.

Give It Up—Anger Doesn't Work

The apostle Paul warns fathers not to make their children frustrated. Children may become bitter and resentful when the father doesn't respond in a loving manner. The father is singled out in this instance, because he is primarily responsible before God for the atmosphere of his home and for how his children are raised. Instead, fathers—and mothers, too—should instruct their children in how to love and trust God, along with giving them consequences for disobedience.

What Others are Saying:

Charles Swindoll: Parents, just because kids are little people doesn't mean you have the right to fire away. If your children are small, get down on their level when you talk with them. Kneel down occasionally for your visits—even before discipline.[3]

Marriage God's Way—We exasperate our children when we scold and nag them. Instead of producing the obedience we desire, it makes our children angry and resentful. Discipline should be applied through consequences, suggestions, and godly advice.

Think about It

Sometimes children disobey out of frustration and anger over the unfairness of a parent's punishment or the inconsistency of a parent's expression of love. They are insecure about being loved and act out their insecurities through disobedience. Therefore, a wise parent will examine a child's behavior and evaluate whether disobedience is coming, not so much from rebellion, but from frustration.

Brewing and Stewing

He Says . . .

LARRY: I frequently saw Kathy's anger boil when Darcy, our toddler, would resist Kathy's instructions with a strong, willful "No!"

I was surprised at Kathy's reaction and commented, "I think you take Darcy's behavior personally."

Confused, Kathy turned to me and said, "I don't get it, how do I take it personally?"

"You see Darcy's disobedience as a commentary on your mothering skills," I said. "Every time she defiantly tells you no, you act like she is really saying, 'You are a bad mommy.' Actually, she's just a kid doing what she does so well: misbehaving by wanting everything her own way."

She Says . . .

KATHY: When Darcy was two years old and Mark was a newborn, I was angry at Larry because I couldn't make him do what I wanted—stay home more and help me around the house. Since he was gone so much and my efforts to communicate my displeasure didn't work, I ended up directing my frustration at Darcy when she disobeyed me. And it seemed like everything she did displeased me. Whether it was because she wouldn't cooperate with my toilet training program, or because she played with the sand in the fireplace, I was constantly unhappy and angry. My responses to her were completely out of control. I realized I was physically abusing her—at times hitting her in the head, kicking her, and one time even choking her. When God didn't answer my pleas for help, I concluded he no longer loved me and had given up on me. I thought there was no hope, and I considered suicide at one point.

Then God began to show me that he did indeed love me, and he began to reveal the underlying causes of my anger. Over the period of about a year, I gained control over my anger, and during that time, God used Larry's comment, "I think you take Darcy's behavior personally," as one of the keys to my healing. For the first time I realized that I did believe she was disobeying me on purpose. When I realized that she was disobeying me because she was a child, I became more patient with her, and I also learned to discipline her consistently. I had been expecting her to act like an adult, but she was just a child. Such a revelation was one of many that God used to bring me to the place where I could be the patient and loving mother that I really wanted to be.

TAKE IT FROM THEM

A goal that Patty and Ted hold high in their parenting is their pursuit to "walk their talk." They make it a point not to compromise their Christian values or standards whether they are in public or in private. They desire to always have clear consciences before the Lord and seek to treat one another as God would desire.

Certainly, there are times when they fall short as parents, when tempers flare, or impatience sets in. There are times when they say things they shouldn't or fail to say things they should. Yet, because of the grace God extends to them, coupled with the standards he sets before all Christians, they openly admit when they have gotten off course and then make a quick commitment to getting back on track. Ted and Patty's children have seen that walking with the Lord is a daily choice, often most clearly lived out in how they treat one another behind the closed doors of their home.

> **Matthew 5:44–45** But I tell you: Love your enemies and pray for those who persecute you, that you may be sons of your Father in heaven. He causes his sun to rise on the evil and the good, and sends rain on the righteous and the unrighteous.

God Doesn't Play Favorites

God is the most loving and gracious parent. As our example for parents and couples, he doesn't play favorites. He is concerned equally with each of us, and he equally loves each and every one of his created beings. Although he says, *"Since you are precious and honored in my sight, and because I love you, I will give men in exchange for you, and people in exchange for your life"* (Isaiah 43:4), he wants that to apply to every person. And it does to those who commit their lives to him.

What Others are Saying:

Randy Carlson: Check to be sure the family rules aren't slanted. Have family meetings and discuss the rules—everything from bedtime to allowances, from chores to homework. Give both children a chance to bring things up that might be bothering them.[4]

REMEMBER  THIS

A primary way for a child to become frustrated and angry is through parental favoritism. Favoring one child over another is contrary to God's example of unconditional love for everyone. Children can sense when a parent treats a sibling with greater love and when they do, devastating emotional feelings erupt. Helplessness and bitterness arise and hinder their spiritual and emotional growth. If a parent realizes they are favoring one child over the other, they should confess their error to God, and ask for his help in treating each child the same.

KEY POINT

The best parent is the one who doesn't play favorites.

Isaac and Rebekah struggled with favoritism. They played the favorites game with their two sons, which wreaked havoc in their family and created disaster in the generations that followed. Rebekah gave birth to twin boys, Esau, the older, and Jacob, the younger. These boys were very different and each parent preferred one of them. Genesis 25:27–28 tells us, *"The boys grew up, and Esau became a skillful hunter, a man of the open country, while Jacob was a quiet man, staying among the tents. Isaac, who had a taste for wild game, loved Esau, but Rebekah loved Jacob."* It's so easy to picture. Isaac loved the idea of a macho son who satisfied his appetite for good food. He must have thought of Jacob as a wimp. Jacob may have sensed his father's disdain and became even closer to his mother, who loved his tender characteristics.

Esau and Jacob saw the favoritism, and, not surprisingly, were jealous of each other. Their relationship started to unravel one day when Esau returned from a day of hunting, completely famished. Jacob had cooked one of his special stews, and Esau willingly sold his **birthright** as firstborn son in order to satisfy his hunger. Jacob had cunningly received what he wanted.

The sons' jealousy and their parents' favoritism caused a crisis when Isaac was about to give the firstborn son's blessing to Esau. Rebekah deceived her blind husband by dressing Jacob to appear as Esau. Because of the deception, Esau threatened to kill Jacob. As a result of the threat, Jacob was sent away to distant relatives for his safety. Rebekah never saw her favored son again, a painful consequence of her dysfunctional favoritism.

Couples in the Bible

☞ **Check It Out:**

Genesis 25:27–28;
27:1–28:9

birthright: inheritance rights of firstborn son

> **Mark 10:9** Therefore what God has joined together, let man not separate.

Child-Proof Your Marriage

Just as God doesn't play favorites and parents should not play favorites among their children, parents should not favor their children over the health of their marriage relationship. As children grow up and leave home, a couple will spend more time alone together than they have previously. The marriage relationship should not be diminished because of children. Children will be more secure and happy knowing their parents love each other enough to make the time and effort to grow in their marriage.

What Others are Saying:

Henry Cloud and John Townsend: Children are built-in intruders on a marriage. They need so much, so often, from a couple. Yet the couple who puts parenting above their marriage has a problem.[5]

Marriage God's Way—Children can "separate" the intimacy between husband and wife when the following happens:

- The children's activities or demands become more important than the marital relationship.
- The children's schedule becomes an excuse not to work on the marriage.
- One spouse feels excessive obligation for the welfare of the children and spends more time and energy on their welfare than the spouse's.
- The overindulgent spouse believes their mate can handle the lack of attention.
- One spouse considers a child more of a friend and confidant than their spouse.
- One spouse shares their marital struggles with the child.
- The children are a source of self-esteem that the spouse should be providing in that aspect of life.

Think about It

Children want most of all for their parents to love each other. Children who face their parents' divorce or separation pray hardest for their parent's love to be restored. They want a whole family. Allowing children to come between parents is actually detrimental to the health of the child.

WARNING

Make time for your relationship. Keep that time separate from the children. Although you may spend a lot of time as a family doing activities centered around the children, that in itself doesn't build love between a husband and wife. A couple needs to plan times alone without the children, talking about themselves.

MIX AND MATCH FAMILIES—
GOD LOVES THEM ALL

> **Joel 2:25–27** I will repay you for the years the locusts have eaten—the great locust and the young locust, the other locusts and the locust swarm—my great army that I sent among you. You will have plenty to eat, until you are full, and you will praise the name of the Lord your God, who has worked wonders for you; never again will my people be shamed. Then you will know that I am in Israel, that I am the Lord your God, and that there is no other; never again will my people be shamed.

God-Style Pest Control

God used locusts (see illustration, page 162) as one <u>plague</u> to force Pharaoh to let the people of Israel leave Egypt. God often used locust swarms as a <u>disciplinary</u> measure to get Israel's attention, so they would repent of their sins and worship only him again.

Locusts, in large swarms, can quickly devastate a land area. They have been known to fly in a swarm of ten or twelve miles long, four or five miles wide, and so <u>deep</u> that they block the sun. As they travel, they <u>eat everything</u> that is green. When they appear in such "<u>armies</u>," as they are called by the local people, nothing stops them, even the fires that people light trying to kill them. They are truly dangerous in such swarms.

Such devastation can sometimes be a metaphor for our lives. When we face destruction, God promises that if we seek him, he can bring <u>good</u> and healing even from that devastation. Although it is never God's perfect will that a couple divorce and marry others, God still wants to bring good and fullness to any family—regardless of their past. God cares about blended families where the parents and children are brought together to be a new family. The locusts may have devastated the Israelites' land but God says he will restore what they ate—and that applies also to spiritual and emotional things. God can do the same thing for blended families as a couple dedicates themselves to him.

☞ **GO TO:**

Exodus 10:4–19
(plague)

1 Kings 8:37–40;
2 Chronicles 7:13–14
(disciplinary)

Judges 7:12 (deep)

Psalm 105:35
(eat everything)

Judges 6:5 (armies)

Romans 8:28 (good)

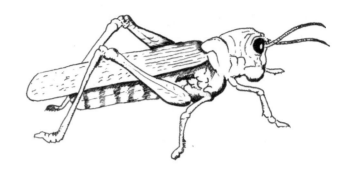

What Others are Saying:

Maxine Marsolini: We are witnessing this in our lives. The dark years of divorce, the struggles to adapt in our own strength to blend our families, the years without prayer, and all the anger and selfishness were devouring days—days given over to the locusts. But when, by God's grace, we chose to recognize them as bearers of death, something wonderful began to happen. A heavy spirit gave way to the light of his presence. Out of the discoveries made by looking back at the years of childhood and desolation came fresh nourishment for our lives.[6]

Think about It

Stepchildren need even more affection, affirmation, firm discipline, support, and unconditional love than other children because of the trauma and uncertainties they have faced—either through divorce or death of a parent. Since they may feel especially vulnerable because of a new parent, they should be treated with sensitivity and given opportunities for honest sharing. Some acting out may surface in their behavior, and should be met with the firm discipline of consequences, not physical or verbal anger or emotional withdrawal.

KEY POINT

There is hope for blended families.

REMEMBER THIS

Because a stepparent is new to the family, allow plenty of adjustment time before the stepparent takes on every role. He or she might not want to give consequences for a while, allowing the biological parent to continue the discipline as before remarriage. Immediate enforcement of the stepparent's authority could cause difficulties that would be more easily avoided after the children have formed a bond with their new stepparent.

Maxine Marsolini: We would all have fared better if the children continued to look to me, their biological parent, for discipline during the first few months we were a blended family. Then, little by little, their stepfather could come alongside me in a slower manner, demonstrating warmth, discussion, interaction, and even prayer with the children. With this delay, the children would have had the chance to become familiar with Charlie and adjust to receiving parental discipline from this new man in their lives.[7]

What Others are Saying:

Dennis and Eva Marie had the ultimate blended family! When they married, Dennis had two children from a former relationship who did not live with them. They soon had a child, Jessica, of their own. Soon after the birth of the baby, Dennis's twelve-year-old son moved in with them. His daughter lived just a mile away and was "the regular visiting family member." This meant a lot of adjustments. New rules and disciplines had to be set. During "visitation" with his eldest daughter, more rules had to be established. Additionally, they made certain that each child knew that no matter *who* the biological parents were each was a part of this family.

TAKE IT FROM THEM

One afternoon, one of the older children made the comment, "Jessica is not my real sister because we don't have the same mother."

Eva Marie quickly, but lovingly, corrected the child. "What is not bound by blood is bound by love," she said. "We are all one family. You are half brother and sisters, but we won't use the word 'half.' We will say 'brother and sisters.'" Eventually the oldest daughter, as an adult, moved in with Dennis, Eva Marie, and Jessica. Even after twenty-one years of marriage, the family still refuses to use the word "half." They are a "whole" family.

STUDY QUESTIONS

1. How does God model unconditional love for parents?
2. How did the apostle Paul describe a child?
3. In order to train children to follow God, what should parents avoid?
4. God treats everyone with equal love, and how is he an example for parents?
5. If God wants nothing to break up a marriage, what should parents avoid?
6. Sometimes parents of blended families can feel like failures, but what does God promise?

- God loves all of his created beings equally and without question. His love is never dependent upon his children's behavior. If they disobey him, there will be consequences but his love never stops. He is the perfect model for parents because God wants mothers and fathers to love their children unconditionally—even as they give consequences for wrong choices.

- Parents can love their children unconditionally by reminding themselves that their children are acting like children—not because they want to punish their parents—but because they are children. As they get older and receive consequences for disobedience, they will mature and learn to make wise choices.

- Parents should avoid becoming angry when trying to teach their child. Anger doesn't produce obedience and can cause frustration in a child who believes he can never please his parent. Favoring one child over another will also make a child exasperated. Parents should treat every child the same: with equal love and similar consequences for disobedience. Parents should not favor their children over the health of their own marriage, because children feel most secure when their parents love each other.

- Although parents of blended families can feel discouraged about past mistakes, God is the God of the impossible. He can bring love within blended families and teach every family how to be healthy and strong.

KATHY & LARRY'S  BOOKSHELF

Kathy and Larry's favorite books about loving our children:

- *Boundaries in Marriage*, Henry Cloud and John Townsend, Zondervan. Helping understand the friction points and move beyond them.

- *Blended Families*, Maxine Marsolini, Moody Press. Creating harmony as you build a new home life.

- *Disciplines of the Home*, Anne Ortlund, Word Books. Choosing a simplified life and family instead of a too-busy one.

- *You and Your Child*, Charles Swindoll, Thomas Nelson Publishers. A biblical guide for nurturing confident children from infancy to independence.

11 HANDLING DISOBEDIENCE

Here We Go

Most couples look forward to having children, but when it comes to responding to a child's disobedience it's frustrating. This is another potential area of disagreement between husband and wife. How each of us was disciplined will influence how we handle a child's disobedience. We tend to parent the way we were parented without considering our actions. Or we may totally reject our past and its ideas, determining that we will parent differently and better. Differences in parenting style can certainly cause a lot of stress in a marriage. The key is to be aware of those differences and to seek a balanced, united approach to discipline.

The Bible contains practical and usable advice about disciplining children. Let's explore God's perspective so that couples can stand united as they respond to a disobedient child.

DISCIPLINE AND ENCOURAGEMENT

> **Hebrews 12:4–6** In your struggle against sin, you have not yet resisted to the point of shedding your blood. And you have forgotten that word of encouragement that addresses you as sons: "My son, do not make light of the Lord's discipline, and do not lose heart when he **rebukes** you, because the Lord disciplines those he loves, and he punishes everyone he accepts as a son."

rebukes: corrects

Discipline Equals Love

If you ask a child, "Do you feel loved when your mommy gives you a consequence for disobeying her?" none of us would be surprised to hear that child say, "No, I don't feel loved. I hate it!" To convince anyone that discipline should make us feel loved is difficult. Yet, Scripture is very clear that discipline really is a very loving thing to do.

We know that God loves us totally, and yet he disciplines us. From his vantage point, discipline is meant for our good. Because it brings us pain—either physical or emotional—we don't see it as a benefit. The Psalmist wrote, *"Do good to your servant according to your word, O Lord. Teach me knowledge and good judgment, for I believe in your commands. Before I was **afflicted** I went astray, but now I obey your word. You are good, and what you do is good; teach me your **decrees**. Though the arrogant have smeared me with lies, I keep your **precepts** with all my heart. Their hearts are callous and unfeeling, but I delight in your law. It was good for me to be afflicted so that I might learn your decrees. The law from your mouth is more precious to me than thousands of pieces of silver and gold"* (Psalm 119:65–72). He recognized that without the "affliction" of the discipline from God, he wouldn't learn God's rules and he couldn't become the person of good character that God wanted him to be.

The verse from Hebrews at the beginning of this section shows the parallel between God's discipline and how parents should discipline their children. God disciplines us because we are his children and he loves us. We discipline our children because they belong to us and we love them.

afflicted: *consequence for disobedience*

decrees, precepts: *rules*

KEY POINT

God gives consequences to his children for their good.

What Others are Saying:

Bruce Narramore: Unfortunately, most English Bible translations use "discipline" and "punishment" interchangeably. Consequently, some passages read as though God is punishing the Christian. This is not so. A careful reading of the context and usage of the words "punish" and "discipline," along with an awareness of the different principles involved, will help avoid confusion on this point.[1]

REMEMBER THIS

The writer of Hebrews is quoting from Proverbs 3:11–12: *"My son, do not despise the Lord's discipline and do not resent his rebuke, because the Lord disciplines those he loves, as a father the son he delights in."* Even back in the "olden days" of the Bible, it was recognized that when someone was disciplined, they were seeing the evidence of love. And in the case of Solomon, who wrote Proverbs, he recognized God's loving hand of correction.

synonyms: words with similar definitions

Think about It

English translations of the Bible use the words "discipline" and "punish" as **synonyms**, but among experts in child development and training, they recognize that there is a difference between the two words. The chart below shows the difference between discipline and punishment.

Discipline	Punishment
Motive of parent to train child for future maturity	Motive of parent to take revenge and pay back the child for disobedience
Parent reacts with calm and loving responses	Parent reacts with frustration and anger, often taking the child's behavior personally
Parent focuses on the maturity and growth of the child	Parent focuses on what the child did wrong
The child feels loved and has a sense of belonging to the family	The child reacts with shame and apprehension

Marriage God's Way—To change our perspective from one of punishment to one of correction, we must evaluate the words we're using when reacting to our children. The more similarly a couple can respond to their children, the more the child will sense unity and feel secure. Parents depict "punishment" when they say, "I'm spanking you because you did that." Instead, they can respond to their child's disobedience by saying, "I'm spanking you so that you will choose to do the right thing the next time." Such a change puts the focus on the future maturity of the child rather than on payback for what they did wrong.

☞ **GO TO:**

Proverbs 3:11–12; Revelation 3:19; Hebrews 9:28 (discipline)

Isaiah 13:9–11; Matthew 25:46; 2 Thessalonians 1:7–9; 2 Peter 2:9 (punish)

> **Hebrews 12:7–8** Endure hardship as discipline; God is treating you as sons. For what son is not disciplined by his father? If you are not disciplined (and everyone undergoes discipline), then you are illegitimate children and not true sons.

No Discipline Equals No Belonging

In Rome at the time of this writing, an "illegitimate child" didn't have any inheritance rights. The writer of Hebrews—most likely the apostle Paul—wanted Christians to understand that the suffering they were experiencing didn't mean they weren't Christians. In fact, it proved they *were* Christians—a part of God's family because they were identified with him and persecuted because of it.

Likewise, a child knows he is truly part of a family when he's disciplined. If he's not disciplined, it would seem that he is not important enough for parents to take the time and make the effort to correct his behavior. Ultimately, he will miss the inheritance of goodness that comes from being corrected.

What Others are Saying:

Zig Ziglar: The acceptance of your child in your family unit with definite responsibilities makes him feel like an important member of the team. This will substantially reduce his likelihood of joining some other close-knit group, perhaps a neighborhood gang, just so he can "be accepted" and "belong."[2]

Think about It

At a school, the fence needed to be torn down for replacement. The teachers worried that without the fence the children would roam too far. But when the fence was gone, instead of playing near the edge or off school property close to the street, the children huddled in fear near the buildings—as far away from the borders as possible. They felt insecure without the protection of the fence. Similarly, children inwardly appreciate the boundaries of rules and consequences—even though they would never admit it. Though all of us say we hate boundaries and restrictions, a child actually feels more secure when there are rules and consequences for breaking those rules.

KEY POINT

Disciplining a child makes him or her feel secure.

TAKE IT FROM THEM

Ted and Elva came up with a cute little response to their children's mishaps—whether a temper tantrum or an accidental fall. If one of the children came in with a cut or bruise, the wound was tended and then as a family everyone sang a little song: "One, two, three, four . . . don't do that anymore." Many times that was just the touch needed to ease the pain. It was a togetherness-type thing and each singing family member knew they might well be the next recipient.

This song was applied to car accidents, temper outbursts, scraped knees, and just about any situation where correction and encouragement were needed. It helped Ted and Elva to respond lovingly—even to a child's disobedience. That little ditty has survived three generations and is still being sung to Ted and Elva's grandchildren.

> **Hebrews 12:9–10** Moreover, we have all had human fathers who disciplined us and we respected them for it. How much more should we submit to the Father of our spirits and live! Our fathers disciplined us for a little while as they thought best; but God disciplines us for our good, that we may share in his holiness.

Discipline Is Spelled "R-E-S-P-E-C-T"

Christians who are honest will recognize that they love and respect God more because he disciplines them. They realize that he intends it for their good and that cooperating with him results in holiness. In that way we are changed into the image of Jesus because we make wiser choices based on the consequences for wrong choices.

Likewise, when children are disciplined and corrected fairly, with love and concern, they inwardly respect their parents. That respect may not be immediately expressed; in fact, children will whine and complain about it, but in the long run, it brings the positive results of respect.

Chuck and Barb Snyder: The root word for discipline is the same one as for disciple. When someone asks us to disciple them, we are patient, kind, loving, and never get angry or loud. We think the best of that person, and are usually willing to give him lots of second chances. Why don't we do the same thing with our kids as we "disciple" them? It's the same word, same principle—just different people.[3]

In order for a parent to discipline in love, and not punish with a desire for revenge, a parent must be convinced that consequences will provide the best lesson for their child. Many parents are afraid to discipline because their own parents responded with anger or abuse. They're afraid that if they try to correct, they'll lose control. Therefore, they do nothing and gamble with their child's character.

Of course, a parent should not respond in anger. They

☞ **GO TO:**

Romans 6:22 (holiness)

Colossians 3:10 (image)

What Others are Saying:

Think about It

can, though, learn to correct and give consequences without anger. The best way to do that is to give a consequence immediately rather than repeated warnings to the child.

> **Hebrews 12:11–13** No discipline seems pleasant at the time, but painful. Later on, however, it produces a harvest of righteousness and peace for those who have been trained by it. Therefore, strengthen your feeble arms and weak knees. "Make <u>level paths</u> for your feet," so that the lame may not be disabled, but rather healed.

Pain Produces Pleasant Payoffs

Discipline through loving correction, whether of an adult Christian by God or of a child by a parent, produces a harvest of good qualities:

- *Righteousness:* The Christian or child makes wise and godly choices.
- *Peace:* The person who receives correction responds in ways that bring less strife to relationships.
- *Strength:* Cooperating with correction makes a person more capable of trusting God. Since they believe God wants what is best for them, they look at life's difficult circumstances as something positive, as an opportunity for growth.
- *Healing:* The corrected Christian or child is more able to look at life through God's eyes rather than through the selfish eyes of a victim who concentrates on his or her own needs.

☞ **GO TO:**

Proverbs 4:26 (level paths)

☞ **GO TO:**

Ephesians 4:24 (righteousness)

1 Peter 3:11 (peace)

Philippians 4:13 (strength)

KEY POINT

Discipline seems painful but it brings great rewards.

What Others are Saying:

Gwen Shamblin: The parents are invited by the children to get with the program or get out of their way. They completely manipulate the parents and use the parents. How does even a one-year-old know he can do this? Because the child can sense that the parent wants fellowship at almost any cost. The parent adores the child and the child adores himself—a nice combination for getting what you want. The parent jumps at the child's yelling or pouting. How difficult it is to discipline an object that you adore.[4]

Remembering the positives of disciplining a child can remove the fear of losing the approval or love of a child. In failing to correct a child, we allow disobedience. We might avoid a temporary battle, but we'll lose the war of building self-control within the child. Friendship with our children most often occurs when they are adults, and is the result of the respect gained through being parents—not "best buddies."

REMEMBER 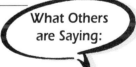 THIS

STATE THE RULES

> **Joshua 1:8** Do not let this Book of the Law depart from your mouth; **meditate** on it day and night, so that you may be careful to do everything written in it. Then you will be prosperous and successful.

meditate: dwell upon

No Rules? No Success!

God told Joshua to meditate and obey his laws—the laws that were given previously in the **Pentateuch**—and promised to bring him prosperity and success. God knows that having rules lets us know exactly what is expected, and that brings security, wisdom, and the ability to handle life in a godly manner. He knew we needed to be certain of his expectations so he spelled them out in the first five books of the Old Testament.

Pentateuch: first five books of the Old Testament

God also knew we wouldn't be able to keep his rules perfectly. That's why Jesus was <u>predicted</u> back in the time of Adam and Eve when God gave them consequences for their disobedience (see GWPB, pages 9–10). The law helped them see their need of living in God's power, and it gave them rules for success—to whatever degree they could obey.

☞ **GO TO:**

Genesis 3:15 (predicted)

Charles Swindoll: Training should prepare the child to think for himself. In many a Christian home a child is told what he may and may not do—but is not trained to understand *why*. As soon as Junior gets out of the nest (actually before) he is a ready target for the enemy's darts. His defenses are weak because he has merely learned his parents' lists.[5]

What Others are Saying:

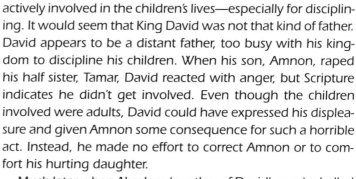

Marriage God's Way—When a couple establishes the rules of their home, they are following God's example of declaring clearly and precisely what they expect from their children. If such rules and guidelines are not communicated concisely, children won't know how to conform and respond obediently.

Establishing seven to ten basic rules for your household, depending upon the age of your children, will bring greater peace into your home, and that's "prosperity and success." If a rule is broken, the consequence—the "discipline"—should already be established. Many parents will draft a chart that is explained at a family meeting, or everyone at the meeting could create the chart. Then after being discussed, it is put on the refrigerator where everyone can refer to it.

Couples in the Bible

☞ **Check It Out:**

2 Samuel 13:1–39

☞ **GO TO:**

2 Samuel 15:7–12
(rebelled)

Good, godly parenting requires a mother or father who is actively involved in the children's lives—especially for disciplining. It would seem that King David was not that kind of father. David appears to be a distant father, too busy with his kingdom to discipline his children. When his son, Amnon, raped his half sister, Tamar, David reacted with anger, but Scripture indicates he didn't get involved. Even though the children involved were adults, David could have expressed his displeasure and given Amnon some consequence for such a horrible act. Instead, he made no effort to correct Amnon or to comfort his hurting daughter.

Much later when Absalom (another of David's sons) <u>rebelled</u> against his father and temporarily took control of the nation as king, David meekly slithered away in the night, unable or unwilling to fight for his God-given throne. In these instances, David shows himself to be a weak father who doesn't correct his children and as a result, suffers the consequences of a broken home with sons who war against him and each other.

Check the Chart

He Says . . .

LARRY: When our children were in elementary school, we knew we needed to make the rules of our home very clear. In a family meeting, we asked questions like, "What are the important rules for our family? If someone breaks a particular rule—even mom and dad—what should the consequence be?" Thus, the Miller

Household Rules, which included a consequence for each rule, were formed.

Kathy and I were surprised that Darcy and Mark were harder on themselves than we would have been in determining a consequence. When we discussed a possible disciplinary action for "make bed neatly before school," the kids spoke up and said, "they must make everyone else's bed the next morning." That got a laugh out of all of us but we wrote it down.

She Says . . .

KATHY: We still have the piece of paper that our first chart was written on. Here is what we developed.

Rule	Consequence for Disobedience
No TV until homework is done	No TV for rest of day
Make bed neatly before school	Make everyone else's bed the next morning
Pick up all articles of possession and place in appropriate place in evening before bed: bedroom floor should be clear and things removed from other parts of house	Any items left out will be put in "time out" basket and will stay for a week. If an item must be used before then, it can only be "redeemed" for ten cents each item.
Brush teeth in morning and before bed	Brush teeth for two minutes
Shower every other day	Stay in house all next day—except for school.
Private Bible reading before bed	Move bedtime earlier by fifteen minutes next night
Do not go into another person's bedroom without knocking and getting permission	Time out in own bedroom for fifteen minutes

Disciplining children isn't just about giving consequences for disobedience. It's also about giving rewards for obedience—to stimulate cooperation. God always offers rewards for obeying the law. Here are just a few of the dividends mentioned in Psalm 119 for following God's rules.

REMEMBER THIS

Psalm 119:	Reward for Obeying God's Law
verse 1	Blessings
verse 11	Ability to resist sin
verse 24	Wise counsel for life
verse 28	Strength
verse 46	Confidence
verse 66	Good judgment
verse 98	Wisdom
verse 99	Insight

Psalm 119:	Reward for Obeying God's Law
verse 100	Understanding
verse 105	Guidance
verse 114	Protection
verse 172	Joy
verse 173	Help

Just as God motivates his children to obey him with such wonderful promises, we can motivate our children to obey through offering rewards.

TAKE IT FROM THEM

Elizabeth and Doug know the value of rewards. At the beginning of summer when Katy and Johnny were home from school and prone to fighting, Elizabeth and Doug chose to be proactive by using rewards to diminish sibling rivalry. Doug drew up a chart and at a family meeting, Elizabeth and Doug explained that whenever the children acted nicely toward each other and their parents noticed, they could put a sticker on the chart. When there were fifty stickers on the chart, the family would take a day trip to anywhere the children wanted to go.

Of course, Doug and Elizabeth knew the children would choose the local amusement park, and that's just what they did. The project was a complete success. Although Katy and Johnny still fought at times, their negative interaction was lessened considerably, and they even seemed to make a point of cooperating so that they could gain more stickers on the chart. Elizabeth and Doug were encouraged to use other reward projects to help their children make wise choices.

TO SPANK OR NOT TO SPANK

> **Proverbs 13:24** He who spares the rod hates his son, but he who loves him is careful to discipline him.

☞ **GO TO:**

Proverbs 10:13; 22:15; 23:13–14; 29:15 (verses)

Proverbs 1:8–9 (instruction)

This Will Hurt Me More Than It Will Hurt You

Spanking isn't a modern concept. It goes way back to the Old Testament and was ordained by God as one of several means of giving consequences to children. Several <u>verses</u> in Scripture refer to it. And <u>instruction</u> should go along with it for it to be considered true biblical discipline.

Bruce Narramore: These and other verses clearly show that God intends that parents spank their children. But this seems to contradict some of the "experts" who hold spanking in disrepute. Much of the reason for this conflict lies in the misuse of spanking. Many parents spank when they do not need to, and others severely punish children physically. This misuse of spanking is no more biblical than failing to spank at all. The biblical attitude is to spank only when necessary, and then only in love.[6]

Spanking should always be done without anger and only with young children. A teenager should never be spanked. If another consequence can be used—like withdrawing privileges or giving "time out"—those techniques should be used first. But toddlers may not understand such consequences; therefore, spanking can be effective if done without anger and with consistency.

Any disciplinary technique, whether spanking or other consequences, will not be effective unless used consistently. If children think they can get away with disobedience because a parent isn't consistent, they will risk disobeying. Consistency brings security and actually better behavior because children know the risk of discipline is greater than the benefit of disobedience.

Not only should parents be consistent toward the child, but they must be consistent between themselves. Unfortunately, most parents have different perspectives of how to discipline children. Some want to be lenient, thinking that time will teach the child; others want to be strict, believing that only a strong hand will create change. When such differences erupt, it's essential that a couple work through their differences so that their marriage will be protected and their children won't be able to use their disagreements against them.

Ellis and Donna faced a unique and difficult challenge in disciplining their son, Nathan, who suffered from Prader-Willi syndrome. Children with this syndrome crave food and easily gain weight, which is highly **detrimental** to them. Ellis and Donna disagreed repeatedly on how to respond to Nathan. For the twenty-seven years that Nathan lived, most of their arguments were about how to discipline Nathan with his unique problems. Donna believed they should be strict

What Others are Saying:

REMEMBER THIS

KEY POINT

Spanking can be effective if done without anger and with consistency.

WARNING

TAKE IT FROM THEM

detrimental: *damaging*

and take charge of everything Nathan ate. Ellis had a more patient perspective and wanted to be lenient. Ellis and Donna learned to relieve the stress of Nathan's daily problems by taking long walks in their pasture or along the nearby creek. Ellis made the rule that they could talk about anything during that hour except the problems with Nathan. They needed that break from the stress, and keeping to that rule helped their marriage survive, especially as they later grieved the loss of their son.

But You Don't Discipline Correctly!

He Says . . .

LARRY: Kathy and I often argued about disciplining Darcy and Mark. I wanted firmer consequences, and Kathy wanted a more gentle approach. When Kathy dealt with their misconduct with too much leniency, I felt compelled to compensate and raise the ante the next time. Of course she would see my raise and respond to misconduct with even more sympathy. I remember telling her, "Life is harsh. Our children need to learn the sting of consequences now, so that life doesn't slap them down later."

Well, you see the cycle. It didn't work. Unified discipline was a joke because Kathy and I felt compelled to offset each other's perceived weaknesses. We were each too busy trying to prove our own approach was superior.

She Says . . .

KATHY: Larry and I fought about this issue more than any other. We were both convinced we were right and the other was totally wrong. I responded to Larry's strictness with a mother's tender heart, saying, "You are harsh, and it makes them feel discouraged." But Larry just couldn't understand, and I knew I was right.

Then we realized after having another heated discussion that we were both right—and we were both wrong. We both had elements of truth, but we were going to extremes. We committed to stop overreacting to each other. I promised to be more faithful in giving consequences, and Larry vowed to include more compassion and encouragement with the consequences. And it worked! We became more balanced and stopped fighting each other. Darcy and Mark saw us as more unified, and there was less friction between us all.

COOPERATE

> **Proverbs 22:6** Train a child in the way he should go, and when he is old he will not turn from it.

Which Way Did He Go?

Many people have interpreted this proverb as a guarantee that raising a child in a Christian atmosphere will produce a godly person. Unfortunately, the Proverbs are general observations of what is usually true—not specific promises from God. In most cases, a child trained in a godly direction will choose that righteous way of living when they are adults. But since God gives each person a free will to choose, it's possible that even with good Christian training, a child could grow up and reject their godly training.

That doesn't mean that parents should abandon the training of their children in godly ways. A loving, nurturing relationship accompanied by consistent training will give a child the best foundation for making godly choices as an adult.

Bruce Narramore: All this is not to say that a child's environment is not important. It certainly is. Proverbs says we must bring up our children properly if they are to maintain their faith as adults. There is a dual responsibility for the development of sinful behavior. Some lies with the child; the rest lies with the parents. Both parent and child share the responsibility for the child's personal development.[7]

What Others are Saying:

Charles Swindoll: God is not saying, "Bring up a child as *you* see him." Instead, he says, "If you want your training to be godly and wise, observe your child, be sensitive and alert so as to discover *his* way, and adapt your training accordingly." *Way* is a Hebrew word that suggests the idea of "characteristic," "manner," "mode."[8]

When a child doesn't follow through on the godly training given them, it's easy for parents to blame themselves. They may feel ashamed or think they were not good parents or that they failed. But parents are not a reflection of their children in every case. Good people

WARNING

can come out of the most horrible family circumstances, and godly parents can raise ungodly children. We do our best and then resist the temptation to blame—or take undue credit. Other factors like personality, trauma from childhood, and the environment in their school can influence a child. Christian couples still need to stand firm, consistently disciplining their children but also understanding that there aren't any guarantees.

STUDY QUESTIONS

1. Why should a person look positively upon God's discipline? And similarly, why should a child look favorably upon his parent's discipline?
2. If a child isn't disciplined, how does he feel inside?
3. What is the primary purpose of discipline?
4. What are the other four results of discipline?
5. What will be the result if a person meditates and obeys God's rules?
6. What is one possible way to discipline a child, especially a toddler?
7. If a child is trained in a godly manner, what is the most probable thing that will happen, even though it's not guaranteed?

CHAPTER WRAP-UP

- Just as God disciplines his children because he loves them, parents must discipline their children in order to communicate love. A child may not acknowledge that he feels loved because of the discipline, but inside, he knows that he is loved because of it. Those who aren't disciplined may wonder if they are important members of the family. Those who are disciplined might not acknowledge it, but they will respect their parents for the discipline.

- Parents should have specific rules and consequences for breaking those rules. If these rules are communicated clearly and followed consistently, there will be more peace in the family and the children will be better behaved.

- Spanking can be an effective technique for disciplining children, especially very young children who don't yet understand consequences like a time out or restrictions for their behavior. Spanking should always be done without anger.

- Scripture tells us that if we will train a child in the correct way, he will most likely follow God's rules as an adult. Although

Proverbs are observations by Solomon and don't give guarantees, parents can find strength and peace in believing their good efforts will most likely bring positive results.

KATHY & LARRY'S  BOOKSHELF

Some of Kathy and Larry's favorite books about disciplining children:

- *Help! I'm a Parent!*, Bruce Narramore, Zondervan. Offers practical answers to the dilemma facing the modern parent.
- *Parent Talk*, Kevin Leman and Randy Carlson, Thomas Nelson Publishers. Straight answers to the questions that rattle moms and dads.

12 LETTING GO

Here We Go

When we hold that new baby in our arms, we don't realize that the "letting go" process has already started, but it has. Even though we'll be the major influence in our children's lives and in what they experience, we will need to learn to let go as we see them grow.

Some couples may never have children and will need to let go of that dream. Other couples will experience the heartache of a child's death, whether due to miscarriage, illness, or accident. Dreams for that child die with the child.

Life is full of times when we must release the ones we love. Despite the heartache God's great faithfulness and love can strengthen us and our faith. Let's look at how some biblical couples let go as they trusted in God.

LETTING GO OF THE DREAM TO HAVE A CHILD

1 Samuel 1:1–8 There was a certain man from **Ramathaim**, a **Zuphite** from the hill country of Ephraim, whose name was Elkanah son of Jeroham, the son of Elihu, the son of Tohu, the son of Zuph, an Ephraimite. He had two wives; one was called Hannah and the other Peninnah. Peninnah had children, but Hannah had none. Year after year this man went up from his town to worship and sacrifice to the Lord Almighty at Shiloh, where Hophni and Phinehas, the two sons of Eli, were priests of the Lord. Whenever the day came for Elkanah to sacrifice, he would give portions of the meat to his

Ramathaim: fifteen miles north of Jerusalem

Zuphite: ancestors of Zuph from tribe of Ephraim

wife Peninnah and to all her sons and daughters. But to Hannah he gave a double portion because he loved her, and the Lord had closed her womb. And because the Lord had closed her womb, her rival kept provoking her in order to irritate her. This went on year after year. Whenever Hannah went up to the house of the Lord, her rival provoked her till she wept and would not eat. Elkanah her husband would say to her, "Hannah, why are you weeping? Why don't you eat? Why are you downhearted? Don't I mean more to you than ten sons?"

Sometimes a Spouse Isn't Enough

Hannah desperately wanted a child. Her husband, who had sons and daughters through his other wife, Peninnah, couldn't understand Hannah's obsession. He thought she should be satisfied with just him, and couldn't understand her longing for children. He did his best to help, giving her a larger portion of food than his other wife and speaking tenderly to her.

Hannah's desperation was so intense that at times she wouldn't eat, especially when Peninnah provoked her. Hannah's grief was most likely caused by two reasons. First, as a woman she wanted a child. Second, according to the cultural view of her day, any woman without children was thought to be <u>cursed</u> by God. Children were a high priority in Jewish society. Couples <u>talked</u> about children even before the wedding. Each family needed children to extend the family line into the next generation. If a woman was barren, the townspeople "<u>reproached</u>" her with ridicule. Even her relatives treated her with pity, looking upon her the same way they looked at a widow—removed from God's blessings.

In time, God did answer Hannah's desperate pleas for a child, and her son, Samuel, was born. But God doesn't always choose to answer every couple's plea for a child and that can bring a divisive tension to even a strong marriage.

☞ **GO TO:**

Deuteronomy 7:13–14 (cursed)

Ruth 4:11–12;
Genesis 24:60
(talked)

Luke 1:25 (reproached)

What Others are Saying:

David and Heather Kopp: Nearly every couple experiences deep disappointment together—the loss of a child, chronic illness, financial disaster, unfulfilled goals. When life is not turning out as we hoped, it's easy to focus on what our mate isn't giving us—or can't give us even if he or she wants to. At such times, small gifts of kindness reassure our mates that we treasure them no matter what.[1]

Charles Swindoll: Don't be frustrated if you are without children. Don't be frustrated if you have seven or eight. Relax. Children are assigned by God. Whether naturally or by adoption into a godly home, he fits certain kinds of children with certain kinds of parents. His Lordship extends even to making your quiver full. Think of it this way: Happiness is a full <u>quiver</u>, no matter what the size.[2]

What Others are Saying:

☞ **GO TO:**

Psalm 127:5 (quiver)

Marriage God's Way—When one person in a marriage has a desperate need for a child and the other person can't understand that need, there can be a lot of tension. Trusting God in the midst of that tension can be difficult. God promises in Psalm 37:4–5, *"Delight yourself in the Lord and he will give you the desires of your heart. Commit your way to the Lord; trust in him and he will do this."* If God doesn't fulfill our desire for a child, we may believe he has failed to keep that promise. A husband and wife need to be very careful during such stress that they don't allow the tension to draw them away from each other.

KEY POINT

God loves you whether or not he gives you children.

> If God seems not to answer your longing for a child, he still loves you and wants only the best for you. Be careful not to **displace** your frustration with God onto your spouse. Be sure to find tender ways to acknowledge each other's pain in your infertility and remind yourselves that you are not enemies, but friends as you travel this painful road together.

WARNING

displace: transfer

I Want What I Want

KATHY: I was raised in a family that highly valued children, and the message I received from my parents, especially my mother, was, "The most fulfilling thing you can do is grow up, get married, and have children." I was excited after Larry and I had been married for a year and a half and we agreed it was time to start our family. As each month went by and I didn't get pregnant, I was disappointed. After unsuccessfully trying to have a child for a year, I began to wonder whether I would ever become a mother. When the second year passed, I really wondered what God had planned for me. It had never occurred to me that he might not want me to be a mother. That was inconceivable. But as I entered my third year of frustration and dashed hopes, I had to consider it—and I

She Says . . .

didn't like the idea! I thought I couldn't be fulfilled unless I was a mother.

As time went by, my prayers were more and more fervent. "Lord, I want to be a mother. You've given me this desire and you've promised to give me the desires of my heart. Please let me conceive." Each month's disappointment made me question God's plan. I knew I should be willing to surrender every desire to him, but giving up the hope of motherhood seemed totally beyond my ability. My plea became almost a demand, "Lord, I must have a child. Don't you love me and want what's best for me?"

In time, my hand developed a skin rash that itched continually. I instinctively knew my stress was being expressed through this physical reaction and nothing relieved it. I tried using skin lotion. I tried telling God I'd cooperate with whatever he wanted—but I didn't really mean it. I wanted to be a mother too much.

After almost three years, my prayers were answered. Graciously, God didn't wait until I had totally surrendered to him on this issue—otherwise, I'm not sure I would have ever conceived. But God taught me a lot about trusting him during that time, even though I was not perfect at relinquishing my own desires.

Looking back, I can see God's purposes in delaying the arrival of our children. I thought Larry and I were mature at that time. I can, in hindsight, see how immature we were. Considering I struggled with abusive anger even as a twenty-seven year old, it could have been much worse if I'd been younger. God really does know what's best. I thank him that he delayed answering my prayer.

 He Says . . .

LARRY: I wasn't too sensitive to Kathy's deep desire for children. Even before we were married, I told her children were not on my radar screen. In fact, I was willing to be a childless couple for life. Later, she told me she just didn't believe me. She couldn't fathom someone choosing to remain childless. As Kathy pressed for children in our early marriage, my opinion began to weaken. I agreed to have children, but out of my selfishness and immaturity, I told her she would take care of the kids and I would take care of our future. Little did I know the stress that would result from our different views toward children.

GRIEVING THE LOSS OF A CHILD

2 Samuel 12:15–24 After Nathan had gone home, the Lord struck the child that Uriah's wife had borne to David, and he became ill. David pleaded with God for the child. He fasted and went into his house and spent the nights lying on the ground. The elders of his household stood beside him to get him up from the ground, but he refused, and he would not eat any food with them. On the seventh day the child died. David's servants were afraid to tell him that the child was dead, for they thought, "While the child was still living, we spoke to David but he would not listen to us. How can we tell him the child is dead? He may do something desperate." David noticed that his servants were whispering among themselves and he realized the child was dead. "Is the child dead?" he asked. "Yes," they replied, "he is dead." Then David got up from the ground. After he had washed, put on lotions and changed his clothes, he went into the house of the Lord and worshiped. Then he went to his own house, and at his request they served him food, and he ate. His servants asked him, "Why are you acting this way? While the child was alive, you fasted and wept, but now that the child is dead, you get up and eat!" He answered, "While the child was still alive, I fasted and wept. I thought, 'Who knows? The Lord may be gracious to me and let the child live.' But now that he is dead, why should I fast? Can I bring him back again? I will go to him, but he will not return to me." Then David comforted his wife Bathsheba, and he went to her and lay with her. She gave birth to a son, and they named him Solomon. The Lord loved him.

Getting Up and Going On

The death of a child is tragic, whether or not it's the result of sin as it was with David and Bathsheba. David did everything he could to prevent his son's death. He <u>confessed</u> his adultery with Bathsheba and his involvement in getting Bathsheba's husband, Uriah, killed at war (see GWMB, pages 99–100). Yet, God's consequences for his sin were final.

The death of a child doesn't always mean the parents have

☞ **GO TO:**

Psalm 51:1–4 (confessed)

sinned, but the grief is still intense. Many parents cry out to God to save their child. Yet for unknown reasons, God doesn't spare that child's life. Every cause of a child's death, whether before or after birth, brings deep hurt and grief to a couple and more tension to their relationship.

Frank Minirth: Miscarriage is much more of an issue than most people will admit. It's a severe loss, and you have to go through the stages of grief. A husband must be supportive of his wife. He has to try to understand her emotions because he probably has them also. It's an insight into his own feelings. He may not realize how much it's affecting him. It is. Men tend to lack a keen awareness of their own emotions. It's not that they're not emotional; it's just that, in general, men are not as acutely aware of their feelings as women.[3]

Marriage God's Way—David gives a wonderful example of a man's expression of emotion that many men should learn to **emulate**. When a man expresses grief, it helps his wife cope with her grief and feel closer to her husband. A man may say that he doesn't have feelings, but he does—he just has to get in touch with them. Making a list of feeling words can often help a man, or woman, become more in tune with their feelings. Looking at such a list will help a couple identify their feelings if they aren't accustomed to naming or describing them.

emulate: follow

WARNING

Wisely, David and Bathsheba dealt with their grief by not withholding sex from each other. Oftentimes, a grieving wife will think her husband is insensitive if he wants to have sex after they experience the loss of a child. She may think he just wants to have pleasure. But for a man, sex is sometimes the only way he knows how to express closeness. An understanding wife will welcome his desire to draw close to her in that way—especially since he may not be able to express his grief as an emotion of sadness.

REMEMBER THIS

Every couple grieves in their own way. Some want to talk about their grief, others might not want to mention the pain. Grief may propel some into activity, while others may want to just sit and reflect. Often a husband and wife grieve in exactly the opposite manner; therefore, it's essential that they accept their spouse's unique method and not assume that his or her reaction disregards the loss. Such understanding will draw them closer together instead of bringing greater tension and confusion. If they are not sympathetic toward each other's grief, they may find their marriage a divorce statistic. Risk of divorce is increased for couples after the death of a child. God wants to prevent that by comforting each couple's heart through empathy for the other.

Jeff and Karen faced the loss of their first baby from a severe birth defect. The person they usually relied on for emotional support—their spouse—was also in very deep pain. Jeff needed Karen's help and Karen needed Jeff's help, but neither of them was able to be much support to the other. As much as they needed each other, they had to allow one another space to grieve individually, in different ways and at different paces. They were both suffering parents, but they did not have the same needs.

Communication was the key, including taking the risk of honestly sharing difficult feelings. For instance, Karen needed to talk and talk and talk about what had happened, but after a while, Jeff needed to stop talking. It was hard for him to tell Karen—and initially it did hurt her feelings—but it was important to recognize they could not meet those needs in each other. Karen found a friend or two who listened to her, which gave Jeff the silence he needed. Each then had the freedom to grieve as they needed, empowering them to heal in their own unique way.

TAKE IT FROM THEM

KEY POINT

Grief is hard to handle, regardless of its cause.

SENDING THEM OFF

Psalm 91:1–6 He who dwells in the shelter of the Most High will rest in the shadow of the Almighty. I will say of the Lord, "He is my refuge and my fortress, my God, in whom I trust." Surely he will save you from the **fowler's snare** and from the deadly **pestilence**. He will cover you with his feathers, and under his wings you will find refuge; his faithfulness will be your shield and rampart. You will not fear the terror of night, nor the arrow that flies by day, nor the pestilence that stalks in the darkness, nor the plague that destroys at midday.

fowler's snare: hunter's trap

pestilence: disease

Fear Versus Trust

Trusting God like David did, as his shelter, fortress, refuge, and shield, takes a lot of faith—especially when it involves letting go of our teenage and young adult children. Finding the balance between what to control and what to release in our children's lives is very difficult, but knowing that they are in our great God's care will help.

Learning to trust God as our child's protector is hard because of the following things:

- It's a dangerous world and many unfortunate things are happening every day. We want to keep our children protected from pain.
- We reflect on our lives and the poor choices we made, and we don't want our child to make those same unwise decisions.
- We may expect them to be perfect. Since they can't possibly meet that standard, we refuse to grant them independence.
- We think controlling them will induce them to seek God in our way.

When we remember that our children are just on loan to us and that they were created by God and belong to him, we can learn to trust God to care for them. He will care for them better than we can because he is with them everywhere—everywhere including their first solo drive. Their first date. Their first day at college. Their first apartment.

Charles Swindoll: Look upon release as a process rather than a sudden event. You don't release your child the day of his marriage. You begin the process of releasing your child on the day of his birth. You plan on it. You anticipate it. Some days you wish it would hurry up![4]

James Dobson: Near-misses make me want to gather my children around me and never let them experience risk again. Of course, that is impossible and would be unwise even if they submitted to it. Life itself is a risk, and parents must let their kids face reasonable jeopardy on their own.[5]

Letting go of our children is not a one-time act when they are eighteen. It's a continuous process all along the way (*see* WBFM, chapter 13). It also involves empowering them to make more and more decisions, as they become capable. Unfortunately, a husband and wife may have a totally different perspective on what is appropriate for children at certain ages. Together the opinions of a husband and wife will form a complete perspective, and a **consensus** can be attained through talking about it.

> **John 16:33** I have told you these things, so that in me you may have peace. In this world you will have trouble. But take heart! I have <u>overcome</u> the world.

Troubles Will Come

Jesus told us that trials and pain are inevitable in this world. As parents, we will never be able to totally protect our children. Of course, when they are very small, it's our responsibility to shield them as much as possible, but as they become older, we must release them to do more things for themselves and go to places where we can't completely protect them.

Charles Swindoll: The young men and women who enter adulthood with confidence are the ones who were taught by their parents how to handle the issues of life. They are the ones whose moms and dads are available, waiting in the wings, to give counsel or support or assistance whenever it is needed and requested.[6]

Marriage God's Way—God intends to use difficulties our children face to draw them closer to him and then <u>use</u> their experiences to help others. Second Corinthians 4:16–18 instructs us, *"Therefore we do not lose heart. Though outwardly we are wasting away, yet inwardly we are being renewed day by day. For our light and momentary troubles are achieving for us an eternal glory that far outweighs them all. So we fix our eyes not on what is seen, but on what is unseen. For what is seen is temporary, but what is unseen is eternal."* God will protect our children from anything that is contrary to his will for them. He wants our children to turn to him with their problems, and he wants to bring an eternal change in their hearts. If we prevent them from having difficulties, we prevent them from learning to depend on God.

REMEMBER THIS

consensus: agreement

☞ **GO TO:**

Luke 10:19; 1 John 2:14 (overcome)

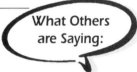

What Others are Saying:

☞ **GO TO:**

2 Corinthians 1:3–4 (use)

KEY POINT

Even if he allows misfortune in our child's life, God will use it for good.

☞ **GO TO:**

1 John 4:8 (loves)

Romans 8:28 (bless)

Acts 17:27 (seek)

Proverbs 8:17 (rewarded)

> **Jeremiah 29:11–13** "For I know the plans I have for you," declares the Lord, "plans to prosper you and not to harm you, plans to give you hope and a future. Then you will call upon me and come and pray to me, and I will listen to you. You will seek me and find me when you seek me with all your heart."

God Has Great Plans for Your Child

God <u>loves</u> each of our children and wants to <u>bless</u> them through the situations he allows in their lives. He desires each circumstance to motivate them to <u>seek</u> him. He promises that such seeking will always be <u>rewarded</u> with knowledge of himself.

What Others are Saying:

Quin Sherrer: No matter how hopeless—no matter how impossible your situation seems—God has the answer. He wants to woo our lost, damaged children back to himself. To do this, he needs us to be faithful in prayer. And we need his wisdom and strength to stand in the gap for our children.[7]

Think about It

Allowing our children to increasingly take greater control over their lives is actually showing our trust in God's amazing <u>sovereignty</u>. He has a plan, and we can cooperate with it by releasing them more and more. We can do that by allowing them the following:

☞ **GO TO:**

Daniel 4:32 (sovereignty)

Hebrews 12:10–11 (consequences)

Deuteronomy 33:27 (everlasting arms)

- To have increasing control over spending their money
- To have increasing control over decisions about their activities, friends, and goals in life
- To suffer the <u>consequences</u> when they don't do their homework or they make unwise financial choices

Allowing these increased responsibilities should happen subtly over time as the child gets older and proves continued maturity. It will require risking failure, but human beings learn more from failure than they do from success. In the midst of success or failure, God's <u>everlasting arms</u> are there to catch them.

> **Psalm 49:7** No man can redeem the life of another or give to God a ransom for him.

God Doesn't Have Spiritual Grandchildren

Spiritual life isn't passed down; it's the choice of each person. We can't give redemption as a gift. We can only encourage others to seek it from God. And we can live a godly life that shows them the blessings of <u>abiding</u> in God's power.

☞ **GO TO:**

John 15:6 (abiding)

James Dobson: Parents can, and must, train, shape, mold, correct, guide, punish, reward, instruct, warn, teach, and love their children during the formative years. Their purpose is to control that inner nature and keep it from tyrannizing the entire family. Ultimately, however, only Jesus Christ can <u>cleanse</u> it and make it "wholly <u>acceptable</u>" to the Master.[8]

What Others are Saying:

Although we might be tempted to dictate how our children should live their spiritual walk, that won't create their own desire for change. Forcing them or nagging them to read their Bible or pray won't produce spiritual hunger. It will only make them resentful and possibly turn from God. We can model for them our own strong prayer life and invite them to participate, but trying to **coerce** them to interact with God will only create problems.

Think about It

☞ **GO TO:**

1 John 1:9 (cleanse)

Romans 15:16 (acceptable)

coerce: force

KEEP PRAYING

> **Luke 22:31–32** Simon, Simon, Satan has asked to sift you as wheat. But I have prayed for you, Simon, that your faith may not fail. And when you have turned back, strengthen your brothers.

Pray! Pray! Don't Stop Praying!

Jesus, even though he faced death within hours, was still concerned about his disciples. He let Simon Peter know that he was praying for him and even indicated that he knew Peter would fail. Jesus encouraged him by letting him know there was hope in the future when he turned back to God.

intercessory: *prayer for
others*

KEY POINT

We can't control
others, but we can
pray.

☞ **GO TO:**

John 17:1 (prayed)

REMEMBER THIS

☞ **GO TO:**

James 5:16 (effective)

Think about It

James Dobson: We are given the powerful weapon of **intercessory** prayer, which must never be underestimated. The Scriptures
teach that we can pray effectively for one another and that such a
petition "availeth much" (James 5:16 KJV). God's answer to our
requests will not remove the freedom of choice from our children, but he will grant them clarity and understanding in chart-
ing their own course. I also believe the Lord will place key
individuals in the paths of the ones for whom we pray—people of
influence who can nudge them in the right direction.[9]

Marriage God's Way—Jesus is the ultimate parent.
He "parented" his disciples while on earth, instructing them and
encouraging them to succeed. He didn't control them, yet he <u>prayed</u>
for them. He could have supernaturally prevented Simon Peter
from denying him, but he didn't. He allowed Peter that experience in order that he may have the additional experience of receiving God's gracious forgiveness. Without undergoing failure
and restoration, Peter could not have effectively spoken of God's
grace later.

As Jesus modeled, the best thing we can do is to pray for our
children. Jesus released Peter to experience failure, but he
supported him in prayer. So often we conclude that our
prayers haven't been <u>effective</u> because our children make
mistakes or fail. Sometimes they even fall into serious sin.
But Jesus didn't consider his prayers ineffective when Peter
failed. He knew that his prayers would keep Peter faithful
over the long haul. Our prayers, likewise, will not prevent
our children from experiencing pain or failure, but we can
trust that God will work through our prayers to draw them
eventually back to himself.

If your adult child is currently not following God or is being openly rebellious, God isn't finished writing the chapters of his or her life. There is always hope. Many children
fall away but return when they see their need for God. Don't
stop praying. God will never stop reaching out his loving,
faithful hand.

After experiencing childlessness for many years, Manoah and his wife were given a challenge by God to raise a strong-willed son named Samson. They were instructed by an angel to make their child a "Nazirite," a person dedicated to God who refrained from cutting his hair. Samson grew up knowing he had a special calling from God, because an angel had predicted that Samson would deliver the Israelites.

Yet, Samson was weak in self-control and frequently had ungodly desires. In spite of that, God had a plan and was directing his life. Judges 14:1–4 tells us, *"Samson went down to Timnah and saw there a young Philistine woman. When he returned, he said to his father and mother, 'I have seen a Philistine woman in Timnah; now get her for me as my wife.' His father and mother replied, 'Isn't there an acceptable woman among your relatives or among all our people? Must you go to the uncircumcised Philistines to get a wife?' But Samson said to his father, 'Get her for me. She's the right one for me.' (His parents did not know that this was from the Lord, who was seeking an occasion to confront the Philistines; for at that time they were ruling over Israel.)"*

Manoah and his wife could have easily despaired over their son's behavior. However, they offered their opinion and godly perspective, but then trusted God enough—even though they didn't know his plan—to release Samson to make his own choices. If they had controlled their son's decision, he would not have accomplished great feats for God.

Of course, this example should not be interpreted as an excuse for parents to help their children sin or to support their ungodly choices. But if our children persist in making unwise choices as adults, we must allow God to work, knowing he is more powerful than we are. We can also keep praying for our child to repent and return to God.

When Shannon was sixteen she declared to her parents, Cherry and Ron, that she wanted to marry her boyfriend. She emancipated herself through the courts and moved in with her nineteen-year-old boyfriend, who promised to marry her within the month. Cherry and Ron repeatedly tried to change Shannon's mind but she was adamant.

Cherry often sat crying in her daughter's old room, and at one point, she received a nudge from God to write Shannon a love letter. She quickly wrote down many of her wonderful memories of Shannon's childhood and expressed her uncon-

Couples in the Bible

☞ **Check It Out:**

Judges 13:1–14:4

TAKE IT FROM THEM

ditional love. She also released her daughter, saying that she knew God would watch over her and care for her. Before signing it, she wrote, "I'll always be here waiting for you," and then placed the letter in the bottom of one of the boxes Shannon would be taking to her new home.

Cherry found out later that Shannon and her boyfriend found the letter and read it together, both of them crying. It touched their hearts, but neither was willing to change their arrangement. After discovering a side of Shannon he didn't like, Shannon's boyfriend postponed their marriage. Their relationship disintegrated, and eventually they broke up.

Since Cherry and Ron hadn't alienated Shannon, slowly she began to come for brief visits. During these visits, the family relationships grew closer and trust was reestablished.

Today, Cherry and Shannon have a close mother-daughter relationship. Shannon is married and has two beautiful daughters. She and her husband are involved in their family and their church and have dedicated their lives to Christ.

STUDY QUESTIONS

1. How could Elkanah have better responded to his wife's grief over being barren?
2. How was David wise in dealing with the grief of his son's death?
3. What comfort can parents take as they release control of their children and let them face the world?
4. When children go through tough times, what should parents remember that Jesus said about living in the world?
5. What can give a couple peace as they release their children?
6. Even when a couple can't control their children, what can they do that is always effective?

CHAPTER WRAP-UP

- The loss of the dream of having a child, or the fear that we won't get pregnant, can be stressful. It takes a strong faith to believe that God really knows what is best for us when we don't agree. God does know what he has planned for each of us, and we can trust him.

- Losing a child through death or miscarriage causes a couple to grieve deeply. It would be easy for a couple to grow apart if they misinterpret how the spouse expresses sorrow. If a husband and wife can be compassionate and understanding of their spouse's unique way of grieving, God can help them both to grow even closer through their trauma.

- Learning to release control of our children is a lifelong process. If we seek to protect them from every danger, we are not demonstrating our belief that God will protect them and that he has a plan for them. God will even use pain to cause them to seek him and grow in character.

- Though parents feel helpless when releasing their child, they do have a strong weapon—prayer. A husband and wife can't always be with their child, but they can pray that God will be with him or her. God honors prayers offered for the good of a child.

KATHY & LARRY'S  BOOKSHELF

Some of Kathy and Larry's favorite books about parenting:

- *How to Pray for Your Children,* Quin Sherrer with Ruthanne Garlock, Regal Books. This book challenges, inspires, and encourages parents to pray for their children.

- *Praying God's Will for My Son*, Lee Roberts, Thomas Nelson Publishers. Gives verses that can be used for prayer in many different categories.

- *Parents & Teenagers*, edited by Jay Kesler with Ronald A. Beers, Victor Books. Compiled articles from the experts on every aspect of parenting teenagers.

Part Three

"DOIN' WHAT COMES NATURALLY"

REVEREND FUN

"You received 739 messages from your wives while you were out."

13 SEX IS GOOD— VERY, VERY GOOD!

Here We Go

Sex was God's idea! He designed this delightful marital act for **procreation** and pleasure. Although some Christians have misinterpreted his intentions over the years, thinking of sex as evil, the Bible doesn't say that. In the very beginning, God created sex as an important and unifying act for a husband and wife. And he declared it good!

God's ideal is for every husband and wife to enjoy their sexual togetherness. He designed sex to bring them together for enjoyment and to make them feel close to each other. That's why we can look to the Bible for the godly and positive attitudes we should adopt about this often misunderstood gift from God.

procreation: to bring forth offspring

GOD CREATED SEX

> **Genesis 2:22–25** Then the Lord God made a woman from the rib he had taken out of the man, and he brought her to the man. The man said, "This is now bone of my bones and flesh of my flesh; she shall be called 'woman,' for she was taken out of man." For this reason a man will leave his father and mother and be united to his wife, and they will become one flesh. The man and his wife were both naked, and they felt no shame.

One Flesh Is Good—and Fun!

When God created a woman to unite with Adam, he designed the concept of sex so that men and women within the commitment of

☞ **GO TO:**

Genesis 3:6
  (disobedience)

Genesis 3:7 (ashamed)

What Others
are Saying:

inundated: flooded

marriage could express love for each other and bring children into the world. In God's original plan, man and woman would be completely free with each other—not aware of their nakedness, not ashamed or embarrassed to expose their total beings. When sin entered the world through Eve and Adam's <u>disobedience</u>, they became <u>ashamed</u> of their nakedness. As a result, each man and woman comes to their new spouse with varying degrees of concern that they will be accepted unconditionally—with all their physical flaws. That is not as God had intended.

Bill and Pam Farrel and Jim and Sally Conway: Today's adults are crying out for a sexual relationship that is intense yet comforting, thrilling yet committed, passionate yet purely romantic. The top forty music charts are **inundated** with desires longing to be fulfilled. Women want a man who is "Shameless" in his love, "Too Sexy" to be resisted, but committed to going to "The End of the Road" in devotion. Women expect a guy to give "Passionate Kisses" yet not create an "Achy, Breaky Heart."

A man wants a woman who looks at him like he's "Romeo," who is "Breathless" at the sight of him. He wants a woman who will "Lose Control" and get "Dangerous" in giving him "Love Deluxe."[1]

David and Claudia Arp: Remember that sex is God's idea. He is the one who put the passion and desire in your heart for each other, and he wants you to celebrate your sensuality by loving each other with abandon.[2]

REMEMBER THIS

God created a man and woman's desire for sex to accompany a lifelong commitment that will bring passion and yet security. It is never wrong to have a longing for sexual unity within the context of marriage, even though in the past, well-meaning Christians have taught that sex was evil or dirty. Sex is God's idea, and he desires for his human creation to enjoy his wonderful gift.

💍 **Marriage God's Way**—God intended for a man and a woman to be united in a committed marriage until death. Today's society communicates falsehoods that cause people to believe they will find true happiness by living with a boyfriend or girlfriend. People believe the lie that they can sleep with multiple partners and find the security they are inwardly seeking. God called that fornication. Only sex within the loving and secure relationship of a committed marriage was called "good."

God made women in particular to need the commitment of marriage to feel secure and to be able to return physical love. One study found that women who were living with their boyfriends were more jealous than married women, their emotional dependency was greater, they had fewer female friendships, and they had less desire to advance within their job.

Wrong Again!

Somehow through the years, church leadership began to believe that God hadn't created sex as completely good. Some theologians and pastors thought of sex only for procreation, and didn't believe it was healthy, desirable, and for pleasure.

The church had a very restrictive view of sex and frequently banned its practice for religious reasons. Between the third and tenth centuries, the church prohibited its members from having sex on Saturdays, Wednesdays, and Fridays, as well as during the forty-day fast periods before Easter, Christmas, and Pentecost. One historian estimates that only forty-four days a year were left for marital sex after taking away the possibility of sex during feast days and days of **female impurity**.

Remember, God doesn't blush about sex. He uses the whole concept to illustrate some important issues in the Bible. Consider his use of sexual imagery through these biblical images:

- The portrayal of Israel as a "prostitute" because God's children worshiped other gods (see GWBI, page 122)
- The identification of the church as the "bride of Christ" (see GWRV, pages 282–283)
- The description of the church as a virgin who should stay pure in order to be presented to Jesus at the wedding of the Lamb

---

Bill Hybels: The **duality** of sexuality and spirituality is theologically incorrect. In Greek and **Gnostic** thought, body and soul were separated on the grounds that the physical couldn't be spiritual and the spiritual couldn't be physical. But the Bible does not teach this. It insists that spirituality involves all of what it means to be human—even sex, that seemingly most carnal of acts. There are no apologies or blushes about the issue.[3]

 GO TO:

Galatians 5:19
(fornication)

Think about It

female impurity: during a woman's period

 GO TO:

Jeremiah 2:20
(prostitute)

Revelation 19:7–9
(bride of Christ)

2 Corinthians 11:2
(virgin)

duality: separation

Gnostic: religious philosophy in first few centuries A.D.

What Others are Saying:

No one need be concerned that they are sinning or doing something evil when expressing their sexuality with their marriage partner. God is not covering his eyes in embarrassment nor is he aghast at his creation's activity during sexual intercourse. He created the whole idea and is actually smiling, because we are enjoying his gift to us.

SEX EQUALS ONENESS

> **1 Corinthians 6:15–17** Do you not know that your bodies are members of Christ himself? Shall I then take the members of Christ and unite them with a prostitute? Never! Do you not know that he who unites himself with a prostitute is one with her in body? For it is said, "The two will become <u>one flesh</u>." But he who unites himself with the Lord is one with him in spirit.

☞ **GO TO:**

Genesis 2:24 (one flesh)

Good-bye Me, Hello Us

In the verse above the apostle Paul warned believers in Corinth of the dangerous sin of prostitution because so much immorality and temptation surrounded them. The temple of the love goddess Aphrodite employed over a thousand prostitutes to help the followers of Aphrodite "worship" by participating in sex. Paul cautioned that uniting a person's soul through sex with a prostitute is against God's intentions. Instead, he desired that a married man and woman become closer through joining their bodies sexually.

What Others are Saying:

Bill Hybels: God didn't design sex just to express his love of passion and energy. He designed it so we could experience intimacy. First Corinthians 6:16 states that sexual intercourse unites a man and woman in a "oneness of spirit." In other words, in the arithmetic of sex, 1 + 1 = 1. The two, in some deep and spiritual way, become one. No other human act or expression has such power or mystery.[4]

Ed Wheat and Gloria Okes Perkins: Intimacy (derived from the Latin *intimus*, meaning inmost) refers to the state of being most private, most personal in relationship. It depicts a special quality of emotional closeness between two people in which both are constantly alert and responsive to fluctuations of feeling and to the well-being of the other. It can mean to understand and to be fully understood by one who cares for us deeply.[5]

Marriage God's Way—The "uniting" that sex brings is certainly a mysterious thing. Although not always experienced every time with equal emotion or active participation, couples can strive toward its ideal. Sex is more than just the physical union of two bodies. It is the union of two souls and spirits as well. In the physical union when there is mutual love, security, and respect, a husband and wife feel like they have been accepted and "known." They feel that they have revealed their innermost being and their gift of themselves has been received with tender concern.

In the perfection of the Garden of Eden, Adam and Eve "knew" each other in that way and were not ashamed. Because of sin and the baggage that each of us brings into marriage, that "knowing" is now limited. It is still God's desire that every married couple enjoy to some degree that special affection that sexual intercourse brings.

KEY POINT

Sex unites two people physically, spiritually, and emotionally.

☞ **GO TO:**

Galatians 4:8–9; Philippians 3:10 (knew)

NEVER STOP

> **Deuteronomy 24:5** If a man has recently married, he must not be sent to war or have any other duty laid on him. For one year he is to be free to stay at home and bring happiness to the wife he has married.

Concentrated Concentration

God so valued the marriage relationship that one of his laws for the Israelites was that nothing—no war, no important work—would hinder a husband's ability to enjoy his wife within their first year of marriage. Such a high priority was placed upon their relationship that God didn't want anything to prevent a couple from getting to know each other. Since the Israelites also valued children, God wanted a man to be protected from the likelihood of death in battle before he had a chance to impregnate his wife.

☞ **GO TO:**

Genesis 25:5–10 (children)

Ed Wheat and Gloria Okes Perkins: Biblically, the Lord allotted one year of concentrated togetherness for newlyweds in order to establish the patterns of intimacy that would last a lifetime. The Hebrew word translated "to cheer up" meant: to delight his wife, to know her, and to discover what would be pleasing to her.[6]

David and Claudia Arp: Schedule time for sex. Yes, actually put it on your calendar (in code, of course). When our children were young, our working schedules were flexible. With the help of a wonderful Moms' Day Out program, we scheduled a couple of hours each Monday morning when we could be alone. This was our time to learn how to be great lovers. Becoming great lovers is an acquired skill—but it is one you can develop if you schedule time for practice.[7]

KEY POINT

Sex is best when it's not spontaneous—but planned and anticipated.

insulate: protect

Marriage God's Way—God knew that putting too much responsibility upon a new husband would be detrimental to the success of a couple's marriage. Yet today, we seem to forget that important concept: that we must **insulate** our marriage from distractions that will prevent its growth. We're so busy that we put other life activities before the importance of our marriage—and that certainly applies to the sexual relationship. Most couples today just don't find quality time to make love to each other. God knew its importance and made a law that protected a new couple's relationship.

WARNING

Planning time to enjoy each other sexually isn't always easy. There are always many other things to be done. Yet, unless we plan for it, it most likely won't happen—or it will occur to meet a sexual need, which is usually unsatisfying. One of the myths about sex is that it should come naturally and spontaneously, but in our busy world, spontaneity must be planned.

Think about It

Sex doesn't start in bed, or even in the bedroom. Sex starts in the everyday affection that communicates value and importance of the spouse, by offering meaningful touching and loving words on an everyday basis—not just when one partner wants sex.

Wives have indicated that romance is essential in preparing them for sex. They considered the following forms of affection to be important:

- Conversation
- Nonsexual touching during the day and as a part of foreplay
- Kind words and the lack of criticism and harshness
- Tender displays of love, like flowers, dinner out, or caring for the children without being asked
- Hearing "I love you"
- Making the relationship a priority over other activities

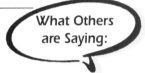

What Others are Saying:

Bill Hybels: What happens between a husband and wife in the kitchen is equally as important as what happens in the bedroom. An environment of trust, love, respect, and security are just as much a part of "foreplay" as is a physical caress.[8]

Gary Smalley: Many women tell me they need as much as three days' preparation for sex, romantically and emotionally, before they can respond to their husbands. A woman is sort of like an iron and a man is like a light bulb. She *warms up* to the sexual expression, while he *turns on* immediately.[9]

Donna and Ellis, now married for over forty years, remember the times when their children were young and romance was difficult. They taught their children that when their bedroom door was shut, they were not to be disturbed. Their children knew they were not to open it without knocking. Later a lock was even put on the door. Donna and Ellis also learned to take the phone off the hook and not worry about the to-do list that was waiting.

TAKE IT FROM THEM

Who Wants Affection When You Can Have Sex?

LARRY: When we were first married I had a different view about affection than Kathy. It seemed during dating and courtship that affection was the ritual used to prepare for marriage and its intimate sharing. After marriage, I was ready to trade affection in on the new and improved model—sex. Who wouldn't want to make the switch? Well . . . Kathy . . . and every other wife! I quickly learned that Kathy expected even more affection after marriage to prepare her for sex. You can imagine the interesting exchanges

He Says . . .

between Kathy and me when I shared my expectation of less affection and more sex.

KATHY: I couldn't believe Larry's attitude. It was obvious to me that we needed both affection and sex, but when I tried to share my perspective, he just couldn't comprehend. I felt unloved and found it harder to respond to him sexually when he didn't communicate his love by holding my hand or putting his arm around me. I began keeping score of how often he touched me—other than for sex. It wasn't a high number. In fact, it was really low.

Unfortunately, keeping score didn't help my attitude. I was testing him. Bitterness and resentment set in. At the time, I didn't realize I was also being tested. But an "ah-ha" experience hit me one day when I realized, "It doesn't even occur to Larry to give me affection. He's clueless!" Previously, I really believed he was consciously thinking, "I know Kathy wants me to hold her hand, but I'm not going to." Now I realized it was up to me to remind him, so I took his hand as we walked along, or I reached out to him in some way. In those moments, he readily reached back.

In time, he began to understand how important affection was for my sexual responsiveness. He read it in books and heard it at several couples' conferences we attended. Since he wanted anything to make me more sexually interested, he began giving me the affection I craved. Now, Larry gives me the touching and affection during the day that prepares me for some wonderful sexual unity in the evening.

Couples in the Bible

☞ **Check It Out:**

Genesis 26:8

There is something very tender in watching an elderly couple hold hands as they walk down the street or stroll through the mall. When we see them pat their spouse's shoulder in affection or smile lovingly while looking deep in each other's eyes, we grin. We are encouraged for our later years.

Isaac and Rebekah were that kind of couple. Even though theirs was an arranged marriage, they quickly fell in love and stayed in love until Rebekah died. After being married many years, they were still affectionate with each other. Genesis 26:8 recounts that Isaac caressed Rebekah, even under circumstances where it was dangerous to do so (see GWGN, page 207). At this point, they had been married for some time because their sons were adults. Their expression of affection was not that of newlyweds; it was the result of experiencing life's challenges together and valuing the other person as a gift from God.

> **1 Corinthians 7:3–5** The husband should fulfill his marital duty to his wife, and likewise the wife to her husband. The wife's body does not belong to her alone but also to her husband. In the same way, the husband's body does not belong to him alone but also to his wife. Do not deprive each other except by mutual consent and for a time, so that you may devote yourselves to prayer. Then come together again so that Satan will not tempt you because of your lack of self-control.

Brief Sexual Pauses Only, Please

In the busyness of life, sex seems like one aspect that can easily be put aside. Yet, Paul wrote that it shouldn't be neglected for anything except prayer, and then only for a short time agreeable to both of you. Paul's exhortation was in response to the immorality that surrounded Corinthian believers—and that can certainly apply to the immoral influences that tempt Christians today.

Because of the prevalent and widespread evil influence in Corinth, some Greek Christians as well as non-Christians had become extreme in trying to resist immorality. They abstained from sex even within marriage, and considered every part of sex to be evil. As a result, Corinthian believers were confused. They asked Paul whether they also should refrain from sex. If abstinence could help them live a godly life, they were willing to do it.

Paul had a firm reply, "Don't stop having sex within marriage. If you do, you'll just have more temptation. Only stop having sex if both of you agree to abstain for a limited time so that you can spend concentrated effort and time praying for your concerns" (1 Corinthians 7:5 paraphrased).

Paul also explained that sex was not to become a weapon where one spouse could withhold it for any reason. Both a husband and wife should be committed to providing for their spouse's sexual satisfaction. Paul reiterates God's perspective that there should be equality between husband and wife.

For attaining good sex, remember to fulfill your spouse's needs, allow your body to belong to your spouse, and deprive each other only by mutual consent for the purpose of concentrated prayer.

KEY POINT

Keep married sex regular—you'll be happier.

fidelity: *faithfulness*

What Others are Saying:

Bill and Lynne Hybels: These verses are not-so-subtle reminders that we each owe our spouse a satisfying sexual relationship. We are, after all, our spouse's only sexual option. The commitment to marital **fidelity**, which every sincere Christian couple must make, means that if we don't find sexual fulfillment in our marriage, we don't find it. It is as simple, and sometimes as tragic, as that. Each of us must take our sexual responsibility seriously, and lovingly and enthusiastically do everything in our power to meet and fulfill our spouse's sexual needs and desires.[10]

 **Marriage God's Way**—Many ways within our society and in television programs like *Married with Children,* give the idea that wives, in general, don't enjoy sex and that they have sex only out of duty or as a means of punishment or reward. Christian women are portrayed as sex-haters who are unable to respond sexually. That attitude isn't what Paul thinks. He stressed that men should fulfill their sexual responsibility to their wives. In that, he says that women enjoy and desire sex just like men.

REMEMBER THIS

Any sexual act, on which both husband and wife agree, is acceptable. Anything that brings discomfort or pain should not be forced upon either of them. A couple should want the greatest pleasure for their mate, finding out what satisfies them and doing it! In the Bible there is no restriction on sexual acts between a married couple.

What Others
are Saying:

Gary Smalley: To get an idea of your husband's sexual appetite, think about your own desire to eat. How often do you feel hungry when you're on a diet? If you're like most of us, it's three times a day—morning, afternoon, and night! The hunger drive hits a woman on a diet about as often as a man's sex drive naturally hits him—especially during the first years of marriage. That's why a man can slip into bed at 10 o'clock at night after not seeing his wife all day, reach over and touch her on the shoulder, and say, "What do you *think*?"[11]

STUDY QUESTIONS

1. When God created Eve and presented her to Adam, how did they feel about themselves?
2. What was God's main purpose for sex?
3. What provision did God make to help a newly married couple get to know each other adequately?
4. What is the only thing that should stop a married couple from having sex?

- God created sex for only good purposes, and he wants men and women to enjoy it within the context of marriage. When Adam and Eve were created and God presented them to each other, they were naked and unashamed. There was no self-consciousness or selfishness during their lovemaking because sin hadn't yet brought its evil influence. That is how God would ideally like every husband and wife to enjoy his gift of sex.

- God designed sex to bring a unity and oneness between a husband and wife. Therefore, the apostle Paul had to write to the Corinthian believers to explain that using a prostitute made them one with her and that was wrong. Each man should only be united with his wife, and spiritually, with God.

- God was so concerned that sex be a positive experience that he made a law that no bridegroom could be sent off to war or be given another military duty during the first year of his marriage. Instead, he should concentrate on pleasing his wife. Today, people can make their marriage and sex a priority by not withholding sex from each other—except for a mutually agreed upon time in order to concentrate on prayer.

KATHY & LARRY'S  BOOKSHELF

Some of Kathy and Larry's favorite books on sex:

- *Love Stories God Told*, David and Heather Kopp, Harvest House. The great romances of the Bible.

- *Romancing the Home*, Ed Young, Broadman & Holman. How to have a marriage that sizzles.

- *Passages of Marriage*, Frank and Mary Alice Minirth et al., Thomas Nelson Publishers. Five growth stages that will take your marriage to greater intimacy and fulfillment.

- *Pure Pleasure*, Bill and Pam Farrel and Jim and Sally Conway, InterVarsity Press. Making your marriage a great affair.

14 ADULTERY IS BAD— VERY, VERY BAD!

Here We Go

God created sex to be enjoyed by a married couple—married to each other, that is! It wasn't designed as a temptation to be used by Satan. Yet in today's society, adultery and other forms of immorality aren't considered wrong, just "different" choices for having a full sexual experience. That kind of "fullness" just leads to a full plate of pain, hurt, guilt, and broken families. That wasn't God's plan!

Instead, God wants to offer the help we need to resist sexual temptation and to continue the love affair with our spouse. Temptation will come because no marriage is perfect, but with God's power we can resist and continue to enjoy the wife or husband of our <u>youth</u>. We'll find within Scripture the strength we need to resist adultery.

☞ **GO TO:**

Proverbs 5:18 (youth)

A BIG NO-NO

> **Exodus 20:14** You shall not commit adultery.

Only One Spouse at a Time

One of the Ten Commandments is God's exhortation that his created beings should not commit adultery. Adultery is having a sexual relationship with a person other than one's spouse. God designed a man and a woman to be exclusively married to each other. When another person is a part of that equation, it is sin and brings pain

☞ **GO TO:**

Matthew 6:24 (hate)

James 1:6, 8
(uncertainty)

illicit: unlawful

What Others
are Saying:

explicit: visually dramatic

Think about It

and destruction. A person cannot stay emotionally and spiritually healthy while maintaining two spousal relationships at once. It creates <u>hate</u> for the original partner and a false love for the new partner. There is guilt, <u>uncertainty</u>, and a split in the unfaithful person's personality as he or she tries to juggle all the facets of an **illicit** relationship and keep from being detected. That is not God's plan for man. This same command also relates to sexual immorality through pornography.

Lois Mowday: Immorality is certainly not the only way that we seek security and significance in the wrong way. There are many others. But to realize that an immoral relationship reflects a deep need in our lives is better than to rationalize it away, justify it, or simply accept it as a weakness and stop trying to change.[1]

James Dobson: As a member of the Attorney General's Commission on Pornography, I listened to testimony by those who thought they could jazz up their sex lives with obscene materials. They discovered that the stuff they were watching quickly began to seem tame and even boring. That led them to seek racier, more **explicit** depictions. And how did it happen? The door was quietly opened and a monster came charging out. My point is this: The restrictions and commandments of Scriptures were designed to protect us from evil.[2]

When a person gives in to adulterous temptations, he or she, without knowing it, is indicating there are deep unmet needs in his or her life. Such a person is hurting and desperate to find anything that will release him or her from the pain. Satan offers the most destructive way to do that, clothed in the array of seeming happiness: an affair. Understanding the causes could help someone resist the temptation to have an affair. Here are some of the potential causes:

- *A lack of self-worth:* a feeling of being unworthy of God's love or insignificant to others. We reach out to those who we think can meet our needs.

- *An emotional handicap:* a weakness to resist temptation during a time when we are wounded or weary. People who are burned out through work or ministry can be susceptible to an affair.

- *Denial:* an unwillingness to accept that there are problems in our marriage, that we're needy, or that the relationship with the other person is becoming more important than that of our spouse.

- *Unrealistic expectations:* an impractical desire or demand that our spouse meet a need of ours that he or she cannot fulfill. We may feel justified in trying to have that need met elsewhere.
- *Pride:* an inner belief that God's rules don't apply to us. We selfishly feel that our needs should be met even if it means breaking God's commandments.

Dave Carder with Duncan Jaenicke: Some sexual feelings towards others (even those we're not married to) is normal. But many believers cannot believe such feelings are OK and so they deny that they experience them. Guilt and shame follow. Denial is the defense mechanism of choice.

Yet denial doesn't solve anything. In fact, it usually **exacerbates** the problem because in the stages of denial, the desire to be around the other person "goes underground," and the **infidel**-to-be actually initiates contact with the partner unconsciously.[3]

What Others are Saying:

exacerbates: *worsens*

infidel: *unfaithful spouse*

> **Proverbs 5:1–6** My son, pay attention to my wisdom, listen well to my words of insight, that you may maintain discretion and your lips may preserve knowledge. For the lips of an adulteress drip honey, and her speech is smoother than oil; but in the end she is bitter as gall, sharp as a double-edged sword. Her feet go down to death; her steps lead straight to the grave. She gives no thought to the way of life; her paths are crooked, but she knows it not.

Watch Your Wants

Although sexual sin looks and feels attractive—like honeyed lips and smooth speech—such disobedience leads to heart-breaking results. It can lead to the death of a family through divorce, or diminished trust if a couple stays together. A couple choosing to stay together will have to journey through the difficult process of restoring their marriage, possibly never fully trusting each other again. (To learn more about the effects of divorce, see WBFT, pages 290–292.)

James Dobson: Infidelity is an addiction that can destroy a life as quickly as drugs or alcohol. Once a man or woman is hooked on the thrills of sexual conquest, he or she becomes intoxicated with its lust for pleasure.[4]

The Book of Proverbs speaks frankly about adultery and prostitution. Solomon, the writer of Proverbs, had many wives, so he may have been writing from experience.

Proverbs	Disadvantages of Sexual Sin
2:16–22	Brings lack of abundant life. God will cut such people off from the land.
5:7–22	Ruin and regret. Realization that the lack of discipline is destructive.
6:20–35	Punishment and discipline from God. Consequences for the sin, sometimes even poverty.
9:13–18	Prostitution is based on lies and deceit. It traps the **gullible** person and leads to destruction.
22:14	An adulteress speaks lies to gain power over a man.
23:26–28	A prostitute is like a robber, lying in ambush to deceive.
27:7–8	Adultery often starts because the married person wasn't satisfied at home.
29:3	Prostitution wastes money.
30:20	Adultery causes the sinning persons to deny their sin.

gullible: naïve and believing

**TAKE IT
FROM THEM**

Ed and Gayle were married only two years before Gayle knew something was very wrong. She discovered that Ed was addicted to cyberspace sex. At first, Gayle was supportive and understanding of his feeble efforts to overcome it, but having no consequences for his actions, Ed didn't stop. They tried counseling, but Ed continued to feel powerless. Finally, Gayle had to apply the principles of "tough love" and separated from Ed, saying they could be a family only after he had worked on his issues. He was then motivated. At the same time, Gayle worked on overcoming the effects of the sexual abuse she'd experienced as a child. In time, Ed stopped acting out his addiction and was able to show that healing had occurred. Their family was reunited, and now their relationship is better than ever.

FATAL ATTRACTION

> **2 Samuel 11:1–4** In the spring, at the time when kings go off to war, David sent Joab out with the king's men and the whole Israelite army. They destroyed the Ammonites and besieged Rabbah. But David remained in Jerusalem. One evening David got up from his bed and walked around on the roof of the palace. From the roof he saw a woman bathing. The woman was very beautiful, and David sent someone to find out about her. The man said, "Isn't this Bathsheba, the daughter of Eliam and the wife of Uriah the Hittite?" Then David sent messengers to get her. She came to him, and he slept with her. (She had purified herself from her uncleanness.) Then she went back home.

Eyes Wide Open

Usually, kings accompanied their armies and helped them fight, which gave the men courage and morale. But for some reason David chose this time to remain home. He was vulnerable to the temptation of adultery by being where he shouldn't have been and by looking where he shouldn't have looked. His restlessness began a dangerous stroll with his eyes wide open. Although he had many wives and concubines, when he saw Bathsheba, he thought he'd found the answer to his cravings.

Bathsheba could have resisted the invitation. Maybe she had secret designs on the king. Her roof (see illustration, page 216) was conveniently within watching distance from the palace and maybe she was missing her husband who was at war, or maybe she was just awaiting the opportunity for a bid for greater power. Regardless, even if it meant danger to her own life by refusing the king, she could have said no to him.

Lois Mowday: People don't lead moral lives one day and have an affair the next. It may appear that way, but it is a process. The process is often overlooked because some stages are not obvious to us, the viewer, and thus they are difficult to detect. That's why it seems to happen overnight.[5]

KEY POINT

Deep sharing and emotional intimacy keeps marriage healthy and protects against adultery.

What Others are Saying:

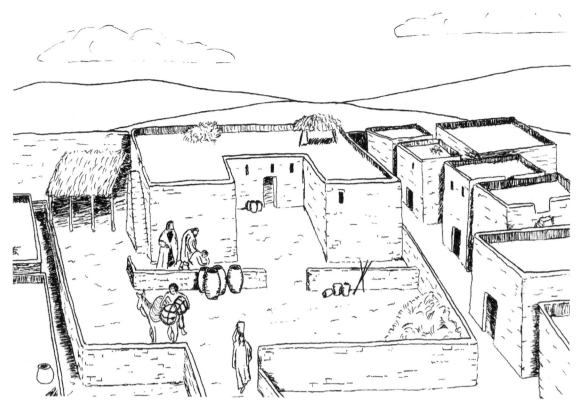

Israelite House

The roofs of homes in Israel were used for activities like sleeping in tents on hot nights, drying linen or fruits, and meditation.

Think about It

☞ **GO TO:**

Ephesians 5:11, 13 (armor)

REMEMBER THIS

David's little stroll seemed very innocent, and often that is where illicit sex begins. It can start with sharing your marriage problems with an understanding coworker of the opposite sex. Or flirting with the man next door. Or planning to meet an attractive woman at the coffeehouse because you know she goes there every Saturday morning. Generally speaking, an affair doesn't suddenly occur. It's actually a process that begins where there is a hurting heart.

David was a very successful king. Sometimes success can be more dangerous to our integrity than times of trial. When we finally reach our desired goal, we can forget to keep on our spiritual <u>armor</u>. It's often the successful periods of life when Satan attacks, because we forget during peaceful times that we do need God's help.

> **2 Samuel 11:5–9** The woman conceived and sent word to David, saying, "I am pregnant." So David sent this word to Joab: "Send me Uriah the Hittite." And Joab sent him to David. When Uriah came to him, David asked him how Joab was, how the soldiers were and how the war was going. Then David said to Uriah, "Go down to your house and wash your feet." So Uriah left the palace, and a gift from the king was sent after him. But Uriah slept at the entrance to the palace with all his master's servants and did not go down to his house.

☞ **Check It Out:**

2 Samuel 11:5–27

Deception: That Light Is an Oncoming Train

After the one-night stand, Bathsheba discovered she was pregnant. David heard the news that Bathsheba was pregnant and knew he was in trouble. What could he do? Instead of confessing his sin, he plotted to bring Uriah back home but Uriah didn't cooperate. Uriah slept in the street instead because he didn't want to dishonor the warriors who were fighting in bad conditions.

Because of the failure of his plan, David had another opportunity to confess his sin, but he didn't. His deception increased as he planned Uriah's murder. Instead of taking responsibility and seeking God's cleansing, he dug himself into a bigger hole.

Dave Carder with Duncan Jaenicke: Marriage is all about honesty, and the spouse who strayed (even though "only once") absolutely needs to reveal his downfall and process it correctly; otherwise the secret amounts to a ticking time bomb. It will either dramatically explode one day or slowly do its damage.[6]

What Others are Saying:

Marriage God's Way—Scripture seems to focus primarily on David's actions because he was king, but Bathsheba had a part in the deception as well. When she discovered she was pregnant, she should have confessed her sin to Uriah, making way for possible healing in their marriage. Instead she sought the assistance of the all-powerful king. God considered both Bathsheba and David guilty. Each adulterous partner must face his or her own responsibility for the sin.

KEY POINT

Both parties in adultery are responsible.

☞ GO TO:

Psalm 31:5 (truth)

Psalm 5:8
  (righteousness)

Psalm 51:4
  (unpunished)

Numbers 32:23
  (hidden)

Isaiah 43:25 (clean)

☞ Check It Out:

2 Samuel 12:1–12

Unconfessed sin always starts a progression that involves more sin and greater deception. Sin becomes the foundation of a house of lies that will eventually tumble down because God is a God of <u>truth</u> and <u>righteousness</u>. He will not allow sin to go <u>unpunished</u> or remain <u>hidden</u>. Sin is too destructive to our souls because it poisons our relationship with God and others. He wants our souls made <u>clean</u> through confession and repentance.

> **2 Samuel 12:9–10** "Why did you despise the word of the Lord by doing what is evil in his eyes? You struck down Uriah the Hittite with the sword and took his wife to be your own. You killed him with the sword of the Ammonites. Now, therefore, the sword will never depart from your house, because you despised me and took the wife of Uriah the Hittite to be your own."

One Finger Pointing Out but Three Pointing Back

David and Bathsheba's child was born, and maybe the passage of time had anesthetized David to his sin. Maybe he had convinced himself that his sin wasn't really that bad or that God had forgotten it. But God hadn't.

God sent the prophet Nathan to David to confront him with his sin. Nathan told David a little story about a poor man who had only one lamb that he loved dearly and kept as a pet. A greedy rich man with a flock of sheep in his pasture swooped in and took the poor man's lamb, turning it into lamb chops.

David was furious and pounded his fist on his throne. "That man must pay for his evil deed!"

"Gotcha!" said Nathan. "You are that evil man." Then Nathan went on to proclaim the punishments that David and his family would suffer because of this sin.

And every consequence that Nathan proclaimed as God's powerful punishment for the adultery occurred. They are as follows:

- The death of the child that Bathsheba and David conceived in sin (2 Samuel 12:19)

- Sexual turmoil in David's family; including the rape of Tamar by Amnon, her half brother (2 Samuel 13:1–19; see also GWWB, pages 218–219)

- A constant threat of murder within David's family (2 Samuel 13:26–30; 18:14–15); Absalom, the brother of Tamar, took vengeance upon Amnon for Tamar's rape by killing Amnon (2 Samuel 13:23–37)
- The grief of David upon Absalom's separation from the family because of Amnon's murder (2 Samuel 13:38)
- Absalom's rebellion against David's reign; upon Absalom's takeover, he had sex on the palace roof with David's concubines (2 Samuel 16:21–22; see also GWMB, page 102)
- The death of Absalom when David's troops return to Jerusalem to restore his reign (2 Samuel 18:9)

Dave Carder with Duncan Jaenicke: Nathan used a "what if" story that would touch David's feelings, one which would provoke pain and cause him to react. Nathan didn't just want David to say it was wrong; Nathan was looking to break David's secret wide open. He wanted David to see it from the other side, from the victim's point of view. Nathan's motivations were that justice be done and that, in love for David, he be restored to God and man. Those motivations certainly apply when approaching an **infidel** too.[7]

infidel: unbeliever

☞ **GO TO:**

Ephesians 1:6 (grace)

Colossians 1:21 (separates)

Hebrews 12:10 (motivate)

Sin always has consequences, although we may think that God will overlook our sin or not take action. Sometimes in his incredible <u>grace</u> we don't suffer the discipline we deserve. But if not confessed, sin still <u>separates</u> us from fellowship with God. God uses consequences to <u>motivate</u> us to avoid wrong choices the next time we're tempted.

WARNING

What Others are Saying:

Bill and Pam Farrel and Jim and Sally Conway: From 1965 to 1985 teen pregnancies rose 553 percent; sexually transmitted diseases in 15- to 19-year olds went up 226 percent. Divorce tripled each year from 1963 to 1984; single parent families increased by 160 percent; unmarried couples living together went up 353 percent. The revolution left its mark on those who are adults today, and the next generation will also be deeply affected.[8]

> **2 Samuel 12:13–14** Then David said to Nathan, "I have sinned against the Lord." Nathan replied, "The Lord has taken away your sin. You are not going to die. But because by doing this you have made the enemies of the Lord show utter contempt, the son born to you will die."

Redemption Always Follows Repentance

To David's credit, when Nathan confronted him, David acknowledged his sin and repented. In God's mercy and grace, he forgave David but the consequence, David's son's death, would still occur. David was restored to fellowship with God, but his actions had brought discredit upon God. Therefore, God needed to deal a very serious consequence—the death of the child conceived in sin. Hebrews 13:4 tells us, *"Marriage should be honored by all, and the marriage bed kept pure, for God will judge the adulterer and all the sexually immoral."*

What Others are Saying:

Dan B. Allender and Tremper Longman III: Immorality attempts to do an end-run around the problems of relationship. And for a time, usually short, it works with fewer complications than marital sexuality. No wonder fantasies are preferred to the frustrations and inevitable incompleteness of failed leaving and incomplete weaving. Sin works for a season, but the wages of immorality are always more disastrous than the recurrent struggles of a growing and struggling marital union.[9]

☞ **GO TO:**

Isaiah 43:25 (motivated)

John 8:3–11 (adulterous)

Leviticus 20:10 (law)

Psalm 51:1–4 (writing)

Marriage God's Way—There isn't anything that can't be forgiven by God, except the "unpardonable sin"—the rejection of God's offer of salvation. Such a merciful God as Jehovah can even forgive adultery and murder. God is <u>motivated</u> to forgive any and every confessed sin. Jesus demonstrated that when an <u>adulterous</u> woman who was caught in the act was brought before him. Even though the <u>law</u> said she should be put to death, Jesus forgave her (see GWLC2, pages 32–34).

Think about It

As David worked through the pain of acknowledging his sin and facing the grief of seeing his infant die, he penned some beautiful <u>writing</u>, expressing his feelings (see GWBI, pages 74–75). Writing out feelings can be a useful and powerful tool for anyone who wants healing from sinful choices.

WATCH THAT THOUGHT

> **Ephesians 5:3–5** But among you there must not be even a hint of sexual immorality, or of any kind of impurity, or of greed, because these are improper for God's holy people. Nor should there be obscenity, foolish talk or coarse joking, which are out of place, but rather thanksgiving. For of this you can be sure: No immoral, impure or greedy person—such a man is an idolater—has any inheritance in the kingdom of Christ and of God.

Don't Even Hint about Immorality

Immorality, including adultery, can begin with tempting thoughts and actions like foolish talk, joking, and flirting; therefore, we must guard ourselves against such temptations. We must also avoid comparing our mate with another person who seems to be perfect. Instead of focusing on the qualities in that person that are attractive and downplaying our spouse's good qualities, we must give thanks for all that our spouse can offer us.

KEY POINT

Don't even daydream about how wonderful it would be to be married to someone else.

Jerry B. Jenkins: Whenever I need to meet or dine or travel with an unrelated woman, I make it a threesome. Should an unavoidable last-minute complication make this impossible, my wife hears it from me first.[10]

What Others are Saying:

Marriage God's Way—Making wise choices about sexual temptation requires God's power. We must each learn to control ourselves by doing the following:

☞ **GO TO:**

1 Thessalonians 4:3–5 (control)

- Resisting any thoughts that put another person on a pedestal above our spouse
- Making sure we don't find ourselves alone and in private with someone other than our spouse
- Being careful in public not to give any subtle messages that we are attracted to the other person
- Refusing to share the difficulties of our marriage with someone of the opposite sex and refusing to hear the problems of that person's marriage

- Confessing to our spouse any attraction we feel toward someone else
- Holding ourselves accountable to a group or counselor for any attractions we might have to someone else

Confess First, Ask Questions Later

KATHY: I couldn't believe that another man was stealing my affections, even when I adored Larry so much. Larry and I had been married for fifteen years, and he had become my best friend. How could I be thinking about that other man so much? Whenever I thought of him, I focused on all his good points—and they were usually the points Larry wasn't quite as strong in. It was driving me crazy. I knew I needed to break the control of these thoughts, but I didn't know how . . . until I realized I should tell Larry about it. Tell Larry about it? That seemed too incredible. Wouldn't he stop trusting me? Wouldn't he want a divorce? Telling him seemed like the most illogical thing to do, but somehow I knew it was the solution.

When I told Larry, he calmly asked me some questions and then affirmed I'd done the right thing. I was relieved. From that point on, the bondage of thinking about the other man was broken.

LARRY: When Kathy shared with me, I was surprised. Our marriage was growing, thriving, in fact. Surprisingly, I didn't feel threatened by Kathy's revelation. Our relationship was strong, and I felt comfortable hearing her confession. But I *was* concerned. I felt responsible to take leadership and make the right call. I confessed to her that thoughts of other women had also troubled me in the past. We discussed our mutual love and began to view these intruding thoughts as Satan's scheme to crumble the foundation of our marriage. This was a wake-up call for both of us to guard our eyes and hearts because if a king could fall, we could be just steps behind.

Temptation is something <u>everyone</u> faces. We need to remember this:

- It's nothing new or unusual. Even Jesus was <u>tempted</u> but <u>didn't sin</u> (see GWLC, pages 65–76). It's a part of being human.
- God understands those temptations and in his power

She Says . . .

He Says . . .

☞ **GO TO:**

1 Corinthians 10:13 (everyone)

Matthew 4:1–10 (tempted)

Hebrews 4:15 (didn't sin)

Think about It

protects each person from anything that is beyond their ability to resist.

- God promises to provide a way to resist temptation. But we each must be willing to take hold of his help in that moment. God won't force us to receive the help he offers but he will make it available.

Walter Wangerin Jr.: When a desire is <u>born</u> in us, we have a choice. When it exists still in its infancy, we have a choice. We can carefully refuse its existence altogether, since it *needs* our **complicity** to exist. We can dread it from the very beginning, naming it straightway as a parasite that intends no good for us. Or else we can attend to it, think about it, fantasize it into greater existence—feed it! We can feed our sexual thoughts with pictures, books, videos, and a wandering eye at work. But if we do the latter, if we give it attention in our souls, soon we will be giving it our souls.[11]

Jerry B. Jenkins: The problem with the temptation verse (1 Corinthians 10:13) is that people apply it too late. Ten minutes into foreplay with the wrong partner, they're ready to seek that way of escape that was supposed to have come with the temptation. That's just it: The escape comes with the temptation. It's preventive medicine, not first aid after you've already set your course on a path toward injury.[12]

Marriage God's Way—God helps us resist sexual temptation:

- We can resist when we remember that sexual sin actually hurts us by damaging the spiritual <u>temple</u> that is the dwelling of the Holy Spirit. We won't be happy or content when we're sinning sexually. Such sin, like any other sin, doesn't bring us the good results we want (1 Corinthians 6:15–20).
- We can resist by turning away from it, even if we must literally run the other way. We must avoid any situations that could put us in a place of temptation. Resisting that initial danger will be easier than after getting ourselves deep into temptation (1 Corinthians 6:18).
- We can resist by focusing on the good qualities of our mate. Being grateful for whatever our husband or wife can

What Others are Saying:

☞ **GO TO:**

James 1:14–15 (born)

complicity: cooperation

☞ **GO TO:**

1 Corinthians 3:16 (temple)

KEY POINT

When tempted, look for God's escape route.

give us protects us from being overwhelmed with discontentment and dissatisfaction (Philippians 4:8).

- We can resist by continually transforming our minds to look at others through God's eyes of *appropriate* love! We can view another man or woman with innocent love but we don't have to give in to inappropriate interest in them (Romans 12:1–2).

Joseph was originally sold into slavery to the Midianites by his brothers who hated him (see GWGN, pages 255–258). Eventually the Midianites sold him to Potiphar, the captain of the guard, who was one of Pharaoh's officials. God gave Joseph favor with Potiphar, and Potiphar put Joseph in charge of his entire household.

Day after day Potiphar's wife made sexual suggestions, but Joseph always avoided her. One day she was too insistent and actually grabbed him. He literally ran away from her to maintain his purity, leaving his garment in her hands. She used the "evidence" against him by claiming he had tried to rape her. Joseph was betrayed again and put into prison because of her false claim. Never once in all his misfortunes did he blame God or become bitter. Later in life, he would say that everything that had happened to him was <u>used by God</u> for good.

Couples in the Bible

☞ **Check It Out:**

Genesis 39:1–23

☞ **GO TO:**

Genesis 50:20
(used by God)

UNFAIR AFFAIR

> **1 Corinthians 7:15** But if the unbeliever leaves, let him do so. A believing man or woman is not bound in such circumstances; God has called us to live in peace.

You Can't Make Me

God never wants a person to leave his or her marriage for any reason—especially sexual sin. Yet, the Bible also acknowledges that we cannot force anyone to do anything, even stay in a marriage. Often by releasing a spouse, God is able to more powerfully work in his or her life to restore the marriage.

Chuck and Barb Snyder: Instead of crying and begging and acting weak, you become strong because Christ's <u>strength</u> is now in you. You picture your husband as handicapped. Picture him as not being able to control himself. He just doesn't have the supernatural ability to do the right thing. Your role, however, is just an observer. The Bible says if the non-Christian husband or wife wants to leave, let them. But usually what happens is they are so taken by your <u>quiet and gentle spirit</u>, they are attracted back to you.[13]

Jim and Sally Conway: Now is the time to act *rationally*, not rashly. Don't force your mate out of the house and don't start divorce proceedings. If adultery has been committed, you have every legal and <u>biblical</u> right to divorce, but God doesn't say you *must* divorce. In the first few days, spend time asking God for wisdom and peace. Quietly take stock of your situation. Whatever you do, don't make decisions you'll later wish you could reverse.[14]

It takes an incredible trust in God to release a spouse after adultery if they want to leave. The fear of being misunderstood in not fighting for your marriage or in being considered at fault can lead to desperate measures to keep the disobedient spouse from leaving. Nagging or begging only make the erring spouse more determined to get away. Showing strength by releasing control over the sinning spouse can sometimes make them reconsider their decision to leave.

LOVE 'EM, DON'T LEAVE 'EM

> **Proverbs 5:18–23** May your fountain be blessed, and may you rejoice in the wife of your youth. A loving doe, a graceful deer—may her breasts satisfy you always, may you ever be captivated by her love. Why be captivated, my son, by an adulteress? Why embrace the bosom of another man's wife? For a man's ways are in full view of the Lord, and he examines all his paths. The evil deeds of a wicked man ensnare him; the cords of his sin hold him fast. He will die for lack of discipline, led astray by his own great folly.

What Others are Saying:

☞ **GO TO:**

Philippians 4:13 (strength)

1 Peter 3:1–4 (quiet and gentle spirit)

Matthew 5:32 (biblical)

Think about It

Rejoice in What You've Got!

The writer of Proverbs must have been thinking about a couple who had become bored in their marriage. A couple whose marriage has become dull might ask, "Is this all there is? I thought marriage would be constantly exciting." Marriage does have periods of routine and boredom, but that doesn't mean someone else will bring the excitement that we crave. What that new person will bring is a different set of problems—to go along with your old ones. Having the right attitude will revitalize a ho-hum marriage. The word "captivated" means to stagger as if drunk, or to be thrilled beyond measure. And the word "satisfy" implies complete contentment and total delight. What great descriptions of sex in marriage!

What Others are Saying:

1 Corinthians 7:1–5 (neglect)

Ed Young: Do you know why most affairs take place? It is so simple. Most affairs happen because people believe they can receive from another person that which they are not receiving from their mate. To <u>neglect</u> sex with one's spouse for too long is to place him or her in a vulnerable position where temptation is concerned.[15]

Think about It

Make a list of the things you appreciate about your spouse, and post it for constant review. Concentrate on the good attributes rather than the disappointing ones. No one else is perfect either! Enjoy the one person God gifted you with, and be happy.

STUDY QUESTIONS

1. Which one of the Ten Commandments is geared toward a married couple's fidelity to each other?
2. What is the ultimate result of following the tempting promises of an adulteress?
3. Why did the sight of Bathsheba bathing especially tempt David?
4. How did David make his sin of adultery even worse?
5. How did God bring David to the point of repentance and cleansing?
6. What were some of the consequences that God gave David because of his sin?
7. To be sexually pure, what should we avoid? And what should we choose to do instead?

8. If an unfaithful spouse wants to leave, what should be the response of their mate?

9. How can a husband or wife resist the temptation of adultery?

CHAPTER WRAP-UP

- God knew that sexual immorality, especially adultery, would be destructive. He dedicated one of the Ten Commandments to its opposition. People are created to be emotionally and spiritually most healthy when they remain faithful to their spouse. Otherwise, the tempting allure of an adulteress quickly turns to a path of spiritual and emotional death.

- David's story of his decline into adultery and the consequences he suffered can be a motivating reminder that sexual sin only reaps death and destruction. He gave in to his desires and ended up a murderer, deceiving himself into ignoring his great transgression. He and his family paid an enormous price for his moment of pleasure. From him we can learn to resist sexual temptation, for it will never bring us what we are seeking.

- Satan uses temptation to attract people to others who aren't their spouse, but God wants us to stay pure and be grateful for the wonderful things our spouse offers us. If we are tempted, God promises a way of escape, but we need to act on his offer immediately, not play around with the temptation.

- If a mate commits adultery and wants to leave the marriage, the remaining spouse cannot force him or her to stay. Releasing him or her may actually set up an atmosphere of love that encourages him or her to stay.

- It will be easier to resist sexual immorality as a husband and wife concentrate on the wonderful ways their spouse meets their needs, even though it's done imperfectly. Remembering the bad things that can happen by succumbing to temptation will also help us resist.

KATHY & LARRY'S  BOOKSHELF

Kathy and Larry's favorite books about avoiding sexual immorality:

- *The Snare*, Lois Mowday, NavPress. Avoiding emotional and sexual entanglements.

- *Torn Asunder*, Dave Carder with Duncan Jaenicke, Moody Press. Recovering from extramarital affairs.
- *Love Must Be Tough,* James Dobson, Word Books. New hope for families in crisis.
- *Loving Your Marriage Enough to Protect It*, Jerry B. Jenkins, Moody Press. Protecting a loving marriage and making it stronger.

15 HAVE A GREAT LOVE LIFE

Here We Go

The Song of Songs is most romantic, and yet it's a very spiritual book of the Bible. It is both a graphic description of human love and a majestic metaphor of God's love for his bride, the church. We will concentrate here on the aspect of marital romantic love and hit the highlights of the stirring relationship between a king and his beloved bride.

Sexual intimacy and passion are described in almost every verse of Song of Songs, also called Song of Solomon. We find advice for keeping love and ardor alive and thriving. Every couple could benefit from reading this imaginative true story aloud to each other—hopefully in the quiet seclusion of a romantic bedroom.

Any hesitation in believing that God favors the sexual union should be dispelled in this book written by him through the fingers of Solomon. God created sex for our enjoyment, and the final evidence is here.

John Trent: If you want a Betty Crocker cake mix to come out right, then you need to follow the directions printed on the label, using the exact ingredients. If you want to have a sexual relationship as beautiful as your wedding cake, then get your baking instructions from the Author of intimacy himself. Right here in the Song of Songs is every ingredient you need to have an exciting, fulfilling sexual relationship.[1]

What Others are Saying:

ANTICIPATION

> **Song of Songs 1:2–6** *Beloved:* Let him kiss me with the kisses of his mouth—for your love is more delightful than wine. Pleasing is the fragrance of your perfumes; your name is like perfume poured out. No wonder the maidens love you! Take me away with you—let us hurry! Let the king bring me into his chambers. *Friends:* We rejoice and delight in you; we will praise your love more than wine. *Beloved:* How right they are to adore you! Dark am I, yet lovely, O daughters of Jerusalem, dark like the tents of **Kedar**, like the tent curtains of Solomon. Do not stare at me because I am dark, because I am darkened by the sun. My mother's sons were angry with me and made me take care of the vineyards; my own vineyard I have neglected.

☞ **GO TO:**

Genesis 25:13 (Kedar)

Kedar: collective name for nomadic Arabic tribes

Love at First Sight

In the beginning verses of this delightful book of the Bible, we are introduced to three main "characters": Solomon, his bride, and a chorus who interjects comments.

Solomon's fiancée was eager to marry her beloved, Solomon, because she loved him so much. Though she is not named, she reveals much about herself. She is dark-skinned from working in the family vineyard or caring for the flocks. This young bride feels self-conscious. Because of her attention to her work, she has neglected her own "vineyard": her appearance. But Solomon doesn't mind and gives her unconditional love and acceptance.

She, in turn, compliments him on the integrity of his "name," in other words, who he is in his character. She considers him an honest, just, and good person. Those qualities are attractive to her, both emotionally and sexually.

What Others are Saying:

Bill and Pam Farrel and Jim and Sally Conway: Solomon realized his young wife was insecure in her looks because she was tanned from the hard work of watching sheep in the fields. The women in Solomon's court were very light-skinned because they had been sheltered from the sun. The young wife also felt insecure about her station in life and her simple background. Solomon picked up on the anxieties of his wife and did two very specific things. First, he used language to build up her self-esteem, especially in the area of her beauty. Then he went out of his way to set up a lavish and very special setting for their intimate times together.[2]

___

Gary Smalley: What Solomon's wife is telling us is a truth about marital passion. The more purified my character, the more attractive I am to my spouse—and the more responsive she'll be to me as a result. Time and again I've seen this principle working in the relationships of people—for good or for bad.[3]

Solomon and his bride, the Shulammite, may be one of the most celebrated romantic couples of history and literature. Her name is never given yet she steals the heart of a mighty and wise king. Some commentators believe that she may have been his first "true" love. His other wives and concubines may have been the result of political arrangements. Solomon and his beloved met when he visited his royal vineyards where she was working. She is called a shepherdess by some commentators. Others believe she worked in the vineyards of Shunem, a farming community about sixty miles north of Jerusalem. After seeing her there, he couldn't forget her and later returned, disguised as a shepherd in order to court her. What better Hollywood plot is there than that? Disguised as a commoner, he woos a working gal. After a whirlwind courtship and wedding, she becomes a queen. No wonder this book of romance, retreat, and restored love is cherished by so many.

   Their devotion to each other was not perfect, for they, like all lovers, went through disillusionment and discouragement. This actuality makes their story even more compelling. What happens to Solomon's dark-skinned beauty at the end of his life is untold. We learn only that his foreign wives and concubines woo him away from his worship of Jehovah. Their example should remind us to keep our love alive through all the years God gives us as a couple.

Solomon was a wonderful fiancé because he wooed the Shulammite with lots of attention. The Shulammite knew well her future husband's scent. He evidently used lots of aftershave! Staying in love has a lot to do with the senses. The wise spouse will continue "romancing" his or her mate through cleanliness and care of appearance.

Couples in the Bible

☞ **Check It Out:**

Song of Songs 1–8

___

KEY POINT

Romance isn't just for the season of courting; it's a marriage-long goal.

Think about It

> **Song of Songs 2:1–7** *Beloved:* I am a rose of Sharon, a lily of the valleys. *Lover:* Like a lily among thorns is my darling among the maidens. *Beloved:* Like an apple tree among the trees of the forest is my lover among the young men. I delight to sit in his shade, and his fruit is sweet to my taste. He has taken me to the banquet hall, and his banner over me is love. Strengthen me with raisins, refresh me with apples, for I am faint with love. His left arm is under my head, and his right arm embraces me. Daughters of Jerusalem, I charge you by the gazelles and by the does of the field: Do not arouse or awaken love until it so desires.

Sweet Talkin' Will Get You Everything

The Shulammite woman, the "Beloved," was a little insecure about the great king's love. After all, he was admired by all the beautiful women of the courts, even women from distant nations, like the <u>Queen of Sheba</u>. Solomon's bride called herself merely a "lily of the valley" which was a common but beautiful flower in Israel (see illustration, page 233). But Solomon wouldn't hear of such nonsense and replied that she was like a lily in comparison to the "thorns" of his court and other women he knew. He valued her more than all others.

Such affirming praise made the bride even more appreciative of him, and she praised him. She loved him because of these things:

- He protected her like a leafy tree on a hot day. He was strong and had the power to take care of her.

- He proclaimed his love of her to others. He wasn't ashamed to let others know he had found the love of his life.

- He proved he was a man who knew how to treat her with tenderness and affection—the qualities women value most.

- He prevented them from getting too intimate before their wedding. She could trust him to do what was best for her and their relationship.

GO TO:

1 Kings 10:1
(Queen of Sheba)

What Others are Saying:

Ed Wheat and Gloria Okes Perkins: Husband, one sentence of criticism directed at your wife in any area may well drive away the desire she would otherwise feel that day. On the other hand, one sentence of praise and approval is going to do wonders for her and for your sense of closeness in the sexual relationship.[4]

Lily of Palestine

The lily of Palestine was often found growing among the wheat and cornfields. They had pink, purple, or blackish-violet flowers. Their stems, when dried, were suitable for fuel in the Israelite ovens.

Gary Smalley: To most women, sex is much more than just an independent physical act. It's the culmination of a day filled with security, conversation, emotional and romantic experiences, and then, if all is right, sex. For the average man, you can reverse the order—or just skip everything that comes before sex![5]

What Others are Saying:

KEY POINT

Praising a spouse is like putting fuel on the fire of passion.

Marriage God's Way—A wise husband or wife will express "I love you" every day and through tender displays indicate to others that "this is my beloved and I am his (or hers)." Expressing love in public, through affection and kindness, fosters security because others can see "this couple is solid."

> **Song of Songs 3:1–4** All night long on my bed I looked for the one my heart loves; I looked for him but did not find him. I will get up now and go about the city, through its streets and squares; I will search for the one my heart loves. So I looked for him but did not find him. The watchmen found me as they made their rounds in the city. "Have you seen the one my heart loves?" Scarcely had I passed them when I found the one my heart loves. I held him and would not let him go till I had brought him to my mother's house, to the room of the one who conceived me.

Love Means Never Wanting to Be Separated

The Shulammite woman had a nightmare that she was separated from Solomon, and it was very frightening to her. In her dream, she searched frantically for Solomon all over the city and finally found him. What relief! She didn't want to let him go again.

Gary Smalley: Being "one flesh" in a marriage is a wonderful gift of a happy marriage. But it's only one part of a successful relationship. Security, meaningful communication, emotional and romantic times . . . and physical intimacy go together like pieces of a puzzle to make a nearly complete picture of a fulfilling relationship.[6]

Marriage God's Way—The Shulammite woman showed by her dream that she would do anything to be with Solomon and take care of him. An attitude of such selflessness is the cornerstone of a good marriage and preparation for a good sexual relationship. The best kind of "lovemaking" is the kind that wants to please the other person. When someone is similarly unselfish, he or she is invariably just as pleased as the spouse is.

The bride wants to cling to Solomon and in a healthy relationship there's nothing wrong with that. However, if it is taken to extremes, it can turn into jealousy and an unhealthy dependence. A solid marriage is where two individuals are strong alone and yet relate to each other with balanced dependence. Each one can enjoy separate activities without feeling anxious or jealous.

HONEYMOON FUN

Song of Songs 3:6–11 Who is this coming up from the desert like a column of smoke, perfumed with myrrh and incense made from all the spices of the merchant? Look! It is Solomon's carriage, escorted by sixty warriors, the noblest of Israel, all of them wearing the sword, all experienced in battle, each with his sword at his side, prepared for the terrors of the night. King Solomon made for himself the carriage; he made it of wood from Lebanon. Its posts he made of silver, its base of gold. Its seat was upholstered with purple, its interior lovingly inlaid by the daughters of Jerusalem. Come out, you daughters of Zion, and look at King Solomon wearing the crown, the crown with which his mother crowned him on the day of his wedding, the day his heart rejoiced.

Talk about a Walk Down the Aisle!

Solomon arrives in high splendor to take his bride to their wedding feast. It is obvious to the Shulammite that she is important to her future husband. Solomon has spared nothing in the lavish procession to the wedding feast, which traditionally lasted seven days.

The procession, including friends of the bride and bridegroom, was protected by sixty of Solomon's valiant warriors. Myrrh and incense created a column of smoke visible from a distance to safeguard against bandits.

Solomon communicated to his bride her importance by providing an elaborate and beautiful carriage. His mother, <u>Bathsheba</u>, contributed to the festivities by giving Solomon a crown, which many commentators believe indicated happiness rather than royalty.

 **GO TO:**

2 Samuel 12:24 (Bathsheba)

John Trent: Solomon and his bride enjoyed just being together, praising each other, looking into each other's eyes, kissing, and caressing. If a spouse only feels that she's being reached for for "one thing," it can bring a hesitant or rejecting response—not a willingness to let the other person near. Like we saw on Solomon's wedding night, enjoy the whole "feast" of physical interaction that God endorses.[7]

What Others are Saying:

Marriage is highly valued by God but belittled by society at large. Couples live together without being married, and our culture no longer considers it detrimental. Yet, the procession and all the trimmings of this royal marriage indicate the importance of the wedding and marriage. Regardless of what a couple plans for their wedding, God wants it to be as significant as the lifelong commitment they are making before him.

WARNING

Solomon brought along plenty of protection for the wedding procession and that can be compared to the financial protection a husband should provide for his bride. He should be concerned about meeting the needs for shelter and food for his family because the Bible says, *"If anyone does not provide for his relatives, and especially for his immediate family, he has denied the faith and is worse than an unbeliever"* (1 Timothy 5:8).

Think about It

> **Song of Songs 4:6–7** Until the day breaks and the shadows flee, I will go to the mountain of myrrh and to the hill of incense. All beautiful you are, my darling; there is no flaw in you.

The Windows Get Fogged Up

During the wedding night, the newly married couple enjoyed each other, and Solomon was very verbal about how much he loved his bride and her delightful body. He expressed his love for his bride in the most creative ways. He called her beautiful and referred to her hair, teeth, lips, temples, neck, and breasts. He used the most artistic metaphors to describe how much he appreciated her beauty, referring to doves, goats, sheep, ribbon, fruit, warrior's shields, and gazelle fawns.

Solomon declared his gratitude that she was a virgin and that she was assertive in their lovemaking. They both delighted in enjoying the other's body and felt satisfied when their intercourse was completed.

What Others are Saying:

John Trent: Did you know that in terms of sexual hormones, they are at their *peak* with most people when they wake up? As an experiment, why not lock your bedroom door before you go to sleep and set the alarm clock early to enjoy a time of intimacy when you're more rested and relaxed? Whether it's picking a "less stressed" time or just lowering the level of stress in our lives, both can add greatly to sexual intimacy.[8]

Marriage God's Way—There is no shyness about sexuality between Solomon and his bride. God's Word reveals his perspective of sexual union and enjoyment. He's all for it! Sex was designed by God to strengthen marriages through delighting in each other's bodies.

REMEMBER THIS

Solomon freely and vividly points out the things he loves about his wife. His expression of love and gratitude is a lesson for every husband and wife about the importance of focusing on the positives. The Shulammite's body most likely wasn't perfect, but Solomon didn't focus on any negatives, only the positives. A couple's love life will improve when they do likewise.

Sally and Danny still laugh when they think of their early years as a married couple and about their sexual habits. Sally was so shy she didn't want Danny to see her before she got into bed. The lights had to be turned off, and they could only make love at night. The daytime would be too revealing. If Danny tried to whisper sweet nothings while they made love, it was just too embarrassing for Sally, who had been raised in a family where sex was not discussed.

Those are all laughable memories sixteen years later. Now Sally loves their sex life. One of the important contributions to Sally's change of perspective was when they began reading the Song of Songs aloud to each other. Putting sex in the framework of God's Word helped Sally see it as an important and valuable gift from God.

Now Sally and Danny enjoy sex on any day that starts with a "T": Tuesday, Thursday, Tunday, Taturday, and Today and Tomorrow; plus, any time of the day—morning, afternoon, or night. Danny has Mondays off and the kids are in school, so that's their time to enjoy "afternoon delight." Sally loves to talk with Danny about their sexual encounters. She realizes that it prepares her to enjoy Danny's selfless love-making. They know they've both come a long way!

TAKE IT FROM THEM

ROMANCE, TAKE TWO

> **Song of Songs 5:2–8** *Beloved:* I slept but my heart was awake. Listen! My lover is knocking: "Open to me, my sister, my darling, my dove, my flawless one. My head is drenched with dew, my hair with the dampness of the night." I have taken off my robe—must I put it on again? I have washed my feet—must I soil them again? My lover thrust his hand through the latch-opening; my heart began to pound for him. I arose to open for my lover, and my hands dripped with myrrh, my fingers with flowing myrrh, on the handles of the lock. I opened for my lover, but my lover had left; he was gone. My heart sank at his departure. I looked for him but did not find him. I called him but he did not answer. The watchmen found me as they made their rounds in the city. They beat me, they bruised me; they took away my cloak, those watchmen of the walls! O daughters of Jerusalem, I charge you—if you find my lover, what will you tell him? Tell him I am faint with love.

Not Now, I've Got a Headache!

Solomon and his wife experienced the indifference that can plague any marriage. Solomon's wife had a dream that symbolized the separation between her and Solomon. He tried to reach her, but she refused his request for admittance, giving some flimsy excuses.

Suddenly, she realized she wanted to welcome him but found him gone. The fact that the watchmen abused her as she searched for Solomon could indicate that she blamed herself for the indifference and emotional separation between them. She felt she deserved the consequences for her unloving choices.

For the husband's part in the problem, Solomon may have been spending a lot of time "at work" and not enough appropriate time with her. Maybe her dream indicated her resentment for not getting the attention she deserved.

KEY POINT

Make sex a high priority for the health of your marriage.

Bill and Pam Farrel: Men rarely confide how much they love it when their wives miss them sexually and are willing to be playful and pursue them. Most often, when a wife has lost the passion for her husband, the simplest solution is for her to slow down and think about her husband's positive attributes—and then let him know she wants him. In focusing on the good characteristics of her husband, sexual assertiveness rises up naturally, rather than by some stilted imitation or Hollywood-type acting.[9]

REMEMBER THIS

☞ **GO TO:**

Ephesians 4:31 (anger)

Proverbs 21:19 (nagging)

Think about It

Insensitivity to our spouse's needs, especially sexually, can be detrimental to a happy relationship. It's easy to let love-making become an inconvenience, but making sex a high priority is worth the effort. Couples who plan time away from children and work responsibilities are ensuring their marriage against the attacks of Satan who wants to destroy marriage.

Indifference is a two-way street; both a husband and wife contribute. When one person in the marriage begins to withdraw, the other can easily become bitter, showing <u>anger</u> or <u>nagging</u>. That doesn't draw the spouse closer, though, it just drives him or her away, producing a downward spiral into disillusionment and misunderstandings. If couples can identify the cycle early, they can take constructive and loving steps to communicate their needs more carefully and clearly.

> **Song of Songs 5:10–16** *Beloved:* My lover is radiant and ruddy, outstanding among ten thousand. His head is purest gold; his hair is wavy and black as a raven. His eyes are like doves by the water streams, washed in milk, mounted like jewels. His cheeks are like beds of spice yielding perfume. His lips are like lilies dripping with myrrh. His arms are rods of gold set with **chrysolite**. His body is like polished ivory decorated with sapphires. His legs are pillars of marble set on bases of pure gold. His appearance is like Lebanon, choice as its cedars. His mouth is sweetness itself; he is altogether lovely. This is my lover, this my friend, O daughters of Jerusalem.

chrysolite: a gem like topaz

Positive Focus

In this wonderful description of Solomon, the Shulammite beautifully depicted the wonders of her lover's body. In a creative way, this adoring wife communicated these things:

- He was handsome.
- His hair was as abundant as the value of gold.
- His eyes were peaceful and gentle like doves.
- His cheeks and lips were delightful and attractive.
- His body was chiseled with strong muscles.
- He was tall like <u>cedars</u>.
- He kissed very romantically.

Most importantly, she called him her lover and her friend—the greatest compliment a spouse can give.

☞ **GO TO:**

Psalm 29:5 (cedars)

Willard F. Harley Jr.: I have counseled hundreds, if not thousands, of women who thought they would never have sexual feelings toward their husband again, only to discover these feelings returning with greater strength than they'd ever known. What changed? Did they have to develop a new attitude about sex? No. In most cases the only change was in the husband, who learned how to stop hurting the wife and started meeting her emotional needs.[10]

What Others are Saying:

☞ GO TO:

Philippians 4:8 (positive)

2 Corinthians 10:5 (training)

Marriage God's Way—Solomon's wife restored the closeness of her marriage with Solomon by focusing on the positive things about him. She dwelt on things that were lovely and concentrated on what was positive. Training the mind to think with affirmation and encouragement is a daily choice but pleasing to God who admonishes us to do that very thing.

Think about It

Especially for a woman, interest in sexual activity has a lot to do with her brain. If she is distracted by the kids or work problems, she hasn't taken the time to think about making love that night. If her husband makes the suggestion, it's most likely a totally new thought—and her body isn't prepared to respond. By preparing her mind to consider a sexual encounter, she prepares her body and will be more responsive. That's what Solomon's wife did. She thought of all the different ways her husband was physically and sexually attractive and that restored her ardor for him.

A husband can help by taking a real interest in his wife, by asking about her day and about how she feels—in areas other than the bedroom. If she feels overwhelmed by pressures at home, a loving husband can pitch in to help bring things under control. If she feels pressure at work, a husband can provide a sympathetic ear and a good back rub.

REMEMBER
THIS

The best marriage is made up of two best friends. Without friendship, a marriage is a dull relationship. A friendship between a husband and wife can be gained through having fun together, staying positive about the other's weaknesses, believing "different isn't necessarily wrong," and finding things in common that they can enjoy together.

My Other Sex Organ Is My Brain

She Says . . .

KATHY: Over the years I had learned to highly value Larry and our sexual relationship, but at times, I found it hard to desire sex because of life's pressures and distractions. I was tired at the end of the day or something Larry did would become a source of irritation. Or the children needed me or I had other, more important, things to do. Lovemaking wasn't the highest priority.

I began writing a Bible study called *Romantic Love: My Father's Gift* based on the Song of Songs. For almost two months, I daily studied the love story of Solomon and the Shulammite. I came to fully realize how much God valued the sexual relationship as a way for couples to express and increase their love. Concentrating on Solomon's tasteful but explicit expressions of love and sex stirred my brain, emotions, and body. Day after day, I couldn't wait for Larry to get home from work. I was impassioned with desire for lovemaking and couldn't get enough.

As never before, I realized that the most important sexual organ is my brain. By priming the pump of desire in my mind, I overcame my lack of interest. It proved to me that I needed to prepare myself for our sexual encounters with plenty of thought—which would turn into desire.

LARRY: I thought I'd died and gone to heaven.

He Says . . .

> **Song of Songs 7:1–9a** How beautiful your sandaled feet, O prince's daughter! Your graceful legs are like jewels, the work of a craftsman's hands. Your navel is a rounded goblet that never lacks blended wine. Your waist is a mound of wheat encircled by lilies. Your breasts are like two fawns, twins of a gazelle. Your neck is like an ivory tower. Your eyes are the pools of **Heshbon** by the gate of Bath Rabbim. Your nose is like the tower of Lebanon looking toward Damascus. Your head crowns you like Mount Carmel. Your hair is like royal tapestry; the king is held captive by its tresses. How beautiful you are and how pleasing, O love, with your delights! Your stature is like that of the palm, and your breasts like clusters of fruit. I said, "I will climb the palm tree; I will take hold of its fruit." May your breasts be like the clusters of the vine, the fragrance of your breath like apples, and your mouth like the best wine.

☞ **GO TO:**

Numbers 21:25 (Heshbon)

Heshbon: *a Moabite city famous for water reservoirs*

Now It's His Turn

In chapters 6 and 7, Solomon focuses on the wonderful things he loves about his wife. It may be that he was gazing at her as she danced. He focused on her feet, legs, navel, waist, breasts, neck, eyes, nose, head, and hair. Each of his descriptions referred to beauty from nature or their geographical area. For instance, when he wrote, "Your head crowns you like Mount Carmel," he was referring to a mountain range that was considered to be among

KEY POINT

Be creatively positive in sensitively describing what you like about your spouse.

the most beautiful in that area, rich with green plants and trees. Although we might not use such a description for our spouse, Solomon meant it as a compliment. After watching his Shulammite wife, Solomon could restrain himself no longer and vowed to "climb" and "take hold" of his wife's lovely body—like climbing a palm tree to pick the dates from a date-palm tree.

What Others are Saying:

Bill and Pam Farrel: The reference to her breasts can be better understood by knowing more about gazelles. They are delicate animals, soft to touch and two-toned in color, a very white and a darker brown. They are frolicsome and playful, yet graceful and quiet. They were also served to kings as delicacies. With this in mind, Solomon was probably delighting in touching and kissing while he admired.[11]

Kevin Leman: Men need to hear from their wives that they are on the right track. It's too easy for us to try to continue a sexual relationship without any words. Rather than be a flaw-picker or completely silent in bed, try reinforcing in a positive and loving way those things that are going on that are exciting and pleasurable. Men and women both have a need to know that they are attractive, prized, and special.[12]

WARNING

There can be lots of misunderstanding and hurt, if a husband and wife don't communicate sensitively in ways that the spouse can appreciate. A husband can say something that a male friend would consider a compliment but his wife would think of as a cut. Male and female gender differences can divide and conquer best friends within marriage. We must each be sensitive to what the other person values.

SECURITY IN MATURITY

> **Song of Songs 7:10–13** I belong to my lover, and his desire is for me. Come, my lover, let us go to the countryside, let us spend the night in the villages. Let us go early to the vineyards to see if the vines have budded, if their blossoms have opened, and if the pomegranates are in bloom—there I will give you my love. The man-

> drakes send out their fragrance, and at our door is every delicacy, both new and old, that I have stored up for you, my lover.

Come Away

Solomon's wife was assertively suggesting that they get away from the busy city so they could enjoy each other's company and lovemaking. She referred to <u>mandrakes</u>, a plant that was used for fertility. Maybe she wanted to become pregnant.

☞ **GO TO:**

Genesis 30:14–15 (mandrakes)

John Trent: Solomon's wife called upon him to "go out into the country" for a respite. I believe every couple (my wife and I included) should get away twice a year to renew and enrich their relationship. It's the best way to escape the breakneck pace of modern life that takes an incredible toll on relationships.[13]

What Others are Saying:

Think about It

This wise wife knew the value of initiating sexual activity between her husband and herself. A husband with a sexually assertive wife is a blessed man. A man will usually feel most loved and desired when his wife initiates sex.

She is also wise in realizing that time away from the demanding pressures and busyness of life can make sexual love blossom and become more **ardent**. The couple who gets away to concentrate on themselves and especially their lovemaking will be stronger and more committed to each other. An emotionally mature couple recognizes the need to escape from stress and to focus on their spouse. A change of scene can spark desire.

ardent: enthusiastic

> **Song of Songs 8:6–7** Place me like a <u>seal</u> over your heart, like a seal on your arm; for love is as strong as death, its jealousy unyielding as the grave. It burns like blazing fire, like a mighty flame. Many waters cannot quench love; rivers cannot wash it away. If one were to give all the wealth of his house for love, it would be utterly scorned.

☞ **GO TO:**

2 Corinthians 1:22 (seal)

Mature Bonds

In the concluding verses of Song of Songs, Solomon and his wife expressed the value of mature love. There was a security between them expressed through their commitment of unending love and complete sharing.

They referred to their love as a "seal." The seal was like a signet ring used to indicate ownership and protection, just as the Holy Spirit is God's <u>seal</u> upon a believer's heart.

☞ **GO TO:**

Ephesians 1:13 (seal)

Statements as powerful as the description of love mentioned in 1 Corinthians 13 were given about the nature of love. The writer says that love has the following traits:

- It is strong as death in that it can't be resisted at times. Hopefully, every married person's love will stay that strong, even in the midst of difficult circumstances or disillusionment.

- Like jealousy, it is often as cruel as the grave. Here "jealousy" refers to a protective love and "cruel" can be translated as "hard" or "unyielding." Therefore, a good kind of love wants only the best for the other person and will do anything to provide that for him or her.

- It burns like the flame of a blazing fire. Some commentators believe that the formation of the Hebrew words refers to God's name, thus saying God inspires the flames of love within those relationships that he establishes. It would be his desire that such relationships never grow cold.

- It is so unquenchable that many waters can't wash it away. Love can't be drowned, no matter how many troubled waters wash over it.

- It is worth more than great wealth. Trying to buy it at any price is foolish because it can't be purchased at any cost.

KEY POINT

Sex can get even better in the latter years.

What Others are Saying:

Ed Young: There is no truth to the notion that as couples age they get more "spiritual" and therefore are able to lay aside all sexual desires. Physical love should increase and improve, becoming more beautiful and more fulfilling with age. Instead of becoming routine or boring, married lovemaking can become more open and creative and satisfying as two partners age. That is part of God's plan.[14]

REMEMBER THIS

As a couple ages, their love doesn't need to diminish, nor does their sexual enthusiasm need to grow cold. Sex is enjoyed by many into their elderly years. Illness can become an obstacle, but with good health, a couple can enjoy sex. The longer a couple is happily married the more they find that their physical love is secure. They enjoy more complete openness and are totally comfortable with one another's bodies and sexual likes and dislikes.

Think about It

Human love is never perfect, but the love described by Solomon and his wife is worth seeking. Although we can never expect our spouse to be perfect, we can enjoy God's perfect love for us. First John 4:16–18 tells us, *"And so we know and rely on the love God has for us. God is love. Whoever lives in love lives in God, and God in him. In this way, love is made complete among us so that we will have confidence on the day of judgment, because in this world we are like him. There is no fear in love. But perfect love drives out fear, because fear has to do with punishment. The one who fears is not made perfect in love."* The greater our love grows over the years, the more we are expressing God's kind of love, and the less fear there will be in our marriage relationship. When we know our spouse wants the best for us, we will increasingly trust him or her. Such mature love takes time to develop and is a wonderful goal.

STUDY QUESTIONS

1. Why did Solomon's bride feel insecure about his love?
2. How did the bride express her appreciation of Solomon's love?
3. How did the bride know that she was missing Solomon more than she realized?
4. How does Solomon show his love in their wedding procession?
5. How does Solomon put his bride at ease on their wedding night?
6. What does the bride say when she doesn't want to respond to Solomon's sexual overture?
7. How does the bride get back in the mood for sex?
8. What does the bride wisely want in order to avoid distraction and have a fulfilling sexual experience?

CHAPTER WRAP-UP

- Falling in love is lots of fun, and yet it has its elements of insecurity. The bride of Song of Songs felt insecure. Solomon showed her in practical and sensitive ways that he valued her and considered her beautiful. She, in turn, complimented him. Couples need to remember to be creative in the way they talk to each other.

- Solomon demonstrated his great love for his bride in the wedding procession by being extravagant. When men and women put forth their best efforts for their wedding and their lifelong relationship, they communicate how important their mate is to them—and that pays dividends of love and sexual satisfaction. Whether it's on their wedding night or years later, every couple needs to show gratitude for their mate's body and attempts to meet their sexual needs. Even advice about pleasing each other should be done gently and without frustration or disgust.

- Every marriage will encounter sexual challenges, and that was true for Solomon and his bride. Initially she rebuffed his sexual advances but after contemplation, expressed her desire for sex. Although no couple will have a mutual desire to make love every time one of them suggests it, they both need to be sensitive to the other's needs and make every effort to cooperate. Getting in the mood for sex can be done best by concentrating on what we like best about our spouse.

- Just as the bride and Solomon choose to make their sexual relationship a high priority by getting away by themselves, every couple can benefit from leaving work and children behind and being by themselves for a while.

KATHY & LARRY'S  BOOKSHELF

Kathy and Larry's favorite books about fulfilling sexual intimacy:

- *Sex Begins in the Kitchen*, Kevin Leman, Regal Books. Renewing emotional and physical intimacy in marriage.
- *A Gift for All Ages*, Clifford and Joyce Penner, Word Books. A family handbook on sexuality.
- *The Gift of Sex*, Clifford and Joyce Penner, Word Books. Encouragement for a fulfilling sexual experience.
- *The Romance Factor*, Alan Loy McGinnis, Harper and Row. Put romance back into your marriage.

Part Four

HURDLES OF HONEYHOOD

REVEREND FUN

"Just look at this mess, Adam! . . . Why do you always have to track mud all over creation?"

16 MONEY MATTERS

Here We Go

For married couples, finances can be a sore spot in their relationship, whether they have little or much. Our attitudes are ground zero for this problem.

The abundance we possess today exceeds anything our parents dreamed possible. Still, many of us are worried about the future. Materialism drives us away from dependence on God and erodes our contentment in God's provision. Our spiritual lives will be richer when we surrender to the Lord the title to our 401K, our savings, and our retirement plan. We must resign as owners of our possessions and become **stewards**.

stewards: *managers of others' property*

FINANCIAL PRESSURE POINTS

> **Psalm 24:1–2** The earth is the Lord's, and everything in it, the world, and all who live in it; for he founded it upon the seas and established it upon the waters.

God's Title and Deed

The issue of ownership always challenges the believer. Who really owns all we possess? Can we claim ownership of our possessions when we claim God as our Lord? The Bible tells us everything <u>belongs</u> to God. There isn't anything that isn't under his sovereign <u>control</u> and power. Many people, especially unbelievers, may think they are in the driver's seat when it comes to their <u>wealth</u> or possessions, but the truth is, God is holding the steering wheel.

☞ **GO TO:**

Job 41:11 (belongs)

1 Chronicles 29:12 (control)

Haggai 2:8 (wealth)

WARNING ▶

☞ GO TO:

Luke 12:33 (hearts)

Proverbs 15:6 (greedy)

Colossians 3:23
(work hard)

1 Timothy 5:8 (provide)

Edwin Louis Cole: Money itself is amoral. The morality of money is given to it by the nature of the man with it. Money can be a blessing or cursing, depending on its use. Man determines the meaning of money.[1]

Our spiritual vision is hindered when our hearts focus on the things we possess. Our financial condition, the investments we make, or the jobs we achieve can turn our <u>hearts</u> away from true worship of God. Rather than basing our value upon material goods or status, we need to focus on a sovereign God who is in control of our lives. When we think we are responsible for creating wealth or even providing for our needs, we can easily become anxious, discontent, ungrateful, and <u>greedy</u>. That doesn't mean we should not <u>work hard</u> or <u>provide</u> for our family. We should. But if we are thinking we can force wealth to happen apart from God's empowerment, we are fooling ourselves. That's saying we are in control, instead of our financial condition belonging to God.

SHOW ME THE MONEY

Luke 16:10–12 Whoever can be trusted with very little can also be trusted with much, and whoever is dishonest with very little will also be dishonest with much. So if you have not been trustworthy in handling worldly wealth, who will trust you with true riches? And if you have not been trustworthy with someone else's property, who will give you property of your own?

Dollar Wise

Jesus makes two important points about money in the verses above. First, money should be used for God's kingdom to spread the Gospel and to help others. Eternal benefits will spring from earthly investments in God's work when we resist making money our servant.

Second, Jesus suggests that the real test of our integrity is measured by how we handle the small details of managing money (see WBFW, pages 138–140). Do we have a budget? Do we spend on impulse? Do we balance our checkbook so we don't overdraw our account? Often we justify poor conduct by rationalizing the little things. Jesus tells us to be honest and <u>faithful</u>. When we demonstrate our worthiness, greater things like *"true riches"* result. This refers to the kingdom's spiritual riches that we will receive.

☞ **GO TO:**

1 Corinthians 4:2 (faithful)

Larry Burkett: If God is the owner and we are simply his stewards, we need only to be concerned with how best to manage his possessions. In so doing, money is no longer our possession, it is God's possession, which we hold in trust. But because we will have to give an account of how well we managed his material goods and possessions, we must to the best of our ability use the money as we feel he would use it and in a manner that is pleasing to Him.[2]

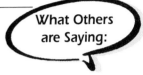

KEY POINT

Everything belongs to and is controlled by the Lord.

Edwin Louis Cole: The deceitfulness of riches is the fact that when you think you have enough, it never is, and you need still more. There is never any contentment. Contentment is necessary because it eliminates monetary deception.[3]

Many of us are begging God for more money or more things and we promise, "I'll be a good steward when you give them to me, Lord." But have we proven ourselves faithful in the little he's already given us? Have we tithed faithfully? Have we been generous with what we have? Maybe we are grumbling about what we have and think that we'll be <u>content</u> when we have more. God's financial philosophy is, "Be faithful in the small things, and I'll bless you with more."

True contentment doesn't come from having more, but from appreciating whatever we do have. We all know those who have more than us and yet they aren't happy. And we all know those who have less than us but they are satisfied. The apostle Paul wrote, *"I know what it is to be in need, and I know what it is to have plenty. I have learned the secret of being content in any and every situation, whether well fed or hungry, whether living in plenty or in want"* (Philippians 4:12). We can take great comfort in knowing even the spiritually strong apostle Paul had to learn the state of contentment, and we will too as we affirm that God will give us everything we truly <u>need</u>—because he's the generous owner of it all. Being a good manager means we're content with whatever he chooses to provide.

REMEMBER THIS

☞ **GO TO:**

Ecclesiastes 5:10 (content)

Philippians 4:19 (need)

KEY POINT

Happiness is something that happens to you. Contentment is something you choose.

Think about It

Solomon wrote Proverbs and, as a very wealthy man, had a lot to say about being a good manager rather than an owner.

Proverbs	Attitudes of a Manager
11:24–25	I can be generous because it brings joy.
11:28	I won't trust riches because they are fleeting.
14:31	I will be generous to the needy because it brings glory to God.
16:8	Riches from honest work are valuable, but money from injustice is unsatisfying.
22:1	My good reputation is more valuable than being dishonest.
22:2	Having the respect of others is more valuable than great wealth.
22:4	Humility is a wonderful accompaniment of wealth.
23:4	Too much work, even with riches, isn't beneficial.

> **Matthew 25:14, 19** Again, [the kingdom of God] will be like a man going on a journey, who called his servants and entrusted his property to them. . . . After a long time the master of those servants returned and settled accounts with them.

Time, Talent, and Treasure

parable: story

talents: form of money

☞ **GO TO:**

1 Kings 9:14 (talents)

Jesus shared a **parable** about a true steward who was faithful. An employer gave money, called **talents**, to three of his employees before leaving on a trip. One received five talents, the second received two talents, and another received one talent. When the master returned, he found that the first man had doubled his money, as had the second. The third had hidden the money in the ground and reported that he had been afraid to do anything with it because his employer was a hard taskmaster.

Two of the servants were faithful in caring for the master's money and shared a financial reward. They also shared in the master's joy. The third servant wanted to keep the money for himself in case his master did not return. He hid the money because he had no sense of duty to care for another's property. He had no sense of honor to protect the trust that was given him by the master. The master called that employee lazy and wicked and gave his talent to the first man.

God clearly expects us to share in his joy as we faithfully serve him with our time, talent, and treasure.

Jesus is not emphasizing the amount that was given back to the master, otherwise he would have also been unhappy with the second man who didn't return as much as the first. He is stressing the importance of being faithful with whatever we have—even if it's one or two talents.

Talents in the day of Jesus were the heavy coins. They were most likely a lump of silver in the form of thick round discs or rings weighing three thousand shekels, about $180 today. Of course, Jesus was referring to money in this parable, but the principles Jesus is sharing about stewardship apply to our time, possessions, and gifts and abilities also.

Larry Burkett: A steward manages someone else's property. We manage that which belongs to God but that he has provided for us as individuals. So, it's important to learn to be a good manager of our abundance from God. The Bible is full of God's financial priorities and investment philosophies, and they are just as applicable for managing a household as they are for operating a large business or maintaining a sound national economy.[4]

Marriage God's Way—One of the servants in the parable was afraid of the owner, and that's why he hid his talent rather than investing it. If we are afraid of God or consider him unfair like the servant did, we also will resist direction or not trust his plan for us. We'll squander the opportunities he gives us because we're afraid he won't be pleased with our results. If we are certain he is leading, we should trust him enough to boldly take advantage of the financial opportunities he gives us.

DEBT LAND

> **Proverbs 22:7** The rich rule over the poor, and the borrower is servant to the lender.

Debt Service

God wants us to only be a servant to him. When we are in debt, we become a servant of others. We are obligated to please our benefactor rather than seeking God's will for our money and our lives. Neither is God's will for us to rule over people to whom we

KEY POINT

The rich rule, but the borrower serves.

have loaned money. Pride or greed can cause us to become insensitive to those who don't have as much as we do. Both positions are dishonoring to God because everything belongs to him.

What Others are Saying:

Ron Blue: We need to have a clear understanding of debt:

- Debt is not a sin! The Bible discourages the use of debt, but does not prohibit it.
- Debt is never the real problem; it is only symptomatic of the real problem—greed, self-indulgence, impatience, fear, poor self-image, lack of self-worth, lack of self-discipline, and perhaps many others.
- Debt can be defined many ways. I define it as "any money owed to anyone for anything."[5]

More Will Than Wallet

He Says . . .

LARRY: Kathy and I have been very conservative in acquiring debt throughout our marriage. When we made home improvements or purchased a car, we waited until we could pay cash or pay off the debt early. I enjoyed the freedom of being debt free, especially after we were able to pay off our house five years before the end of the mortgage. Because our money was not dedicated to monthly payments, we could provide for others in need and were blessed to be able to do so. It often happened that when Kathy and I would hear of a financial need, we would look at each other and smile, knowing we would contribute. We could give because we were free from debt.

She Says . . .

KATHY: Over the thirty years of our marriage, we can look back and see God's faithfulness because we've tried to have the attitude that we are steward/managers, not owners of our money and possessions. If we were financially strapped, God often provided in special ways. Many years ago we had a bill due and no extra money for it. We wondered how God would pay his bill. We knew we'd managed our money as well as possible, but there was still a need for more. Without warning, we heard a crash in our backyard and discovered that a car had careened into our block wall. The driver's insurance company sent someone to estimate replacement cost, and we got a check. Our neighbor did the repair work at almost half the normal cost—and we used the extra to pay the other bill. God certainly is trustworthy—and creative.

As Christians, the <u>payment</u> of debt is the honoring of a vow. It is clear throughout Scripture that we must always <u>pay back</u> any debt we take on. This principle of honesty is strongly supported because God labels those who fail to repay debt as "<u>wicked</u>" people, pledging that they won't <u>prosper</u>. Our testimony is compromised, and the kingdom is hurt when we fail to meet our obligations.

REMEMBER THIS

☞ **GO TO:**

Psalm 37:21 (payment)

Ron Blue: There are four questions to ask [before borrowing]:

1. Does it make sense?
2. Do my spouse and I have unity about taking on this debt?
3. Do I have the spiritual peace of mind or freedom to enter into this debt?
4. What personal goals and values am I meeting with this debt that can be met *no* other way?[6]

What Others are Saying:

☞ **GO TO:**

Romans 13:7–8 (pay back)

Proverbs 29:7 (wicked)

Proverbs 11:24 (prosper)

Dan and Robin have spent the last several years tithing and getting out of debt because they wanted to help others. In January of 1999, they felt motivated by God to tithe on the gross amount of their income and to give their van to a couple without a safe car. Dan and Robin went from a two-car to a one-car family, but they looked at God's covenant promises instead of circumstances and trusted God to take care of them. That year Robin unexpectedly received $15,000 from a former employer. They were able to pay off their 30-year mortgage early and give ten times their usual donation to God's work. When Dan was unemployed for four months, God blessed them with the gift of a new Mercedes.

TAKE IT FROM THEM

TITHING MAKES A TREASURE

Malachi 3:10–12 "Bring the whole **tithe** into the storehouse, that there may be food in my house. Test me in this," says the Lord Almighty, "and see if I will not throw open the floodgates of heaven and pour out so much blessing that you will not have room enough for it. I will prevent pests from devouring your crops, and the vines in your fields will not cast their fruit," says the Lord Almighty. "Then all the nations will call you blessed, for yours will be a delightful land," says the Lord Almighty.

tithe: 10 percent gift

A Flood of Blessings

☞ **GO TO:**

Deuteronomy 28:1–14
(promised)

1 Kings 7:51;
Nehemiah 10:38
(tithed grain)

In the Old Testament, God <u>promised</u> that if his people obeyed him, he would bless them abundantly, but if they disobeyed him, they would experience disasters. One of the ways they were to obey him was in bringing 10 percent of their produce to the Temple to be dedicated to God. The storehouse refers to the special room(s) within the Temple where the tithed grain to be used by the priests was kept. The importance of this <u>tithed grain</u> was not so much that it provided for the priests who didn't have their own land, but it symbolized the people's declaration that God had provided the grain in the first place. In a tangible way, they were saying, "We are the stewards, Lord. You are the owner and provider." When the people acknowledged God's Lordship and gave their tithe, they prospered. But when they neglected to give God the credit he was due, their nation plunged into problems. God kept his word—for good or bad.

What Others are Saying:

Edwin Louis Cole: Men cannot outgive God. God will be debtor to no man. Giving to God without his giving more in return would essentially make God a debtor to the giver. That can't be done. Of course, God doesn't always give back the way men do.[7]

Larry Burkett: One of the first standards of giving found in the Bible is the tithe, a word which means "tenth." Abraham tithed in Genesis 14 after returning from the daring rescue of his nephew Lot from four enemy kings. He encountered the priest Melchizedek and voluntarily surrendered to him one-tenth of all the spoils he had taken from his enemies. It's often said that the tithe is Old Testament "legalism," but Abraham tithed some 430 years before the Law was given to Moses.[8]

Marriage God's Way—Although there is no command in the New Testament of an exact tithe, 10 percent of our income, there is a general principle of giving a portion to God. The apostle Paul wrote to the Corinthians, *"Now about the collection for God's people: Do what I told the Galatian churches to do. On the first day of every week, each one of you should set aside a sum of money in keeping with his income, saving it up, so that when I come no collections will have to be made"* (1 Corinthians 16:1–2). Therefore, it's common among believers to give a portion, usually 10 percent, toward the local church and other Christian ministries or mission-aries (see WBFW, pages 141–144).

God is more interested in our attitude of giving than the amount we give. Here are some principles from Scripture for giving in a way that pleases God.

REMEMBER THIS

Passage	Principle for Giving
2 Corinthians 9:6	If we give generously, God will bless us generously.
2 Corinthians 9:7	God wants us to give cheerfully without feeling pressured about how much to give.
2 Corinthians 9:8	Giving sets us free to receive all the good things that God intends for us.
Galatians 6:6	We need to support those who minister to us.
Galatians 6:7	Whatever we reap, we will sow.
Galatians 6:9	Even though we may not reap immediately, God will bring good eventually and in his good time.
Galatians 6:10	We should give to everyone, but especially believers.
Philippians 4:18	When we give to God's work, especially when it's a sacrificial gift, God is very pleased.
Philippians 4:19	God promises to meet the needs of his children, when they obey him.

In the early days of the Body of Christ everyone sold their personal assets, giving them to the church leaders for the provision of all. Ananias and his wife, Sapphira, agreed to sell some land and donate proceeds to the church. They told the leaders that they were donating the full selling price. They thought this would bring them great respect and power within the church. But the Holy Spirit revealed to the apostle Peter that they hadn't given all the money—only a portion. When Peter gave each of them an opportunity to tell the truth, they continued their original lie. As a result, God struck both of them dead. Their error was not in keeping some of the money, but in their deceit and selfish motive in giving. They weren't giving sacrificially and cheerfully as a means of blessing others but as a way to bring esteem to themselves.

Couples in the Bible

☞ **Check It Out:**

Acts 5:1–11

KEY POINT

The more we give to
God, the more we will
be blessed.

Several years ago, Dan and Bonnie started a new business. Often, after paying expenses, there wasn't enough money for Dan and his partners to get paychecks. Although Dan and Bonnie had very little money, they continued to give a tenth to their church as a tithe. They saw that God did supply all their needs. He provided for physical, emotional, and spiritual needs. On one cold November day, Bonnie headed for the mailbox, lamenting that she needed to buy a coat for their one-year-old son. She hated to spend the money because he would outgrow it so quickly. Unexpectedly, there was a package in the mailbox. It was a winter coat, a ten-month-belated baby gift from a former student of Bonnie's! Dan and Bonnie's attitude toward "needing" things changed. Less was suddenly better, healthier, and more fun. Spiritually, they were united as a family with a mission of frugality, and they were more grateful for all they actually had.

STUDY QUESTIONS

1. Although some people think they are the captains of their own financial ships, who is really in charge and why?
2. How does God determine the level of surrender and obedience in a couple's heart regarding finances?
3. What was Jesus trying to teach when he shared the parable of the talents?
4. Why is being in debt a disadvantage?
5. Why does God want couples to tithe their income?

CHAPTER WRAP-UP

- God created everything, and therefore he is sovereignly in control, especially of the finances each couple has. Although some people think they own what they have, they are actually only managers, because God is the owner. Christian couples need to surrender control over their finances and trust that God will provide for their needs.

- It is essential that couples be faithful in handling whatever God gives them. If they are trustworthy with small things and honest in their financial dealings, God may decide to give them even more to manage.

- Although being in debt is not a sin, it's not the best way to manage the finances God has given. Couples need to work hard at getting out of debt, so they can fully obey God's directions, rather than being concerned about indebtedness to someone.

- Tithing is God's way of helping couples remember that he is the owner of everything they have and if they will obey him, he will bless them abundantly. He wants them to give generously and cheerfully because that shows they trust him.

KATHY & LARRY'S  BOOKSHELF

Kathy and Larry's favorite books about finances:

- *Master Your Money,* Ron Blue, Thomas Nelson Publishers. A step-by-step plan for financial freedom.
- *Communication, Sex & Money,* Edwin Louis Cole, Honor Books. The three most common obstacles that challenge relationships between men and women.
- *Giving and Tithing,* Larry Burkett, Moody Press. How to have a godly attitude in your giving.
- *Investing for the Future,* Larry Burkett, Chariot Victor. A guide to understanding the economy and other financial challenges.
- *Debt-Free Living,* Larry Burkett, Moody Press. How to get out of debt and stay out.

17 THE TRAINING ROOM OF TROUBLE

WHAT'S IN THIS CHAPTER

- Great Expectations
- God Makes Good
- Gain from Pain

Here We Go

We each got married looking toward a bright and happy future, and we certainly don't like the idea of bad things happening. But by the end of our lives many traumatic events will have occurred. Each incident can make us bitter and resentful, or it can draw us closer to God. Trials can divide our marriage or be the mortar that brings us together. None of us is exempt.

How will we cope? With God's help, we can make the best of difficulties and even see God's hand of blessing.

GREAT EXPECTATIONS

> **1 Peter 4:12–13** Dear friends, do not be surprised at the painful trial you are suffering, as though something strange were happening to you. But rejoice that you participate in the sufferings of Christ, so that you may be overjoyed when his glory is revealed.

The Trouble with Troubles

Troubles. Trials. Traumas. Tragedies. They are to be expected. The apostle Peter wrote that no one should be surprised by what they experience. Instead they should <u>rejoice</u>. That's not easy, but it may help to know that we're all in this together. Every person and every couple in the Bible experienced trauma of some kind. Every person on earth has experienced and is experiencing trauma of

☞ **GO TO:**

James 1:2 (rejoice)

some kind! It's the way of the world. Only in heaven will we be without trouble. We know this intellectually, but our hearts keep saying, "I don't deserve this! I shouldn't have to go through this! Why *me*?"

What Others are Saying:

Frank and Mary Alice Minirth: Crises arise in every passage of marriage, of course, but they seem to have more profound implications as you grow older. A crisis you could bounce back from in youth becomes overwhelming in later age. You have little time left of your life to repair some crises—financial setback, personal problems, career difficulties. Therefore, confronting crisis becomes a major task. Handling it well is an important goal.[1]

REMEMBER THIS

Some people became Christians because they were promised a rosy life if they committed themselves to Christ. But Jesus never promised that rose garden. From the very beginning he said, *"I have told you these things, so that in me you may have peace. In this world you will have trouble. But take heart! I have overcome the world"* (John 16:33). It's inaccurate and wrong to encourage a person to become a Christian with the promise of a perfect life on earth. If anything, becoming a Christian makes a person more open to <u>attacks</u> from Satan. Satan doesn't like a person committing to God, and he'll do everything he can to try to stop their growth.

☞ **GO TO:**

2 Corinthians 2:11 (attacks)

> **Job 2:7–10** So Satan went out from the presence of the Lord and afflicted Job with painful sores from the soles of his feet to the top of his head. Then Job took a piece of broken pottery and scraped himself with it as he sat among the ashes. His wife said to him, "Are you still holding on to your integrity? Curse God and die!" He replied, "You are talking like a foolish woman. Shall we accept good from God, and not trouble?" In all this, Job did not sin in what he said.

KEY POINT

Bad things *will* happen; don't be surprised. God isn't.

Stop the Blame Game

Job wasn't surprised that these terrible things were happening to him, and he didn't blame anyone—not even God. However, Job's wife had difficulty coping and blamed God. She was so traumatized that she couldn't believe anything good could come from their losses and pain. Having completely lost hope, she believed that death was the only remedy to Job's suffering—both physically and emotionally.

Blaming begins when we assume that someone else or someone's sin is responsible for our misfortune. Yes, sin is often the cause of pain in this world, but not always. Job's troubles arose when Satan identified him as a righteous man. According to Satan, Job only trusted in God because God had blessed him. Yet, the Bible identifies Job as a man *"blameless and upright; he feared God and shunned evil"* (Job 1:1). Job might not have suffered such difficulty were he not a man who trusted God.

What Others are Saying:

Frank and Mary Alice Minirth: The blamer is projecting all his or her own pains and frustrations onto the projection screen of the spouse. It's easy to do and far less painful than admitting pain and frustration. By focusing all that blame on someone else, the blamer escapes the white heat of the spotlight on his or her own actions.[2]

Marriage God's Way—When bad things happen, it's easiest to blame the person closest to us: our spouse. Job's wife looked around at the loss of her ten children, the destruction of her possessions, and the physical pain of her husband and took out her own pain on him. Instead of focusing on how she could cope, she played the blame game, diverting her energies and attention onto Job and God.

During tough times, a spouse needs to first focus on how he or she can respond in a godly manner, and then help their spouse work through the trouble. Avoid comments like, "If only you hadn't . . ." or "I know why this has happened, it's because you. . . ." Blaming only concentrates on the trouble, instead of dealing with it in a constructive way.

When our lives aren't <u>trouble-free</u> as expected, we tend to place blame. We may think that affixing the blame will bring a solution and even protection from future problems. But life happens! And with it comes <u>trouble</u>.

☞ **GO TO:**

2 Corinthians 7:4 (trouble-free)

Job 5:7 (trouble)

WARNING

 **TAKE IT FROM THEM**

Chuck and Marita have been married for sixteen years. As part of her job, Marita travels a great deal. On her return flights after several stressful days away, Marita likes to read a light, Christian romance novel and envision how Chuck will romantically greet her at the airport. Of course, the reality is that when she arrives home after a late flight Chuck is already in bed asleep. Hardly the romantic scene Marita had painted in her mind.

Marita really wanted that romance novel scene when she arrived home on their sixteenth anniversary. So she took action rather than risking disappointment and the temptation to blame. Before she returned, she had flowers sent to Chuck's office with a card that said "Happy Anniversary! Hurry home!" She had the flowers delivered in the morning—in case he forgot what day it was.

Marita made sure she arrived home before Chuck got off work so that she could prepare a lovely dinner. When she went into the bedroom, she found something small and black hanging on their four-poster bed with an anniversary card. He hadn't forgotten after all! She relaxed in a bubble bath, put on her present, and lit candles in the bedroom. As time neared for Chuck to arrive, she crawled up on the bed and read her romance novel. When the dogs barked, heralding his arrival, Marita placed herself artfully across the bed. Marita knew she would be able to write a new chapter in a romance novel with the results of her efforts—and she wasn't disappointed!

Wisely, Marita realized that instead of being angry with Chuck for not living out her romance novel images, she could help them happen. She created the same atmosphere for her next return trip and enjoyed the same wonderful results. Even though neither of them likes her being away, they both love the reunions upon coming home. Instead of blaming and pouting, Marita took positive action.

> **Ecclesiastes 3:1** There is a time for everything, and a season for every activity under heaven.

Count on Change

All of life involves change and different seasons of life. We become surprised by trouble when we're experiencing a pleasant time of life and believe that everything will stay the same. But the only thing that won't change is change. Just when you think, "Yes, I like this stage of life, I'd like to keep it just as it is," things will change. We must be prepared. We can enjoy that stage, but don't depend on it for contentment or happiness.

Bill Blackburn: Each new stage of a family brings its particular agenda, its particular problems and joys. Each is different and requires a new set of skills. And each new stage brings its own particular set of stresses.[3]

Only God <u>doesn't change</u> and knowing that gives us security in life. Circumstances change. People change. But God never changes. We must focus on him, not life or our spouse for our security and joy.

GOD MAKES GOOD

> **Romans 8:28–31** And we know that in all things God works for the good of those who love him, who have been <u>called</u> according to his <u>purpose</u>. For those God <u>foreknew</u> he also <u>predestined</u> to be **conformed** to the likeness of his Son, that he might be the <u>firstborn</u> among many brothers. And those he predestined, he also called; those he called, he also **justified**; those he justified, he also glorified. What, then, shall we say in response to this? If God is for us, who can be against us?

Diamonds Come from Coal

None of us eagerly asks for, prays for, or welcomes trauma or troubles that marriage brings. It's against our very nature. At a heart level, we want everything to go smoothly, especially in our marriage. We marry in order to gain happiness, not to be bombarded by life's troubles. So endorsing an attitude that welcomes trauma can be hard.

Yet, God wants us to have the attitude expressed by Paul. God allows only that which he uses for good. The primary "good" that he desires is that we become more like Jesus—that we become conformed to the image of his Son. The disappointments and difficulties of marriage have a way of smoothing our rough spots

KEY POINT

People and life change, but God is always the same: holy and good.

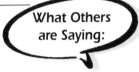
What Others are Saying:

REMEMBER THIS

☞ **GO TO:**

Malachi 3:6;
    Hebrews 13:8
    (doesn't change)

☞ **GO TO:**

Romans 1:7 (called)

2 Corinthians 5:5
    (purpose)

Romans 11:2
    (foreknew)

Ephesians 1:5
    (predestined)

Colossians 1:15
    (firstborn)

Romans 3:24 (justified)

conformed: molded

justified: made free of sin in God's eyes

KEY POINT

God sovereignly causes everything to work for good as we let him be in charge of our lives.

and conforming us to Christ's image. We must choose whether we will become more like Jesus, or the opposite, more selfish.

If we choose love and are willing to be conformed to Christ, we'll reap the benefits of making the right choice. We'll discover by experience that God isn't opposing us by allowing trouble—he actually *can* bring benefits from it.

What Others are Saying:

Kay Arthur: If you are experiencing neither happiness nor fulfillment in your marriage, or any other relationship, and you have done all you should have in light of his Word, rest! God will see to it that even your heartbreak will work together for good. So bow your knee and say, "I will give Thee thanks forever, because thou has done *it*, and I will wait on Thy name, for *it* is good" (Psalm 52:9). Because he is God, he will satisfy your thirsty soul, he will fill your hungry soul with what is good (Psalm 107:9).[4]

TAKE IT FROM THEM

Charlene and Greg don't always agree on how to handle their daughter's rebellion, but they realize that their marriage is more important than the difficulty Kristen is experiencing. Their twenty-one-year-old daughter is on drugs and pregnant out of wedlock. Initially Charlene and Greg were frantic, trying to convince Kristen she needed their help, although she believed she didn't. They fought about how to respond. Charlene wanted to rescue Kristen from the streets and make sure she couldn't use drugs. Greg thought she should suffer the consequences of her actions, and they became increasingly divided.

Eventually they realized that Satan was attacking their family and creating a distance between them, along with destroying Kristen's life. They made a new commitment to work through the problem together, making sure that Kristen's problems weren't the only thing on which they focused. They made plans to have fun together, sometimes not even talking about Kristen at those times. They realized that they were both right—and wrong—in how they wanted to handle the situation. Rather than an either-or approach, a balance was needed. They reached out to Kristen by taking her food and blankets but didn't force her off the streets. Although they don't know how this situation will end, they won't let Satan destroy their marriage. What they do know is that their marriage is stronger because of this difficulty.

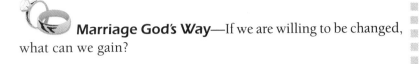 **Marriage God's Way**—If we are willing to be changed, what can we gain?

Reference	Verse and Benefit
John 15:2	***Verse:*** "He cuts off every branch in me that bears no fruit, while every branch that does bear fruit he prunes so that it will be even more fruitful." ***Benefit:*** Ability to handle life and help others come to know Jesus through our witness—to be more accepting of the weaknesses of our spouse because love will permeate our reactions.
Romans 5:3–4	***Verse:*** "Not only so, but we also rejoice in our sufferings, because we know that suffering produces perseverance; perseverance, character; and character, hope." ***Benefit:*** Perseverance, character, and hope—the ability to cope with life or our spouse's inability to completely meet our needs.
1 Peter 1:6–7	***Verse:*** "In this you greatly rejoice, though now for a little while you may have had to suffer grief in all kinds of trials. These have come so that your faith—of greater worth than <u>gold</u>, which perishes even though refined by fire—may be proved genuine and may result in praise, glory and honor when Jesus Christ is revealed." ***Benefit:*** Stronger faith and stronger witness of God in our lives—the belief that God will help us handle anything and that our strong marriage will be an example to others.
James 1:2–4	***Verse:*** "Consider it pure joy, my brothers, whenever you face trials of many kinds, because you know that the testing of your faith develops perseverance. Perseverance must finish its work so that you may be mature and complete, not lacking anything." ***Benefit:*** Perseverance, maturity, and emotional wholeness—the ability to avoid becoming easily upset, depressed, and irritated because we're committed to our spouse until death.

Jeremiah 29:11–14 "For I know the plans I have for you," declares the Lord, "plans to prosper you and not to harm you, plans to give you hope and a future. Then you will call upon me and come and pray to me, and I will listen to you. You will seek me and find me when you seek me with all your heart. I will be found by you," declares the Lord, "and will bring you back from captivity. I will gather you from all the nations and places where I have banished you," declares the Lord, "and will bring you back to the place from which I carried you into exile."

KEY POINT

Difficulties and problems result in good character and the ability to handle life.

KEY POINT

Everything he brings into our lives is meant to make us depend upon him more.

☞ **GO TO:**

Philippians 3:10 (know)

What Others
are Saying:

☞ **GO TO:**

Isaiah 45:7 (creates)

Think about It

☞ **GO TO:**

Psalm 105:28; Isaiah
31:2; 42:15 (creator)

REMEMBER THIS

☞ **GO TO:**

James 1:14 (arises)

Romans 3:23 (heart)

Closer, Still Closer

Trauma and trouble are intended by God to force us to seek him. God doesn't want to harm us by allowing difficulties, but to help us understand that he wants the best for us: prosperity, hope, and a future. If we're far from God, he allows problems to turn our attention to him. When we're overwhelmed, we'll realize how much we need him. When we think we can't <u>know</u> him any more than we do, we'll draw even closer. God wants us to find him and know him better. He doesn't distance himself; he stands ready to receive us when we call.

Kay Arthur: This eternal God who <u>creates</u> prosperity and adversity has neither beginning nor end. He is not confined to the finiteness of time or to man's reckoning of time. He is never early, never late, and never in a hurry. And whether we understand our immediate circumstances or not, he views our whole earthly pilgrimage through the eyes of eternity. He knows where we are going. He knows how it all fits together. He knows how to extract maximum good and maximum glory out of every situation, *no matter what!*[5]

Many people have difficulty believing God can be the <u>creator</u> of bad things that happen in our lives, yet Scripture tells us that he is. We may identify unfortunate or painful events as "evil," and believe that God can't create evil, but the difficulties we face aren't "evil" in themselves. They are neither right nor wrong—our response to them makes us judge them as evil or good. All circumstances are meant by God to be useful in our lives. If we look at them as God's resource for drawing us to him, we won't consider them "evil," but "good."

God's sovereignty doesn't mean that man isn't accountable for his own evil actions and choices. God doesn't force anyone to do evil; it <u>arises</u> out of our own selfishness and sinfulness. God knows what is in the <u>heart</u> of man, but he doesn't make us respond with evilness.

Marriage God's Way—As a couple, we should look at each difficulty and ask, "How can this draw us closer to God?" Maybe it will force us to pray together more often. It may help us evaluate our ideas about God and change some of our misconceptions or identify poor choices. God desires that each couple seek his presence through their experiences—not be pushed away.

How Can Cancer Be Used for Good?

He Says . . .

LARRY: One December morning over ten years ago, I noticed a mole on my chest that had changed. I made a mental note to monitor it because a dear friend had recently died of melanoma, the most deadly form of skin cancer. Six months later fear gripped me when I realized I had forgotten to monitor the mole. Fear turned to dread when I noticed the mole was completely black. Something was very wrong.

My worst fears were confirmed after surgery. I had let malignant, invasive melanoma grow on my chest for over six months. After the cancerous mole was removed, the waiting game began. Would it reappear?

Suddenly, I couldn't spend enough time with Kathy. Walks, evenings out, and long talks in bed became the norm. Cancer changed our lifestyle. I was surprised that conversation and affection, normally a woman's needs, became priceless to me. I couldn't get enough time with Kathy.

She Says . . .

KATHY: We saw that God was using Larry's cancer positively in our marriage, but I couldn't understand how it could be used for good in our family. At that point, our fifteen-year-old daughter, Darcy, was rebelling and I feared that the danger to Larry's life would make her rebel completely. Would she run away? Would she start taking drugs? I questioned God's wisdom in allowing those two circumstances to happen simultaneously. We didn't need two intense stress factors—but we had them!

During Larry's medical trauma, we tried to no avail to reach out to Darcy. She was angry and yelled at us each evening before leaving with a boyfriend—someone she wasn't even supposed to be dating. When we tried again, she sat across from us, glaring, her arms folded, defying us to reach through her armor-plated soul.

Then, miraculously, Darcy began opening up to us about what

was bothering her, and we knew God had done something amazing. It wasn't until our conversation was concluded that we found out *how* he had done it. "I don't know why I've been talking with you like this," Darcy said, pausing. "But it's because Daddy has cancer."

We suddenly understood that the possibility of losing her father had cracked Darcy's rebellion and that God knew that timing those circumstances would bring good. The healing within our family began at that point, and we are grateful that Larry's melanoma never returned.

GAIN FROM PAIN

Malachi 2:10–16 Have we not all one Father? Did not one God create us? Why do we **profane** the <u>covenant</u> of our fathers by breaking faith with one another? Judah has broken faith. A **detestable** thing has been committed in Israel and in Jerusalem: Judah has **desecrated** the sanctuary the Lord loves, by marrying the daughter of a foreign god. As for the man who does this, whoever he may be, may the Lord cut him off from the tents of Jacob—even though he brings offerings to the Lord Almighty. Another thing you do: You flood the Lord's altar with tears. You weep and wail because he no longer pays attention to your offerings or accepts them with pleasure from your hands. You ask, "Why?" It is because the Lord is acting as the witness between you and the wife of your youth, because you have broken faith with her, though she is your partner, the wife of your marriage covenant. Has not [the Lord] made them one? In flesh and spirit they are his. And why one? Because he was seeking godly offspring. So guard yourself in your spirit, and do not break faith with the wife of your youth. "I hate divorce," says the Lord God of Israel, "and I hate a man's covering himself with violence as well as with his garment," says the Lord Almighty. So guard yourself in your spirit, and do not break faith.

profane: curse

detestable: disgusting

desecrated: destroyed

☞ **GO TO:**

Genesis 6:18 (covenant)

Draw Even Closer to Each Other

At the time of Malachi, the prophet, Jewish men had divorced their wives and married foreign women who didn't believe in Jehovah. God was disgusted with such behavior and caused the men to suffer consequences so they would return to him and obey his commands to restore and commit to the marriages with their Jewish wives.

David Augsburger: Life and growth should be **redundant** words, but observation of others and reflection on oneself reveals embarrassing periods of being stuck in routine. Growth and marriage should also be repetitive, but most marriages alternate quiet periods of stability with brief passages of change and maturation. Growth and change are not ends in themselves. In fact, growth for growth's sake is the philosophy of the cancer cell. The goal of growth is wholeness, completeness, maturity.[6]

What Others are Saying:

redundant: *repetitive*

Marriage God's Way—Some people never change without being forced. Likewise, some marriages will never change until they are pressed. God intends for each couple to use their difficulties to recommit to love and cherish each other. For those not following God's guidelines for marriage, he wants them to return to the commitment with their spouse.

God desires for each person to view their troubles like the Psalmist who wrote, *"Teach me knowledge and good judgment, for I believe in your commands. Before I was afflicted I went astray, but now I obey your word. . . . It was good for me to be afflicted so that I might learn your decrees"* (Psalm 119:66–67, 71).

There are more examples in the Bible of couples who didn't use their trials for growth than there are of those who did, yet we can learn from them all.

Abraham and Sarah: Abraham and Sarah seemed to grow closer over the years after facing infertility and the apparent delays in God's promises. Even though they made mistakes at times, they stayed faithful to each other in the long run.

Jacob and Rachel: Jacob and Rachel lacked the intimacy that God desired for them. Jacob adored Rachel, but Rachel never

Couples in the Bible

☞ **Check It Out:**

Genesis 11–25

☞ **Check It Out:**

Genesis 27–36

☞ **Check It Out:**

1 Samuel 1–2

☞ **Check It Out:**

2 Samuel 11:6–27

☞ **Check It Out:**

2 Samuel 12–13

☞ **Check It Out:**

Luke 1–3

expressed love or even favor for her husband. She was only interested in the competition between her and her sister, Leah, of having children. Rachel didn't learn from her difficulties and remained a depressed woman, focusing on the child, Joseph, that God eventually gave her. Her heart never enjoyed the love that Jacob had for her.

Hannah and Elkanah: In the beginning Hannah's initial infertility caused her to reject Elkanah's loving outreach. Yet, once she believed that God would grant her a child, she chose to trust him and become content (see WBFM, pages 49–52).

Uriah and Bathsheba: Uriah and Bathsheba evidently lacked good communication, and the challenges they faced increased their problems. When Bathsheba became pregnant by King David, instead of waiting to deal with her husband, she contacted David. David called Uriah back from battle, hoping he would sleep with his wife and thereby claim the child. Although Uriah chose to sleep on the street so as not to dishonor the sacrifices of his fellow soldiers, his lack of devotion was apparent when he didn't even contact Bathsheba. David's scheme thwarted, he returned Uriah to the battlefield with a death sentence and, after the customary grieving time, Bathsheba meekly became David's wife.

David and Bathsheba: The poor choices of David and Bathsheba caused them to face the trauma of their child's death and seemed to draw them closer together. Bathsheba seemed to have greater influence upon David than his many other wives. In later years when David faced death, he responded to Bathsheba's plea that their son, Solomon, become the king after David.

Joseph and Mary: Joseph and Mary faced the possibility of persecution together, and it solidified their commitment to God. When Mary, as a virgin, was pregnant, the law demanded she be stoned to death. Joseph stood by her (see GWLC, pages 20–21) and together, with their faith and confidence in God's guidance, they faced a disbelieving world.

Make a Fresh Commitment

God wanted the men in these biblical couples to make a fresh commitment to their wives. He desires for our trials and difficulties to create the same kind of fresh commitment between a husband and a wife. We will only be able to do that as we trust that God has something positive planned for the difficulty we are facing.

What Others are Saying:

Dan B. Allender and Tremper Longman III: Marriage requires a radical commitment to love our spouses as they are, while longing for them to become what they are not yet. Every marriage moves either toward enhancing one another's glory or toward degrading each other.[7]

Think about It

As you make this fresh commitment and work through the problems you're facing as a couple, share your feelings honestly. Do it in a loving manner, being aware that emotions fluctuate. Your feeling of anger or impatience may seem justified at the moment, but in time, it will change. Share your feelings, but be conscious of the fickleness of those emotions, which **vacillate**, especially in the face of crisis. Hurting your spouse by threatening, blaming, using harsh words, or criticizing won't solve anything. Avoid regret by thinking through what you want to say.

vacillate: *waver*

STUDY QUESTIONS

1. What attitude should we have about troubles?
2. What was Job's response to trials, and what was his wife's response?
3. What can we be certain of regarding change?
4. Why does God allow difficulties in our lives?
5. How does God bring good from our difficulties?
6. What does God want a couple to do when facing troubles?

CHAPTER WRAP-UP

- Although it's against our nature, we can actually rejoice as a couple about trials because we know that God will use them for our good—especially in our marriages. We can accomplish that by not blaming each other for our troubles and by understanding that trial doesn't necessarily stem from sin.

- God desires to bring good out of every situation we face, and as that happens we will grow closer to him. Along with the blessings of growth, we will also become more like Jesus because our character is being transformed.

- God hates divorce because he knows the pain and destruction it brings. He wants a couple to recommit themselves to each other over and over again—especially when they are facing hard times. Regardless of the feelings that a husband and wife each experience, they can make the loving—yet difficult—choice to stay strong in the midst of difficulties, growing closer together and closer to God.

KATHY & LARRY'S  BOOKSHELF

Kathy and Larry's favorite books about dealing with crisis:

- *The Making of a Marriage*, Thomas Nelson editors, Thomas Nelson Publishers. Everything you need to know to keep your relationship alive and healthy.

- *Walk This Way*, Tim Woodroof, NavPress. An interactive guide to following Jesus.

- *Lord, Only You Can Change Me*, Kay Arthur, Multnomah. A devotional study on character.

- *Spiritual Spandex for the Outstretched Soul*, Jeanne Zornes, Harold Shaw Publishers. Practical and inspirational ideas for reaching God's best.

18 THE GREENHOUSE OF MARRIAGE

Here We Go

The potential for a successful and satisfying marriage is within the "seed" of every marriage relationship. It takes hard work and lots of devotion to produce an environment or soil that will not only support the seed but provide it with the nutrients to make it sprout, grow, and flourish into a strong marriage that will give glory to God through its fruit.

Jesus told a parable about seeds and soil that we can apply to "growing" our marriage in spite of the traumas and trials that might assail our "sprouting" marriage. Satan will attempt to steal the seed of love. The shallowness of lack of commitment can starve it. A busy life can choke it, but through loving choices, a marriage can not only survive, but also thrive—and bear much fruit. We'll learn how that can happen in this chapter.

THE DEVIL'S PLAYBOOK

> **Matthew 13:1–4, 18–19** That same day Jesus went out of the house and sat by the lake. Such large crowds gathered around him that he got into a boat and sat in it, while all the people stood on the shore. Then he told them many things in **parables**, saying: "A farmer went out to sow his seed. As he was scattering the seed, some fell along the path, and the birds came and ate it up. . . . "Listen then to what the parable of the sower means: When anyone hears the message about the kingdom and does not understand it, the evil one comes and snatches away what was sown in his heart. This is the seed sown along the path."

parables: stories with hidden meanings

Satan's Seedy Business

Jesus wanted to communicate to his listeners the importance of their choices in making the kingdom of God important in their lives. He used the example and **metaphor** of a farmer sowing seed in a field. God is that farmer, sowing the seed of the good news about his Son, Jesus, who died for the sins of the world. The good news is heard by many kinds of people with different attitudes. They will receive the seed or reject it or allow things to take away the seed.

We can use the same metaphor to emphasize the "heart" conditions we might have to help the seed of our marriage flourish. Jesus mentions several things that can take away the effectiveness of the seed of the kingdom in people's hearts. Likewise, different trials, traumas, and situations can diminish our ability to make our marriage successful.

In Jesus' metaphor, the first thing that steals away the seed of the Gospel—the "good news"—is Satan, the "evil one." Satan doesn't want people to receive the seed of the good news, and he also doesn't want Christian marriages to succeed. Since God intended marriage to be an example of his unity with the church, when Christian marriages fail, Satan has been successful in diminishing the power of God's example of that unity. Satan tries to divide and destroy marriages in many different ways.

metaphor: figure of speech where one word stands for something else

KEY POINT

God sows the seed of the good news about Jesus in every heart, but that heart must be willing to receive it.

What Others are Saying:

Donald R. Harvey: Happy and fulfilling marriages are products of extreme efforts. They are desired, sought after, fought for, and planned. They never *just* happen. Couples frequently complain to me how their marriage *just* fell apart. Nothing *just* happens.[1]

WARNING

Satan's tactics in trying to divide husbands and wives against each other can come in many different forms:

- He can foster misunderstandings between spouses based upon erroneous assumptions, like "my husband can read my mind" or "my happiness is dependent upon my wife's behavior" or "my way is the only way," so that a husband or wife will concentrate on negative qualities in each other.

- He can remind a spouse of hurts and disappointments, making forgiveness difficult.

- He can give the impression that God can't forgive infidelity, making the sinning party feel condemned and hopeless.

- He can cause work or busyness, even in church involvement, to seem so attractive that spouses neglect each other.
- He can create the allusion that all our needs can be met through pornography, affairs, or other sinful activities that society considers acceptable—even helpful.

Marriage God's Way—In order to combat Satan's schemes to destroy marriage, we must work hard. Marriage requires effort and thought! We need to think through the destructive messages that Satan whispers in our ears and the subtle, ungodly ideas from the world. We have to make the difficult choices to forgive and be understanding of our spouse's inadequacies and weaknesses. If we are going to be successful in marriage, we must fight Satan by doing the following:

- Refusing to be deceived by ungodly ideas about marriage or to respond selfishly to our mate (2 Thessalonians 2:3)
- Understanding that we can be forgiven regardless of the sinful choices we've made against our marriage (1 John 1:9) and also forgiving our spouse for their harmful choices
- Walking in the power of the Holy Spirit so that we can resist our fleshly, selfish desires and urges (Galatians 5:17)
- Dressing our minds and souls with the armor of God that empowers and protects us with faith, truth, righteousness, and accurate thinking to reject Satan's false ideas (Ephesians 6:10–17)

James 4:7 says, *"Submit yourselves, then, to God. Resist the devil, and he will flee from you."* Resisting Satan can also take the form of verbally telling him to leave the area or situation. At those times we recognize his evil influence, we can say out loud, "Satan, I resist you in the name of Jesus. You will not have success in bringing evil into this circumstance. Get out of here!"

> ### KEY POINT
> Look out for Satan's efforts to steal the joy and strength from your marriage.

REMEMBER THIS

Attacks on Joint Ministry

LARRY: Kathy and I often speak on marriage at couples events and retreats. Days before a speaking engagement we pray for prepared hearts and open minds. Knowing our effectiveness is showcased through our love for each other, we also pray for our closeness. And we need it. It never fails that Kathy and I will start bickering with each other the day of the event, sometimes just hours before we are due to speak.

Kathy and I can anticipate and prepare for those challenges now. We have learned that couples who actively minister together—especially about marriage—will face Satan's attacks. Satan wants to shatter their oneness and unity, and undermine their confidence that God can use them.

KATHY: Even though we know Satan's attacks are bound to come, we often can't see through the smoke of our irritation to our enemy's schemes. Instead, I focus on Larry's failure to do things the way I think they should be done. Because of our different temperaments, we go into ministry differently. I want to keep our presentations the same. Larry wants to rewrite our talks a week before the event. I like to be at events extra early, but Larry doesn't mind if we arrive at a reasonable time. In each situation, it's easy for me to think Larry is trying to aggravate me, and I begin to look at him as the enemy.

The actual enemy, however, is Satan, who is trying to tear apart our unity. As soon as we stop concentrating on each other, recognize Satan's fingerprints on the conflict, and turn our eyes toward Jesus we get back on the right track. Remembering Ephesians 6:10–12 helps: *"Finally, be strong in the Lord and in his mighty power. Put on the full armor of God so that you can take your stand against the devil's schemes. For our struggle is not against flesh and blood, but against the **rulers**, against the **authorities**, against the **powers** of this dark world and against the spiritual forces of evil in the heavenly realms."*

rulers, authorities, powers: *all of Satan's evil helpers*

REJECTING SHALLOWNESS

> **Matthew 13:5–6, 20–21** Some fell on rocky places, where it did not have much soil. It sprang up quickly, because the soil was shallow. But when the sun came up, the plants were scorched, and they withered because they had no root. . . . The one who received the seed that fell on rocky places is the man who hears the word and at once receives it with joy. But since he has no root, he lasts only a short time. When trouble or persecution comes because of the word, he quickly falls away.

Hang On

Jesus talked about shallow soil. He meant some people hear about Jesus and his sacrificial death and quickly agree with the premise but don't make a true commitment. As soon as difficulties or persecution for being a Christian come, they think their decision is not worth the effort to maintain.

Marriage can be like that. We fall in love, and we "receive it with joy." We love being in love. But when the troubles assail us, we "fall out of love." We wonder if marriage is worth the effort. Troubles come in a variety of forms: our spouse may not look as attractive as when we were dating; he or she may now be sick or even disabled; we might have to care for family members or struggle with a wayward or seriously ill child; or our job may cause us to travel extensively or live apart from our husband or wife for a time.

KEY POINT

Stay committed and strong even in times of sickness or disability.

Regardless of the difficulty, it is up to us to accept the circumstances and our spouse. If we don't we are being shallow. In marriage, shallowness could be expressed as selfishness, anger, or unfaithfulness.

Joni Eareckson Tada: The neat thing about Ken is that he helps me look at my disability as an asset rather than a liability. We choose to believe that my disability will strengthen our sense of commitment. It will press us to be unified (sometimes whether we want to or not!) as we tackle problems together.[2]

What Others are Saying:

Think about It

☞ **GO TO:**

2 Corinthians 12:9
(surrendering)

camaraderie:
togetherness

You can deepen your marriage during trials by making wise choices. If your spouse is ill, consider creating greater depth in your marriage by doing the following:

- Praying for healing, yet allowing for God's glory. It's not always God's will to heal every illness, but if he allows the illness to continue, he promises to bring good from it (Romans 8:28).

- Surrendering your spouse to God's will. You cannot control the situation. Trying to do so could make you blame your spouse for being sick or make you become stressed over your need to be in charge. Instead, understand that only God is powerful enough to control the situation.

- Joining a support group. The **camaraderie** of others going through similar circumstances will strengthen you and fortify your commitment to your partner.

- Learning about the illness. Ignorance will only create fear and an inability to make wise choices. It's essential that patients take charge of their own health. If your spouse is ill and unmotivated to ask bold questions, then step in and love by taking charge. Doctors aren't gods; they aren't perfect nor do they have all the answers.

- Taking care of yourself. If you're not well, you can't care for your spouse. Find the help you need in order to have private time to replenish your own energy.

- Expressing your commitment to your ill spouse. An ill spouse may feel insecure about your loyalty and love. You can't tell them too often that you love them and will stay by their side.

- Discovering your spouse's true needs. Don't assume you know. Ask how you can best make them feel loved and comfortable.

- Preparing for the death of your spouse. It's not pleasant to think about or plan for, but it's necessary, even if your spouse isn't ill. Each spouse should know about insurance plan(s) and what agencies and services are available. Having a will is essential. Knowing what financial investments have been made will give peace to the spouse who will have to deal with them alone in the future.

For Dennis and Eva Marie, not dealing with an illness would be unusual. From their early marriage, Eva Marie battled illnesses that seemed unconnected. It wasn't until Eva Marie, a typical workaholic, took a nosedive physically that extensive tests were given and the couple learned that the illnesses were all connected. The greatest moment of fear came when, having lost twenty-one pounds in seventeen days, Eva Marie looked at Dennis and said, "I'm going to die . . . and they aren't going to know from what." Dennis didn't say anything, nor did he try to pacify her. He simply wrapped his arms around her and held her close. It was all Eva Marie needed to get through that night. She survived, and their marriage is stronger than ever.

TAKE IT FROM THEM

REFUSE TO BE USED

> **Matthew 13:7, 22** Other seed fell among thorns, which grew up and choked the plants. . . . The one who received the seed that fell among the thorns is the man who hears the word, but the worries of this life and the deceitfulness of wealth choke it, making it unfruitful.

Busy Bother

Jesus identified another cause of the good news about Jesus not being received: a person's heart soil being full of thorns. The seed landed on their consciousness but the busyness and concerns of life caused them to be too focused on making a living or being involved in activities.

The same thing can happen in marriage. The breadwinner of the family may spend so much time and energy earning a living that he or she doesn't have energy left to focus on building the relationship with the spouse. Even if husbands or wives don't work, they may get so involved in volunteer work or the children's activities that they fail to spend time on their spouse.

☞ **GO TO:**

Psalm 127:1–2 (labors)

Even church work and socials can become a hindrance to the marriage. "Working for the Lord" may seem noble, but if God's emphasis on marriage is neglected, our labors for the kingdom will be disgraced through an unhappy or failed marriage.

◄ **WARNING** 💣

Donald R. Harvey: Far too often, we have a heightened sense of attention for things that really deserve less priority in our lives. This is not to say that having concerns for the cares of this life are necessarily bad. However, when our concerns become excessive, our adversary subtly claims more and more of our energies. In a state of physical, mental, and emotional exhaustion, our marriages drift into bankruptcy.[3]

Think about It

Most of us have a hard time saying no to the many opportunities we are offered. There are a number of reasons why we say yes, even while wondering if we have the time or energy. Here are some of those reasons:

- Being asked to participate makes us feel needed and important. If we say no to the present opportunity, we may not get another chance to feed our craving to feel needed and important.

KEY POINT

Learn to say yes to only that which God desires for you and which will build up your marriage.

- We don't want to hurt someone's feelings. If we say no we risk rejection or disapproval. We want to make everyone happy, and we want everyone to like us!

- We don't want to appear to be less than a "super Christian." We fear that turning down an opportunity means we aren't spiritual enough to handle it. We could incorrectly think that if we are empowered by the Holy Spirit, we should be able to do everything asked of us.

- We see a need and think we are capable of doing a good job. Our perfectionism can compel us to say yes for fear that the job won't be done or won't be done perfectly!

- We don't want to miss out on interaction with the group. We want to be included in all the fun, and we fail to think about all the work involved.

- We are building a smoke screen of activity, so we don't have to face our problems. Busyness dulls the hurt and pain, so that we don't have to deal with challenges in our personal lives or our marriage. We think that what we don't acknowledge we won't have to change!

REMEMBER THIS

In order for us to make wise choices and avoid busyness that depletes the energy that should be spent on building our marriage, we can do the following:

- Learn humility. We are not God. We can't do everything. Even <u>Jesus</u> didn't meet all the needs of everyone around him while on earth.

- Reply promptly to a request, saying, "Thank you for thinking of me. I'll be glad to pray about it and get back to you." Don't feel obligated to make an immediate decision. Pray about it first, talk it over with your spouse, and give an answer later.

- <u>Count the cost</u> of supporting the project. Most of the time, involvement takes more time and energy than was originally described. Find out what is really involved before saying yes.

- Become secure enough not to say yes in order to feel needed, important, and valuable.

- Diminish perfectionistic thinking. Instead, allow others to participate and grow by delegating—even if it's not done as well as we might have done.

☞ **GO TO:**

Luke 5:15–16 (Jesus)

Luke 14:28 (count the cost)

Barbara and Orris know that what happens to one of them affects both of them. Recently, Barbara needed open heart surgery to repair her mitral valve. Orris said yes to his beloved wife and no to the needs of others by rearranging his work schedule and using vacation time to be with Barbara during appointments, tests, and surgery. He continued to faithfully minister to her during her recovery period. Orris and Barbara shared their fears during that frightening time and often prayed together. They held and encouraged each other. Orris continued to say yes to Barbara by helping with her personal care as well as doing practical chores. During those months, they fell even more in love and experienced a closer intimacy that came from saying no to that which would have made Barbara feel less important in their marriage.

TAKE IT FROM THEM

Galatians 6:2–5 Carry each other's burdens, and in this way you will fulfill the law of Christ. If anyone thinks he is something when he is nothing, he deceives himself. Each one should test his own actions. Then he can take pride in himself, without comparing himself to somebody else, for each one should carry his own load.

Burdens or Loads

We may find the above verses confusing. Are we supposed to help carry something or not? What's the difference between "burden" and "load"?

We can understand the disparity between "carry each other's burdens" with "carry his own load" by defining a "load" as those challenges which a person can take care of himself. If we step in to help such people, we are <u>rescuing</u> them from a task God wants them to depend upon him for. We will deprive them of the joy of growing closer to God as they seek him.

In contrast, "burdens" are the responsibilities or tasks that a person can't handle alone due to lack of adequate skills, emotional energy, or wisdom. They may not possess the faith or inner strength to depend upon God and will likely fail in their endeavor. Those are the people God wants us to help—not necessarily by doing everything for them, but by assisting them in making wise choices.

We hurt our marriage when we help others with loads. We may even hurt our marriage if we help carry too many burdens. And we can't help with others' burdens if we aren't doing a good job carrying our own loads. Asking for our spouse's advice before agreeing to help with another's burden is one way to prevent overcommitment.

☞ **GO TO:**

Proverbs 19:19
(rescuing)

What Others are Saying:

Bill and Lynne Hybels: When we do something we don't really want to do, when we say yes but we mean no, when we do things for people who are capable of and should be doing them for themselves, when we do more than our fair share when our help is requested, and when we fail to ask for what we want, need, and desire, we are involved in unhealthy caretaking, or rescuing.[4]

Marriage God's Way—Spreading ourselves too thin because we want to be of service to others can be detrimental to our marriage. Yet, it can be hard to know how much to help others when they are needy. Our neighbor might want help building a fence while our spouse is complaining that our own yard isn't cleaned up. Maybe a couple at church with a sick baby needs meals, but our husband wants to go away for the weekend. Maybe a friend who is having difficulties wants to talk on the phone every evening, but our husband, who is having trouble at work, really needs our attention. When we allow the needs of others to take **precedence** over the needs of our mate, we allow thorns to choke out the goodness and closeness in our marriage.

precedence: priority

The woman who seemingly did everything—the "Proverbs 31 Woman"—might appear to have ignored God's instructions for keeping the thorns of busyness out of her marriage. After all, she helped the poor, ran a business, cared for her family, directed her household help, sewed her own clothes, and so on. With no hint of stress, she always had a kind word on her tongue, spoke with wisdom, knew what to do in any situation, and encouraged everyone around her. She *did* it all. She *has* it all. She *was* it all. Yet, her efforts did not impair her marriage. Her husband adored her. She must have done something right in her marriage. He complimented her saying, *"Many women do noble things, but you surpass them all"* (Proverbs 31:29).

We can remember that this woman fulfilled her many activities over the span of her life. She didn't do everything all at one time. She said no to the things that weren't right for a particular stage of life and yes to the things that were. When a wife is likewise discerning, her husband will praise her also.

Couples in the Bible

☞ **Check It Out:**

Proverbs 31:10–33

Gene and Arlene have learned to recognize the true "burdens" of the other in their marriage of forty-three years. Gene is disabled, and Arlene is the breadwinner. When Arlene arrives home from a hectic day, Gene is ready for her attentiveness but recognizes her need for "alone time" before connecting with him again. She reads the mail and unwinds alone, then emerges refreshed for dinner and to meet his need for conversation. Gene, the "night" person, would prefer that she stay up late with him, but recognizes her need for an early 9:30 P.M. bedtime. For a time, he tried different ways to keep her up with him, but soon recognized her need for a good night's sleep to face the burdens of the workday. Now he cheerfully supports her early bedtime. They recognize that they are both working hard to make their marriage fruitful—even after forty-three years.

TAKE IT FROM THEM

MARITAL MIRACLE GROW

> **Matthew 13:8–9, 23** Still other seed fell on good soil, where it produced a crop—a hundred, sixty or thirty times what was sown. He who has ears, let him hear. . . . But the one who received the seed that fell on good soil is the man who hears the word and understands it. He produces a crop, yielding a hundred, sixty or thirty times what was sown.

Heart Harvest

Jesus explained in his parable of the soils that when the seed of the Gospel fell on good soil, there was a bountiful crop: sometimes one hundred, sixty, or thirty times more than the initial single seed. He then applied it to a man's heart that not only hears but also understands the importance of the good news that Jesus died for him. That man's faith matures, and he guides others into the kingdom of God. God desires this outcome for everyone.

Likewise, it is God's desire for every marriage to reach its full potential, producing one hundred times the fruit of enjoyment, encouragement, and enrichment. In the beginning, God provided <u>Adam and Eve</u> with everything they needed to enjoy each other. He blessed them and wanted them to appreciate the concept of marriage as he had created it.

Today, we can't expect trouble-free circumstances to surround our marriages because we live in a world that has sin, but God still wants husbands and wives to champion each other and represent him to a needy world.

☞ GO TO:

Genesis 1:27–28
(Adam and Eve)

What Others are Saying:

Gary Smalley: I believe the more we help others achieve their full potential in life, the closer we are to maturity. Demonstrating a selfless desire for others to gain is the strongest base for building lasting relationships. How can you go wrong when you develop a love that is primarily concerned with discovering your wife's specific needs and looking for creative ways to meet them?[5]

REMEMBER THIS

We can enjoy the hundredfold fruit of a good and godly marriage as we prepare the soil of our marriage to be rich with ingredients that

- identify Satan's schemes to destroy us,
- make a commitment to love and support regardless of the troubles, and
- eliminate the thorns of busyness that choke out love and intimacy.

As a result, we'll have a marriage that shows, not perfectly of course, that we desire to meet each other's needs and that we love each other.

Think about It

Each couple's interpretation of a hundredfold marriage will be different, depending on their definition of love and the circumstances of their relationship. Comparing our own marriage with another serves no purpose and can actually harm our relationship. Measure the bountifulness of your marriage only with your own marriage relationship. Rejoice in the good, and seek to understand what's harmful in order to correct it.

A bountiful marriage is ultimately tested when one partner dies. The fruitful marriage that Sylvia and Jack had developed was the foundation for facing their last days together with courage. Jack was terminally ill, but Sylvia and Jack wanted to make the most of their time left together. The challenge was to exchange their restless, sorrowful energy for an awareness of God's peace and comfort.

*TAKE IT
FROM THEM*

They focused on creating memories of peaceful times— memories that would last long after Jack's death. Sylvia recorded many such moments in her journal. She took photographs of Jack taking pictures of their new granddaughter, enjoying baby robins in a nest over the kitchen window, and laughing at a view through their grandson's kaleidoscope. Sylvia and Jack thought of other ways as well:

- Tape-record the ill person's recitation of a favorite poem or hymn.
- Discuss favorite Bible verses with the ill partner and videotape the discussion.
- Label a journal "The Living-On Book," and fill it with stories of peaceful times.

These ideas for focused memories may work well during any time of recuperation from illness, surgery, or accidents. They remind the sick person that their bodily health is not their spiritual health.

Jack is gone now, but Sylvia continues to appreciate the fruits of their bountiful marriage even as she grieves.

STUDY QUESTIONS

1. In Jesus' parable about the soils, what happened to the seed that fell along the path and how does that relate to marriage?
2. How does shallow soil compare to marriage?
3. What happens to the seed among thorns, and how does that apply to marriage?
4. How can a husband or wife know how to respond to other people's requests for help?
5. The good soil produced what kind of results from the seed, and how does that relate to marriage?

- Jesus' parable of the different soils can be applied to marriage. Birds eating the seeds that fall on the path can be related to Satan trying to steal the seed of a loving marriage by bringing unhappiness through misunderstandings, anger, and selfishness. To keep our marriage strong, we need to identify Satan's attacks and fight against him with God's armor and truth.

- A marriage can become shallow when trials surface and the spouses have trouble coping. They disregard their decision to love and only look out for their own interests. Such a couple grows distant, unable to share at a deep emotional level with each other. To prevent that, we need to meet our spouse's needs, especially during illness, and commit to loving no matter what.

- Many husbands and wives forget or neglect to focus on their marriage's growth because they are too busy making a living or with other activities. A successful marriage takes time and the work of selflessness. A couple needs to make sure that nothing, even church involvement, chokes out their commitment to each other by learning to say no to that which God doesn't require. They can confidently say yes to whatever God directs, knowing it won't detract from their relationship.

- God wants every couple to experience the good soil of love in their marriage. He wants them to bear an abundant crop of love, selflessness, devotion, and faithfulness—until death separates them.

KATHY & LARRY'S  BOOKSHELF

Kathy and Larry's favorite books about strengthening marriage:

- *The Proverbial Woman*, Robin Chaddock, WinePress Publishing. Reflections on Proverbs 31 for being a wise woman in a wild world.

- *Husbands and Wives*, Howard and Jeanne Hendricks, eds., Victor Books.

- *As for Me and My House*, Walter Wangerin Jr., Thomas Nelson Publishers. Crafting your marriage to last.

19 MIDLIFE MAYHEM

Here We Go

No husband or wife intends for it to happen. No one plans to go through it. Each one actually thinks that the transitions of midlife won't turn into a midlife crisis. But it can happen to anyone. Feelings may range from mild discontentment and dissatisfaction to deep fear and depression. Behavior may even take a turn into adultery or other sins.

Each husband and wife needs to prepare for the potential difficulties of midlife. Even if that stage doesn't include a "crisis," there are always transitions with which to deal. We can take steps and precautions to avoid a difficult passage. The Word of God is relevant—even for midlife mayhem.

ACCEPTING THE INEVITABLE

> **Ecclesiastes 1:1–3** The words of the Teacher, son of David, king in Jerusalem: "Meaningless! Meaningless!" says the Teacher. "Utterly meaningless! Everything is meaningless." What does man gain from all his labor at which he toils under the sun?

Solomon Goes over the Hill

Solomon had reached a midlife crisis. He had climbed his world's highest mountain of wealth, wisdom, and status only to find the peak desolate and unfulfilling. He thought, "Hey! Wait a minute! I worked all these years for this? How come I feel yucky?" He was forced to reevaluate his priorities, and the Book of Ecclesiastes is about his inner journey to find meaning.

When Solomon was first crowned King of Israel, he sought God with his whole heart. In a dream, God offered Solomon anything he wanted. Instead of asking for great wealth, Solomon asked for wisdom to rule: *"Now, O Lord my God, you have made your servant king in place of my father David. But I am only a little child and do not know how to carry out my duties. Your servant is here among the people you have chosen, a great people, too numerous to count or number. So give your servant a discerning heart to govern your people and to distinguish between right and wrong. For who is able to govern this great people of yours?"* (1 Kings 3:7–9).

God was pleased with Solomon's request and granted him wisdom, along with great riches and fame. Gradually, surrounded by wealth, women, and song, Solomon turned away from God and his commandments. As a result, he saw all of life as "meaningless." We could say that Solomon had a "midlife crisis" and Ecclesiastes is the record of his crisis. Several things contributed to Solomon's crisis:

- He married Pharaoh's daughter who did not worship Jehovah.
- He <u>married</u> seven hundred women who worshiped foreign gods.
- He had three hundred concubines in his harem.
- He added continually to his own wealth and found it in the end unsatisfying.
- He experienced all of the sensuality of his age and tired of it.

The influence of ungodly women, the worship of wealth, and the lure of sensuality destroyed his love for God and his desire to be the kind of man God wanted him to be.

What Others are Saying:

culprit: lawbreaker

☞ GO TO:

Nehemiah 13:26 (married)

Joseph M. Stowell: Our need for significance is not the **culprit**. We were built for significance. The culprit is our struggling, stumbling attempts to manufacture our own sense of significance and in the process place at risk that very thing for which we strive, the very people we need and love, the society in which we move, and the cause of Christ for which we have been redeemed.[1]

Sally Conway: Some research shows that as much as 80 percent of American men suffer moderate to severe symptoms in making the midlife transition, while other studies show the figure to be almost 100 percent.[2]

Everyone experiences a midlife transition, but not everyone has to have a midlife crisis. Midlife is a time to evaluate the importance of activities and attitudes that we value. Are they really the important things of life? Are the long hours we've always worked really that important? Has climbing the ladder of success only made us reach the wrong building? Have we really loved the important people in our lives the way they want to be loved?

A crisis occurs when the things of life, which were previously important, become meaningless. It can happen when a person fails to make adjustments in attitudes and perspectives as he or she grows older. Those erroneous ideas of younger years are no longer useful as the end of life creeps toward him or her. But a crisis doesn't have to be bad. We can evaluate things and make positive changes.

A marriage can suffer a similar midlife crisis with husband and wife drifting and growing apart if adjustments aren't made by each person throughout the years.

What the world offers—the lure of sex, wealth, and fame—are insufficient ways to fill the craving for significance that God originally built into us. God intended that the drive for significance would force us to seek our value in him and, to some degree, our marriage relationship. God wants us to feel significant because we are his children, his valuable created beings. Although society gives the impression that things of the world will fulfill us, they don't. Only by knowing how much we are loved and valued by God and living out that love through selfless giving to our spouse will we find our true purpose.

REMEMBER THIS

WARNING

Think about It

GOAL SWITCHING

Ecclesiastes 12:1–8 Remember your Creator in the days of your youth, before the days of trouble come and the years approach when you will say, "I find no pleasure in them"—before the sun and the light and the moon and the stars grow dark, and the clouds return after the rain; when the keepers of the house tremble, and the strong men stoop, when the grinders cease because they are few, and those looking through the windows grow dim; when the doors to the street are closed and the sound of grinding fades; when men rise up at the sound of birds, but all their songs grow faint; when men are afraid of heights and of dangers in the streets; when the almond tree blossoms and the grasshopper drags himself along and desire no longer is stirred. Then man goes to his eternal home and mourners go about the streets. Remember him—before the silver cord is severed, or the golden bowl is broken; before the pitcher is shattered at the spring, or the wheel broken at the well, and the dust returns to the ground it came from, and the spirit returns to God who gave it. "Meaningless! Meaningless!" says the Teacher. "Everything is meaningless!"

Gravity Wins

Solomon noticed that things were different as he aged. There wasn't as much pleasure from life. The "light," representing joy, and the "darkness," representing death, were coming just as clouds return after the rain. In the days of Solomon, the Hebrews believed that any decline in the zest of a person, even a younger person, was the beginning of death. To them, it was a longer process than it is to us.

Solomon continued by describing the characteristics of old age or declining health:

- "keepers of the house tremble"—arms and hands grow weak
- "the strong men stoop"—backs hunch over
- "grinders cease because they are few"—teeth become loose and fall out
- "those looking through the windows grow dim"—eyes can't see as well
- "the doors to the street are closed"—lips sink in because teeth are missing
- "the sound of grinding fades"—teeth are no longer there to grind food
- "men rise up at the sound of birds"—inability to sleep
- "all their songs grow faint"—inability to hear

- "men are afraid of heights and of dangers in the streets"—increase in fear of common things previously unfeared

- "the almond tree blossoms"—hair grows gray or silver

- "the grasshopper drags himself along"—body is bent and walk is slowed

- "desire no longer is stirred"—the appetite is lessened

Then Solomon described a person's death and gave his exhortation "everything is meaningless," which was repeated many times in his essay. Solomon wanted the reader to know that the <u>fear of God</u> was necessary to fight the feeling of meaninglessness in life.

☞ **GO TO:**

Ecclesiastes 11:8
(fear of God)

What Others are Saying:

Sally Conway: Our own work with midlife people as well as other research indicates that the midlife crisis range may be wider, occurring as early as thirty-five for some men and as late as fifty-five for others. Sometimes an external event, such as loss of a parent or friend or a drastic change in job status, forces a man into an open battle with the internal evaluation that is going on. Sometimes, however, a tragedy causes him to suppress the questions until later.[3]

A midlife transition more often turns into a midlife crisis when we don't accept that life will end in illness and eventually death. People who convince themselves otherwise may frantically search for something that gives purpose. By not seeking God's perspective, they will find only greater pain. Others, who are selfish and focus on succeeding by the world's definition, will find only a lack of fulfillment. Whatever the cause, a midlife crisis is characterized by the following:

REMEMBER THIS

KEY POINT

Be alert to any erroneous ideas about life and marriage so that you can adjust them to the truth.

- A desire to reevaluate. Beliefs previously accepted as fact or as being sensible are now accompanied by doubt.

- A sense of time passing quickly. We realize that important goals may not be reached.

- A sense of purposelessness. We realize that accomplishments don't bring actual fulfillment.

- A loss of identity. After giving extensively to others, we have a feeling of emptiness and of not knowing ourselves.

- A loss of physical prowess or ability. The strength and agility of our body declines.

- A disappointment. Although we have new insights, we realize maturity does not bring fewer problems.
- A reduced ability to deal with stress. At a time in life when fewer worries are expected, we may feel unforeseen stress from the need to care for aging parents or the concern about adult children.

A man often experiences these challenges between the ages of forty-five and fifty-five. While on the contrary a woman experiences an unsettling time in her later thirties. Thirty-five is the most common age for a wife to run away from home.

Unresolved trauma from earlier in life can create a midlife crisis. Women and men who were sexually abused as children or those who grew up in dysfunctional families must work through the pain of those years and bring healthy closure through forgiveness. Otherwise, the emotional weakness and illness that come with aging will no longer be able to push down the negative feelings, making a person susceptible to the desire to escape into unhealthy and sinful behavior.

Transition, Not Tragedy

He Says . . .

LARRY: There is one exception to the onset time for midlife troubles in men. I have learned that law enforcement officers frequently experience these feelings as early as age thirty. There is something about the us-versus-them attitude in law enforcement that hinders healthy marriage relationships between police officers and their spouses. I have watched countless police marriages fail when the men get lost in these powerful feelings.

I was prepared for these feelings after reading Jim and Sally Conway's books about the midlife years. I began preparing for the time both children would be gone and I would retire from law enforcement. Knowing life was changing, and that men tended to live in the present without planning for the future, gave me an edge. I began to embrace the changes as challenges. I tried new approaches at work. I became more concerned with my duty to develop those who worked for me rather than in promoting myself. I became more interested in growing our marriage, practicing what I preached across the country. These choices helped insulate me from the assault of the midlife years.

KATHY: Now that Larry and I are over fifty, we are grateful for the foundation that God helped us lay early on. We may still have further changes to make, but awareness of midlife questioning helped us deal with it right away. It does seem that the important things of life have changed, and knowing that such a change of perspective is normal removes the fear of unmet expectations or the doubt of God's goodness.

For instance, I recently hurt my back and was disappointed that I had to take four weeks off from my step-aerobics class. But I told myself that these kinds of things could happen more as I age and that I need to be patient with myself. Rather than becoming discouraged, I just need to accept the limitations of being older and adjust my expectations. I will get back to exercising as soon as possible and in the meantime, I can do stretching exercises and gentle walking. Adapting my thought process has prevented me from becoming depressed. I can focus on my value in Christ.

TAKE IT FROM THEM

Jim and Candy never anticipated the struggles his diabetes would bring to their marriage. Although the potential complications had been explained, they seemed distant, unlikely, and far in the future. As a newlywed, Candy's greatest challenge regarding Jim's diabetes was learning to cook without sugar. Twenty years later, diabetes is an ongoing midlife crisis, affecting every area of their marriage. The greatest element is fear. The complications from diabetes are progressive, affecting Jim's vision. His bathroom counter resembles a drugstore, with medications for blood pressure, kidney function, depression, heart, and lungs. The struggle to regulate and control blood sugars has become a tedious balancing act of diet, exercise, and insulin in an ever-changing combination. What worked yesterday will not necessarily work today or tomorrow.

How do they cope with the real possibility of death and function in a healthy marriage relationship? Communication is the key. Honestly expressing fears and frustrations and making them a matter of prayer has helped. Living each day in an attitude of thankfulness and love diminishes the fear of the future.

TAMING THE SHREW

> **Proverbs 15:1** A gentle answer turns away wrath, but a harsh word stirs up anger.

Listen, Don't Lecture

An angry person—which describes a person going through a midlife crisis—doesn't need or learn from a spouse who responds in kind. That will only "stir up" more anger. Instead, gentle answers laced with understanding, compassion, and support will help struggling spouses work through the transitional phase they are going through. Even if our spouse blames us for his or her problems, we can remember that our spouse is going through "a phase." Telling ourselves this will help us to be patient.

Sally Conway: Producing guilt, however, is not your job. It is God's. Your job is to make sure your own slate is clean and then to do what is necessary to restore your marriage. Reminding your husband of his sinfulness and his obligations to the family will not do anything to rebuild your relationship.[4]

REMEMBER THIS

Our spouse is struggling with not feeling significant and loved. What had previously offered significance now seems . . . well . . . insignificant. As the end of life gets closer, he or she wonders if the long work hours, emphasis on fitness, or striving for success is really important. Even in working for Christ's kingdom and glory, hidden motives may now be revealed. Maybe our spouse realizes that unexpressed hopes won't be achieved. Trying to force our spouse to think logically about these things, or trying to quote Scriptures to make him or her see errors in thinking, will only raise more feelings of failure. While expressing the truth and validity of their feelings, we must let God do the work from the inside out.

Marriage God's Way—People in midlife crisis can't understand what they are going through. They only know they feel frustrated and angry, and usually end up blaming the closest and dearest person to them—their spouse. What's the spouse to do? Scripture gives extensive advice for responding to an angry person. Here are some passages to help.

Reference	Verse and Benefit
Psalm 37:8	**Verse:** "Refrain from anger and turn from wrath; do not fret—it leads only to evil." **Benefit:** Realize that anger won't get the results you desire.
Proverbs 15:18	**Verse:** "A hot-tempered man stirs up dissension, but a patient man calms a quarrel." **Benefit:** Be patient. "This too will pass."
Proverbs 19:3	**Verse:** "A man's own folly ruins his life, yet his heart rages against the Lord." **Benefit:** Understand that your spouse is actually angry with himself or herself but is taking it out on you and the Lord. In time, they will probably realize the truth.
Proverbs 19:11	**Verse:** "A man's wisdom gives him patience; it is to his glory to overlook an offense." **Benefit:** Being patient may make you feel taken advantage of, however, showing your own good character will bring glory to God.
Proverbs 21:9	**Verse:** "Better to live on a corner of the roof than share a house with a quarrelsome wife." **Benefit:** Quarreling will not bring spouses to their senses; it will only cause them to seek distance—either emotionally or physically.
Matthew 5:22	**Verse:** "But I tell you that anyone who is angry with his brother will be subject to judgment. Again, anyone who says to his brother, 'Raca,' is answerable to the Sanhedrin. But anyone who says, 'You fool!' will be in danger of the fire of hell." **Benefit:** Though it may seem justifiable to respond in anger, God doesn't want you to respond in kind and will hold you responsible.
Ephesians 4:26–27	**Verse:** "'In your anger do not sin': Do not let the sun go down while you are still angry, and do not give the devil a foothold." **Benefit:** The transition process your spouse goes through can take months or even years, so deal with your anger each day. Professional Christian counseling and sharing your feelings with trusted friends may help.
James 1:19–20	**Verse:** "My dear brothers, take note of this: Everyone should be quick to listen, slow to speak and slow to become angry, for man's anger does not bring about the righteous life that God desires." **Benefit:** Though tempted to respond in anger or unkind words, or to try to control or change your hurting spouse, such responses will not help them or honor God. Instead, believe that God can do the work within your spouse that you can't do from the outside.

Self-employed as a painting contractor for twenty years, Ken realized at age forty that he would not meet some of his professional goals. In addition, his father became terminally ill and retired from Ken's business. Ken was forced to reevaluate his priorities but found it difficult to talk about his feelings.

Deb, his wife, tried her best to be supportive, but couldn't understand the depth of his turmoil until they hit upon a useful word picture. Ken said he was in a rowboat in the middle of the ocean with no motor, oars, or navigation tools. Every few evenings at bedtime, Deb would ask how Ken felt—if he had found an oar that day or if he could see land on the horizon.

Some days Ken said a dense fog settled over his boat. Other times a storm threatened. But gradually over the weeks and months, Ken gained oars, sighted land, and finally was able to get out of the "boat" and walk safely to shore.

Couples in the Bible

☞ **Check It Out:**

Genesis 16:1–16

Abraham and Sarah had a "midlife crisis" when they chose to have a child through Sarah's maid, Hagar. As they evaluated their old age and realized again that they hadn't accomplished their "goal" of having a child, even though God had promised it—and *especially* because God had promised it—they created a crisis by making wrong choices. Their trust in God wavered as they saw the end of their lives getting closer and the promise of a child becoming more elusive. In the midst of contemplating that "truth," they concluded they must have deluded themselves about God's plan. He must have meant any child from Abraham's loins. Since their society accepted a child from one of the wife's maids as a legitimate child, they choose to have a child through Hagar.

DIVORCE DISASTER

> **1 Corinthians 7:15** But if the unbeliever leaves, let him do so. A believing man or woman is not bound in such circumstances; God has called us to live in peace.

Separation Anxiety

Sometimes, a midlife crisis brings the most dreaded circumstance—separation, with the threat or expectation of divorce. The natural reaction is to panic, to try to force the spouse to return, or to shake some sense back into him or her. But God, who <u>hates</u> divorce, says that we can let them go. Although this Scripture specifically names an "unbeliever," the principle is clear. God knows we can't force anyone to do anything, so we must let him or her go and let God work.

☞ **GO TO:**

Malachi 2:16 (hates)

Jim and Sally Conway: The people who usually have the most success in saving their marriages are those who keep their panic under control. Most are not naturally serene people, but they develop a surprising degree of composure and find strength they didn't know they had.[5]

What Others are Saying:

Sharon Marshall: Release the one you love to the God who loves him far more than you ever could! It was a great morning when I awoke to discover that God loved my love far more than I did; that God was far wiser than I in how to lead him back; that God could go wherever he was, but I couldn't any longer handle the wondering and worry about him; that I could trust the one I love into the hands of the God who loves us both.[6]

Marriage God's Way—If you're feeling overwhelmed with the prospect of a midlife crisis in your marriage, it's hard to feel that God is still working. Panic can easily set in and then unwise or bitter reactions could push your spouse even farther from you. Remembering that God is the God almighty and sovereign Lord of the Universe will infuse you with hope and strength. He says, *"Be still, and know that I am God; I will be exalted among the nations, I will be exalted in the earth"* (Psalm 46:10–11).

KEY POINT

Don't panic. God is still in control.

> **Malachi 2:15–16** Has not [the Lord] made them one? In flesh and spirit they are his. And why one? Because he was seeking godly offspring. So guard yourself in your spirit, and do not break faith with the wife of your youth. "I hate divorce," says the Lord God of Israel, "and I hate a man's covering himself with violence as well as with his garment," says the Lord Almighty. So guard yourself in your spirit, and do not break faith.

God Hates Divorce

KEY POINT

Even if your spouse wants a divorce, God still loves you as much as before.

It is never God's plan for a couple to divorce, because he knows and hates the evil consequences that divorce brings—especially upon the children. Therefore, he exhorts believers to remain faithful and stay married. If a spouse chooses to divorce in disobedience to God's command, the faithful spouse can't prevent it, but he or she can trust that God still loves both of them and wants the best for them.

What Others are Saying:

Bill and Lynne Hybels: Some people imagine divorce as an easy way out, but we learned through other people's experiences that husbands, wives, and children all pay a heavy price when marriages fail. People who opt for divorce unwittingly trade one set of problems for another, and the postdivorce problems are often far harder to resolve than the marital problems would have been.[7]

TAKE IT FROM THEM

Candy and Chad had been married for over twenty years when Chad confessed to having an affair. Candy was devastated and had a mental breakdown, but couldn't share the cause with her psychiatrist. Candy and Chad were reconciled, but Chad's relationship with God deteriorated. He began participating in wife-swapping groups and tried to convince Candy to participate. She was confused and angry. She wanted to be a submissive wife but didn't understand how to do that while refusing to participate in things she knew were wrong.

Her shame prevented her from reaching out to others, and she felt unloved and lonely. While at a night meeting with her boss, they began flirting, which led to a sexual encounter even though both were Christians. When she confessed her sin to Chad, he wasn't upset at all and suggested they get a divorce.

Candy incorrectly believed God must be leading them, and they were divorced. Looking back after many years, Candy can identify how confused she was about her role as a Christian wife and the sins they committed. She wishes she had sought professional Christian counseling because the divorce has caused severe emotional injuries to her children, who have struggled in their own marriages. Candy has grown closer to God, but she regrets the pain the divorce brought to her family.

If you are seeking divorce because of your own midlife crisis, or if you're weary from waiting out your spouse's midlife crisis, consider these ramifications of divorce:

Think about It

- Divorce doesn't eliminate your spouse from your life. You'll still have to deal with him or her under even more stressful circumstances.

- Divorce is costly and usually creates greater financial drain on both spouses who have to support two households.

- The children of divorcing parents are impacted negatively for the rest of their lives. They feel more insecure, unloved, guilty, and traumatized than do children of parents who stay together. Their grades suffer, they are more prone to suicide, and they are more likely to abuse drugs and alcohol.

- Divorce causes many of the important issues of your life to be decided by a judge who may or may not have your best interests at heart.

- If you choose to remarry after divorce, second marriages have a less than 30 percent chance of surviving five years or more.

If you did not want a divorce but your spouse divorced you, the consequences still affect your life. That is an even greater reason to trust God and believe that he is a father to the <u>fatherless</u> and a husband to those without husbands. It is not God's will for spouses to divorce. But if your partner divorces you, you can know that it is God's will for you to experience a divorce and his faithful watch over you. He understands your heart's desire to keep your family together, and he will honor your faithfulness. You can trust him to provide for your true <u>needs</u>—even in separation or divorce.

In the meantime, take steps to maintain the best possible attitude by

- taking a divorce-recovery class,
- finding professional Christian counseling,
- becoming accountable to a support group,
- building a circle of wise friends who can support you,
- reading books about preventing divorce and dealing with midlife crisis,

REMEMBER THIS

☞ **GO TO:**

Deuteronomy 10:18 (fatherless)

Philippians 4:19 (needs)

- avoiding separation from your church out of embarrassment,

- releasing anger and bitterness and learning to forgive and let go, and

- avoiding another relationship until you have healed from the hurt and pain.

STUDY QUESTIONS

1. What is the attitude of people in midlife, as expressed by Solomon?
2. How does Solomon describe the aging process?
3. What is the best thing a spouse can do if their mate is going through a midlife crisis?
4. If one spouse actually leaves because of a midlife crisis, what should the other spouse do?
5. How does God feel about divorce, and what does he want divorcing people to do?

CHAPTER WRAP-UP

- Marriages can be affected, often detrimentally, when spouses go through midlife. Midlife transitions don't have to turn into a crisis. But midlife is a time when a person questions the meaning of life and that can affect the way he or she responds to a mate.

- As each person ages, changes take place in the body. If husbands or wives can't accept these changes, they may become angry and think that leaving their marriage will bring renewed happiness. Actually, by accepting changes, husbands and wives will learn to see each other and themselves through God's loving eyes.

- It can be frightening to watch your spouse go through a midlife crisis. Remember to respond to anger in a calm manner and not to take it personally. God will work in his or her heart from the inside out.

- If a mate wants to separate, or even divorce, trying to make him or her stay won't really help. Instead, be strong by not taking his or her behavior personally. Believing that God can work more effectively on his or her heart and soul will bring peace—as much as possible in such a stressful circumstance. The hurting spouse can trust that because God hates divorce, he will do everything possible to help the mate return.

KATHY & LARRY'S  BOOKSHELF

Kathy and Larry's favorite books about midlife:

- *Perilous Pursuits,* Joseph M. Stowell, Moody Press. Coping with our obsession with significance.
- *Your Husband's Midlife Crisis,* Sally Conway, Victor Books. What a woman can do when her husband comes "unglued" in midlife.
- *When a Mate Wants Out,* Sally Conway and Jim Conway, Zondervan Publishing House. Secrets for saving a marriage.
- *Surviving Separation and Divorce*, Sharon Marshall, Baker Book House. How to keep going when you don't really want to.

20 SENIOR SCENARIO

Here We Go

As Barbara Bush watched, her husband, former President George Bush, jumped from an airplane. He celebrated his seventy-fifth birthday by skydiving with only a parachute attached—and no assistant. "Old guys can still do stuff," George said, "and you might as well go for it. It was heaven. It was exhilarating. I feel like a spring colt."[1] After being asked if she was proud of her husband's exploit, Barbara commented, "Not particularly, I expect the best from George Bush."

There's an older couple who is enjoying retirement and each other! That's an example of what God has for married couples as they grow older. He wants married people not only to stay together, but also to enjoy every moment. Even when we face difficult problems caused by aging, we can still make loving choices for our marriage.

Someone has quipped that old age is defined by four things: bifocals, baldness, bridges, and bulges. Another person wisecracked that old age is the contagious disease of "too": too tired, too late, too far, too much, too long, too hard, too fattening, too noisy, too quiet. Those disadvantages don't have to make marriage unhappy. We can actually grow closer together.

GRACEFUL AGING

> **Ecclesiastes 9:9** Enjoy life with your wife, whom you love, all the days of this meaningless life that God has given you under the sun—all your meaningless days. For this is your lot in life and in your toilsome labor under the sun.

A Reason to Revel

Solomon wrote Ecclesiastes in the ebb of his life. Throughout the book he examined all the different things that people value, and in the end, he said, they were all meaningless—without God. Even though his viewpoint seems dismal, Solomon advised people to enjoy their human endeavors as a gift from God's hand. He included marriage in that evaluation.

With Christ at the center of our marriage, we can not only enjoy marriage in our later years, but we can revel in it. Our relationship with our spouse can get increasingly better if we continually act with selflessness and understanding.

What Others are Saying:

☞ **GO TO:**

Job 12:12; Psalm 90:12 (wisdom)

Think about It

Couples in the Bible

☞ **GO TO:**

Genesis 7:6 (six hundred)

David and Claudia Arp: We've got great news! Contrary to popular opinion, you are never too old to grow wiser. So many times we get set in our ways and just assume we're too old or don't have the energy to make wise changes. However, the Scriptures tell us that both <u>wisdom</u> and understanding—which are attributes of the aged—enable us to make needed changes.[2]

One of the ways to keep a positive attitude about marriage in the elder years is to reflect on the positive growth and change you have experienced because of the relationship with your spouse. How has he or she made you better as a person? The common idea is that a husband and wife begin to look like each other physically, but hopefully their souls are also growing alike—in wisdom and godliness.

Old age is not a hindrance to God. Never once in the Bible is a person disqualified from serving God because of youth or old age. Psalm 92:12–15 encourages us by saying, *"The righteous will flourish like a palm tree, they will grow like a cedar of Lebanon; planted in the house of the Lord, they will flourish in the courts of our God. They will still bear fruit in old age, they will stay fresh and green, proclaiming, 'The Lord is upright; he is my Rock, and there is no wickedness in him.'"*

Our culture values youth and scorns age. God evaluates us on our availability to him and our willingness to submit to his plans, not our age. Consider these biblical characters:

- When the flood came, Noah was <u>six hundred</u> years old, and we assume his wife was of similar age. Although we don't live to be that old these days, Noah and his wife are still an example of a couple who were used by God in their senior years.

- Abraham and Sarah fulfilled God's promise to have a baby when they were both well <u>past childbearing</u> ages, one hundred years and ninety years, respectively. Their infertility of many years was not a problem for God. When the angel announced to them that they would have a child, the angel clarified, *"Is anything too hard for the Lord?"* (Genesis 18:14).

- Moses didn't begin to serve God until he was eighty years old and then he led the Israelites through many difficulties for forty years. When he <u>died</u> on the edge of the Promised Land at the age of 120, *"his eyes were not weak nor his strength gone"* (Deuteronomy 34:7).

- Aaron, Moses' brother, and Miriam, Moses' sister, served the Israelites along with Moses for many years. Miriam even played the <u>tambourine</u> to praise God in her senior years.

- Solomon, unfortunately, is an example of a man who served God for <u>forty years</u>, but was not a spiritual success in his efforts. The lure of his wives' foreign religions stole away his first love for God, yet God used him on the throne for many years.

- <u>Anna</u>, age eighty-four, and <u>Simeon</u>, of unknown age but old, greeted the baby Jesus and declared him the Messiah. They had both served God in the Temple for many years.

☞ **GO TO:**

Genesis 21:2
(past childbearing)

Deuteronomy 34:7
(died)

Exodus 15:20
(tambourine)

1 Kings 11:42
(forty years)

Luke 2:36–38 (Anna)

Luke 2:25–35 (Simeon)

KEY POINT

Old age doesn't have to be negative: it's your attitude that counts.

Jill Briscoe: I began to research the "oldies" in the Bible for my peace of mind. This began to restore my confidence and helped me to get a heavenly perspective. I was amazed how old Moses was (80) when God set him off on his life's work. Aaron was 84 and Miriam was even older! Miriam, in fact, was still bashing a mean tambourine in her mid 80s, dancing around praising the Lord. Anna, a happy octogenarian, smiled at me from the New Testament, not to mention Elizabeth, Zechariah, and Simeon. Yes, there seemed to be plenty of lively old folk around Christ's world when he came.[3]

What Others are Saying:

☞ **Check It Out:**

Genesis 20:1–18

> **Genesis 20:1–2** Now Abraham moved on from there into the region of the Negev and lived between Kadesh and Shur. For a while he stayed in Gerar, and there Abraham said of his wife Sarah, "She is my sister." Then Abimelech king of Gerar sent for Sarah and took her.

Meet My Sister, Sarah

Old age doesn't mean we won't repeat the mistakes we made in the past. We're supposed to grow older, but we never become perfect. Even though Abraham had <u>lied</u> about his relationship to Sarah before, he again failed to trust God to protect his life. Abraham certainly hadn't learned his lesson. He was afraid other men would want Sarah because of her great beauty and would kill him to get her. Same fear, same result (see GWGN, pages 115–117 and 161–165). Just what he feared happened, but minus his own murder.

☞ **GO TO:**

Genesis 12:10–20 (lied)

It's amazing that Sarah was still so beautiful at ninety years old that a stranger wanted to take her for his wife. Since God was about to fulfill his promise for Sarah to become pregnant, he had evidently protected Sarah's body from the full effects of old age. She was attractive and Abimelech wanted her! But before Abimelech became intimate with Sarah, God intervened and made it known that Sarah was a married woman.

KEY POINT

Even in old age, we'll make mistakes. And God will continue to forgive.

Wayne Barber, Eddie Rasnake, and Richard Shepherd: [Abraham and Sarah's] lies, instead of protecting them, put Sarah in harm's way. Even when we are faithless, God remains <u>faithful</u>, for he cannot deny who he is.[4]

☞ **GO TO:**

2 Timothy 2:13 (faithful)

As we age, we will repeat some of the mistakes we made in our younger years. We must be alert to Satan's schemes in order to protect our marriage. We are a work in progress no matter how old we are. Philippians 1:6 applies to anyone at every age: ". . . *being confident of this, that he who began a good work in you will carry it on to completion until the day of Christ Jesus."* God is continuing his work in our marriage as well. We can always learn more about our mate.

Thankfully, God's <u>grace</u> and <u>mercy</u> are available to us all of our lives. Satan may try to whisper that God won't be as forgiving because we should have learned our lesson previously, but God's <u>forgiveness</u> has no time limits or age limits. Every person, regardless of age or experience, can receive God's mercy and grace.

DON'T PROTEST THE EMPTY NEST!

> **Ecclesiastes 3:1–8** There is a <u>time for everything</u>, and a season for every activity under heaven: a time to be born and a time to die, a time to <u>plant</u> and a time to uproot, a time to kill and a time to heal, a time to tear down and a time to build, a time to weep and a time to laugh, a time to mourn and a time to dance, a time to scatter stones and a time to gather them, a time to embrace and a time to refrain, a time to search and a time to give up, a time to keep and a time to throw away, a time to tear and a time to mend, a <u>time to be silent</u> and a time to speak, a time to love and a time to hate, a time for war and a time for peace.

Just Us Two

God designs life to be a series of beginnings and endings—stages when different things are appropriate. None of us will live forever; therefore, there is a time to die. None of us should only plant; there's also an appropriate time to pull up roots and start over. In this beautiful and poetic writing above, Solomon reminds us that life never stays stagnant. There is always a new challenge or a new stage to encounter.

New stages make life interesting, and one of the most interesting stages of life for a couple is the empty nest! Many people are thrilled about it, and many people fear it. It need not be any more difficult than any other stage, for God is with us even in this transitory time of life.

H. Norman Wright: Often a love recession occurs when couples move from one stage of marriage to another (e.g., childlessness to parenting) or when they go through one of the transitions of life (30s, midlife, etc.). You feel alone or isolated, and think that some-

REMEMBER THIS

☞ **GO TO:**

Romans 5:1–2 (grace)

Romans 9:23 (mercy)

Matthew 26:28 (forgiveness)

Ecclesiastes 8:6 (time for everything)

Isaiah 28:24 (plant)

Esther 4:14 (time to be silent)

What Others are Saying:

thing is wrong with you. You begin questioning whether you ever loved your partner in the first place and wondering if the diminished love can ever become strong again. No, you are not the only person who has ever experienced this phenomenon. Don't panic. It is important to remember that, with honest acceptance of the situation and some positive action, your love can and will increase.[5]

WARNING

KEY POINT

An empty nest means no interruptions!

> Our response to the "empty nest syndrome" is an attitude that we choose just like any other. There's bound to be some initial sadness when the children leave. The relationship between husband and wife is for a lifetime, but parenting children in the home is a limited commitment. If a couple lives into their later years, they may experience as much time without the children as with the children in the home. A husband and wife need to develop their own hobbies and have mutual interests to keep the marriage healthy.

TAKE IT FROM THEM

Dennis and Eva Marie have found that "empty nest" means "love nest!" Now that all of their children are grown, Dennis and Eva Marie have rediscovered the joy of time alone. Years ago, when they were dating, Dennis and Eva Marie enjoyed eating delivery pizza or Chinese takeout while sitting on the floor watching television or listening to music. Today they "re-enjoy" that same concept . . . and it's nice to be back!

What Others are Saying:

Bill Blackburn: The marriages that thrive in the launching stage and the empty nest are those in which the partners are constantly rediscovering the good qualities of each other, are willing to forgive hurts and slights and differences, and have a high commitment to growing in marriage and expressing that growth through affection, valuing each other, time together, and a sense of adventure.[6]

KEY POINT

Keep touching and loving.

Ed Wheat and Gloria Okes Perkins: Some people dread the loss of their youthful vigor, or they fear their sex life will become boring and empty through much repetition. But this need not be the case. People growing together in love find that their sexual relationship provides more meaning and enjoyment all the time. In middle age and later years, overabundant sexual energy can be exchanged for mature, sensitive, skilled lovemaking with a beloved partner whose responses are understood intimately.[7]

Marriage God's Way—As we've seen in chapter 13, sex is a blessing from God and intended for every married couple—including aged couples. The apostle Paul names only one thing to prevent a couple from enjoying sex by choice—and it's not old age. It's prayer. He wrote, *"Do not deprive each other except by mutual consent and for a time, so that you may devote yourselves to prayer. Then come together again so that Satan will not tempt you because of your lack of self-control"* (1 Corinthians 7:5). So take advantage of the empty nest and make love on the living room floor—with plenty of padding underneath.

The Empty Nest Test

LARRY: Would it be as good as I thought? Would it be as much fun as the years before the children came? It didn't take long to get the answer. When Mark, our youngest, went off to college, the empty nest test was on.

It was great! There was no comparison to our early married years. Our maturity, seasoned love, and improved financial status made this test seem like a holiday. During one month we went to out to lunch over twenty times. There is nothing better than a robust, mature love expressed in freedom, intimacy, and time alone.

KATHY: Even though I adore my children and have thoroughly enjoyed them over the years, I always thought I'd love the empty nest. It sounded delightful to enjoy each other, without the children interrupting or creating tension. When the subject came up among my friends, I'd proudly say, "I can't wait for the empty nest. It'll be wonderful." Some friends eyed me with suspicion.

I began to wonder. Would I really love it? Would I suddenly have regrets? Was I being proud by saying I was looking forward to it? Maybe the Lord would humble me by making me pine over having no children at home.

When the nest was actually empty, I absolutely loved it! No regrets! No sudden or unexpected sadness. Larry and I could make love without interruption or pick up and go any time we pleased.

KEEP FEAR TO THE REAR

> **Psalm 92:12–15** The righteous will flourish like a palm tree, they will grow like a cedar of Lebanon; planted in the house of the Lord, they will flourish in the courts of our God. They will still bear fruit in old age, they will stay fresh and green, proclaiming, "The Lord is upright; he is my Rock, and there is no wickedness in him."

Becoming a Fruitful Tree

We may fear old age, illness, and the death of a spouse. But those who know the Lord need never fear. Even though our bodies deteriorate, our souls can flourish like the strong cedar trees in Lebanon. Each of those trees stands fresh and green, and God wants our souls to do the same.

We can trust him as our rock and our strength to face calamities, problems, or physical failings. We can have that confidence since God is not a wicked God. He doesn't allow adversity in our lives for evil purposes or from hateful motives, but he does <u>allow</u> unfortunate things to happen. He uses the hard times to readjust our focus on him as our rock and nourishment.

☞ **GO TO:**

Isaiah 45:7 (allow)

What Others are Saying:

Think about It

Bill Blackburn: If issues have been dealt with reasonably well at earlier stages of the marriage, the stresses of the senior years can be more easily handled and handled in a way that is positive for the marriage.[8]

God can use the difficulties of midlife to deepen our relationship with our spouse. The older couples who still look at each other with passion and joy are often the couples who have faced the greatest challenges. They've gone through the "fire" together and seen the other respond with love and faithfulness. Without being singed, their love wouldn't be as strong.

Marriage God's Way—Regret is one of Satan's schemes for breaking apart a midlife couple. The "if only's" of living can make a husband or wife blame the other for past problems. Whatever the past trouble, blame over past decisions isn't going to make the consequences disappear. Resist living in regret and blaming either yourself or your spouse. Instead, forgive as Ephesians 4:32 says, *"Be kind and compassionate to one another, forgiving each other, just as in Christ God forgave you."* Believe that God can make you bear fruit in your old age—and stay fresh and green.

Here are some tips to help you enjoy your senior years:

REMEMBER THIS

- Keep busy through volunteer work at your church, local hospital, hospice program, schools, or senior citizen center.
- Continue to learn by reading, traveling, or researching on the internet.
- Help others through babysitting for a single mom or sorting clothing at a thrift store.
- Work at a part-time job. Recent changes in the law allow retirees to make more money than before and still earn full social security benefits.
- Be the best grandparent you can be. Don't be negative with the grandkids or wish for the good old days. Instead, be positive about life. Take an interest in their activities and learn about what's important to them. When you talk about their current activity, whether it's soccer, playing drums, or taking a biology class, they will value you and want to spend time with you.

Elaine and Charles were married for eleven years before pancreatic cancer took Charles's life. As Elaine learns to live alone, she can see God bringing good out of this very painful time of her life. She is more sensitive than before, giving a sympathetic smile to the driver who turns in front of her or to the person in the cashier's line who can't find her checkbook. She has more grace because she's hurting and wonders whether they are, too.

TAKE IT FROM THEM

Elaine has learned greater coping skills because she doesn't demand more from her physical or emotional being than she can give. She doesn't berate herself for her lack of emotional stamina, and she gives herself permission not to worry about things that don't get done around the house. Little by little, she is building her emotional reserves and trusting God for continued healing.

Elaine marvels at God's timing and how he has worked out every detail of her life's tapestry. Even though it has unraveled, God has kept the pattern and the colors clear in her memory of her life with Charles.

PARENTING AGAIN

> **1 Timothy 5:8** If anyone does not provide for his relatives, and especially for his immediate family, he has denied the faith and is worse than an unbeliever.

Parenting Your Parents

The apostle Paul wrote to Timothy and gave an important principle for all of God's children: be responsible for your family, including your relatives. When this was written, there was no social security, retirement benefits, or welfare. Every family was supposed to provide for their own members.

Even though support programs now exist, the principle still stands and God would prefer that, instead of the government, people take care of their own parents. Taking care of our relatives in their need, especially our elderly parents, shows God's love to them and others who are watching us. If a person doesn't provide for his or her parents, either physically or financially, he or she is not living out God's sacrificial love.

REMEMBER THIS

The caregiving of a parent or another relative can put stress on a marriage. Both husband and wife must take extra precautions to nurture the marriage. Here are some tips to help:

- Express appreciation for any help your spouse gives in the situation—even if it's not all you would like it to be.
- Keep a sense of humor. Find the fun in the situation, even when everything seems overwhelming. Share a joke, laugh at a child, look at old photos, or do a crossword puzzle together—but do something to find joy together in the midst of stress.

- Pray together for the person who needs your care and for each other. Express your appreciation for your spouse to God in prayer.
- Talk positively. Don't belittle your spouse for mistakes. Don't continually talk negatively about the problems the caregiving brings. Don't blame your spouse for problems or focus on his or her inadequacies. Instead, think and act positively. Find something good to say in all situations.

Caring for ailing parents, or grieving from their sudden death, can put great strain on a marriage relationship. It is vitally important that both husband and wife release their parent to God. Whether the parent was loving or hurtful to their child, saying "good-bye" and bringing closure is necessary and will help the marriage relationship. Unhealed or ignored grief about a parent can cause anger or bitterness to spill over on the spouse.

Psychologists suggest taking some of these steps to bring about release of the potential loss or actual death of a parent:

- List the good times you experienced with your parent and rejoice by expressing gratitude to your parent.
- List the bad times you experienced with your parent and choose to forgive them for each item on the list.
- Write a letter to your parent saying the things you've always wanted to say. Either read them the letter or read it to a caring spouse or friend if your parent is dead.

Think about It

Frank and Mary Alice Minirth: Even if a parent is senile or comatose or unreceptive, you can say hello and good-bye to him or her with a monologue or a letter. Take the good times and the bad times you remembered and write about them. Then emotionally wave good-bye to that relationship.[9]

What Others are Saying:

Joan and Emmitt cared for several relatives over the past years: her mom, dad, two aunts, and an uncle. They found that they needed to go out of their way for each other by being keenly aware of the other's needs. They realized that in spite of the demands of caregiving, the spouse is still the most important person in life.

They found that it's the little things that count. They taped

TAKE IT FROM THEM

a love note to the bathroom mirror or brought a cup of coffee to their spouse in bed. Taking a short walk together while holding hands relieved some of the stress they experienced. They frequently told each other, "I love you." Expressing their appreciation and gratitude made them never take each other for granted.

One morning Emmitt seemed a little grumpy from loss of sleep after sitting up all night with Joan's aunt in the hospital. They took turns and he had taken the night shift. Joan embraced him and said, "I bet you a quarter I can't kiss you."

"Okay," he said.

Joan planted a big kiss on him and exclaimed: "You win!" They found that flirting was a great stress reliever. They made sure they were affectionate with each other and found that it cushioned the stress and strain.

STUDY QUESTIONS

1. Even when life is seemingly meaningless, especially in old age as Solomon describes, what does he advise couples to do?
2. What do we learn from Abraham's continuing problem with calling Sarah his sister rather than his wife?
3. Solomon eloquently wrote about the different seasons of life. What can an older couple gain from his perspective?
4. Using Isaac and Rebekah as an example, what should older couples never stop doing?
5. What does God want older folk to experience?
6. Who does God want an older couple to care for, if they have the opportunity?

CHAPTER WRAP-UP

- As we grow older, we may think that the later years can't be as good as when we were young—or we may be afraid the pain from the earlier years will continue. But it doesn't have to be that way. There can be healing, forgiveness, and growth toward a loving and caring relationship. God wants to use even those who are older, as he did with Noah, Abraham and Sarah, and many older couples described in the Bible.

- As we age, we could believe that eventually we'll reach perfection—or pretty near it. But even Abraham, who walked closely with God, continued to struggle with some of the same issues as when he was young. We can understand that God is patient and will continue to work in our lives until we die.

- Some people struggle with the empty nest and some don't. It, like other stages of life, needs preparation by placing more importance on the couple relationship than the children. Seeing the absence of the children as a way of renewing love and fun times will help to make the empty nest enjoyable.

- Fear can become an older couple's enemy if they let it ruin their enjoyment of life. Yes, bad things will happen, but God wants to use each circumstance to draw a couple closer to each other and to him. That can happen by avoiding "if only's" and "regretitis."

KATHY & LARRY'S  BOOKSHELF

Kathy and Larry's favorite books about keeping love strong:

- *The Drifting Marriage*, Donald R. Harvey, Fleming H. Revell Company. The most common cause of marital failure among Christian couples.

- *Stress Points in Marriage*, Bill and Deana Blackburn, Word Books. How to recognize the stress points in your marriage.

- *Give and Take*, Willard F. Harley Jr., Fleming H. Revell Company. The secret to marital compatibility.

- *Straight Talk*, James C. Dobson, Word Books. What men need to know and what women should understand.

APPENDIX A—THE ANSWERS

CHAPTER 1

1. He means someone who would complement Adam in his needs, strengths, and weaknesses. (Genesis 2:18)
2. He did this because God wanted Adam to realize he was lonely and needed Eve. (Genesis 2:19–20)
3. "Woman" means "from man." (Genesis 2:23)
4. Esther spent twelve months getting ready with spices, cosmetics, and oil of myrrh. (Esther 2:12)
5. She revealed her quality personality by humbling herself in front of David, by recognizing him as God's anointed, and by taking quick action in the face of danger. (1 Samuel 25:2–44)

CHAPTER 2

1. God is interested in every area of our lives and wants to guide and lead us. (Psalm 73:23–24)
2. God does not want Christians to marry those who have not made a commitment to him because they will have opposing goals and desires. (2 Corinthians 6:14–15)
3. Jezebel caused Ahab to worship the idols she worshiped because she was a strong personality who thrust her opinions and ideas upon her husband. (1 Kings 16:29–33)
4. Just as Abraham sent his servant to find a wife for Isaac, God the Father sends his Holy Spirit to call each Christian to be the Bride of Christ. It is also an analogy for how God leads a man or woman to their future spouse through the Holy Spirit. (Genesis 24:1–67)
5. Love is patient, kind, not envious nor boastful. It is not proud, rude, self-seeking, easily angered, nor does it keep a record of wrongs. Love doesn't delight in evil but in truth. It protects, trusts, hopes, perseveres, and never fails. (1 Corinthians 13:4–8)
6. Delilah wanted Samson's destruction and not his good. (Judges 16:4–6)

7. Jesus was wise, physically mature, and he had good relationships with God and people. (Luke 2:52)

CHAPTER 3

1. God wants us to avoid sexual immorality so that we can learn self-control and be an example to unbelievers. (1 Thessalonians 4:3–5)
2. He questioned God's motives and suggested God didn't want what was best for her. (Genesis 3:1–5).
3. Forbidden things look "good, pleasing, and desirable for wisdom." (Genesis 3:6)
4. His love was so great that he didn't mind waiting for seven years to marry Rachel. (Genesis 29:16–20)
5. Dinah went to visit the pagan women. (Genesis 34:1–2)
6. The Bible says we shouldn't even speak of sexual immorality so that we won't be tempted by it. (Ephesians 5:1–4)

CHAPTER 4

1. It is important to make plans because if you don't, you won't know where you're going or whether you've arrived. (John 8:14)
2. A Family Mission Statement empowers a couple to know specifically how they want their marriage to work and operate. (Proverbs 28:19)
3. The word "commit" means "to roll," and a couple can "roll" their plans into God's care. (Proverbs 16:3)
4. A couple can consider their marriage more important than anything else by abandoning attitudes from their former single's life that hamper development of a relationship with their spouse. (Philippians 3:3–11)

CHAPTER 5

1. Words have the ability to be as valuable as silver and gold, but they need to be shared and given in the right context. (Proverbs 10:20; 25:11)

2. Michal, David's wife, criticized David possibly because she was jealous of his relationship with God and because she thought royalty should act in a distinguished manner. (2 Samuel 6:16–23)
3. God woos his children to him with tender words and a message of hope. Couples can learn from that by speaking tenderly and kindly to their mates and offering hope for their relationship. (Hosea 2:14–16)
4. By seeing that they should avoid becoming enemies, and work on finding a compromise that is acceptable to both parties. (Proverbs 20:3)
5. Anger in itself is not wrong or sinful but we shouldn't let it fester and give Satan an opportunity to use it against us. (Ephesians 4:26)

CHAPTER 6

1. Even though to him we weren't living pleasing lives, God sent Jesus to die for our sins. That's an example of love based not on feelings but on a choice—something couples need to do. (Romans 5:8)
2. Love is patient, kind, not envious nor boastful. It is not proud, rude, self-seeking, easily angered, and it doesn't keep a record of wrongs. Love is truthful and always protects, trusts, hopes, and perseveres. That kind of love never ends. (1 Corinthians 13:4–8)
3. God used Jesus' sacrificial death to express his love for us; he gave up his only Son (John 3:16). In marriage each person has his or her own definition of love that the other needs to learn and fulfill. Each spouse should give up his or her own demands and love sacrificially.
4. Couples can appreciate their spouse's differences by understanding that God created each person to be different and unique for his own purposes. (1 Corinthians 12:4–6)
5. Each person can reflect aloud the other person's feelings, making that person feel understood. (Romans 12:15)
6. They can love their mate as much as they love and care for themselves. (Ephesians 5:28–30)

CHAPTER 7

1. Spiritual oneness is having no shame or embarrassment, being "emotionally naked," as a couple. (Genesis 2:22–25)
2. A couple's "one flesh" experience represents oneness between God and his church. (Ephesians 5:31–32)
3. Sex is the only thing couples are permitted to refrain from so they can spend more time in prayer. They are to refrain for only a short time by mutual agreement. (1 Corinthians 7:3–5)
4. Husbands should listen before answering. (Proverbs 18:13)

5. Solomon's bride. (Song of Songs 5:16)
6. Abimelech saw them caressing each other in ways that only husbands and wives touch. (Genesis 26:8–9)
7. Husbands are to love their wives as Christ loved the church by leading through sacrifice and care. (Ephesians 5:25–33)
8. Wives are to submit to their husbands as if they were submitting to Jesus. (Ephesians 5:22–24)

CHAPTER 8

1. They should emotionally and physically leave their parents and unite with each other. (Genesis 2:22–24)
2. Couples should still honor their parents. (Exodus 20:12)
3. God wants us to provide for immediate relatives, otherwise we have behaved worse than an unbeliever and have turned away from our faith. (1 Timothy 5:8)
4. Couples can listen to parents' counsel and honor their wisdom. (Proverbs 15:22)
5. Jesus said that we should love him above all else and all others. If we obey parents without considering Jesus' teachings, then we are loving them above him. (Matthew 10:37)
6. We can respond with concern and patience. Ruth responded that way with Naomi, her depressed mother-in-law. (Ruth 1:19–21)
7. They should speak the truth in a loving and caring way. (Ephesians 4:15)

CHAPTER 9

1. According to Proverbs 22:17–19, wisdom comes from seeking advice and knowledge from wise people.
2. Don't make unbelieving couples your total source of knowledge and encouragement. (2 Corinthians 6:14–18)
3. God wants couples to be involved in a church so they may receive the encouragement that every couple needs. (Hebrews 10:25)
4. One purpose for investing in others is to give God the glory for the work he's done in our lives. (Psalm 34:3)
5. The early church ministered to each other's needs by spending time together, even to the point of selling everything and living communally. (Acts 2:42–47)
6. They weren't helpful because they wouldn't accept Job's claim that he was without unconfessed sin, and they didn't listen well. (Job 16:2)

CHAPTER 10

1. God models unconditional love by disciplining his children but not withdrawing love from them, even

when they are disobedient. (Psalm 89:30–34)

2. Paul described a child as someone who talks, thinks, reasons, and acts like a child. (1 Corinthians 13:11)

3. Parents, especially fathers, should avoid making their children frustrated. (Ephesians 6:4)

4. Parents shouldn't play favorites with their children. They should treat and love each child the same. (Matthew 5:44–45)

5. Parents must not make a child more important than their marriage. (Mark 10:9)

6. God can resolve problems and restore even broken marriages. (Joel 2:25–27)

CHAPTER 11

1. Discipline shows that a person is loved and a part of the family. (Hebrews 12:4–6)

2. An undisciplined child feels like he's not a part of the family. (Hebrews 12:7–8)

3. The purpose of discipline is to promote holy and righteous behavior. (Hebrews 12:9–10)

4. Some results of godly discipline are righteousness, peace, strength, and healing. (Hebrews 12:11–13)

5. Prosperity and success will result when a person obeys God's rules. (Joshua 1:8)

6. One way to discipline a young child is with a spanking, if it's done correctly without anger. (Proverbs 13:24)

7. The child will most likely follow God's commands. (Proverbs 22:6)

CHAPTER 12

1. Instead of saying she should be happy with just him, he could have communicated that he understood her grief. (1 Samuel 1:1–8)

2. David put off his fasting clothes, readied himself for other work, and made love to Bathsheba. (2 Samuel 12:15–24)

3. Parents can take comfort in knowing that God can protect their child even more than they can. (Psalm 91:1–6)

4. Parents should remember that Jesus said every person will have trouble in this world. (John 16:33)

5. Parents find peace in knowing that God has a wonderful plan for their child's life. (Jeremiah 29:11–13)

6. They can pray. (Luke 22:31–32)

CHAPTER 13

1. The man and woman were both naked, and they felt no shame. (Genesis 2:25)

2. God planned sex as a way to create a unity and oneness between a husband and wife. (1 Corinthians 6:15–17)

3. God said that a bridegroom should not be sent off to war or have any other duty assigned to him during the first year of his marriage. (Deuteronomy 24:5)

4. Couples should refrain from sex only for a short time when they want to concentrate on prayer. (1 Corinthians 7:3–5)

CHAPTER 14

1. They should not commit adultery. (Exodus 20:14)

2. The end result of adultery is death and destruction. (Proverbs 5:1–6)

3. David was vulnerable because he wasn't where he should be, at war. He was most likely bored, and her beauty thrilled him. (2 Samuel 11:1–4)

4. He conspired to have Bathsheba's husband, Uriah, killed so that he could marry Bathsheba. (2 Samuel 11:5–27)

5. God sent the prophet Nathan to tell a story that convicted David of his own sin. (2 Samuel 12:1–12)

6. David's consequences included death of the child, sexual turmoil and murder within his family, rebellion by his son, and death of more of his children. (2 Samuel 12–18)

7. Those who want to be sexually pure should avoid mentioning or teasing about sexual immorality, along with obscenities and coarse joking. Instead, God's people should concentrate on gratitude. (Ephesians 5:3–5)

8. Let them leave. (1 Corinthians 7:15)

9. We can resist the temptation of adultery by focusing on the good things about our mate and be satisfied by what our spouse can give us. (Proverbs 5:18–23)

CHAPTER 15

1. The bride was insecure because she was dark-skinned, unlike the beautiful light-skinned women of Solomon's court. (Song of Songs 1:4–6)

2. She referred in positive terms to nature's examples of beauty and strength and complimented him on how he caressed her. (Song of Songs 2:1–7)

3. She had a dream that she couldn't find him. (Song of Songs 3:1–4)

4. He used perfume, an impressive carriage, sixty warriors, and spent a lot of money. (Song of Songs 3:6–11)

5. He complimented everything about his new bride's body in a very graphic but positive way. (Song of Songs 4:1–16)

6. She gave flimsy excuses, such as she was already asleep and didn't want to get her feet dirty getting out of bed. (Song of Songs 5:2–8)

7. She concentrated on all the things she liked about Solomon. (Song of Songs 5:10–16)

8. She wanted to leave the city with him and spend time alone in the country. (Song of Songs 7:10–13)

CHAPTER 16

1. God really owns everything because he created it all. (Psalm 24:1–2)
2. He may give them a little and see what they do with it. (Luke 16:10–12)
3. Jesus was teaching that it's not how much you have, but whether you faithfully manage the finances God provides. (Matthew 25:14–30)
4. It makes the borrower a servant to the lender, concerned about pleasing the lender rather than God. (Proverbs 22:7)
5. It shows their dedication to him and their acknowledgment that he is the owner of it all. (Malachi 3:10–12)

CHAPTER 17

1. Trials are something that will happen. We can't prevent them. We should actually rejoice because of them. (1 Peter 4:12–13)
2. Job seemed at peace about them, but his wife was angry and wanted Job to curse God and then die.
3. Everything changes including change. (Ecclesiastes 3:1)
4. God wants us to draw closer to him and be glorified through our troubles by bringing good from it. (Romans 8:28–31)
5. Because in his sovereignty, he already knows exactly how he's going to use it—so that we'll seek him. (Jeremiah 29:11)
6. He wants them to recommit themselves to each other and to obeying God. (Malachi 2:10–16)

CHAPTER 18

1. Birds came and ate it. It refers to how Satan tries to destroy marriages or make them weak. (Matthew 13:1–3, 18–19)
2. Shallowness refers to being weak when trouble or persecution comes. In marriage, it could be expressed as selfishness, anger, or unfaithfulness. (Matthew 13:5–6, 20–21)

3. The seed among thorns gets choked out, and that can happen within marriage when a couple gets caught up in making money or doing activities. The joy of their marriage is choked out. (Matthew 13:7, 22)
4. Evaluate whether a person's need is a burden or a load. A burden is something that they need help with. A load is something that God wants them to carry themselves. (Galatians 6:2–5)
5. The seed in the good soil produced a hundred, sixty, or thirty times what was sown. That can be related to a marriage where a couple makes the choice to love each other through the good times and the bad and is rewarded with a long, happy marriage. (Matthew 13:8–9, 23)

CHAPTER 19

1. All life is meaningless. (Ecclesiastes 1:1–3)
2. He talks about the body being affected: arms, hands, back, teeth, eyes, hearing, graying hair, and appetite. (Ecclesiastes 12:1–8)
3. He or she should respond without anger but with gentle understanding. (Proverbs 15:1)
4. He or she should let the spouse leave and trust that God will work. (1 Corinthians 7:15)
5. God hates divorce, and he wants divorcing couples to reconcile. (Malachi 2:15–16)

CHAPTER 20

1. Enjoy life with your spouse. (Ecclesiastes 9:9)
2. In old age, we can continue to make the same old mistakes. (Genesis 20:1–7)
3. Everything changes. Each new season of life can bring new joy or sorrows—but it's up to us how we respond to each one.
4. Never stop being affectionate. (Genesis 26:6–11)
5. God wants us to enjoy the fruit of walking with him and growing even closer together. (Psalm 92:12–15)
6. God wants us to care for our own parents, rather than making them depend solely upon government assistance. (1 Timothy 5:8)

APPENDIX B—THE EXPERTS

Dan B. Allender teaches and counsels at Colorado Christian University and presents workshops about sexual-abuse recovery and counselor training. He is also an author and speaker.

Michael J. Anthony chairs the Department of Christian Education at Talbot School of Theology, Biola University. He has counseled hundreds of teens and young adult singles.

Claudia Arp, with her husband, David, is the cofounder and director of Marriage Alive International. She is a popular speaker, seminar leader, columnist, and author.

David Arp, with his wife, Claudia, is the cofounder and director of Marriage Alive International. He is a popular speaker, seminar leader, columnist, and author.

Kay Arthur is a well-known Bible teacher and best-selling author. She and her husband, Jack, are the founders of Precept Ministries, which reaches hundreds of thousands of people internationally through a radio ministry and inductive Bible studies.

David Augsburger is a writer and speaker with a Ph.D. in pastoral psychotherapy and family therapy. He has served two pastorates.

Wayne Barber is the Senior Pastor-Teacher of Woodland Park Baptist Church in Chattanooga, Tennessee, and is an author of books and a magazine column.

Bill Blackburn and his wife, Deana, have led family-life conferences and marriage-enrichment retreats extensively, along with authoring several books, individually and as cowriters, including *You TWO Are Important.*

Ron Blue is a Certified Public Accountant who has written several books about Christian financial matters. He is the managing partner of Christian Financial Management in Atlanta, Georgia.

Jill Briscoe is a world-renowned author and speaker, focusing on women's spiritual growth and marriage.

Stuart Briscoe has worked with youth, pastors, missionaries, and lay leaders in more than one hundred countries. He is the pastor of Elmbrook Church in Brookfield, Wisconsin, and the author of many books.

Rich Buhler is an author of several books, a speaker, and syndicated radio personality.

Larry Burkett is the founder and president of Christian Financial Concepts. He is the author of numerous books on financial matters and hosts two national daily radio programs, *How to Manage Your Money* and *Money Matters.*

Ross Campbell is the author of many popular books, including *How to Really Love Your Child* and *How to Really Love Your Teenager.*

Dave Carder is assistant pastor at First Evangelical Free Church of Fullerton, California, and the author of several books, including *Secrets of Your Family Tree.*

Randy Carlson is the founder and president of Today's Family Life, Inc. and Parent Talk, Inc. and the cohost of *Parent Talk,* a nationally syndicated radio program. He is also an author.

Henry Cloud is a licensed psychologist and cohost of the nationally broadcast *New Life Live!* radio program. He has authored several books and is a frequent speaker.

Edwin Louis Cole is an internationally acclaimed lecturer, public speaker, and author who conducts rallies and seminars encouraging men to reach their maximum potential in all areas of life.

William L. Coleman is an author and leader of family seminars.

Jim and Sally Conway are the founders and presidents of Midlife Dimensions, a ministry helping people through their midlife transitions.

Larry Crabb is a well-known speaker, author of numerous best-selling books including *God of My Father* and *Men and Women*, and Distinguished Scholar-in-Residence at Colorado Christian University in Morrison, Colorado.

Linda Dillow is a wife, mother, speaker, and author who often speaks on being a creative wife. She and her husband, Joseph, train Christian leaders in different parts of the world.

James Dobson is founder and president of Focus on the Family, a nonprofit organization that produces his nationally syndicated radio program heard on more than two thousand stations. He is a best-selling author of many books including *Hide or Seek*.

Elisabeth Elliot is the author of numerous books, including *A Chance to Die, Passion and Purity*, and *Shadow of the Almighty*. She is also a popular seminar leader and the speaker on her radio program, *Gateway to Joy*.

Bill Farrel is the pastor of Valley Bible Church in San Marcos, California. He is also a speaker at couples' and men's events, and the author of several books including *Marriage in the Whirlwind*, coauthored with his wife, Pam Farrel.

Pam Farrel is a pastor's wife, author, and speaker. She lives in southern California and has authored *Pure Pleasure: Making Your Marriage a Great Affair*.

Wayne Grudem is Associate Professor of Biblical and Systematic Theology at Trinity Evangelical Divinity School. He is the author of several books.

Michelle McKinney Hammond is a popular speaker at singles' conferences and retreats. She is a freelance writer, art director, producer, singer, and voice-over announcer for commercials and short films.

Willard F. Harley Jr. is a clinical psychologist and marriage counselor. He is also an author of several books, including *His Needs, Her Needs*.

Donald R. Harvey has his doctorate in Marriage and Family Therapy and is clinical director of Christian Counseling Services in Nashville, Tennessee.

Robert Hemfelt is a psychologist who specializes in the treatment of chemical dependencies, codependency, and compulsivity disorders. He is also an author and speaker.

Harville Hendrix has more than twenty years experience as an educator and therapist. He specializes in working with couples, teaching marital therapy to therapists, and conducting couples' workshops across the country.

Bob and Cinny Hicks minister in churches. Bob has served as Minister of Family Life Development for the Church of the Savior in Berwyn, Pennsylvania.

Liz Curtis Higgs has addressed audiences from more than thirteen hundred platforms all over the world. She is the award-winning author of thirteen books.

Albert Y. Hsu is employed at InterVarsity Press. He has also served on the leadership team of Kairos, the single adult community of Blanchard Road Alliance Church, Wheaton, Illinois.

Bill Hybels is pastor of Willow Creek Community Church, the second largest congregation in America. He is the author of many books, including *Honest to God?*.

Lynne Hybels is a busy wife and mother of two children. She is also an author, editor, freelance writer, and speaker.

Joy Jacobs is a popular speaker at women's conferences and an author of several books including *They Were Women Like Me*.

Duncan Jaenicke is a writer and editor of several books on psychological subjects.

Jerry B. Jenkins is the former vice president for publishing and currently writer-at-large for the Moody Bible Institute in Chicago. He is the author of over one hundred books, including the best-selling *Left Behind* series.

Carolyn A. Koons has become a spokesperson for a generation of unmarried Christian adults and frequently addresses the Christian education needs of singles at conferences and seminars. She is also the author of many books, including *Beyond Betrayal*.

David Kopp is a former editor of *Christian Parent Magazine* and a writer and speaker.

Heather Kopp is a writer and speaker.

Kevin Leman is a Christian psychologist, author, speaker, and regular guest on the radio program, *Parent Talk*.

Paul Lewis is the editor of the *Dads Only* newsletter, which gives encouragement to fathers.

Georgia Curtis Ling is an award-winning newspaper columnist and author of *What's in the Bible for . . .*™ *Women*.

Florence Littauer is the founder of Christian Leaders, Authors, and Speakers Seminar (CLASS). She is the author of many best-selling books and speaks throughout the world.

Marita Littauer is the president of Christian Leaders, Authors, and Speakers Seminar (CLASS). She is a best-selling author and professional speaker.

Tremper Longman III is the author of *How to Read the Psalms* and other books. He is a professor of Old Testament at Westminster Theological Seminary.

Max Lucado is the pastor of Oak Hills Church of Christ in San Antonio, Texas. He is the author of several best-selling books and speaks at Promise Keepers stadium events.

Sharon Marshall is the Score for College program coordinator for Orange County, California, Department of Education. She is also an author and a speaker.

Maxine Marsolini is a freelance writer, author, poet, and pastor's wife.

Josh McDowell is a widely sought after lecturer and best-selling author. He has written *Evidence That Demands a Verdict*, *More Than a Carpenter*, and many other books.

Paul Meier received an M.S. degree in cardiovascular physiology and is the cofounder of the Minirth-Meier Clinic. He is an author and speaker.

Andrea Wells Miller is an author/editor in the field of Christian music. She was formerly the director of music marketing and promotion for Word, Inc.

Kathy Collard Miller is the author of forty books and a nationally and internationally traveled speaker.

Keith Miller is the best-selling author of books such as *A Taste of New Wine, Please Love Me*, and *The Passionate People*.

Frank Minirth is a diplomat of the American Board of Psychiatry and Neurology and is the cofounder of the Minirth-Meier Clinic. He is an author and speaker.

Mary Alice Minirth is an author, homemaker, and mother of four.

Lois Mowday was married for over thirteen years before her husband was killed in a tragic hot-air balloon accident. She is an author and speaker.

Bruce Narramore is a licensed psychologist and author of several parenting books, including *Parenting with Love and Limits* and *Why Children Misbehave*.

Ruth Stafford Peale is the wife of the late Norman Vincent Peale and formerly a writer/editor for *Guideposts* magazine.

Gloria Okes Perkins is a writer of several books and a biblical counselor.

Eddie Rasnake worked in business before joining the staff of Campus Crusade for Christ. Currently, he serves at Woodland Park Baptist Church in Chattanooga, Tennessee, as Associate Pastor of Discipleship and Training.

Bobbie Reed has a Ph.D. in psychology and has authored several books for single adults.

Gwen Shamblin has had extensive experience in the field of nutrition both as a consulting registered dietitian and an instructor of nutrition at Memphis State University. She is the author of two books, *Weigh Down Diet* and *Rise Above*.

Charlie Shedd is a former pastor and the author of more than thirty-five books, including *Letters to Karen*.

Richard Shepherd has ministered at several different churches and since 1983, Woodland Park Baptist Church in Chattanooga, Tennessee. He also has traveled extensively training pastors and church leaders in the United States and abroad.

Quin Sherrer is a speaker and author of many books, including *Miracles Happen When You Pray*.

Gary Smalley is a husband, father, pastor, seminar leader, and author who ministers to crippled and whole marriages. He is the author of many best-selling books, including *If Only He Knew* and *For Better or for Best*.

M. Blaine Smith, a Presbyterian pastor, is director of Nehemiah Ministries, a resource ministry based in the Washington, D.C., area. His work includes giving seminars, lectures, and conferences.

Barb Snyder speaks at marriage seminars along with her husband, Chuck Snyder.

Chuck Snyder owns and operates an advertising agency and is an author and speaker, particularly about marriage.

Joseph M. Stowell is president of Moody Bible Institute and speaks frequently at churches and conferences. He also writes columns for *Moody* magazine and *Today in the Word*.

Deborah Strubel is an editor and writer serving both Christian and secular clients.

Charles Swindoll is a pastor, best-selling author, and president of Dallas Theological Seminary.

Joni Eareckson Tada is president of Joni and Friends, a ministry to the handicapped. She is also an author and speaker.

Jim Talley was an Associate Minister of Single Adults at First Baptist Church in Modesto, California, and now teaches singles' seminars.

Paul Tournier is a former doctor and counselor. He is the author of many books, including *Guilt and Grace*.

John Townsend is a psychologist and cohost of the nationally broadcast *New Life Live!* radio program. He is an author and speaker.

John Trent is president of Encouraging Words, a ministry dedicated to strengthening marriage and family relationships worldwide. He teaches seminars and is an author of many best-selling books.

Donna Vann is the coauthor of *Secrets of a Growing Marriage* and a missionary with Campus Crusade for Christ.

Roger Vann has worked alongside his wife, Donna, with couples in the "Here's Life Europe" minis-

try through Campus Crusade for Christ. He is the author of *Secrets of a Growing Marriage*.

Walter Wangerin Jr. is an author of books in many genres: fiction, nonfiction, short stories, poetry, and children's literature.

Neil Clark Warren is a practicing clinical psychologist and the founder of Associated Psychological Services in Pasadena, California. He authored *Make Anger Your Ally*.

Ed Wheat is a physician and certified sex therapist. He is also an author and speaker.

Mary Whelchel is the author of *The Christian Working Woman* and founder of a radio ministry by the same name.

Jerry White is president of The Navigators, a parachurch organization based in Colorado Springs, Colorado. He is also a writer and speaker.

Mary White is the wife of Jerry White and a writer and speaker.

Tim Woodroof is the pulpit minister at Otter Creek Church in Nashville, Tennessee. He also has authored several books and speaks at retreats and colleges.

H. Norman Wright has written over fifty-one books including the best-selling *Communication: Key to Your Marriage*. He is a licensed marriage and family counselor, and founder/director of Christian Marriage Enrichment.

Ed Young is pastor of the Second Baptist Church of Houston, Texas. He is well known for his renowned preaching and extensive teaching on marriage and family issues.

Zig Ziglar is a popular professional speaker and author of several books.

NOTE: To the best of our knowledge, all of the above information is accurate and up to date. In some cases we were unable to obtain biographical information.

—THE STARBURST EDITORS

ENDNOTES

Introduction

1. *Henry Cloud and John Townsend, Boundaries in Marriage* (Grand Rapids, MI: Zondervan Publishing House, 1999), 10.

Chapter 1

1. Neil Clark Warren, Ph.D., *Finding the Love of Your Life* (Colorado Springs: Focus on the Family Publishing, 1992), 1.
2. Michelle McKinney Hammond, *What to Do until Love Finds You* (Eugene, OR: Harvest House, 1997), 91.
3. Liz Curtis Higgs, *Bad Girls of the Bible* (Colorado Springs: WaterBrook, 1999), 23.
4. Larry Crabb, *The Marriage Builder* (Grand Rapids, MI: Zondervan Publishing House, 1982), 34.
5. Wayne Barber, Eddie Rasnake, and Richard Shepherd, *Following God* (Chattanooga: AMG Publishers, 1999), 107–108.
6. Mary Whelchel, *Common Mistakes Singles Make* (Old Tappan, NJ: Fleming H. Revell Company, 1989), 32.
7. Warren, *Finding the Love of Your Life*, 66.
8. Ibid., 68.
9. Ibid., 76.

Chapter 2

1. M. Blaine Smith, *Should I Get Married?* (Downers Grove, IL: InterVarsity Press, 1990), 36.
2. Ibid., 110.
3. William L. Coleman, *The Engagement Book* (Wheaton, IL: Tyndale House Publishers, 1980, 1990), 16.
4. David and Heather Kopp, *Love Stories God Told* (Eugene, OR: Harvest House, 1998), 25.
5. Coleman, *The Engagement Book*, 41.
6. Whelchel, *Common Mistakes Singles Make*, 47.
7. Warren, *Finding the Love of Your Life*, 5.
8. Smith, *Should I Get Married?*, 68.
9. Ibid., 79–80.
10. Ibid., 120.

Chapter 3

1. Josh McDowell and Paul Lewis, *Givers, Takers and Other Kinds of Lovers* (Wheaton, IL: Tyndale House Publishers, Inc., 1980), 30.
2. Carolyn A. Koons and Michael J. Anthony, *Single Adult Passages* (Grand Rapids, MI: Baker Book House, 1991), 147.
3. McDowell and Lewis, *Givers, Takers and Other Kinds of Lovers*, 31.
4. Higgs, *Bad Girls of the Bible*, 26.
5. Ibid., 29.
6. Albert Y. Hsu, *Singles at the Crossroads* (Downers Grove, IL: InterVarsity Press, 1997), 153.
7. Higgs, *Bad Girls of the Bible*, 34–35.
8. Joseph M. Stowell, *Perilous Pursuits* (Chicago: Moody Press, 1994), 88.
9. Joy Jacobs and Deborah Strubel, *Single, Whole & Holy* (Camp Hill, PA: Horizon Books, 1996), 87.
10. Whelchel, *Common Mistakes Singles Make*, 58–59.
11. Ibid., 52.
12. Keith Miller and Andrea Wells Miller, *The Single Experience* (Waco, TX: Word Books, 1981), 12.
13. McDowell and Lewis, *Givers, Takers and Other Kinds of Lovers*, 60–61.
14. Jim Talley and Bobbie Reed, *Too Close, Too Soon* (Nashville: Thomas Nelson, 1982), 142.
15. Hammond, *What to Do until Love Finds You*, 43.
16. Elisabeth Elliot, *Quest for Love* (Grand Rapids, MI: Fleming H. Revell Company, 1996), 203.

Chapter 4

1. Roger and Donna Vann, *Secrets of a Growing Marriage* (San Bernardino, CA: Here's Life Publishers, 1985), 111–112.
2. Bill and Pam Farrel, *Marriage in the Whirlwind* (Downers Grove, IL: InterVarsity Press, 1996), 84–85.
3. Harville Hendrix, Ph.D., *Getting the Love You Want* (New York: HarperCollins Publishers, 1988), 105.
4. Vann, *Secrets of a Growing Marriage*, 113.
5. David and Claudia Arp, *Marriage Moments* (Ann Arbor, MI: Servant Publications, 1998), 100.

6. Gary Smalley, *The Joy of Committed Love* (Grand Rapids, MI: Zondervan Publishing House, 1984), 46–47.

Chapter 5

1. Dan B. Allender and Tremper Longman III, *Intimate Allies* (Wheaton, IL: Tyndale House Publishers, 1995), 99.
2. Barber, Rasnake, and Shepherd, *Following God*, 129.
3. Smalley, *The Joy of Committed Love*, 93.
4. Florence Littauer and Marita Littauer, *Talking So People Will Listen* (Ann Arbor, MI: Vine [Servant], 1998), 77.
5. John Trent, *Love for All Seasons* (Chicago: Moody Press, 1996), 65.
6. Charlie Shedd, quoted in Cecil Murphey, compiler, *The Encyclopedia of Christian Marriage* (Old Tappan, NJ: Fleming H. Revell Company, 1984), 115.
7. David Augsburger, *Cherishable Love and Marriage* (Scottsdale, AZ: Herald Press, 1971), 69.
8. Bill and Lynne Hybels, *Fit to Be Tied* (Grand Rapids, MI: Zondervan Publishing House, 1991), 123.
9. David Augsburger, *Caring Enough to Confront* (Ventura, CA: Gospel Light, 1973), 51.
10. Hybels, *Fit to Be Tied*, 125.

Chapter 6

1. H. Norman Wright, *Romancing Your Marriage* (Ventura, CA: Regal Books, 1987), 117.
2. Willard F. Harley Jr., *Give & Take* (Grand Rapids, MI: Fleming H. Revell Company, 1996), 21.
3. Dr. James Dobson, *Love for a Lifetime* (Sisters, OR: Multnomah Books, 1987), 54–55.
4. Kopp, *Love Stories God Told*, 91.
5. Chuck and Barb Snyder, *Incompatibility: Grounds for a Great Marriage* (Sisters, OR: Questar Publishers, Inc., 1988), 227.
6. Rich Buhler, quoted in Thomas Nelson Editors, *The Making of a Marriage* (Nashville: Thomas Nelson Publishers, 1993), 78.
7. Dobson, *Love for a Lifetime*, 38.
8. Donald R. Harvey, *The Drifting Marriage* (Old Tappan, NJ: Fleming H. Revell Company, 1988), 193.
9. Kopp, *Love Stories God Told*, 65.
10. Farrel, *Marriage in the Whirlwind*, 24.
11. Hybels, *Fit to Be Tied*, 163.
12. Tim Woodroof, *Walk This Way* (Colorado Springs: NavPress, 1999), 74.
13. Hammond, *What to Do until Love Finds You*, 194.

Chapter 7

1. Linda Dillow, quoted in Thomas Nelson Editors, *The Making of a Marriage*, 58.
2. Arp, *Marriage Moments*, 109.
3. Crabb, *The Marriage Builder*, 22.

4. Barber, Rasnake, and Shepherd, *Following God*, 186.
5. Arp, *Marriage Moments*, 45.
6. Wright, *Romancing Your Marriage*, 72.
7. Farrel, *Marriage in the Whirlwind*, 24.
8. Dobson, *Love for a Lifetime*, 59.
9. Hybels, *Fit to Be Tied*, 162.
10. Snyder, *Incompatibility: Grounds for a Great Marriage!*, 236.
11. Hybels, *Fit to Be Tied*, 161.
12. Ed Young, *Romancing the Home* (Nashville: Broadman & Holman Publishers, 1994), 90–91.
13. Dr. James Dobson, *Straight Talk to Men and Their Wives* (Waco, TX: Word Books, 1980), 64.
14. Wayne Grudem, quoted in John Piper and Wayne Grudem, editors, *Recovering Biblical Manhood and Womanhood* (Wheaton, IL: Crossways Books, 1991), 194–195.
15. *Life Application Bible* (Wheaton, IL and Grand Rapids, MI: Tyndale House Publishers and Zondervan Publishing House, 1991), 2261.

Chapter 8

1. Robert Hemfelt, Frank Minirth, and Paul Meier, *Love Is A Choice* (Nashville: Thomas Nelson Publishers, 1989), 211.
2. Max Lucado, *He Still Moves Stones* (Dallas: Word Publishing, 1993), 44.
3. Dobson, *Love for a Lifetime*, 103–104.
4. Hemfelt, Minirth, and Meier, *Love Is A Choice*, 209.
5. Kathy Collard Miller, *Since Life Isn't A Game, These Are God's Rules* (Lancaster, PA: Starburst Publishers, 1999), 88–89.
6. Hemfelt, Minirth, and Meier, *Love Is A Choice*, 209.
7. Stuart Briscoe, *The Ten Commandments* (Wheaton, IL: Harold Shaw Publisher, 1986, revised 1993), 75.
8. Jill Briscoe, quoted in Stuart and Jill Briscoe, *Pulling Together When You're Pulled Apart* (Wheaton, IL: Victor Books, 1991), 148–149.
9. Briscoe, *Pulling Together When You're Pulled Apart*, 148.
10. Briscoe, *The Ten Commandments*, 76.
11. Ibid., 84.
12. Ruth Stafford Peale, quoted in Thomas Nelson Editors, *The Making of a Marriage*, 250.
13. Ibid., 244.

Chapter 9

1. Kay Arthur, *Lord, Only You Can Change Me* (Sisters, OR: Multnomah, 1995), 156–157.
2. Paul Tournier, *To Understand Each Other* (Atlanta: John Knox Press, 1967), 62–63.
3. Augsburger, *Cherishable Love and Marriage*, 46.
4. Jerry and Mary White, quoted in Howard and Jeanne Hendricks, general editors, with LaVonne

Neff, *Husbands and Wives* (Wheaton, IL: Victor Books, 1988), 149.

5. Arp, *Marriage Moments*, 172–173.
6. Vann, *Secrets of a Growing Marriage*, 153.
7. Bob and Cinny Hicks, quoted in Hendricks, *Husbands and Wives*, 168.
8. Georgia Curtis Ling, *What's in the Bible for. . .*™ *Women* (Lancaster, PA: Starburst Publishers, 1999), 171.
9. Higgs, *Bad Girls of the Bible*, 144.
10. Bob and Cinny Hicks, quoted in Hendricks, *Husbands and Wives*, 168.

Chapter 10

1. Ross Campbell, quoted in Jay Kesler, editor, *Parents and Teenagers* (Wheaton, IL: Victor Books, 1984), 242.
2. Dr. James C. Dobson, *Parenting Isn't for Cowards* (Waco, TX: Word Books, 1987), 24.
3. Charles Swindoll, *You and Your Child* (Nashville: Thomas Nelson, 1990), 61.
4. Randy Carlson, quoted in Dr. Kevin Leman and Randy Carlson, *Parent Talk* (Nashville: Thomas Nelson Publishers, 1993), 163.
5. Henry Cloud and John Townsend, *Boundaries in Marriage*, 167.
6. Maxine Marsolini, *Blended Families* (Chicago: Moody Press, 2000), 88.
7. Ibid., 115.

Chapter 11

1. Bruce Narramore, *Help! I'm a Parent!* (Grand Rapids, MI: Zondervan Publishing House, 1972), 41.
2. Zig Ziglar, quoted in Thomas Nelson Editors, *The Making of a Marriage*, 275.
3. Snyder, *Incompatibility: Grounds for a Great Marriage!*, 221.
4. Gwen Shamblin, *Rise Above* (Nashville: Thomas Nelson, 2000), 211.
5. Swindoll, *You and Your Child*, 70.
6. Narramore, *Help! I'm a Parent!*, 84.
7. Ibid., 34–35.
8. Swindoll, *You and Your Child*, 23.

Chapter 12

1. Kopp, *Love Stories God Told*, 65.
2. Swindoll, *You and Your Child*, 57.
3. Frank Minirth, quoted in Frank and Mary Alice Minirth et al., *Passages of Marriage* (Nashville: Thomas Nelson Publishers, 1991), 114.
4. Swindoll, *You and Your Child*, 157.
5. Dobson, *Parenting Isn't for Cowards*, 214.
6. Swindoll, *You and Your Child*, 157.
7. Quin Sherrer with Ruthanne Garlock, *How to Pray for Your Children* (Ventura, CA: Regal Books, 1998), 20.
8. Dobson, *Parenting Isn't for Cowards*, 202.
9. Ibid., 76–77.

Chapter 13

1. Bill and Pam Farrel and Jim and Sally Conway, *Pure Pleasure* (Downers Grove, IL: InterVarsity Press, 1994), 18.
2. David and Claudia Arp, "Sex After Kids?" *Marriage Partnership*, Spring 2000, 34.
3. Bill Hybels, quoted in Bill Hybels and Rob Wilkins, *Tender Love* (Chicago: Moody Press, 1993), 14–15.
4. Ibid., 36.
5. Ed Wheat and Gloria Okes Perkins, *Love Life for Every Married Couple* (New York: HarperCollins Publishers, 1980), 172.
6. Ibid., 176.
7. Arp, *Marriage Partnership*, 26, 34.
8. Hybels, *Tender Love*, 36–37.
9. Smalley, *The Joy of Committed Love*, 75.
10. Hybels, *Fit to Be Tied*, 169–170.
11. Gary Smalley, *Love Is a Decision* (Dallas: Word Publishing, 1989), 146.

Chapter 14

1. Lois Mowday, *The Snare* (Colorado Springs: NavPress, 1988), 79.
2. Dobson, *Love for a Lifetime*, 106–107.
3. Dave Carder with Duncan Jaenicke, *Torn Asunder* (Chicago: Moody Press, 1992), 108.
4. James C. Dobson, *Love Must Be Tough* (Waco, TX: Word Books, 1983), 56.
5. Mowday, *The Snare*, 84.
6. Carder with Jaenicke, *Torn Asunder*, 53.
7. Ibid., 184.
8. Farrel and Conway, *Pure Pleasure*, 10.
9. Allender and Longman III, *Intimate Allies*, 223.
10. Jerry B. Jenkins, *Loving Your Marriage Enough to Protect It* (Chicago: Moody Press, 1993), 69.
11. Walter Wangerin Jr., *As for Me and My House* (Nashville: Thomas Nelson Publishers, 1987), 195.
12. Jenkins, *Loving Your Marriage Enough to Protect It*, 58.
13. Snyder, *Incompatibility: Grounds for a Great Marriage!*, 222.
14. Jim Conway and Sally Conway, *When A Mate Wants Out* (Grand Rapids, MI: Zondervan Publishing House, 1992), 53–54.
15. Young, *Romancing the Home*, 112.

Chapter 15

1. John Trent, *Love for All Seasons* (Chicago: Moody Press, 1996), 127.
2. Farrel and Conway, *Pure Pleasure*, 116.
3. Gary Smalley, *Love Is a Decision* (Dallas: Word Publishing, 1989), 151.
4. Wheat and Perkins, *Love Life for Every Married Couple*, 87.
5. Smalley, *Love Is a Decision*, 146.

6. Ibid., 156.
7. Trent, *Love for All Seasons*, 138.
8. Ibid.
9. Bill and Pam Farrel, quoted in Farrel and Conway, *Pure Pleasure*, 123.
10. Harley Jr., *Give & Take*, 193.
11. Bill and Pam Farrel, quoted in Farrel and Conway, *Pure Pleasure*, 119.
12. Kevin Leman, *Sex Begins in the Kitchen* (Ventura, CA: Regal Books, 1981), 155.
13. Trent, *Love for All Seasons*, 176.
14. Ed Young, quoted in Wheat and Perkins, *Love Life for Every Married Couple*, 104.

Chapter 16

1. Edwin Louis Cole, *Communication, Sex & Money* (Tulsa: Honor Books, 1987), 169.
2. Larry Burkett, *Giving and Tithing* (Chicago: Moody Press, 1991), 25–26.
3. Cole, *Communication, Sex & Money*, 174.
4. Larry Burkett, "Possessions and Spiritual Accountability," July 2000, <http://money.crosswalk.com/articles/item/1,1237,4174,00.htm> (July 2000).
5. Ron Blue, *Master Your Money* (Nashville: Thomas Nelson Publishers, 1986), 55.
6. Ibid.
7. Cole, *Communication, Sex & Money*, 182.
8. Larry Burkett, *Giving and Tithing*, November 15, 1999, http://www.cfcministry.org/articles/viewarticle.asp?id=10.

Chapter 17

1. Minirth et al., *Passages of Marriage*, 217.
2. Ibid., 220.
3. Bill Blackburn, quoted in Bill and Deana Blackburn, *Stress Points in Marriage* (Waco, TX: Word Books, 1986), 208.
4. Arthur, *Lord, Only You Can Change Me*, 88.

5. Ibid., 92.
6. David Augsburger, *Sustaining Love* (Ventura, CA: Regal Books, 1988), 15.
7. Allender and Longman III, *Intimate Allies*, 11.

Chapter 18

1. Harvey, *The Drifting Marriage*, 44.
2. Joni Eareckson Tada, quoted in Hendricks, *Husbands and Wives*, 445.
3. Harvey, *The Drifting Marriage*, 103.
4. Hybels, *Fit to Be Tied*, 195–196.
5. Smalley, *The Joy of Committed Love*, 29.

Chapter 19

1. Stowell, *Perilous Pursuits*, 28.
2. Sally Conway, *Your Husband's Midlife Crisis* (Colorado Springs: Victor Books, 1987), 23.
3. Ibid., 24.
4. Ibid., 87–88.
5. Conway, *When a Mate Wants Out*, 18.
6. Sharon Marshall, *Surviving Separation and Divorce* (Grand Rapids, MI: Baker Book House, 1988), 55.
7. Hybels, *Fit to Be Tied*, 213.

Chapter 20

1. *USA Today*, June 10, 1999, 3A.
2. Arp, *Marriage Moments*, 115.
3. Briscoe, *Pulling Together When You're Pulled Apart*, 217.
4. Barber, Rasnake, and Shepherd, *Following God*, 18–19.
5. Wright, *Romancing Your Marriage*, 148–149.
6. Bill Blackburn, quoted in Blackburn, *Stress Points in Marriage*, 222.
7. Wheat and Perkins, *Love Life for Every Married Couple*, 77.
8. Bill Blackburn, quoted in Blackburn, *Stress Points in Marriage*, 224.
9. Minirth et al., *Passages of Marriage*, 247.

INDEX

Boldface numbers indicate defined (What?) terms in the sidebar.

Aphrodite, 202
Apollos, 53, 144
Apostle Paul, the (see Paul)
Apostle Peter, the (see Peter)
Apostles (see Disciples)
Appearance:
    aging and, 308
    maintaining, after marriage, 232
    (See also Beauty)
Appreciation:
    approval, showing, 232–233
    of differences, 89
    (See also Encouragement; Praise;
        Thankfulness)
Aptly, 63
Aquila and Priscilla, xii, 53–54, 110, 141,
    144
Ardent, 243
Ark, 67
Arp, David and Claudia, 142
    on Couples' Nights Out, 143
    on elderly couples, 306
    on goal-setting, 57
    on intimacy, Bible secrets for, 98
    on marital intimacy, 102
    on sex, as God's idea, 200
    on sex, scheduling, 204
Arrogance (see Pride)
Arthur, Kay:
    on friends, influence of, 136
    on God, nature of, 268
    on good, God as causing, 266
Asherah, 20–21
Asia Minor, 53
    map of, 54
Attitude, as choice, 93
Augsburger, David:
    on conflict resolution, 73
    on confrontation, the art of, 76
    on growth, life and, 271
    on ministry, partnership in, 141
Authorities, 278
Autonomy, 122

B
Baal, 20
    illustration of, 21
Barak, 144–145
    Barak and Deborah's battle, map of,
        145
Barber, Wayne, Eddie Rasnake, and
    Richard Shepherd:
    on Abraham and Sarah, lies by, 308
    on Esther, 8
    on the marriage bond, 101
    on words, the power of, 64

Barren, barrenness, 11, 181–184, 194
    Hannah as, 90, 181–182, 272
    Sarah as, 271, 298
    stigma of, 182
Bathsheba:
    David and, 185–186, 215–220, 272
    Solomon as son of, 234–235
Beatitudes, 93
Beauty:
    of Abigail, 12–13, 94
    of Bathsheba, 215
    cosmetics, 7–8
    of Esther, 8
    external and internal, 8
    maintaining after marriage, 232
    of Sarah, at age ninety, 308
    of Solomon, 239
    of Solomon's bride, 230–231, 236,
        241
    treatments, 7–8
Belial, 19, 137
Benjamin, 74
Bible, the, xi
    the New International Version (NIV),
        xiii
    studying with spouse, 104
    as truth, xi
    as Word of God, xi
Birthright, 159
Bitterness, avoiding, 75
Black Sea, 53
Blackburn, Bill:
    on empty nest, 310
    on life's stages, 265
    on old age, preparing for, 312
Blaming, 75, 263, 273
    responding to, 296
    (See also Criticism)
Blended family, 161–164
Blessed:
    giving to God as, 257
    meekness as, 93
Blessing others, 68
Blessings:
    children as, 153
    of receiving ministry, 147
    thankfulness for, 105 (See also
        Thankfulness)
Blue, Ron:
    on borrowing money, 255
    on debt, 254
Boaz and Ruth, 25–27
Body, as temple of Holy Spirit, 30, 223
Bondage, 81
Books, of Bible (see individual names)
Boone, Wellington, 92

Boredom, in marriage, 226
Born again, 139
Breaking of bread, 146
Breakups:
    divorce (see Divorce)
    ending an engagement, 25
Briscoe, Jill:
    on mother-in-law, attitude toward,
        127
    on Naomi and Orpah, 128
    on old folk, Bible examples of, 307
Briscoe, Stuart:
    on extended family, value of, 129
    on Jesus before family, 131
    on love languages, 87
    on parents, honoring, 127
Burdens, bearing, 284–285
Burkett, Larry:
    on stewardship, 251, 253
    on tithing, 256
Burnt offerings, 67
Bush, George and Barbara, 305
Busyness (see Overcommitment)

C
Camaraderie, 280
Camels, Rebekah watering, 22
Campbell, Ross, on unconditional love,
    154
Canaan, 21, 45
Canaanites, Israelites, battling, 144–145
Cancer, 269–270, 313–314
Candor, 109
Carder, Dave, with Duncan Jaenicke:
    on adultery, 217
    on David's adultery, 219
    on sexual attraction, extramarital,
        213
Caregiving, 280
    of elderly parents, 314–315
    spouse, consideration for during,
        315–316
Carlson, Randy, on children, avoiding
    favoritism among, 158
Catapults, 82
Celebration, marriage as source, 99
Celibacy, Jesus and, 40 (See also Purity)
Championship, 110
Change:
    changing your spouse, 93
    as from God, 93
    inevitability of, 264–265
    love as causing, 83
    positive, 271
    versatility and, 31
    willingness for, 267

Character:
    hardship as developing, 265–267, 312
    husband's, wife's sexual response to, 231
    strengthening, 133
    traits (see Personality; Qualities; Temperaments)
Characteristics, **10**
Charity, 252
Cheating, on spouse (see Adultery)
Childlessness, 11, 181–184, 194
    of Abraham and Sarah, 271, 298
    Hannah's grief regarding, 90, 181–182, 272
    stigma of, 182
Children, 52
    abuse of, 157
    adult (see Adult children)
    anger at, 156–158, 164, 167, 169
    boundary-setting for, 168
    characteristics of, 154–155
    childlessness, 11, 181–184, 194
    Christian upbringing for, 171, 177–178, 191
    confidence-building in, 189
    death of, 218–220
    developmental differences among, 155
    disagreements about having, 183–184
    disciplining (see Discipline)
    disobedience of, handling, 154, 156–158, 165–179
    divorce and, 160, 162, 301
    empty nest, 309–311
    favoritism, avoiding, 158–159, 164
    as gifts, 153
    God, entrusting to, 187–191
    as individual, 155
    involvement in lives of, parental, 172
    Israelites as valuing, 182, 203
    Jesus with, 31
    letting go of, 181–195
    longing for, 181–184
    losing a child, 185–187, 194
    loving unconditionally, 153–164
    manipulation by, 170
    marriage, children's effect on, 159–160, 164
    maturity level of, 155, 157, 190
    nature of, 155, 157
    overprotectiveness, avoiding, 189–195
    planning for, 11
    potential of, 155
    praying for, 192, 195
    "problem children," 190
    rebellious, 192, 266
    responsibility, giving increased, 190
    rules and, 168, 172–173
    security vs. insecurity in, 168
    special-needs, 104–105
    spiritual life of, 191
    teenage (see Teenagers)
Choice(s), **63**
    and consequences, giving children, 154, 162, 166–168, 171
    good, Jesus as making, 30
    love, as choice, 76, 81–85, 94
    loving, xii
    temptation and, 223
    unwise, 193
Choleric, 31
Chrestus, 53
Christ (see Jesus Christ)
Christians, Christianity:
    difficulties of, 262
    early, Aquila and Priscilla as, 53–54
    friendships with other, 135–139
    persecution of early, 59, 168
    as representing Christ, 47
    (See also Ministry; Witness, Christian)
Chrysolite, **239**
Church, Christian, 52
    as bride of Christ, 23, 201
    as bride of God, 97, 100
    early, 144–147
    finding the right, 139–141, 150
    Holy Spirit and, 23
    of Priscilla and Aquila, 144
Circumcision, **58**, 74
City of David, **67**
Claudius, Roman emperor, 53
Closeness (see Intimacy)
Cloud, Henry, and John Townsend:
    on living each day, xi–xii
    on marriage, children's effect on, 160
Coerce, **191**
Cole, Edwin Louis:
    on God and giving, 256
    on money, 250
    on riches, 251
Coleman, William L.:
    on 1 Corinthians 13:4–8, 23
    on marriage without love, 22
Comfort, 109
    "miserable comforters," 148–149
    tips for comforting others, 147–150
Commit, **56**
Commitment, 109, 275, 279–280, 286
    to God, 158
    during illness, 280
    in marriage, 235, 273–274, 279–280, 286, 288
    marriage as lifelong, 235
physical, 28
renewing, 273–274
Communication, 109, 295
    gender differences in, 106
    guidelines for good, 65–66
    listening and (see Listening)
    of needs, 87
    positive, 68
    sex and, 242
    during tough times, 273
    as vital to marriage, 117
Communion (breaking of bread), 146
Communion (encouraging spouse's spirituality), 109
Companionship, 109
    of Adam and Eve, 3–4
    between Ruth and Naomi, 128
Compassion, 296
Compassionate, **26**
Compatibility, **27**–28
    determining, 34
Compels, **147**
Compiled, **64**
Complements, **5**
Complicity, **223**
Compliments (see Praise)
Compromise, 32, 106, 285
    in conflict resolution, 76–77
Concubines, 219
    of Solomon, 290
Confidence, fostering in children, 189
Conflict resolution, xii, 73–79
    praying together, 103
    principles for, 76–77
Conformed, **265**
Confrontation, 89
    constructive aspect of, 76
Connotations, **132**
Consensus, **189**
Consequences:
    for Adam and Eve's sin, 42
    for David's adultery, 218–219, 227
    in disciplining children, 154, 162, 166–168, 171
    giving spouse, for sexual sin, 214
Contentment, happiness vs., 251
Control, 69
Convert, **19**
Conway, Jim and Sally, 294
    on adultery of a spouse, 225
    on midlife crisis, 290, 293, 296
    on saving a marriage, 299
    (See also Farrel, Bill and Pam, and Jim and Sally Conway)
Corinth, **53**–54, 144
Correction, of children (see Discipline)

Cosmetics, 7–8
Counseling, 11
   choosing a counselor, 138
   Christian, 77, 300–301
   for couples, 55
   godly friends as counselors, 135
   opposite sex and, 221
   premarital, 25, 57
   support groups, 280
   tips for counseling others, 147–149
Couple, your mission as, 51
Couples:
   comparisons with other, avoiding,
     286–287
   elderly (see Elderly couples)
   friendship with others, 135–150
   God and, xi
   relationship vision, defining, 55
   (See also Dating; Engagement;
     Marriage; Spouse; individual
     topics)
Couples in the Bible:
   Abraham and Sarah, xii, 74, 271, 298
   Adam and Eve (see Adam and Eve)
   Ananias and Sapphira, 146, 257
   Aquila and Priscilla, xii, 53–54, 110,
     141, 144
   Boaz and Ruth, 25–27
   David and Abigail, xii, 12–13, 94
   David and Bathsheba, 185–186, 215–
     220, 272
   David and Michal, 67–68, 133
   Deborah and Lappidoth, 144
   Esther and Xerxes, 75, 138
   Hannah and Elkanah, 90, 181–182,
     272
   Hosea and Gomer, 86
   Isaac and Rebekah, 110–111, 159,
     206
   Jacob and Leah, 74
   Jacob and Rachel, 44, 74, 271–272
   Job and his wife, 72–73, 148, 262–263
   Joseph and Mary, 36, 272
   Manoah and his wife (Samson's
     parents), 193
   Moses and Zipporah, 74
   Samson and Delilah, 27–28
   Solomon and his bride, 229–246
   Uriah and Bathsheba, 272
   "Couples' Nights Out," 142–143
Courtship (see Dating)
Covenant, Ark of, 67
Crabb, Larry:
   on Christian marriage as witness,
     100–101
   on fulfillment through Jesus, 6

Crises, handling, 262 (See also Trouble)
Criticism, 68–70, 75, 232–233, 273
   "constructive," 70, 78
Culprit, **290**

D

Dancing, David before the Ark, 67–68
Dating, 3–50
   compatibility, determining, 27–29
   finding the right person, 17–34
   purity during, 37–50
   self-esteem and, 10–15
   unbelievers, 19–21
   (See also individual topics)
Dating your spouse, 58, 109, 142
David, King, xii
   and Abigail, 12–13, 94
   and Absalom, 172, 219
   and Bathsheba, 185–186, 215–220,
     272
   City of David, Jerusalem as, 67
   deception by, 217
   as a father, 172
   in-law problems of, 133
   Jesus as descendant of, 26
   with Michal, 67–68, 133
   and Nabal, 12–13, 94
   Nathan and, 218–220
   Obed as grandfather of, 26
   Saul as father-in-law, 133
   sin of, 215–220
   wives and offspring of, 48
   writings of, 220
Daydreaming, dangers of, 221–224
Death, 99, 287–288, 315
   fear of, 312
   of a parent, 315
   preparation for, 280
   as punishment for Sapphira and
     Ananias, 146
   of spouse, 313
Deborah, 145
   Deborah and Barak's battle, map of,
     145
   and Lappidoth, 144
Debt, 253–255, 258
Deceiver, Satan as, 40–43
Deception:
   by Abraham and Sarah, 308
   by Ananias and Sapphira, 146
   by David, 217
   by Delilah, 27–28
   of Eve by Satan (the serpent), 19, 38–
     41
   by Rebekah, 159
Decisionmaking, responsibility for, 156

Decrees, precepts, **166**
Deify, **131**
Delilah, 27–28
Denial, 28
   adultery and, 212
Dependency:
   healthy and unhealthy, 234
   on parents after marriage, 122–125,
     134
Depression:
   during midlife crisis (see Midlife
     crisis)
   of Naomi, 131
   suicidal thoughts, 157
Desecrated, **270**
Desire, sexual, 43, 45, 208, 243
   and gender differences, 111–112,
     203–206, 208, 232, 242
   and purity (see Purity)
Despair:
   seeking God in, 161
   (See also Trouble)
Destitute, **26**
Detestable, **270**
Detrimental, **175**
Devil (see Satan)
Devotions, sharing, 104
Diabetes, 295
Diabolical, **138**
Differences:
   accepting and appreciating, 88–89
   problems resulting from, 34
   resolving, 11–12
   understanding, 95
   (See also Conflict resolution)
Difficulties (see Trouble)
Dillow, Linda, on Adam and Eve's
     intimacy, 98
Dinah, 45
Disability, 285
Disagreements:
   working out, 11–12
   (See also Conflict resolution;
     Differences)
Disappointment, 182
   patience in, 10
Discerning, **66**
Disciples, 169
   of Jesus, 191–192
   Jesus' treatment of, 155
Discipline, 165, 178
   of children, 156, 164, 167
   consequences, giving, 154, 162, 166–
     168, 171
   consistency in, 156, 175
   disagreements regarding, 175–176

encouragement and, 169
fairness in, 169
God's, of Adam and Eve, 171
God's, of us, 166, 169
loving, 166–171
punishment vs., 166–167
respect, as fostering, 169–170
result of, 170–171
rewards as part of, 173–174
security vs. insecurity and, 168
spanking, 174–175
Discontentment, 69
Disdainful, **69**
Dishonesty, 15
of Ananias and Sapphira, 257
Disillusionment, **82**, 88
in love, overcoming, 81–85
Disobedience:
causes of, evaluating, 156
consequences, giving children, 154, 162, 166–168, 171
to God, consequences of, 42, 256
handling children's, 154, 156–158, 165–179
unconditional love and, 154
(*See also* Discipline)
Disparage, **89**
Disposition (temperament), **31**–33, 34, 155
Distrust, 6
Divorce, 25, 29, 99, 298–303
adultery and, 213, 225
children and, 160, 162, 301
Christian counseling and, 301
God as hating, 270–271, 274, 299–300, 302
God's love despite, 161–162, 164
not an option, 76, 109
ramifications of, 301
recovering from, 301–302
spouse as wanting, 301
Divorce rate, 219
Dobson, James:
on adultery, 214
on childrearing, 191
on children and risk, 188
on children, individual temperaments in, 155
on compromise, 106
on differences, gender-based, 88
on disillusionment, overcoming, 84
on husband as leader, 113
on infidelity, 214
on parents, separating from, 122
on pornography, 212
on prayer, intercessory, 192

Dominating, refraining from, 103, 113–114
Dreams, of Solomon's bride, 233–234, 237–238
Drug abuse, 266
Duality, **201**
Dynasty, **13**
Dysfunctional family, 159, 294

E
Early church, 144–147 (*See also* Aquila and Priscilla)
Eastern sheepfold, illustration of, 116
Ecclesiastes, Book of, 289–292, 306, 309
Eden, Garden of, 39–42 (*See also* Adam and Eve)
Egypt, 71
Elderly couples, 206, 244–245, 305–312
enjoying senior years, 313
enjoying sex, 310–311
(*See also* Aging; Old age)
Elders, wisdom of, 129–130, 134, 306
Eli, 181–182
Elijah, and Ahab, 20
Elixir, **74**
Elizabeth, 307
Elkanah and Hannah, 90, 181–182, 272
Elliot, Elisabeth, on sexual foreplay, 49
Emancipated, **122**
Emotional compatibility, 28
Emotional health, 10–13, 15
Emotions, unreliability of, 23, 34, 84
Empathy, 149
Employment (see *Work*)
Empty nest, 309–311, 317
Emulate, **144**, **186**
Encouragement, 69
disciplining children and, 169
in effective communication, 66
(*See also* Appreciation; Praise)
Engagement:
breaking, 25
evaluating future spouse, 5, 17–35
preparation for marriage, 3–50
purity during (*see* Purity)
(*See also* individual topics)
Enmity, **73**
Envy, 23–24, 69
Ephesians, Book of, 14
Ephesus, 144
Ephraim, tribe of, 181
Equality, between spouses, 113
Equally yoked oxen, illustration of, 20
Esau, 159
Esther (Queen), 138
beauty of, 8–9

Book of, 8
Xerxes and, 8, 75
Eternity, 268
Ethics, compatibility regarding, 28
Evangelism (*see* Ministry; Witness, Christian)
Evangelist, **59**
Apollos, 53, 144
Eve:
as Adam's helper, 3–5
creation of, 4–6, 97, 121, 199–200
deception of by serpent, 19, 38–41
submission to Adam, 42
temptation of, 19, 39–40, 116
(*See also* Adam and Eve)
Evil, 23–24, 268
Ahab, repenting of, 20
Haman's plot as, 138
Jezebel as, 20
knowledge of, 39
(*See also* Satan; Sin)
Exacerbates, **213**
Exalt, **141**
Exasperate, **156**
Explicit, **212**
Extinction, **8**
Extramarital sex (*see* Adultery)
Extroversion, 31

F
Fabrics, Bible time, 64
Failure, learning from, 190
Faith, 267, 277
and marriage, 139
personal, 47
Faithfulness, 10, 28, 207, 288
Fall, the, 39–42
aftermath of, 14
Family, families:
blended, 161–164
dysfunctional, 159, 294
extended, 129, 307
mission statement, developing, 55–56, 61
putting Jesus first, 131, 134
responsibility in, 314
rules, establishing, 172–173
strengths and weaknesses within, 132
as a team, 168
(*See also* Children; In-laws; Parents)
Fantasies, 48–50
controlling, 221–224
Farrel, Bill and Pam:
on intimacy, 105
on priorities, 55
on reflecting spouse's feelings, 91

on sex, women initiating, 238
on the Song of Songs, 242
Farrel, Bill and Pam, and Jim and Sally
Conway:
on extramarital sex, effects of, 219
on sex, 200
on the Song of Songs, 230
Father of lies, Satan as, 38
Father:
David as, 172
responsibility of, 156
(*See also* Children; Parenting;
Parenthood)
Fatherhood, Paul on, 156
Faultfinding (*see* Criticism)
Favoritism (parental):
avoiding, 158–159, 164
of Isaac and Rebekah, 159
Fear, 317
diminishing, 295
of God, 42
God's help for, 312
of illness, 312
love and, 245
result of, xi–xii
trust vs., 188
Feelings:
acknowledging and reflecting
spouse's, 90–91, 95
unreliability of, 23, 34, 84
Fellowship offerings, **67**
Female impurity, **201**
Fidelity, **207**
Finances (*see* Money)
Financial opportunities, taking, 253
1 Corinthians 13:4–8, on love, 23–24, 34,
84, 244
Flax plant, illustration of, 65
Flirting, 216, 221
with spouse, 316
Foibles, **132**
Forbidden fruit, 39–42
Foreplay, 204–205
Forgiveness, 77
in conflict resolution, 76, 79
God's, 14, 276–277, 308–309
by Hosea, of Gomer, 86
intimacy, as protecting, 98–99
in marriage, 313
of parents, 125
Fornication (*see* Premarital sex)
Fowler's snare, **187**
Friends, friendship:
choosing, 135–138
Christian, 135–139
couples and, 135–150

influence of, 136
Job's, "miserable comforters," 148–
149
with other couples, 142, 150
parents as, 125
spouse as best, 89, 109–110, 118,
136–137, 240
unbelievers as, 136–138
Frugality, 257
Fruit, forbidden, 39–42
Fruit of the Spirit, 47
Fulfillment:
God as, 6
Jesus as, 6
in marriage, 275–276
of spouse's sexual needs, 207–209,
238, 246
Fun, Jesus as, 31

G

Garden of Eden, 39–42 (*See also* Adam
and Eve)
Gender differences, 88
in communication, 106
in love, 32
in sex, 111–112, 203–206, 208, 232,
242
Gender roles, 28
Generosity (giving) 10, 252
attitude of, 257
in family life, 52–53
with pure motives, 146
to spouse, 92
without strings, 146
Genesis, Book of, 98
Gentleness, 10
Glean, **26**
Glorify, **141**
Gnostic, **201**
Goal-setting, 57
Goat hair, sackcloth, 64
God:
Church as bride of, 97, 100, 229
as in control, 299
discipline by, 178
as father, 122
as greatest gift, 11
good news of, 275–276
honoring, 49
hope, as offering, xi, 161
imitating, 48
Jehovah, 20, 220
Jesus, relationship with, 30, 51
knowing, 190–191
as leading us, 17
love for us, 14, 30, 153–154, 291

nature of, 268
our importance to, 17–18
personal relationship with, 52
power of, 10, 14
relationship, as our ultimate, 6, 11,
14, 84–85
seeking, 267–269
as selfless, 85
serving (*see* Ministry; Witness,
Christian)
sovereignty of, 268
spiritual oneness with, 41
trust in, 69, 188, 312
unconditional love from, 14, 30, 153–
154, 291
worshiping together, 141
(*See also* individual topics)
God's law, rewards for obeying, 173–174
God's Word (*see* Bible)
Godliness, striving for, 47
Gods, false, 20, 72
Aphrodite, 202
Asherah, **20–21**
Baal, **20–21**
Golden altar of incense, 106
illustration of, 107
Goliath, 68, 133
Gomer, Hosea and, 86
Good:
everything working for, 265–266
God as causing, 266
knowledge of, 39
Goodness, striving for, 47
Gossip, 66
Government, sitting at the city gate,
illustration of, 66
Grace, God's, 309
parental shortcomings and, 158
sin and, 219–220
Grandparenting, 313
Greece, Greek, 53
Greed, 254
Grief:
coping with, 185–187, 194–195, 315
of David, 220
of Hannah, 90, 181–182, 272
of Naomi, 131
Growth, 271
in marriage, 271–274, 288
Grudem, Wayne, on submission, wife's,
115
Guilt, premarital sex and, 42–43, 46–47

H

Hagar, 74, 298
Haman, **8**, 138

God's for us, 14, 86–87, 153–154, 245, 291
godly, 94
healthy, 27
being "in love," 81
individual perceptions of, 86–87, 94
between Isaac and Rebekah, 22, 206
of Jesus, 30
languages of, individual, 87, 94
and letting go, 26–27
liking and, 109–110, 118
living life of, 48
and marriage, 3
mature, 243–245, 311
Paul on, 84
public expression of, 233
rekindling, xii, 68, 82–83, 92
romantic, 82
sacrificial, 314
selfless, 286
self-love, 12
between Solomon and his bride (Song of Songs), 229–246
of spouse as self, 91
staying in, 84
true, 23–24, 27, 34, 81 (See also Unconditional love)
the ultimate, 86
unconditional (see Unconditional love)
unhealthy, 27
withdrawing, 153–154
Love languages, individual, 87, 94
Lovemaking (see Sex)
Lovers, spouses as, 111
in Song of Songs, 229–246
Loving choices, making, xii
Loving extravagantly, 85
Loyalty, to spouse above parents, 122–124, 127, 134
Lucado, Max, on God as father, 122
Lust, of Amnon (rape of Tamar), 48–49
Lying (see Deception; Lies)

M

Magazines (see Media)
Malachi, 271
Man, men:
and midlife crisis, 289–299, 301–303
sexual nature of, 208, 111–112, 242
Manager, qualities of good, 249–252, 258
Mandrakes, 243
Manoah and his wife (Samson's parents), 193
Mara (Naomi), 131

Marriage:
arranged, 17–18, 206
Bible as help for, xi
bountiful, 286–287
change, positive, in, 271
children's effect on, 159–160 (See also Children)
Christ as center, 306
Christian beliefs regarding, 18
as commitment, 235, 273–274, 279–280, 286, 288
comparing to others, 286–287
compromise in, 285
conflict, inevitability of, 73–79
couples, Bible (see Couples in the Bible)
dating your spouse, 58, 142
death as only end, 99
dependency in, healthy/unhealthy, 234
desire for, when single, 4
differences, coping with, 88–89
disillusionment in, overcoming, 81–85
elderly couples (see Elderly couples)
enduring, 29
expectations in, 11, 69
failed, 25
finding the right partner, 5, 17–35
friendship in, 89, 109–110, 118, 136–137, 240
fulfilling, 275–276
God (Jesus Christ) ultimate relationship in, 6, 11, 14, 29, 67, 134
God's guidance in, 23–24, 56
finding God's plan in, 51–52
God's purpose for, 18, 99, 267
as good, 99
growth in, 271–274, 288
happy, 11, 25, 29, 51, 275–276
hard work of, 275–276
hardships, coping with (see Trouble)
healthy, 10, 215, 238, 240–241
Holy Spirit's guidance in, 57
as intensifying existing problems, 11, 15
intimacy in (see Intimacy)
leaving (see Divorce; Separation)
loving spouse as self, 91 (See also Love)
as ministry, 141–150, 267
mission statement in, 51–58
monogamy, 99, 200–202, 211–212
myths of intimacy in, 99–100
nurturing, 204
obedience in (submission), 113, 115–117, 118

parents, spouse vs., 122–124, 127, 134
potential, reaching full, 286
premarital purity, maintaining, 45–46
preparation for, 3–50
problems and struggles in, 22, 221 (See also individual topics)
responsibility, as lifetime, 99
restoring closeness, 239–240
Satan as attacking, 275–278, 286, 288
second, 29
seeking God regarding, 25, 269
selflessness in, 234, 286, 288
sexual unity in, 200 (See also Intimacy; Sex)
solid, 234
spouse as best friend, 89, 109–110, 118, 136–137, 240
stages of, 309–310
strong, as example for others, 267
successful, 10, 51, 234, 288
supporting other couples, 136
thankfulness in, 221, 223–224, 226–227
trouble, in times of, 263, 279–280, 288
trust in, 245
two becoming one, 100–101
to unbelievers, 19–21, 28, 34, 270–271, 290
unhappy, preventing, 25
unrealistic expectations of, 11, 69
valuing spouse, 60
(See also Couples; Spouse; individual topics)
Marriage Alive Seminars, 142
Marriage preparation, 3–50 (See also Dating; Engagement)
Marriage vows, repeating/renewing, 109
Marshall, Sharon, on separation, 299
Marsolini, Maxine:
on blended families, 162
on stepparenting, 163
Martyred, **53**
Mary and Joseph, 36, 272
Mate (see Spouse)
Maturity:
children, level of, 155, 157, 190
emotional and spiritual, 14–15, 28, 243
hardship as developing, 267
McDowell, Josh, and Paul Lewis:
on love, 83
on purity, self-control and, 47
on sex, Christians and, 38
Media, portrayal of sex in, 41, 45, 49
Meditate, **171**

Mediterranean Sea, 53
Meekness, 93, 252, 283
Meier, Paul (*see* Hemfelt, Robert, Frank
    Minirth, and Paul Meier)
Melancholy, 31
Men, sexual nature of, 208, 111–112, 242
Mentoring others, tips regarding, 147–149
Mercy, God's, 6, 309
Mesopotamia, 22
Messiah, Anna and Simeon recognizing,
    307
Metaphor, **276**
Michal, 67–68, 133
Midianites, 224
Midlife crisis, 289–299, 301–303
    characteristics of, 293–294
    of Solomon, 289–290
    of spouse, dealing with, 296–298, 302
Midlife difficulties, benefits of, 312
Military activity, of Deborah, 144–145
Miller, Kathy Collard, on parents,
    honoring, 125
Miller, Keith, on purity, setting sexual
    limits, 45
Miller, Larry and Kathy (He says, She
    says):
    on childlessness, 183–184
    on children and disobedience, 157
    on church, attending, 140–141
    on criticism vs. encouragement, 70
    on dating your mate, 58
    on debt, 254
    on disciplining children, 176
    on disillusionment in love, 82–83
    on empty nest, 311
    on family rules, 172–173
    on first meeting, 7
    on leadership, 114
    on midlife troubles, 294–295
    on parents, dealing with, 123–124
    on praying together, 104
    on purity, 43
    on Satan's attacks, 278
    on serving one's spouse, 92–93
    on sex, affection and, 205–206
    on sexual attraction, extramarital, 222
    on teasing and humor, 9
    on temperament, understanding
        beloved's, 32–33
    on trouble, benefits of, 270
Minirth, Frank, on miscarriage, 186
    (*See also* Hemfelt, Robert, Frank
        Minirth, and Paul Meier)
    Frank and Mary Alice:
        ing, 263
        handling, 262

on elderly parents, caring for, 315
Ministry:
    of Aquila and Priscilla, xii, 53–54,
        110, 141, 144
    Christian marriage as, 141–150, 267
    early church, 144–147
    good reasons for, 147–148
    of Paul, 144
    Satan's attacks on, 278
    selfless motives in, 147
    together with spouse, 141–150
    (*See also* Witness, Christian)
Miriam, 307
Miscarriage, 186
Misfortune (*see* Trouble)
Mission statement:
    family, 55–56, 61
    marriage, 51–58
Missionaries:
    Aquila and Priscilla, xii, 53–54, 110,
        141, 144
    early, 110
    Paul, 110
Mistakes:
    God as forgiving, 308
    lifelong (even in old age), 308
Misunderstandings, 11, 77
    communication and, 242
Moms' Day Out, 204
Money, 235, 249–259
    acquisition of, 113
    children and, 190
    conflict, as source of, 249
    contentment and, 251
    debt, 253–255
    financial opportunities, taking, 253
    get-rich-quick schemes, 53
    God as controlling, 250
    God as providing, 254
    integrity, as testing, 250
    management of, 250–251, 258
    ownership vs. stewardship, 249
    preoccupation with, 113
    prosperity, 267
    riches, true, 250–251
    right use of, 250
    rules as fostering prosperity, 172
    ten talents, parable of, 252–253
    tithing, 255–259
Money-changers, 31
Monogamy, 99, 200–202, 211–212
Mordecai, 138
Moses:
    and Jethro (father-in-law), 129–130
    old age of, 307
    and Zipporah, 74

Motherhood:
    longing for, 181–184
Mother-in-law:
    changing attitude toward, 127
    getting along with, 128–129
    Naomi as Ruth's, 26, 128, 131
    (*See also* In-laws; Parents)
Mount Carmel, 241–242
Movies, portrayal of sex in, 41, 45, 49
Mowday, Lois:
    on adultery, 215
    on immorality, 212
Murder:
    of Amnon, 219
    God's forgiveness and, 220
    of Uriah, 217–218
Myrrh, 7–8
    illustration of, 8

N

Nabal, 12–13, 94
Naboth, 21
Nagging, 69
    alternatives to, 70–71
    of children, 156
Nahor, 22
Nakedness, 98–99
    of Adam and Eve, 6, 41–42, 97, 200
Naomi, 26, 128, 131
    depression of, 131
    and Orpah, 128
Narramore, Bruce:
    on children, raising, 177
    on discipline, 166
    on spanking children, 175
Nathan, 185, 218–220
Nazirite, Samson as, 193
Neediness, 14, 84–85
    God as answer to, 91
Negativity, eliminating, 68
Negotiating, in conflict resolution, 76–77
New International Version (NIV), xiii
New Testament, xiv
Newlyweds, Solomon and his bride as
    (*see* Song of Songs)
Noah, old age of, 306–307

O

Obed, 26
Obedience:
    to God, 42, 256
    submission, meaning of, 113, 115–
        117, 118
Offerings:
    burnt, 67
    fellowship, 67

Old age, 306–312
  of Abraham, 307
  enjoying, 313
  fear of, 312
  of Moses, 307
  of Noah, 306–307
  of Sarah, 307
  Sarah's beauty in, 308
  of Solomon, 307
  (*See also* Elderly couples)
Old Testament, 256
  Pentateuch, 171
  as the Scriptures, xiv
Oneness (*see* Intimacy)
Openness, 11, 15, 98
Optimistic, **31**
Original sin, 39–42
Orpah, 128
Outserving one's spouse, 92–93
Overcommitment, 281–286, 288
Oxen, equally yoked, illustration of, 20

P

Pain:
  grief, 185–187
  inevitability of, 189, 192
  (*See also* Trouble)
Parable(s), 31, **252**, **275**
  of the sower, 275–276, 288
  of the talents, 252–253
Parameters, **45**
Parenting, parenthood:
  Christian, 157–158, 171–172, 177,
    190–191
  consistency in, 175
  different approaches to, 165, 169–
    170, 175–176
  God as perfect parent, 122, 158, 164
  Jesus as model for, 155, 192
  shortcomings, God's grace and, 158
  unified, 175–176
  (*See also* Children)
Parents:
  Adam and Eve as original, 14
  death of, 315
  dependence on after marriage, 122
  detaching from at marriage, 122–125
  elderly, caring for, 127, 314–315
  financial dependence on, 123
  friendship with, 125
  healthy relationship with, 125–126
  honoring, 125–129, 134
  as imperfect, 125, 133–134
  leaving, at marriage, 122–123
  listening to, 129–130, 134
  proximity, pitfalls of, 122–123

problems with, tackling, 130–134
  spouse as priority over, 122–124, 127,
    134
  unhealthy relationships with, 122
Partner (*see* Spouse)
Passion:
  character and, 231
  praise vs. criticism and, 232–233
  premarital purity and, 37–38
  renewing, in marriage, 111
  untrustworthiness of, 23
Passivity, 113–114
  avoiding, 74
Patience, 10, 23–24, 296–297
  parents as needing, 155, 157
  purity and, 44
Paul, 53–54
  on children, 154–155
  on contentment, 251
  on family, responsibility for, 314
  on fatherhood, 156
  Hebrews, as writer of, 168
  on love, 84
  ministry of, 144
  as a Pharisee, 59
  on sex, 207
  on tithing, 256–257
  on unbelievers, 19
Peace:
  discipline as causing, 170
  rules as fostering, 172
  amid stress, 10
Peale, Ruth Stafford, on in-laws, 132
Peloponnesus, 53
Peninnah, 90, 181–182
Pentateuch, **171**
Perfection, 14
  of Jesus, 30–31
  in marriage, 10
  pursuit of, 17
Perfectionism, 69–70, 103, 283
Perfume, 7–8
Perkins, Gloria Okes (*see* Wheat, Ed, and
    Gloria Okes Perkins)
Persecution, of Christians, early, 168
Perseverance, 23–24, 47, 267
Personality, personalities:
  child's individual, 155
  marriage preparation and, 30–33
Personality styles, **31**
Pessimistic, **31**
Pestilence, **187**
Peter (the Apostle):
  and Ananias and Sapphira, 146
  Jesus and, 191–192
  on marriage and prayer, 106–107

on troubles, 261
Phalti, 68
Pharaohs, 161, 224, 290
Pharisee(s), 21, **59**
Philistines, 110–111
  Delilah as, 27
  Samson and, 193
Phlegmatic, 31
Physical compatibility, 28
Physical intimacy (*see* Intimacy; Sex)
Piqued, **75**
Plague, of locusts, 161
Planning, Holy Spirit's guidance, 56–57
Plan(s):
  committing to the Lord, 61
  God's for us, 265–270
  marriage mission statement as, 51–58
Playboy philosophy, 38
Police, problems specific to, 294
Pontus, 53–54
Populating the earth, 4
Pornography, 49, 212, 277
Positive action, taking, 264
Possessions:
  God as controlling, 250
  ownership vs. stewardship, 249
  (*See also* Money)
Possessiveness, true love and, 27
Potiphar's wife, 224
Poverty, of Ruth and Naomi, 26
Power, of God, 10, 14
Powers, **278**
Prader-Willi syndrome, 175–176
Praise:
  of God (*see* Prayer; Worship)
  power of, 68, 72, 79
  in the Song of Songs, 232, 236
  of spouse, 232–233, 236, 242
  (*See also* Encouragement;
    Thankfulness)
Prayer, 283
  blessings, thankfulness for, 105
  for children, your, 190, 192, 195
  with a clean heart, 103
  in conflict resolution, 76, 79
  after disagreements, 67
  and illness, 280
  as important to God, 106
  intercessory (for others), 192
  of Jesus for Peter, 191
  marriage and, 106–107
  as priority, 102
  simple requirement for, 103
  before speaking, 66
  together with spouse, 29, 102–105
Praying God's Will for My Husband, 102

S

Sackcloth, 64
Sacrifice(s):
    animal, 21, 67
    burnt offerings, 67
    Elkanah's, 181–182
    fellowship offerings, 67
    on God's altar, 270
    Jesus as, 86, 279
    leadership as involving, 113, 118
    love, sacrificial, 314
    in marriage, 99–100
    willingness for, by Priscilla and
        Aquila, 144
Saida, 21
Salvation, **19**
Samaria, 21
Samson, 27–28, 193
Samuel, 182
Sanctified, **37**
Sanctity, **44**
Sanguine, 31
Sapphira and Ananias, 146, 257
Sarah, xii
    and Abraham (see Abraham and
        Sarah)
    beauty of, at ninety, 308
Satan:
    as attacking us, 266
    Eve, temptation of, 19, 39–40, 116
    as father of lies, 38
    God, as casting doubt on, 40
    and Job, 72–73, 262–263
    marriage, as undermining, 275–278,
        286, 288
    resisting, 277
    as serpent, 19, 39–40
    and sex, temptation of, 40, 45
    tactics of, 276–277
    temptation as from, 39–42, 50
Saul, King, 94
    David as son-in-law of, 133
    Michal as daughter of, 67–68, 133
Saved, 139
Savior, Jesus as, 139
Scripture(s), xiv (See also Bible)
Seal:
    Holy Spirit as, 244
    love as, 243–244
Security:
    discipline as fostering, 168
    in God's love, 14
    human need for, 5
    inner, 15
Seduction, resisting, 223–224
Self-centeredness, 113

Self-concept, **12**
Self-control, 10
    sexual, 38, 47–48 (See also Purity)
Self-esteem, 15
    adultery and, 212
    in children, 189
    low, 12
Selfishness, 75–76, 98
    evil and, 268
    motives of, 147
    Satan and, 277
    shallowness and, 279
    unselfishness vs., 91–92
Selflessness, 286, 288
    of God, 85
Self-seeking, 23–24
Senior years, enjoying, 313
Separation, 298, 301, 302
Sermon on the Mount, 93
Serpent, 19
    Satan as, 39–40
Servants:
    Abraham's, finding Isaac a wife, 22
    ten talents parable, 252–253
Service:
    leadership as, 113–114, 118
    living life of, 52–53
    ministry as, 141
    outserving spouse, 92–93
    overcommitment, avoiding, 281–286,
        288
Sex, sexuality:
    abstinence from marital, 101–102,
        117, 207–209
    acts, acceptable, 208
    Adam and Eve and, 39, 199–200, 203
    adultery (see Adultery)
    affection and, 111–112, 118, 203–206
    attraction, extramarital, 221–224
    casual, 40
    Christian women and, 208
    Christians and, 38 (See also Purity)
    "chemistry," 23, 28
    church view of, 201
    commitment to, married, 207–209
    communication and, 242
    desire for (see Desire)
    elderly couples and, 244–245, 310–
        311
    enjoying, xii
    extramarital (see Adultery; Premarital
        sex)
    fantasies, 48–50
    fidelity, 207–209, 211–228
    foreplay, 204–205
    fulfilling, 207–209

    gender differences regarding, 111–
        112, 203–206, 208, 232, 242
    as gift from God, 39, 200–202, 236–
        237, 240
    good, 41, 226, 234, 236–237
    grieving and, 186
    healthy approach to, 40
    and intimacy, 202–203
    marriage, as strengthening, 236
    married, 226
    mature, 243–244
    media portrayal of, 41, 45, 49
    men and, 208, 242
    needs, communicating, 238
    neglect of, 226, 238
    older couples enjoying, 244–245,
        310–311
    Paul on, 84
    planning for, 204–205
    Playboy philosophy, 38
    as for pleasure, 199–201, 229, 236–
        237
    praise vs. criticism and, 232–233
    premarital (see Premarital sex)
    prioritizing, 238, 240–241, 246
    privacy from children, 205
    as for procreation, 199–201
    regular, benefits of, 207–208, 226
    rekindling interest in, 239–241
    romance and, 204–205
    as sacred, 39, 200–202, 236–237, 240
    Satan as tempting with, 40, 45
    secular views of, 41, 45, 49, 277
    self-control and, 47–48
    Song of Songs, 229–246
    spouse's needs, fulfilling, 207–209,
        246
    stewardship of, 38
    as strengthening marriage, 236
    stress and, 236, 240, 243
    temptation (see Temptation)
    thoughts of, controlling, 48–50
    as uniting souls, 39
    woman initiating, 238, 243
    women and, 203–206, 208, 232–233,
        238–240, 243
Shackles, **28**
Shallowness, 288
    rejecting, 279–281
Shamblin, Gwen, on children,
    disciplining, 170
Shame, **6**
    of Adam and Eve, 41–42
Shechem, 45
Shedd, Charlie, on the power of praise,
    72

on honeymoon of Israelites, 203–204
on intimacy, 202–203
Whelchel, Mary:
    on emotions as untrustworthy, 23
    on idolizing marriage, 11
    on purity, avoiding tempting
        situations, 45
    on purity, secular view of, 44
White, Jerry and Mary, on ministry, 141
Wisdom:
    Bible as offering, xi
    of Deborah, 144
    of elders, 129–130, 134, 306
    of godly friends, 135
    of Jesus, 30
    of Jethro, 129–130
    in Proverbs, Book of, 53
    of the Proverbs woman, 65
    sharing our own, 150
    of Solomon, 53
    Solomon's request for, 290
    true, 42
Witness, Christian, 52, 267
    Christian marriage as, 100–101
    as ministry, 141–142
Wives:
    Proverbs woman as ideal, 64–65, 78,
        285

Solomon's, seven hundred, 290
submission and, 113, 115–117, 118
(See also Spouse; Woman)
Woman, women:
    as appreciating affection, 111–112,
        118
    creation of, 3–6, 15, 121, 199–200
    as helper, 3–5
    ideal, in Proverbs, 64–65, 78, 285
    and sex, 203–206, 208, 232–233,
        238–240, 243
Woodruff, Tim, on meekness, 93
Wool, 64
Word of God (see Bible)
Words:
    power of, 63–64, 78, 98
    talk, too much, 103, 149
    wise, of Proverbs woman, 65
    (See also Communication)
Work, 52
    importance of, 53
    marriage as, 275–276
    overcommitment, 281–286, 288
    senior citizens and, 313
    too much, 252
Worship, **58**
    sharing together, 141
    (See also Ministry; Prayer)

Wright, H. Norman:
    on developing intimacy, 108
    on intimacy, 102
    on marriage, stages of, 309–310
    on unconditional love, 82
Writing, of David, 220
Wrongdoing, acknowledging (see Sin)

X

Xerxes, King, 7–8, 138
    Esther and, 75

Y

Yoked, **19**
Young, Ed:
    on affairs, 226
    on expressing affection, 111
    on sex, mature, 244

Z

Zeal, **59**
Zechariah, 307
Ziglar, Zig:
    on child as family member, 168
    on family as team, 168
Zipporah, Moses and, 74
Zuphite, **181**

Books by Starburst Publishers®

(Partial listing—full list available on request)

The **What's in the Bible for . . .™** series focuses on making the Bible applicable to everyday life. Whether you're a teenager or senior citizen, this series has the book for you! Each title is equipped with the same reader-friendly icons, call-outs, tables, illustrations, questions, and chapter summaries that are used in the *God's Word for the Biblically-Inept*™ series. It's another easy way to access God's Word!

What's in the Bible for . . .™ Couples
Larry and Kathy Miller

Restore love, unity, and commitment with internationally acclaimed relationship experts Larry and Kathy Miller as they explore God's Word on such topics as dating, sex, money, and trauma. Don't miss the "Take It from Them" feature, which offers wisdom from couples who have lived and learned, and the "Couples of the Bible" feature that spotlights the experiences of such couples as Adam and Eve, Abraham and Sarah, and Joseph and Mary. (Available Spring 2001.)
(trade paper)   ISBN 1892016028 $16.95

What's in the Bible for . . .™ Women
Georgia Curtis Ling

What does the Bible have to say to women? Women of all ages will find biblical insight on topics that are meaningful to them in four sections: Wisdom for the Journey; Family Ties; Bread, Breadwinners, and Bread Makers; and Fellowship and Community Involvement. This book uses illustrations, bullet points, chapter summaries, and icons to make understanding God's Word easier than ever!
(trade paper)   ISBN 1892016109 $16.95

What's in the Bible for . . .™ Mothers
Judy Bodmer

Is home schooling a good idea? Is it okay to work? At what age should I start treating my children like responsible adults? What is the most important thing I can teach my children? If you are asking these questions and need help answering them, *What's in the Bible for . . .™ Mothers* is especially for you! Simple and user-friendly, this motherhood manual offers hope and instruction for today's mothers by jumping into the lives of mothers in the Bible (e.g., Naomi, Elizabeth, and Mary) and by exploring biblical principles that are essential to being a nurturing mother.
(trade paper)   ISBN 1892016265 $16.95

What's in the Bible for . . .™ Teens
Mark Littleton and Jeanette Gardner Littleton

This is a book that teens will love! *What's in the Bible for . . .™ Teens* contains topical Bible themes that parallel the challenges and pressures of today's adolescents. Learn about Bible prophecy, God's plan for relationships, and peer pressure in a conversational and fun tone. Helpful and eye-catching "WWJD?" icons, illustrations, and sidebars included. (Available Fall 2000.)
(trade paper)   ISBN 1892016052 $16.95

(see page 351 for purchasing information)

The **God's Word for the Biblically-Inept**™ series is already a best-seller with over 100,000 books sold! Designed to make reading the Bible easy, educational, and fun! This series of verse-by-verse Bible studies, topical studies, and overviews mixes scholarly information from experts with helpful icons, illustrations, sidebars, and time lines. It's the Bible made easy!

The Bible—God's Word for the Biblically-Inept™
Larry Richards

An excellent book to start learning the entire Bible. Get the basics or the in-depth information you are seeking with this user-friendly overview. From Creation to Christ to the Millennium, learning the Bible has never been easier.
(trade paper)   ISBN 0914984551 $16.95

Daniel—God's Word for the Biblically-Inept™
Daymond R. Duck

Daniel is a book of prophecy and the key to understanding the mysteries of the Tribulation and End-Time events. This verse-by-verse commentary combines humor and scholarship to get at the essentials of Scripture. Perfect for those who want to know the truth about the Antichrist.
(trade paper)   ISBN 0914984489 $16.95

Genesis—God's Word for the Biblically-Inept™
Joyce L. Gibson

Genesis is written to make understanding and learning the Word of God simple and fun! Like the other books in this series, the author breaks the Bible down into bite-sized pieces making it easy to understand and

incorporate into your life. Readers will learn about Creation, Adam and Eve, the Flood, Abraham and Isaac, and more.
(trade paper)   ISBN 1892016125 $16.95

Health & Nutrition—God's Word for the Biblically-Inept™
Kathleen O'Bannon Baldinger

The Bible is full of God's rules for good health! Baldinger reveals scientific evidence that proves the diet and health principles outlined in the Bible are the best for total health. Learn about the Bible diet, the food pyramid, and fruits and vegetables from the Bible! Experts include Pamela Smith, Julian Whitaker, Kenneth Cooper, and T. D. Jakes.
(trade paper)   ISBN 0914984055 $16.95

John—God's Word for the Biblically-Inept™
Lin Johnson

From village fisherman to beloved apostle, John was an eyewitness to the teachings and miracles of Christ. Now, readers can join in an easy-to-understand, verse-by-verse journey through the fourth and most unique of all the gospels. Witness the wonder of Jesus, a man who calmed storms, turned water into wine, healed the blind, and walked on water. (Available Spring 2001.)
(trade paper)   ISBN 1892016435 $16.95

Life of Christ, Volume 2—God's Word for the Biblically-Inept™
Robert C. Girard

Life of Christ, Volume 2, begins with events recorded in Matthew 16. Read about Jesus' transfiguration, his miracles and parables, triumphal ride through Jerusalem, capture in the Garden of Gethsemane, and his trial, crucifixion, resurrection, and ascension. Find out how to be great in the kingdom of God, what Jesus meant when he called himself the light of the world, and what makes up real worship.
(trade paper)   ISBN 1892016397 $16.95

Life of Christ, Volume 1—God's Word for the Biblically-Inept™
Robert C. Girard

Girard takes the reader on an easy-to-understand journey through the gospels of Matthew, Mark, Luke, and John, tracing the story of Jesus from his virgin birth to his revolutionary ministry. Learn about Jesus' baptism, the Sermon on the Mount, and his miracles and parables.
(trade paper)   ISBN 1892016230 $16.95

Men of the Bible—God's Word for the Biblically-Inept™
D. Larry Miller

Benefit from the life experiences of the powerful men of the Bible! Learn how the inspirational struggles of men such as Moses, Daniel, Paul, and David parallel the struggles of men today. It will inspire and build Christian character for any reader.
(trade paper)   ISBN 1892016079 $16.95

Prophecies of the Bible—God's Word for the Biblically-Inept™
Daymond R. Duck

God has a plan for this crazy planet, and now understanding it is easier than ever! Best-selling author and End-Time prophecy expert Daymond R. Duck explains the complicated prophecies of the Bible in plain English. Duck shows you all there is to know about the end of the age, the New World Order, the Second Coming, and the coming world government. Find out what prophecies have already been fulfilled and what's in store for the future!
(trade paper)   ISBN 1892016222 $16.95

Revelation—God's Word for the Biblically-Inept™
Daymond R. Duck

End-Time Bible prophecy expert Daymond R. Duck leads us verse by verse through one of the Bible's most confusing books. Follow the experts as they forge their way through the captivating prophecies of Revelation!
(trade paper)   ISBN 0914984985 $16.95

Romans—God's Word for the Biblically-Inept™
Gib Martin

The best-selling *God's Word for Biblically-Inept™* series continues to grow! Learn about the apostle Paul, living a righteous life, and more with help from graphics, icons, and chapter summaries. (Available Spring 2001.)
(trade paper)   ISBN 1892016273 $16.95

Women of the Bible—God's Word for the Biblically-Inept™
Kathy Collard Miller

Finally, a Bible perspective just for women! Gain valuable insight from the successes and struggles of such women as Eve, Esther, Mary, Sarah, and Rebekah. Interesting icons like "Get Close to God," "Build Your Spirit," and "Grow Your Marriage" will make it easy to incorporate God's Word into your daily life.
(trade paper)   ISBN 0914984063 $16.95

•   **Learn more at www.biblicallyinept.com**   •

God Things Come in Small Packages: Celebrating the Little Things in Life

Susan Duke, LeAnn Weiss, Caron Loveless, and Judith Carden
Enjoy touching reminders of God's simple yet generous gifts to brighten our days and gladden our hearts! Treasures like a sunset over a vast sparkling ocean, a child's trust, or the crystalline dew on a spider's web come to life in this elegant compilation. Such occasions should be celebrated as if gift wrapped from God; they're his hallmarks! Personalized Scripture is artfully combined with compelling stories and reflections.
(cloth)   ISBN 1892016281 $12.95

God Things Come in Small Packages for Moms: Rejoicing in the Simple Pleasures of Motherhood

Susan Duke, LeAnn Weiss, Caron Loveless, and Judith Carden
The "small" treasures God plants in a mom's day shine in this delightful book. Savor priceless stories, which encourage us to value treasures like a shapeless, ceramic bowl presented with a toothy grin; a child's hand clinging to yours on a crowded bus; or a handful of wildflowers presented on a hectic day. Each story combines personalized Scripture with heartwarming vignettes and inspiring reflections.
(cloth)   ISBN 189201629X $12.95

God Things Come in Small Packages for Friends: Exploring the Freedom of Friendship

LeAnn Weiss, Susan Duke, and Judy Carden
A heartwarming combination of true stories, para-phrased Scripture, and reflections that celebrate the simple yet cherished blessings shared between true friends. A new release from the elegant *God Things Come in Small Packages* series that combines the beauty of gift books with the depth of devotionals. Includes reflective meditation, narrative vignettes detailing powerful moments of revelation, and encouraging scripture passages presented as letters to a friend.
(cloth)   ISBN 1892016346 $12.95

God Things Come in Small Packages for Women: Celebrating the Unique Gifts of Women

LeAnn Weiss, Susan Duke, and Judy Carden
Women will experience God's love like never before through powerfully translated Scripture, true stories, and reflections, which celebrate the unique character of women. A new release from the elegant *God Things Come in Small Packages* series combines the beauty of gift books with the depth of a devotional. Includes reflective meditation, narrative vignettes detailing powerful moments of revelation, and encouraging scripture passages presented as letters from God.
(cloth)   ISBN 1892016354 $12.95

The Weekly Feeder: A Revolutionary Shopping, Cooking, and Meal-Planning System

Cori Kirkpatrick
This revolutionary meal-planning system is a way to make preparing home-cooked dinners more convenient than ever. At the beginning of each week, simply choose one of the eight preplanned menus, tear out the corresponding grocery list, do your shopping, and whip up each fantastic meal in less than 45 minutes! The author's household management tips, equipment checklists, and nutrition information make this system a must for any busy family. Included with every recipe is a personal anecdote from the author emphasizing the importance of good food, a healthy family, and a well-balanced life.
(trade paper)   ISBN 1892016095 $16.95

God Stories: They're So Amazing, Only God Could Make Them Happen

Donna I. Douglas
Famous individuals share their personal, true-life experiences with God in this beautiful new book! Find out how God has touched the lives of top recording artists, professional athletes, and other newsmakers like Jessi Colter, Deana Carter, Ben Vereen, Stephanie Zimbalist, Cindy Morgan, Sheila E., Joe Jacoby, Cheryl Landon, Brett Butler, Clifton Taulbert, Babbie Mason, Michael Medved, Sandi Patty, Charlie Daniels, and more! Their stories are intimate, poignant, and sure to inspire and motivate you as you listen for God's message in your own life!
(cloth)   ISBN 1892016117 $18.95

God's Little Rule Book: Simple Rules to Bring Joy & Happiness to Your Life

Starburst Publishers
Let this little book of God's rules be your personal guide to a more joyful life. Brimming with easily applicable rules, this book is sure to inspire and motivate you! Each rule includes corresponding Scripture and a practical tip that will help to incorporate God's rules into everyday life. Simple enough to fit into a busy schedule, yet powerful enough to be life changing!
(trade paper)   ISBN 1892016168 $6.95

Life's Little Rule Book: Simple Rules to Bring Joy & Happiness to Your Life

Starburst Publishers
Let this little book inspire you to live a happier life! The pages are filled with timeless rules such as, "Learn to cook, you'll always be in demand!" and "Help something grow." Each rule is combined with a

reflective quote and a simple suggestion to help the reader incorporate the rule into everyday life.
(trade paper)   ISBN 1892016176 $6.95

Stories of God's Abundance for a More Joyful Life
Compiled by Kathy Collard Miller
Like its successful predecessor, *God's Abundance*, this book is filled with beautiful, inspirational, real-life stories. Those telling their stories of God share Scriptures and insights that readers can apply to their daily lives. Renew your faith in life's small miracles and challenge yourself to allow God to lead the way as you find the source of abundant living for all your relationships.
(trade paper)   ISBN 1892016060 $12.95

More God's Abundance: Joyful Devotions for Every Season
Compiled by Kathy Collard Miller
Editor Kathy Collard Miller responds to the tremendous success of *God's Abundance* with a fresh collection of stories based on God's Word for a simpler life. Includes stories from our most beloved Christian writers, such as Liz Curtis Higgs and Patsy Clairmont, that are combined with ideas, tips, quotes, and Scripture.
(cloth)   ISBN 1892016133 $19.95

God's Abundance for Women: Devotions for a More Meaningful Life
Compiled by Kathy Collard Miller
Following the success of *God's Abundance*, this book will touch women of all ages as they seek a more meaningful life. Essays from our most beloved Christian authors exemplify how to gain the abundant life that Jesus promised through trusting him to fulfill our every need. Each story is enhanced with Scripture, quotes, and practical tips providing brief, yet deeply spiritual reading.
(cloth)   ISBN 1892016141 $19.95

Treasures of a Woman's Heart: A Daybook of Stories and Inspiration
Edited by Lynn D. Morrissey
Join the best-selling editor of *Seasons of a Woman's Heart* in this touching sequel where she unlocks the treasures of women and glorifies God with Scripture, reflections, and a compilation of stories. Explore heartfelt living with vignettes by Kay Arthur, Elisabeth Elliot, Emilie Barnes, Claire Cloninger, and more.
(cloth)   ISBN 1892016257 $18.95

Seasons of a Woman's Heart: A Daybook of Stories and Inspiration
Edited by Lynn D. Morrissey
A woman's heart is complex. This daybook of stories, quotes, Scriptures, and daily reflections will inspire and refresh. Christian women share their heartfelt thoughts on seasons of faith, growth, guidance, nurturing, and victory. Includes Christian writers Kay Arthur, Emilie Barnes, Luci Swindoll, Jill Briscoe, and Florence Littauer.
(cloth)   ISBN 1892016036 $18.95

Why Fret That God Stuff?
Edited by Kathy Collard Miller
Subtitled: *Stories of Encouragement to Help You Let Go and Let God Take Control of All Things in Your Life.* Occasionally, we all become overwhelmed by the everyday challenges of our lives: hectic schedules, our loved ones' needs, unexpected expenses, a sagging devotional life. *Why Fret That God Stuff* is the perfect beginning to finding joy and peace for the real world!
(trade paper)   ISBN 0914984500 $12.95

More of Him, Less of Me
Jan Christiansen
Subtitled: *A Daybook of My Personal Insights, Inspirations & Meditations on the Weigh Down™ Diet.* The insight shared in this yearlong daybook of inspiration will encourage you on your weight-loss journey, bring you to a deeper relationship with God, and help you improve any facet of your life. Each page includes an essay, Scripture, and a tip-of-the-day that will encourage and uplift you as you trust God to help you achieve your proper weight. Perfect companion guide for anyone on the Weigh Down™ diet!
(cloth)   ISBN 1892016001 $17.95

Desert Morsels: A Journal with Encouraging Tidbits from My Journey on the Weigh Down™ Diet
Jan Christiansen
When Jan Christiansen set out to lose weight on the Weigh Down™ diet she got more than she bargained for! In addition to *losing* over 35 pounds and *gaining* a closer relationship with God, Jan discovered a gift—her ability to entertain and comfort fellow dieters! Jan's inspiring website led to the release of her best-selling first book, *More of Him, Less of Me*. Now, Jan serves another helping of her wit and His wisdom in this lovely companion journal. Includes inspiring Scripture, insightful comments, stories from readers, room for the reader's personal reflection, and *Plenty of Attitude* (p-attitude).
(cloth)   ISBN 1892016214 $17.95

Purchasing Information

www.starburstpublishers.com

Books are available from your favorite bookstore, either from current stock or special order. To assist bookstores in locating your selection, be sure to give title, author, and ISBN. If unable to purchase from a bookstore, you may order direct from STARBURST PUBLISHERS. When ordering please enclose full payment plus shipping and handling as follows:

Post Office (4th class)
$3.00 with a purchase of up to $20.00
$4.00 ($20.01–$50.00)
7% of purchase price for purchases of $50.01 and up

Canada
$5.00 (up to $35.00)
15% ($35.01 and up)

United Parcel Service (UPS)
$4.50 (up to $20.00)
$6.00 ($20.01–$50.00)
9% ($50.01 and up)

Overseas
$5.00 (up to $25.00)
20% ($25.01 and up)

Payment in U.S. funds only. Please allow two to four weeks minimum for delivery by USPS (longer for overseas and Canada). Allow two to seven working days for delivery by UPS. Make checks payable to and mail to:

Starburst Publishers®
P.O. Box 4123
Lancaster, PA 17604

Credit card orders may be placed by calling 1-800-441-1456, Mon–Fri, 8:30 A.M. to 5:30 P.M. Eastern Standard Time. Prices are subject to change without notice. Catalogs are available for a 9 x 12 self-addressed envelope with four first-class stamps.

NOTES